Sociology of Mass Communication

Sociology of Mass Communication

Dr. Poonam Rani

Sociology of Mass Communication

ISBN 978-93-5111-625-7

Published in 2015 in India by

RANDOM PUBLICATIONS

4376-A/4B, Gali Murari Lal, Ansari Road
New Delhi-110 002
Phone : +9111-43580356, 011-23289044, 011-43142548
e-mail: sales@randompublications.com,
info@randompublications.com, randomexports@gmail.com
Reprinted 2022

Type Setting by : Friends Media, Delhi-110089
Digitally Printed at : Replika Press Pvt. Ltd.

Preface

Sociology of mass communication is an arm of sociology that seeks to study the relationship between the society, social phenomena and the mass media, it archieves this through the application of sociological concepts and empericism. It is necessary to understand that the sociologists study all factors that affects social reality.

Mass media dominate the mental life of modern societies, and therefore are of intense interest to sociologists. The national organization of the press and broadcasting (radio and television) has been a distinctive feature of these mass media throughout this century. Access to the new technologies looms large in this argument, and with it questions of social marginalization, where groups are denied opportunities to express themselves via these new means of representation. What is striking here is the enormous concentration of ownership across media production, reproduction, and distribution.

The sociological study of communication is an attempt to answer the simple question of 'who says what, in which channel, to whom and with what effect?' This definition implies overt intention, avowed purpose, and communicative efficiency. However, some sociologists take the view that a greater emphasis on the role of society and external social forces in defining the roles of 'sender' and receiver' is more appropriate. The former view further assumes that messages are as much received as sent and that motives for receiving are as significant as motives for sending. Thirdly, it further assumes the media are not neutral but complex social institutions with motives. Fourthly, messages are sent by media that have encoded purposes with many possible interpretations of origin and function.

This book has been written to cater to the needs of all those who are in the field of mass communication and Media, and who may feel interested in knowing more about the evolution of technology in the media field.

I would like to thank my team for standing beside me throughout my career and writing this book. My special thanks go to "Random Publications" who have published the book.

– Dr. Poonam Rani

Contents

1

Process and Effects of Mass Communication

INTRODUCTION

Between about 1930 and the early 1980s, a number of studies were published that led to significant advances in understanding the process and effects of mass communication. Sometimes referred to as *milestones,* these were well-funded, large-scale efforts, conducted with important objectives in mind, and based on standards of methodology respected in their time. A few were much more modest in scale, but whether large or small, they yielded important concepts, generalizations, and theories that are now part of the accumulated knowledge of how the U.S. media function and the kinds of influences that they have on individuals and society.

Since that period, there has not been a similar level of production of such seminal studies. No widely heralded investigation has been produced in nearly two decades-one that provoked wide discussion and changed the way scholars think about the mass communication process. Many noteworthy studies, even hundreds of well-conducted and interesting investigations, have been reported. However, most focus on restricted topics or hypotheses, or are efforts to explore issues raised by the earlier milestones. When asked by my publisher to revise a book summarizing the existing milestones and adding new ones, I could not identify even one that fit the same criteria as the earlier investigations.

It is the purpose of this chapter to suggest some of the reasons why the field of mass communication has changed in this respect. The reasons advanced include a change in the agendas of the social sciences, a lack of a programmatic approach by media scholars, a shift to non-quantitative and critical modes of analysis by many writers, and changes in the work conditions of the professorate.

IMPORTANCE OF COMMUNICATION

Although the Internet may be portrayed as a communication technology unique to the 1990s, this depiction is somewhat misleading. The Internet's origins are in fact traceable to the 1960s development of the military-funded communication network, ARPANET, with the Internet officially making its debut as a civilian tool for communication in 1983.

However, widespread public awareness of the Internet's existence did not occur within the United States until the early 1990s when it was privatized and online services such as America Online (AOL) were developed to serve the general public. Hence, there is a tendency to think of it as a turn-of-the-twenty-first-century phenomenon.

Prior to the 1990s, early public access to the Internet was limited mostly to government agencies, universities, and computer-related organizations, such as hardware and software developers. Initially, users experienced the Internet in the form of text-based communication applications such as e-mail and navigation systems such as Telnet. In 1992, the World Wide Web (WWW) became publicly available in the United States and began to diffuse widely in 1993 with the release of the iconbased web browser Mosaic, which made web navigation more "user friendly" and visually appealing. Subsequently, use of the Web helped to popularize the Internet in general. As use of the Internet has shifted from a small community of researchers and government employees to a worldwide community, researchers recognize the Internet as an important area in need of study. The widespread diffusion and adoption of the Internet in the United States and abroad provides scholars with numerous research opportunities. Because the Internet functions as a channel for communication, this is especially true for the field of communication. However, as with any innovation, it can be difficult at first to know how to approach the investigation of an innovation's contribution to and effects on the society into which it is introduced.

With regard to the Internet, communication researchers, as well as others, must grapple with numerous decisions, such as determining how applicable existing theories and methods of enquiry are to this newest communication technology.

While the arguments for why and how to study the Internet vary, a common theme to arise within our discipline concerns the unique opportunity that today's communication scholars have to witness and record, first hand, the introduction of a major communication technology.

Scholarly journals are one forum where communication researchers record the results of their research for the benefit of current and future generations of scholars. Published articles inform other researchers of the types of approaches being used to study a wide variety of topics, including the Internet.

A number of disciplines are conducting Internet research as is evident when searching electronic databases. For example, a simple keyword search conducted in December 1999 in the Social Sciences Abstracts database on the term "Internet" yielded a return of 969 articles published across a diversity of disciplines, most notably in the areas of business, demographics, law, and policy studies. Each discipline, including communication, typically contains a core set of journals considered to be "leaders" among all others in terms of their coverage of subject matter, length of publication, and quality of published articles. The question asked in this study concerns how leading journals in the field represent Internet-based research conducted by communication scholars, because an important goal of scholarly journals is to document a field's evolution over time.

This study examines the content, frequency, and pattern of published Internet-based research articles-studies that focus on some aspect of the Internet-in leading communication journals for the purpose of assessing how these journals are keeping pace with the Internet's influence on the communication process. It also considers how these journals represent our response to these changes to other disciplines in the social sciences.

MODEL FOR COMMUNICATION

Models for communication are useful to mass media professionals because they offer ways of analyzing the communication situation and anticipating problems that may be avoided or mitigated through design strategies.

At the same time, however, authors need to be aware that all models are reductive approximations of actual communication, and that some models will represent a particular situation more usefully than others. For that reason, this chapter presents a number of different approaches to modeling mass communication and suggests their strengths and weaknesses.

Let's begin with a generalized communication model. The model above combines elements and the general logic of Shannon and Weaver's process model and Stuart Hall's encoding/decoding model, which have provided the bases for the two main approaches to mass communication: process modeling and audience reception modeling.

This model will itself prove useful in analyzing many communication problems, as we shall see, and here it will also serve to introduce some key terms for communication theory.

Westley and MacLean's Model

x = information source

A = sender

B = receiver

C = editorial function

f = feedback path

Westley and MacLean's communication model was the first to attempt to model the mass communication process specifically. It takes into account several factors that are especially prominent in, if not peculiar to, mass communication situations:

- The sender (which is often a team rather than an individual) generally derives information from a variety of sources and combines it in some way to create a message

- The message generally passes through some kind of editorial gatekeeper before being passed on to audiences (this again may be group, and the editorial process may have several layers, including governmental regulation of content, editors, corporation management, and investors or advertisers
- The editorial functions may have direct access to relevant sources of information, some of which the sender may not have access to (*e.g.* an editor who has inside sources in the government or a corporation)
- Feedback from the audience is sometimes directed to the sender, but in many cases is directed to some part of the editorial function, who may modify or expand upon it in transmitting it to the sender

SEMIOTICS I

One weakness of both Shannon and Weaver's and Westley and MacLean's communication models that the meaning of the message is taken for granted (as identical to the sender's intended meaning, aside from noise or editorial effects). A corollary of this assumption is that the audience is taken to be one homogeneous lump-they either get the message or they don't, and if they do, then presumably they understand it in the same way.

Semiotics, on the other hand, is concerned with the interpretation of messages, regardless of the source and of the sender's intended meaning. Semiotics is valuable to the analysis of mass communication in that it provides a model for thinking about how different parts of an audience might interpret messages differently. The basic assumption of semiotics is that messages are made of signs. On the next page we will look at the general notion of sign.

SEMIOTICS II

The signifier is some physical token (a sound, a written word, and image, etc.) that is conventionally understood to stand for some idea. The signified is the idea that the signifier stands for (cat stands for furry domestic creatures that meows). The referent is some thing in the experiential world that the sign is associated with (we associate cat with those actual furry creatures that run around some of our houses).

The line between the sign and the referent is dotted because, according to semiotics, the referent isn't essential to the process of signification, or making meaning. Instead, meaning depends on the relationship between signs in a system called a language.

The sign, then, gives meaning to the referent rather than getting its meaning from the referent. This may seem counter-intuitive, but consider this: if I explain to you what a cat is, entirely in words, could you not understand the meaning of the word without ever having seen an physical cat? Furthermore, isn't it easier to understand why cats are considered cuddly pets in one culture and asocial pests in another if we consider the meaning of cat to be determined by a system of signs rather than any natural quality of cats?

In fact, semioticians argue that the nature of things in the experiential world is to a large extent determined by our sign systems. For instance, if we think of cats as asocial pests, we will try to keep them out of our houses; cats, then, will have to fend for themselves on the street, and are likely to be scrawnier, dirtier, and afraid of the humans who shoo them away instead of petting and feeding them. So far, so good, but to fully grasp the power of semiotic analysis, we need to remember that we generally do not communicate through individual signs, but rather through groups of signs called utterances (a sentence or a paragraph, for example, or film or picture made of many images). On the next page, we'll look at the way semiotics models the interpretation of utterances.

SEMIOTICS III

The two axes of interpretation involved in the interpretation of an utterance. The two axes represent two different mental operations that work simultaneously, and in most cases so habitually that we are not consciously aware of them. As we process a sentence, word by word, on the one hand we are placing the word in paradigms, or categories of signs. Most signs belong to multiple paradigms: cat for instance, is a member of such categories as pets, animals, nouns, words that rhyme with hat, old slang terms for certain kinds of people, metaphors for stealth, cunning, predatory nature, contentment, and so forth.

In any particular utterance, some of these paradigms will come into play, but others will be irrelevant. Among those that are important, some will be more important than others in determining the meaning of this particular chain of signs.

We decide which paradigms are important by processing along the syntagmatic axis-in other words, by considering the sign in relation to the other signs that make up the utterance. In the case of familiar ideas, what information theory would call a highly redundant message, we will have no trouble figuring out which paradigms to invoke to construct the meaning of the message. In the case of new ideas, we will be forced to work harder, in some cases deciding that some signs have to be realigned in different paradigms in order to make sense of the syntagmatic relations.

THE COMMUNICATION PROCESS

The research process in communication begins with a good question, perhaps later developed into a hypothesis, tested in the most rigorous and appropriate way. Research, then, advances the theory behind the question/hypothesis, leading to refinements in the research, and so forth.

Few explorers discovered new lands or routes without some knowledge of those who went before them. Each explorer makes new headway for the next. But metaphors are never perfect, and the communication process studied by communication re-searchers is not exactly like finding a new land: As far as the communication process is concerned, there is no final "place" to be discovered, where a theoretical "flag" can be planted. Yet there is something to be gained by acquiring knowledge about a process that may never be completely understood. The integration of theory and research methodology and the communication process are similar processes. Each begins with information gleaned from some source, and integrates that information into a message of some form (*e.g.*, verbal or non-verbal) or some medium (*e.g.*, interpersonal or mass mediated) that conveys meaning. Information takes on different forms at different times in both processes; sometimes it merely exists, much like background noise or something noted in the environment; sometimes it consists of symbols and signs, such as the words on this page, only written in a language you may not understand.

Either way, there is no intent, it is just there. To some, to be considered communication, the information must be intentionally sent *and* intentionally received. Dittman (1972) pointed out that a message may be subliminal—not consciously received—and yet still impact our thoughts, attitudes, and behaviours. Burgoon and Ruffner (1978) argued that communication has not occurred unless both source and receiver perceive a message to be intentional. Others (Malandro, Barker, and Barker, 1989; Hickson and Stacks, 1993) considered communication to occur if either sender or receiver perceive intent. Either way, information often leads to communication, depending on how the researcher has defined *communication*.

Perhaps the phrase *human communication* is all too often used to describe all communication. This is not feasable when it is necessary to distintinguish mass mediated communication from non-mediated communication.

The research process begins when the researcher reviews the literature relevant to the question or hypothesis of interest, yielding the *literature review*. Previous theory and research form the basis for a new approach, model, or theory that interprets communication differently. Thus, information is basic to both the communication and the theory-research process; it begins the process by pointing to something new, either in the environment (such as Newton's apple leading us to gravity) or in a specific literature (such as theories of how the brain operates coming from neurophysiological studies).

We all are familiar with the cliche that "knowledge is power." But what does this really mean? Knowedge about the communication processes has very practical applications for a variety of purposes—persuading other people to do what you want, for good or evil purposes; teaching elementary students; launching an information campaign to reduce AIDS risk behaviours; selling soap; educating the public about some important issue; brainwashing the people, aggrandizing all power and becoming an absolulte dictator; and so forth.

Thanks to our explorer-researchers, we have refined many of our ideas about human and mass communication processes. With some historical perspectives, we see that the communication process was once guided by naive theories, some as simple as those used to understand language acquisition. Language was once conceived as arising from physical exertion (*yo-he-ho*), from imitation of nature sounds (onomatopoeic, *e.g.*, *bow-wow*), or when the mouth and vocal organs tried to pantomime body gestures (Gray and Wise, 1959). The mass communication process was once guided by a simplistic notion of a direct and universal "hypodermic-needle" effects model on a malleable and passive audience. This model, too, is now in disrepute.

Today we can look back on the earlier generation of communication researchers who gave us various language acquisition and hypodermic-needle models of communication and wonder how they could have ever been so naive. Perhaps future generations will see us in much the same way.

THE RESEARCH PROCESS

We begin our journey by fleshing out the relationship between theory and research. In exploring this relationship we focus on the asking of "good" research questions that lead to important hypotheses. We then examine how the question dictates the method-ology used to test the theoretical relationships. Finally, we examine the research process as a whole, coming full circle to understanding and predicting communication.

The research process begins by asking research questions. Research questions are drawn from the systematic study of an area of communication interest. Whereas a systematic study of the literature is necessary, "good" questions are also derived from old-fashioned common sense.

Questions can be derived either deductively or inductively. The scientific method gives more credence to the inductive process, or hypothetico-deductive logic, in which questions are induced from general principles. That is, they take a law-like approach, much like that found in Berger and Calebrese (1975) interpersonal communication model of uncertainty reduction. Deduction, on the other hand, arrives at truth and questions from rationale observation (Westley, 1958). Deduction can be as simple and elegant as the syllogism, "All humans are mortal; Judy is a human; therefore, Judy is mortal" or as complex as the rule-based, practical syllogism, "Jim wants good grades; to get good grades he must study; therefore Jim must study to get good grades." The two examples differ in their range of generality.

The former has low generalizability, it is simple logic in a lawlike manner; the latter is midrange and more practical, and it requires a mediating factor. Deduction is the way of everyday common sense and rationalism. But induction has its own logic. The logic of induction serves to restrain the dangers of total reliance on common sense that Albert Einstein warned against.

THE CHALLENGE OF COMMUNICATION

What contributions have African communication scholars made to the perennial questions of definition of mass communication research or to the debates over what constitute appropriate problems or appropriate modes of enquiry for studying communication problems? As a group, the contributions by African scholars in these debates have generally been minimal. Although some creative ideas are beginning to emerge from the African group, as we shall see later, these ideas have not yet been systematized and projected into the dominant discussions that have guided the directions of the field. In fact, African communication research has been characterized as 'epiodic, casual, serendipitous and non-systematic. Most tragically, these efforts are not informed by any identifiable philosophies, be they indigenous or foreign' (Okigbo 1987).

The late 1950s and the 1960s represent a watershed in the history of Africa, a period that signalled not only the end of an era, but also the beginning of a new one.

This new era ushered in a crisis of sorts in which African aspirations have been aimed at the total elimination of the forces of exploitation and oppression that have for so long worked against the interests of the continent. But despite political independence, colonialism has simply refused to die and has now taken on a new mask, what some call neo-colonialism.

And despite the emergence of so-called neo-political and neo-economic philosophies and ideologies, Africa still remains in the firm grip of the tentacles of external forces. But even if one concedes the dethronement or demise of the 'old order', the 'new order' is simply not being elevated in its place. In mass communication, as in politics, economics, or cultural affairs, African scholars and those sympathetic to African aspirations have vehemently berated the old and dominant paradigms that have guided the study of communication problems yet they have not quite succeeded in constructing new models to replace them.

Lerner's (1958) and Schramm's (1963) studies provoked much of the debates in the 1960s and 1970s in mass communication research over the role of communication in national development. Upon publication, Schramm's book instantly became a handbook for many African development planners who uncritically embraced its tenets in their development policy considerations. Hence, for many African nations, transistor radios and newspapers were viewed during the 1960s not only as important indices, but sometimes as if they were the primary indicators of development, as Schramm and others had espoused. By the 1970s, however, it became evident that although the works of Schramm and Lerner on development communication demonstrated superb scholarship with 'paramount academic qualifications', such works had little social relevance to the African context (Ugboajah 1985).

MEANWHILE, EVERETT

Rogers (1978), in an intellectual about face, described the demise of the old models of communication and development and the purported emergence of a new paradigm. Much of the literature on development communication by African scholars in this period constitutes what may be called reactive scholarship, in which the concerns expressed were mainly in reaction to what Schramm, Lerner, Rogers, and others had said about Third World development communication problems. Still, new models of communication and development that were inherently African in perspective as well as in orientation were (and still are) either hard to find or-non-existent in the literature.

Hence, the debate over the critical-administrative approaches to mass communication research should be seen as an opportunity through which African communication scholars can influence the dominant views (or paradigms) that have guided the field of communication. Both the administrative and critical schools of thought should be seen merely as two different sides of the same coin, *i.e.* the Eurocentric philbsophy and ideology. Drawing from the unique African cultural and historical experience, the African contribution should be geared towards generating either a hybrid approach that takes into account the operations of both the modern and traditional modes of communication, or an altogether authentic African perspective of the study of communication problems. This elephantine task undoubtedly falls on the shoulders of the African intellectual in communication. By an intellectual in this context, we mean one who constantly apprises himself of aspects of his environment in order to impart his experience to his fellow men for the purpose of increasing awareness (knowledge) of that environment.

From the African perspective, therefore, we may identify two kinds of intellectuals:

(1) traditional intellectuals, those without formal (college or university) education but who have acquired certain skills over time that enable them to collect, store, retrieve, and analyse certain kinds of information about their environment. In this context, the African groat would be considered to be a traditional intellectual;
(2) the modern intellectual who has acquired formal education that enables him to play the kind of roles that the traditional intellectuals play but in a formal way through the modern channels of communication. Edward Shills (1972) states that:

There is in every society a minority of persons who, more than the ordinary run of their fellow men, are enquiring, and desirous of being in frequent communication with symbols which are more general than the immediate concrete situations of everyday life and remote in their reference in both time and space. In this minority, there is a need to externalize this quest in oral and written disconrse, in poetic or plastic expressions, in historical reminiscience or writing, in ritual performance and acts of worship.

This interior need to penetrate beyond the screen of immediate concrete experience marks the existence of the intellectuals in every society. We might, therefore, consider the African musician, the African artist, the African medicine man, the story teller, the town crier and, perhaps, even the African witch doctor as intellectuals who could contribute to our understanding of African communication variables. It can be argued that these intellectuals are constantly engaged in distinct forms of communication that are peculiar to the African social and cultural milieu.

For the traditional intellectual, the primary modes of observation include authority or tenacity, where the views of authority or arguments which our instincts lead us to consider as reasonable may be used to establish the validity of our propositions.

For the modern intellectual, it is science, or the social scientific methods. Considering the inherent threats to validity in both science and authority as methods of knowing, how might African scholars reconcile these two modes in their attempts to generate a hybrid approach to the study of communication?

In using survey research and interview, for example, Obeng-Quaidoo (1986) suggests that researchers begin to experiment with interviewing family groups instead of individuals. The rationale is that in the African context, 'children and young adults are not supposed to talk when older people are talking... (and) due to the male dominance in most African societies, wives at times want their husbands to answer all questions, even those relating to contraception and family planning.' Further, it has been suggested that African scholars undertake studies involving the possible integration of folk media with modern mass media, or the effectiveness of one compared with the other (Ugboajah 1985:).

Another useful approach to the study of African modes of communication is to view communication as a form of culture, for it is culture that determines how members of a society communicate with each other and what meanings they assign to various symbols. The cultural basis for the study of communication draws our attention to, *inter alia,* two levels of analysis of the variables and constructs of mass communication research, namely, the universal and contextual levels. In this respect, we may study the agenda-setting function of the mass media, the ability of the media to determine the important issues of the day, as a universal construct from society to society and wherever forms of the modern media of mass communication are found. We may also study the same construct at the contextual level in a traditional African/rural environment where the modern media might be non-existent. In this case we may ask: to what extent do folklore and traditional media lend salience to certain issues?

The context in this case will be defined on the basis of the cultural factors that guide the channels of African communication — folklore, dance, rituals, arts, etc., and the operations of African traditional media. ditionally, this cultural perspective may help resolve the contending issue of Eurocentric bias — the tendency by Westerners or Western-trained scholars to interprete non-Western phenomena from Western perspectives. Asante (1980) suggests that Africans adopt a posture of 'intellectual vigilance' towards scholarship that ignores the origin of civilization in the highlands of East Africa (1980); that they become 're-creative' intellectuals by taking the visions of our ancestors to new heights.

This evidently would require that the African intellectual goes all the way back into time and re-examines the historical facts about Africa's contribution to world civilization. That Africans were in the vanguard of scientific development, pioneers in medicine, writing and architecture has been widely documented by many African historians (DuBois 1965, Williams 1976, James 1976). One has to study that history to discover the African heritage.

As a way of determining the true African heritage, Chancellor Williams (1976) approached this problem by segregating traditional African institutions from those influenced by Islamic Asia and Christian Europe. 'In this way, and in no other, we can determine what our heritage really is and, instead of just talking about 'identity', we shall know at last what purely African body of principles, value systems or philosophy of life — slowly evolved by our forefathers over countless ages — from which we can develop an African ideology to guide us onward. In other words, there can be no real identity with our heritage until we know what our heritage really is. It is all hidden in our history, but we are ignorant of that history. Because of such ignorance, African intellectuals sometimes embrace the idea that mass communication was introduced in Africa by Europeans.

That is not so. Our history is replete with many creative uses of the drum as a form of mass communication before the advent of the modern media. Consider, for instance, the amazing feat of ingenuity by Queen Nzinga, a 17th century Angolan ruler of valor who inspired her people to continue the war of resistance against the Portuguese.

Dethroned and exiled by the Portuguese, Queen Nzinga mobilized an army and orchestrated many guerilla attacks against the Portuguese, eventually winning the war and regaining her crown. Meanwhile, news of her war efforts was being simultaneously spread among her people through coded messages of the drum (Williams 1976).

Makinde (1986) makes a strong argument for the modern use of the town crier in an African context, noting that 'town criers, like the village minstrel, the drums, the gongs, and various musical devices, have been used since time immemorial as veritable means of disseminating information in rural communities'.

It is not unreasonable, therefore, to suggest that not only did the drum as a channel of mass communication exist in Africa before the advent of the modern media, but that genuine research and development in African communication must take serious interest in the drum and other modes of African communication from both historical and contemporary perspectives.

It is important to remember that conventional (Western) definition of mass communication, with its stipulation of an institutionalized source, and newspapers and the electronic media (radio and television) as channels, precludes the purely African modes of communication. For this reason, the parameters of African mass communication research do not necessarily have to conform to such obviously delimiting, and culturally influenced (Eurocentric) definition. Ideally, African mass communication research efforts should be geared towards syncretization, as exemplied, for example, in Makinde's (1986) conceptualization of the town crier for rural communication:

The modern town crier, as is being proposed for use in rural communication, would retain some of the trappings of his olden counterparts; he would be well known to the community in which he operates; he would be able to speak in the language in which his audience is versed; he would understand the culture and traditions of his audience, and would, possibly, be a resident of the area in which he operates. He would as well imbibe the attributes of the modern communicator: fairly educated, knowledgeable of government policies, programmes, objectives, and activities and armed with government publications and a loudspeaker. He would be able to accommodate questions and measure people's reaction for eventual feedback to government. The modern day town crier would move about on four wheels which enables him to cover long distances within a short time.

Several propositions have been made tor a formulation of a philosophical foundation for African communication research.

For example, Asante's Afrocentricity, which advocates that the African heritage become the primary frame of reference for the African in his day-to-day existence, could be viewed as a philosophical treatise that can provide guidance for African communication research. For, ' Afrocentricity seeks to modify the traditional where necessary to conform to the demands of modern society rather than to abandon those systems that have lasted through the centuries' (1980). Okigbo (1987) argues for a philosophy of communication derived from the African tradition that could give meaning and direction to African communication research. Such philosophy, 'if fully articulated, developed and nurtured, will contribute immensely in improving our thinking and activities concerning our important daily problems'. Similarly, Blake (1979) argues for the 'pedagogical bases for communication studies in Africa', that take into account 'the philosopical influences that guide our structure and practice of teaching', particularly in regard to the practical aspects of structure/content and instruction in African institutions of higher learning. Although the parameters of some of these propositions are not so well defined as yet, they are interesting and important ideas that should be a part of the African communication research agenda.

The thesis or dissertation process might seem intimidating, especially as critics harp on such seemingly trivial matters as measuring tools, study designs, statistical or interpretative procedures, tests for reliability and validity, units of analysis, metaphor, meaning, and historical significance. But theory and research, despite the fact that their qualities seem mysitcal to the initiate, are by no means extraneous to understanding the communication process—whether it be an understanding of the theoretical or applied aspects of communication.

The purpose of the thesis or dissertation exercise is to master a skill that has its own common sense standards that differ from traditional standards.

The purpose of the thesis or dissertation is more than simply to master the content. It involves learning via a mode of conceiving and conceptualizing in which hypotheses or research questions are derived from theory. The hypotheses or research questions are then tested in a manner adhering to agreed-upon standards for gathering evidence, be they quantitative or qualitative in nature. Mastering narrow and perhaps esoteric bodies of research and conducting research based on the literature has, admittedly, little value for students unless they plan to continue in that area. But mastering theoretically based research skills are immensely valuable to the student, scholar, or practitioner who plans to generate or consume primary or secondary research in the future.

WHERE NO ONE HAS GONE BEFORE

Theory organizes and refines our ideas, like a map for exploring unexplored territories. Imagine exploring new lands without at least examining the maps and writings of past explorers to see what rivers and lands they traversed. Although we do not put complete faith in old adventurers' maps and writings, we would be foolish to ignore what others have done.

The novice researcher or the seasoned scholar, excited by a new idea while in the bath, almost always emerges from the bathroom proclaiming that "no one has ever thought of this before." That researcher is like the explorer who believes no one has ever gone, or tried to go, where he or she plans to go. Even cursory investigation, however, usually reveals that others have gone—or tried to go—where the novice researcher plans to go. Theoretically driven research involves building and testing on the knowledge of previous explorers. In this opening chapter, we examine the link between theory and research method-ology, and integrate these two primal aspects of academic study in communication. Our approach is simple: The *research* process itself is integrated. One cannot conduct good research without theory and good theory development requires good verification.

THE CHANGING RELATION BETWEEN THE MEDIA

A number of trends in U.S. society would seem logically to lead to a prediction that important research on the process and influences of mass communication would have increased, rather than decreased. Specifically, the media have expanded and become more complex; their labour force has grown considerably; and colleges and universities now offer far more instruction related to work in the media labour force than ever before. Yet, as already mentioned, there has been no corresponding increase in the production of ground-breaking studies.

THE GROWTH OF THE MEDIA LABOUR FORCE

It is now widely understood that over the last half-century the United States increasingly became an information society. In the older manufacturing-based economy, blue-collar employees worked on factory floors producing things with their hands and machines. However, after midcentury, more than half of our workers were manipulating words and numbers to provide both products and services. With the coming of the computer revolution and the increasing globalization of the economy, the pace of that change has accelerated.

One reason that the percentage of the workforce manipulating symbols, as opposed to things, has increased greatly is that our media system has continued to expand. Before midcentury that system included only telegraph, telephone, print, radio, and film. Today, it includes not only all of the earlier media, but also fax, cellular phones, video-cassette recorders, television, cable, satellite television delivery, and the Internet — with its e-mail, local networks, and World Wide Web. As the media system expanded, a corresponding need for communication specialists and practitioners grew. This, in turn, increased the need for media-related education and has expanded the number of communication professors, scholars, and researchers.

THE GROWTH OF MEDIA-RELATED CURRICULA

Preparing a well-educated labour force for the media industries posed a new challenge for colleges and universities. At the close of World War II, there was a very limited relation between the mass media and the U.S. academy.

Journalists had been educated on campus for decades, but that was not the case for other media professionals. Only a limited number of fledgling programmes existed to prepare students for careers in movie making and radio broadcasting or other media employment. No degree programmes existed in such fields as advertising or public relations.

As television usage spread, a similar situation prevailed. Institutions were slow to offer industry-related curricula. In the more general field of mass communication studies, there certainly were no advanced academic programmes designed around studies of research and theory development. The 1960s saw the beginnings of a gradual and long-term expansion in the number of programmes, departments, schools, and other academic units with curricula focused specifically on the mass media. Some were theory- and research-based programmes. Others were professionally oriented, providing for media-related career training. At present, undergraduate, master's, and doctoral degree programmes in mass comm-unication exist on many campuses. Professional programmes prepare students with the skills needed in such fields as advertising, public relations, film production, and broadcast news. Some programmes remain theory oriented, preparing students to conduct basic research on mass communication. In the professional schools, in particular, many of the courses are now taught by part-time professors, often brought in from the media. In such settings, the study of research methods and theory development may be marginal at best or simply ignored.

Today, students can graduate with a degree in, or at least a major in, media-related communication at the majority of U.S. institutions of higher learning. The numbers rise or fall from time to time, but somewhere between 5 per cent and 10 per cent of all undergraduate and graduate degrees now granted in the United States are in various fields of media-related communication.

That change has not always been a smooth one. Media-related studies are still regarded with suspicion by many traditionalists on campus. They are not always respected by professors, or even administrators, from the physical, biological, and social sciences. Nevertheless, course work in such fields as advertising, public relations, marketing communication, magazine publishing, film and television production, broadcast journalism, and the use of the Internet as a medium for public communication are now providing an annual pool of college graduates that can be hired to exercise the many specialized skills that are at the heart of those industries.

THE DECLINE IN THE PRODUCTION OF RESEARCH MILESTONES

From these three trends one might logically predict that there would be a corresponding increase in significant research on the process and effects of mass communication. Few would disagree with the conclusion that the growing presence and importance of mass communication in the lives of individuals has increased the need to understand their nature and influences. It follows, then, that scholars in the communications disciplines should now be formulating and testing more and better theories, many with practical importance, to explain how the media function and how they influence people, both individually and collectively.

However, in fact, that has not been the case. The development of media theory seems stalled. For a time, earlier in the 20th century, scholarly enquiry and the development of research-based theories to explain the process and effects of mass communication did increase at a rapid rate. Starting even before World War II, and continuing until the early 1980s, scholars conducted a number of seminal studies aimed at understanding the nature, functions, and consequences of mass communication.

As the scientific study of media influences got underway, it was psychologists and sociologists who provided leadership. Some of the Payne Fund studies concluded that movies had powerful influences on children. Later, in 1938, a quantitative study reported that a radio programme prompted millions of people to panic. These findings reinforced beliefs in the *magic bullet* theory, an earlier and now discredited formulation explaining that the media had immediate, uniform, and powerful effects on all who were exposed to their messages. Later, as additional studies were reported, the concept of powerful media began to be questioned.

The results from studies of the influences of training films by the U.S. Army led to a new formulation, now termed the *selective and limited influence theory.* It explained that the media could change beliefs, opinions, attitudes, or behaviour for only some people under some circumstances. The classic Erie County study of media influences on a presidential election campaign showed that belief in powerful, immediate, uniform, and widespread effects was no longer tenable. This milestone also led to important theoretical concepts, such as the two-step flow of communication and personal influence. Clearly, empirical research was beginning to reveal with greater accuracy the complex relation between the mass media and their audiences.

Additional milestone research revealed that the media were not particularly powerful, that the audience was highly selective, and that the process of shaping people's beliefs, attitudes, and behaviour with mass communications is very complex. Studies now regarded as classics yielded such insights as the *uses and gratifications theory,* explaining that audiences used content from the media as guides for their personal choices and derived many psychological rewards from exposure to mass communications. Another modest experiment led to *modeling theory,* which explained the influence of media-depicted models of actions or situations on acquiring new forms of behaviour.

A study of Iowa farmers in a relatively obscure journal provided the foundation for *adoption of innovation theory,* describing the pattern followed when people begin using new products or processes after obtaining information from the media. Other classic research yielded theories of persuasion, explaining how the structure and other features of a message were related to changing beliefs, attitudes, and behaviour.

A study of a small community showed how personal influence was exercised in the two-step flow of communication from the media to opinion leaders, and from them to others who did not attend directly. More recently, *agenda-setting theory* was formulated to explain how levels of prominence selected by the media in forming their agenda play a part in setting personal agendas among their audiences. At one point, attention to television almost crowded out research on other media. Its influences on individuals and society were addressed in literally thousands of studies. A major focus was on the relation between portrayed violence on TV and aggressive conduct in children and youth. This issue was a special focus for psychologists. Their interest was not so much on the process of mass communication, as such, but on media-provided stimulus factors that produce aggressive or violent behaviour. By the end of the 1970s, it seemed clear that under certain circumstances, the portrayal of violence in television content could increase somewhat the probability of aggressive behaviour in some kinds of children. That generalization still represents what we now know about that issue.

In retrospect, then, the decades from the 1930s to the early 1980s, appear to have been a kind of golden age of research on mass communication. During that period a significant number of studies had especially high theoretical yield. Some were large-scale efforts like the massive Payne Fund studies; others were methodological masterpieces, like the Erie County investigation. Few were programmatic — an exception being the Yale studies of persuasion. Others were small in scope, but theoretically important.

Early in the 1980s, however, the golden age all but came to an end. That is not to imply that research on mass communication ceased. During the last two decades thousands of studies have been published. However, most explored very specific issues or narrowly focused hypotheses; some retested or studied extensions of ideas generated by the original milestones.

Perhaps many scholars will challenge these conclusions, or claim that their personal research, or their favourite recent study, should be regarded as truly seminal. Perhaps they would be right. Overall, however, there has been a conspicuous decline in theoretical advances in the study of mass communication compared to the earlier period.

A major question is, Why? Are today's researchers less creative? Are the questions of media functioning and influences any less important? Are members of the public apathetic and uninterested in how mass communications influence them and their children? Is research on mass communications unrewarding, either in terms of personal interest or academic advancement? The answers to all of these questions seem to be a resounding "no." Today's researchers are equally smart and energetic; they have research methods and computer tools at their command that the older generation lacked; the public is still concerned; scholars still need research to develop reputations for career advancement. Where, then, have all the milestones gone?

The answer to why there has been a decline in theoretical productivity in the study of the mass media has no easy answer, but a case can be made that it lies in a complex set of changes that have taken place, both in society as a whole, and in the academy more directly. The sections that follow discuss those changes in an attempt to provide an explanation of why the production of influential research has slowed, or even stopped.

One factor has been the withdrawal of social scientists — who conducted most of the early milestones — from the mainstream of media research. A second is the failure to develop and establish a programmatic approach to the investigation of media processes and influences. A third is the shift away from science to qualitative studies and a focus on criticism within the communication disciplines. A fourth factor is the loss of talented researchers who leave the low pay of the academy to earn high salaries elsewhere. A fifth is that funds for studies of mass communication, especially from federal sources, are more difficult to obtain at present than was the case during the golden age of media research.

Sixth, and finally, there have been changes in the work environment of college and university professors in the field of mass communication that may limit their ability to conduct research resulting in significant scholarly publication. Each of these factors can be discussed more fully.

MASS-MEDIATED COMMUNICATION

There is little doubt that mass-mediated communication has become both more visually oriented and more technologically complex in recent years. Sophisticated graphical interfaces on the Web, seamless photo imaging in TV and print advertisements, and intricate colour information graphics in newspapers are evidence of this emphasis on presentation and its technologies.

This marriage of presentation and technology, however, is not a new phenomenon. Advances in one historically have gone hand-in-hand with advances in the other, from the invention of half-tone technology and new photo equipment to the introduction of colour television. More recently, the arrival of digital imaging technology has strengthened the marriage, and a much-anticipated move towards newsroom "convergence" points to the integration of technological and graphical knowledge with traditional journalistic knowledge.

Anecdotal evidence suggests media managers aggressively seek staffers with the skills to operate today's new technologies, and this demand necessitates training. Training may be gained in school or in the work place, but for those just out of college, school experiences may be the only option. This study explores the relative importance of knowledge of presentation technologies gained in school to the job-finding success of graduates of journalism and mass communication.

The study seeks to determine if level of technological skill predicts job-finding success even after accounting for more traditional school-related predictors such as grade point average, internship experience and curriculum sequence. As such, the study extends earlier work on the predictors of success in the journalism and mass communication labour market. In so doing, it draws on the sociological literature on the relationships between the skills of prospective employees and their likelihood of being hired. The hypotheses generated come from what is termed screening theory, which helps to contextualize the hiring decisions made by communication employers.

TECHNOLOGY AND MEDIA PRESENTATION WORK

Work involving presentation technology is not only becoming more advanced, it is apparently making this type of activity more central to overall work processes in media organizations by facilitating the integration of job tasks. Tasks are integrating because new technologies allow the bundling of work routines from previously separate tasks.

Digital technologies seem especially to facilitate convergence of tasks and roles within media organizations because the underlying language -information as a series of 0's and 1's-can be used in the production and networking of a variety of communicative symbols. Text, photos, video, sound, and the juxtaposition of all of these symbolic elements may all be translated into digital language. A convergence of broadcast, print, and Web technology is already taking place in isolated newsrooms around the country.

In addition, so-called WYSIWYG ("what you see is what you get") software such as pagination programmes, photo-imaging programmes, and Web-editing programmes facilitate task integration.

They do this by allowing those who write and edit text also to visualize and shape page designs, graphics, and photos, all at the same work station or at least in closer quarters. In Web work the tasks of presentation and content creation are perhaps most thoroughly integrated, as Web editors often design and produce images and pages, troubleshoot technical problems, edit copy, and write headlines. Of course, technological change is not the only explanation for task integration. Organizational size and structure are also strong influences.

Industry trade publications, anticipating technological convergence in newsrooms, are abuzz over a perceived need for journalists who can write, research, design graphics, shoot video, and build Web pages. Research also indicates media managers and staff value knowledge of technology highly.

Relevant studies include the following findings: computer skills are considered highly important in assessing applicants for reporting, editing, and design positions; newspaper editors who design list technological knowledge as the skill they most wish they possessed; and "digital darkroom skills" are second only to "good portfolio" in hiring criteria for photojournalism positions.

Technological expertise appears to be rivaling professional journalism knowledge in online work. A 2000 survey of online news managers found managers value both traditional journalism skills and Web knowledge such as the ability to write HTML. A 1999 study found that managers in online newspaper publishing give multimedia skills and computer knowledge greater weight than journalism experience in hiring decisions.

SKILLS, SCREENING, AND HIRING DECISIONS

Hiring is a highly uncertain activity, and frequent turnover and retraining are costly. According to sociological literature on skills and hiring, this in part explains why employers value specific skills learned through job experience, such as technological skills, more highly than a candidate's broader educational experience. Screening theory provides a framework for examining employer assessment of candidates' credentials. In contrast to human capital theory, in which education is viewed as increasing individuals' productive capacity, in screening theory educational credentials are viewed as a tool for employers. As a tool, however, they are inexact. These credentials are merely a proxy for reducing uncertainty in the early stages of the hiring process.

Employers do not focus on specific educational credentials but instead roughly correlate notions of job competencies with a general assessment of educational attainment. In addition, employers view educational attainment as much less important when evidence of productive capacity through on— the-job experience is available.

Often educational attainment is used only in the initial sorting of the candidate pool, while specific job experiences, if available, are used both in the initial sorting and as criteria in the final hiring. Employers for professional and technical jobs tend to focus on technical skills more than behaviour or trainability. Previous job performance and technical expertise have been found to be more important than educational record or personality traits in hiring decisions. However, a number of studies suggest personality fit plays a role as well, especially in the final hiring stages. In these final stages, employers tend to rely heavily on a less formal, but more specific, assessment of "fit" between a candidate, the hiring criteria, and organizational culture. Employers look among the final pool of candidates for highly specific elements of skill, experience, and personality fit called "hot buttons." A hot-button match may be more a result of good fortune than of successful preparation by the candidate.

Previous research findings on hiring for mass communication jobs are largely consistent with the findings of the broader sociological literature. Studies show that job candidates who have tangible experience in the media fields they are pursuing have more success finding work in these fields. Success in the classroom alone-as measured, for example, by grade point average-does not strongly predict job-finding success.

Internships and college media activities provide graduates with practical media work experience, and graduates with these experiences are better positioned in the job market. Other research has shown that media employers value results of practical skill-based tests by prospective employees more highly than they do classroom achievement. Studies also show that graduates who specialize in the media fields in which they seek work have more success finding jobs than those with a more general background or than those who specialize in something other than the field in which they seek work.

Research Questions and Hypotheses

The literature suggests the media are becoming more visually sophisticated and more technologically complex, and that managers may value technological know-how in a job candidate more than professional knowledge about media content. This makes sense from an organizational standpoint. In order to function at all, media organizations must first reduce uncertainty by ensuring that they control the technology necessary to produce and disseminate content. The urgency of this first step heightens in an atmosphere of technological ambiguity. Ensuring quality of content is an important step, but it is not as crucial as the first. The news media, for example, whether print, Web, or TV, do not require staff-created content to function. They may fill all of their pages, Web space, or airtime with syndicated content.

In addition, knowledge of presentation technologies is a specialized knowledge; both the sociological and mass communication literature on hiring indicate that job candidates who have job-specific skills and knowledge are most likely to find work. Therefore it is proposed here that skill with presentation technology should significantly impact degree of job-entry success by those seeking media positions.

This study focuses on the potential benefit of learning such skills in school prior to entering the job market. While screening theory suggests employers only rely on educational attainment (*e.g.*, GPA and type of degree) for sorting the initial pool when evidence of job-specific experience is unavailable, schools do play a role in training candidates for highly specialized skills. Students' experiences beyond the classroom, such as internships and involvement with campus media activities, provide more exposure to job-specific skills. By its very nature, technological skill is highly job-specific, thus rendering the issue of where the skill was learned less important.

For example, computer programmes comprise specialized rules by which work is accomplished, thus making it unnecessary for media organizations to teach these procedures and routines if they have been learned in school. In contrast, the procedures for tasks like writing headlines or conceptualizing the design of information graphics, while also embodying routines, are less constrained by rules and involve more uncertainty. These more malleable, content— oriented tasks allow, or even require, more specific shaping by the hiring organization.

Technological skills, therefore, are more likely to meet the specific "hot-button" needs of employers, especially when technology in the school and in the work place are identical or similar. Experiences tailored to specialized "hot-button" needs of the industry are most valuable to employers, whether learned during school internships or on the job.

Transferred to the individual level of the employee, these arguments suggest that graduates with specific skills will have more success in the job market than those without those specific skills. Consequently these specific skills will explain variance in job-seeking success once other less general skill sets are controlled for. This argument can be restated as the following two hypotheses.

- *H1a*: The greater the degree of skill with presentation technologies possessed by graduates, the greater the degree of success the graduates will have in the job market.
- *H1b*: The greater the degree of skill in presentation technologies possessed by graduates, the greater the degree of job-finding success graduates will have, even after controlling for traditional school-related predictors of job-finding success.

This study also addresses several other research questions, which are of a mostly descriptive nature. These include: Are those graduates who have knowledge of particular presentation technologies upon graduation likely to use these technologies in their work after school? And, in which media jobs are these particular technologies likely to be used?

Method

Data used in addressing these questions come from the 1999 Annual Survey of Journalism and Mass Communication Graduates, which tracks the experiences of a sample of graduates of journalism and mass communication programmes once they leave their universities.

The surveys are conducted at the Henry W. Grady College of Journalism and Mass Communication at the University of Georgia. Each year a sample of schools is drawn from those listed in the Journalism and Mass Communication Directory, published annually by the Association for Education in Journalism and Mass Communication, and The Journalists' Road to Success, published annually by the Dow Jones Newspaper Fund, Inc. Selection of schools is probabilistic, so that those chosen represent the population of schools listed in the two directories. In 1999, 102 schools were drawn from the 456 unique entries of four-year programmes in the United States in the two directories.

A questionnaire was mailed to the 6,613 spring graduates receiving either a bachelor's degree or a master's degree from the selected programmes. Two follow-up questionnaires were mailed to graduates as necessary. Included in the instrument were questions about university experiences, job seeking and employment, salaries and benefits, and experiences with media technology.

A total of 2,826 usable questionnaires were returned, producing a return rate of 47.4 per cent. Return rate, when computed as the number returned divided by the number mailed minus the bad addresses, was 50.8 per cent. Data used in the present study only include results gathered from full-time employed bachelor's degree recipients. Bachelor's degree recipients are the majority of graduates of journalism and mass communication programmes each year.

The independent variable, "skill in presentation techno-logies," was operationalized via self-reported level of proficiency by survey respondents with five different types of presentation software: pagination, graphic illustration, photo imaging, Web-site building, and non-linear editing. Degree of job-finding success, the dependent variable, was operationalized as the number of job offers graduates report receiving upon graduation. The traditional school-related predictors used here as controls were grade point average, sequence specialization, involvement with campus media activities, and involvement with media internships.

Specialization in media presentation was not common for graduates of the schools of journalism and mass comm-unication. In 1999, just slightly more than 1 per cent of bachelor's degree recipients reported selecting graphic design as a major, and roughly the same per cent reported photojournalism as a major. These figures have changed little over the last ten years.

Not only did few graduates report graphic design as a curricula specialization, few reported being proficient with presentation technology at the time of graduation. Data also showed that a relatively low percentage of bachelor's degree recipients reported using presentation technology in their current full-time jobs.

For four of the five software types measured in the graduate survey, one in five or fewer graduates reported being proficient. The percentages of those actually using these software in their current jobs were similarly low. The notable exception was page-design software. About half of the graduates reported being proficient with page-design software while more than 80 per cent reported being at least somewhat proficient. Nearly 60 per cent reported using this software for their jobs. It seems that the technological skill of assembling elements for print layout on computers is widely diffused in the work place. For most software types, close to half of the fulltime employed graduates who reported proficiency with a software upon graduation ended up using this software on their jobs. Again the exception is page-design software for which more than three-quarters reported use on the job. The chart reveals a substantial difference in actual use of software by all graduates and use of software by only those who said they were proficient upon graduation. This chart gives the first hint that the acquisition of expert technological skills in school may predict future use of these technologies in the workplace.

SOFTWARE USE ACROSS MEDIA TYPES

The work in each type of media industry involves unique technological processes, therefore necessitating the use of some graphic software programmes more than others. The data show that skill with page-design software is highly important to the work processes of graduates working at all media types, with the single and not surprising exception of television. Somewhat surprising is the high percentage of online-publishing workers who use page-design software. This may be explained by the fact that designers sometimes first design Web pages in page-design software and then use these designs as templates in Web-site building programmes. It may also be that many respondents who categorized their work as online publishing actually design print material as well. Graphic-illustration software is most heavily used by those in online publishing. Once again, the percentage of graduates working in television who use this software is the lowest.

Similarly, the percentage of graduates working for online publishing companies who use photo— imaging software was much higher than the percentages for other media types. Graduates working for newspapers, public relations, and advertising reported using this software in fairly high percentages, relative to percentage use of other software types.

The results for questions about non-linear editing software, which is used in television work, may reflect a measurement problem. While the percentage of those working in television using this software was the highest, followed by use in online publishing, the relatively high rate of reported use in newspapers is not tenable given the nature of print-media production processes (and most newsrooms aren't "converged" yet). It seems likely that the word "editing" in the question choice "non-linear editing" may have led to confusion by some respondents.

Not surprisingly, the percentage of graduates working in online publishing who reported actually using Web-site building software was much higher than were the percentages of those working for all other media types. The percentage of graduates working in public relations and in advertising who use Web-site building software was low, but it was higher than the percentages working for print media and TV who use this software.

It is clear that knowledge of presentation technology is more necessary to online publishing work in general than to work in the other traditional media industries.

Presentation technology may be more intricately woven into the fabric of the overall work process in online publishing organizations than in the work processes of print media, television, public relations, or advertising. The fact that Web work converges media forms-video, sound, photos, and text-is also a likely explanation.

REGRESSION ANALYSES: SOFTWARE PROFICIENCY AND JOB-FINDING SUCCESS

In order to test the hypotheses and determine the impact of technological knowledge on job-finding success, a zero-order correlation analysis and several regression analyses were conducted. To obtain the overall measure for the independent variable software proficiency, measures of proficiency in four of the five software types were summed.

Non-linear editing, which did not scale well with the other measures, was excluded from the scale for two reasons. First, there is a conceptual distinction between this technology and the other four.

Non-linear editing deals with moving imagery only, while the other software types are largely oriented towards still imagery and design. Second, as previously mentioned, results indicated some respondents might have been confused about the meaning of the term "non-linear editing." The alpha coefficient for reliability among the remaining four items was.

The dependent variable, degree of job-finding success, was measured by the number of job offers graduates reported having upon completing school. The analysis includes only the 1,897 bachelor degree recipients who sought employment with a communication employer, which is 72.7 per cent of the total sample. The mean of the dependent variable was 2.19 (number of jobs offered) and the standard deviation was 1.85. To test H1a, number of job offers received by under-graduates who sought communication jobs was correlated with degree of presentation software proficiency. The coefficient was.064 and was significant at the.01 level. H1a therefore received support.

Overall, the model shows these variables explain a significant though small amount of variance in job-finding success-2.6 per cent of the variance. The finding is consistent with the earlier work in the field of journalism and mass communication both in terms of the predictors and the relatively small amount of variance explained. Having an internship, participating in campus media and being a public relations major are the strongest predictors. The only other significant predictor is being a broadcasting major, and this relationship is negative. In the next model, the variable Degree of Presentation Software Proficiency is entered as a second block. The increase in variance explained is fairly small-from 2.6 per cent to 2.9 per cent-but the incremental change in R-square is significant at the.05 level. H1b receives support, as Presentation Software Proficiency does prove to be a significant predictor, even when accounting for the traditional predictors. Internships, Campus Media Activities, and Public Relations Major continue to be the strongest predictors. In neither model is GPA or Advertising Major a significant predictor.

While the model was significant, the amount of variance explained was quite small. In an attempt to clarify the role of proficiency with presentation technology in job success and improve the overall predictive model, regression analyses next were conducted to test predictors of receipt of a job offer in only the online publishing field. It was anticipated that proficiency with presentation technology would be a better predictor of success finding work specifically in online publishing than it was as a predictor of general job-finding success. This should be the case both because of the apparent importance of presentation software knowledge to Web work and because the model is more specifically targeted.

In the models predicting job-finding success in online publishing the dependent variable was scored as a dichotomy because variance was minimal beyond the 0/1 level. One is equal to receipt of at least one job offer in online publishing work at graduation, and zero is equal to the absence of such a job offer. Only the 300 bachelor degree recipients who sought work in online publishing were included in this analysis, and this number was 12.4 per cent of the total sample. Among these, 38.3 per cent received at least one job offer in online publishing. Because the dependent variable is dichotomous, both OLS regression and logistic regression models were used to assess predictors. There were negligible differences between the models, and OLS regression results will be shown here to make comparison with the earlier regression analysis easier.

The first model includes the traditional predictors of job-finding success, entered as a block. The R-square of the model is not significant. In the next model Proficiency with Presentation Software is entered as the only variable in a second block, and it and Campus Media Activities have the highest beta weights, at.089 each. The R-square of the new model is.026, but neither the change in the R-square nor any of the model's predictors test as significant.

Next, job-finding success in online publishing is regressed on more specific predictors-Campus Media Activities and Proficiency with Presentation Software are replaced with Campus Web Activity and Proficiency with Web-site building Software. In the first model only the traditional predictors are entered as a block (including Campus Web activity), and the R-square is.037. In the second model Proficiency with Web-site building Software is added as a second block, and this second model's R-square is.052. Proficiency with Web-site building Software, with a beta of.131, is the strongest predictor, followed by Campus

Web Each of these predictors are significant, and change in R-square is significant as well. It appears then that as independent variables are tailored more narrowly to the criterion variable, they become better predictors. It also appears that the nature of online publishing work is such that it requires a particularly high level of skill with the requisite presentation software.

However, it may be that Web work is no more demanding of software skills than other media work and that any model made more specific would predict more successfully. To assess this possibility, a final regression model was run for comparative purposes. This model also predicted receipt of a specific type of media job offer, but here the offer was from a daily newspaper job. Included in this model were GPA, sequence, internships, campus newspaper involvement, and proficiency with page-design software, the software most likely to be used by newspaper staffers. While being a print journalism major and working with a campus newspaper were the most important predictors, proficiency with page-design software was not a significant predictor. Neither was the model improved significantly. The results of this comparative analysis lend support to the conclusion that the importance of software proficiency to landing Web job offers is due at least in part to the nature of Web work, and not entirely to specificity of the model.

Study results show that degree of skill with presentation technologies matters to the job-finding success of journalism and mass communication graduates. Skill with presentation technology stands as a significant predictor of job-finding success, even when controlling for GPA, sequence specialization, number of internships, and campus media activities. If media technology and media processes continue to converge, as many industry experts predict, it seems likely presentation software skill will grow in importance.

For those seeking work in online publishing, knowledge of presentation software for the Web surpasses the importance of all the other school-related predictors traditionally associated with job-finding success. Given recent findings from the Annual Survey of Journalism and Mass Communication Graduates that the percentage of graduates taking jobs in online publishing is growing faster than all other media, it seems advisable for journalism and mass communication programmes to increase technological instruction for their graduates. Yet the present study finds that proficiency in online publishing technology (or any presentation technology) is not widespread among graduates of journalism and comm-unication schools. The recent downturn in the economic fortune of tech industries should be acknowledged here, and this focus on technological competence in hiring may change as media industries evolve. On the other hand, it is hard to imagine the industry becoming less visually oriented.

This study lends support to previous findings that media employers-and employers in general-tend to favour job candidates with jobspecific skills. According to screening theory, employers only rely on educational attainment when candidates in the pool lack job-specific, or so-called "hot button," skills. Educational credentials such as GPA serve only as a less-than-perfect proxy for assessing candidate fit. However, skills with presentation technology are job-specific by nature, and they may be taught through school curricula. The rules and routines embodied in these software are the same in school as in the workplace. As a result, employers may view skill with presentation software as a more reliable measure of evaluation than other credentials gained during schooling. Employers may be more likely to hire candidates with these skills because it is a convenient way to reduce uncertainty in the highly uncertain hiring process.

Study findings may also reflect the importance of technological processes to organizations undergoing technological change and indeterminacy. Online publishing is a relatively new field with relatively new technologies that are presently in flux. But as with the production of most mediated information, online production involves time constraints. In Web work, content may be disseminated on a constant, ongoing basis, and increasingly Web-savvy audiences expect sites to be always accessible. Securing the means of production necessarily takes priority over ensuring quality of content: the newspaper must come out, the show must go on, and the site must stay up. Technical skills and knowledge of production would be prioritized over skills and knowledge involved with crafting content. After all, it is possible for a Web site (or any media product) to be produced without using locally generated content. In fact many Web-site producers choose to fill their sites with nothing but "repurposed" text and images and links to the content of other sites.

Perhaps then it is not the degree of technological complexity of a media form that determines how important technological skills are to the operation of a media organization, but rather the degree of uncertainty about technological processes. Older, more established media forms have been able to routinize technological processes and the learning of these processes to a greater degree than has the new field of online publishing. The structural framework for the instruction of older technologies (*i.e.*, school curricula and training sessions in media and professional organizations) has been in place longer, and the principles and conventions adopted for instruction are more established. Such structures for learning are only now being established in online publishing. Once these structures are in place and processes are more routinized, employers in online publishing should be able to turn more attention to content quality.

The study does not directly address the issue of where graduates learned these skills. They may have learned them in classes, in internships, in campus media activities, or even in the privacy of their dorm rooms. Analyses not tabled show that graduates with media internships reported slightly higher levels of software proficiency. This issue should be addressed more directly in future studies.

While this study addresses the importance of technological knowledge to finding jobs, it does not explore the relative quality of such jobs. Knowledge of the software may be enough to help a graduate get hired, but not enough to put the graduate in a good job and foster promotion. There is some evidence to suggest that tasks involving presentation technology eat into time spent performing occupational tasks of a more conceptual nature. Workers relegated to routine technological procedures are less likely to control their work than those whose work knowledge is more abstract and less tied to specific technologies. Findings here suggest schools of journalism and mass communication benefit students through rigorous training in technological skills, but this need not be a zero-sum game. Ways must be found to teach skills in conjunction with more conceptual curricula.

Finally, while the data presented here suggest that job specific skills contribute to the success of graduates in the labour market, and that the more specific the skills the better they predict to success, these skills clearly play only a small role in the hiring decision. In fact, the analysis conducted here show that the vast majority of the variance in hiring is not explained by the job specific skills identified here or even by the more general attributes such as scholastic performance, represented by grade point average.

As noted, the hiring process involves not only an assessment of specific skills, but also an assessment of personality fit, the extent to which an individual will mesh with the organizational culture, and the extent to which candidates are able to match the highly specific and hard— to-anticipate "hot-button" needs of employers. How the applicant presents herself or himself in the interview situation is not measured by any of the variables included in the analysis here. As a result, it is possible to argue, based on the data at hand, that specific skills are important predictors of job market success for journalism and mass communication graduates, but it is not the case that these are the main determinants of success. The main determinants of success will be identified only with additional research in this area.

In recent years, radio and television stations consistently have offered entry-level news salaries below those provided by daily newspapers, public relations, and advertising employers. Yet the broadcast industries report no difficulty in finding people willing to take their jobs. One possible explanation for low salaries in broadcast news is that universities are producing a surplus of graduates, holding down the salaries that are offered. Another explanation is that the lure of jobs in radio and television - the appeal of being a part of these "glamour" industries - is enough to fill the jobs available and keep wages low.

This chapter draws on roughly parallel surveys of hiring patterns in the daily newspaper, radio, and television industries to provide a test of these expectations. The results of these surveys are linked to data on recent graduates of journalism and mass communications programmes to make assessments of the fit between the demand for labour and the supply of labour in these industries. The Annual Survey of Journalism and Mass Communication Graduates, conducted at The Ohio State University, has shown a consistent gap between the entry-level pay of graduates who found full-time work at radio or television stations and those who found work elsewhere in communications. Survey respondents graduated about a year before being surveyed, so the term "entry-level workers" here describes new college graduates taking their first job after graduation. In 1994, only those graduates going to work for weekly, biweekly or triweekly newspapers earned salaries as low as those in television and radio.

The evidence available shows that the low entry-level salaries continue through the career of broadcast journalists. Drawing on data from his surveys of radio and television news directors over the last ten years, Stone shows low pay across almost all job categories in both types of organizations. Television pays well in the large markets and particularly well for anchors. Radio news directors even in large markets earn only about half as much as their TV counterparts. A disparity between the pay for broadcast and print journalists has appeared in the last twenty years. Although a survey conducted in 1971 by Johnstone, Slawski, and Bowman found journalists in television earning slightly more than those at newspapers, later surveys by Weaver and Wilhoit found broadcast journalists' pay lagging behind pay for print journalists. In 1991, the highest median salaries were earned by journalists at news magazines and wire services. They were followed by journalists at daily newspapers, television, weekly newspapers, and radio. Theoretical Issues Stone offers at least two explanations for the low pay in broadcasting. First, in the view of news directors, there is an excess supply of applicants. Second, broadcasting is seen as an attractive field, and people are willing to work for low pay. It seems likely that the attractiveness of the field encourages the excess supply in the first place, but there may be other factors that add to the excess supply as well.

The news directors' notion of excess supply is consistent with the general economic theory that demand and supply work in the labour force as well as the marketplace. According to the labour market application of the demand and supply model, the low pay reflects the fact that there are too many qualified individuals seeking a limited number of jobs. When there is a surplus or excess supply of labour, employers offer low wages, and the supply decreases.

The labour supply curve is a positively sloping straight line illustrating an increasing supply of workers as wages offered increases. The labour demand curve is a negatively sloping line illustrating a declining demand for workers as the wages increase. The intersection of the demand and supply curves is the equilibrium wage, which is what the industry should offer.

The argument that the field is attractive and therefore pay need not be high is frequently heard for various occupations and should not be dismissed out-of-hand. Professors, for example, do not earn salaries comparable to what persons with their education or training would earn in industry. They accept positions at the university, however, because of other benefits. In American society, few institutions are as prominent as television. Broadcasting offers public visibility and star status not provided by many other occupations. These are "benefits" that may compensate for low pay, at least in the view of young persons seeking entry-level work. In the language of labour economics, these "benefits" must be offset with higher wages by competing media industries. The newspaper industry, if this interpretation is correct, must offer its employees a "compensating wage differential" since broadcasting is such an attractive alternative.

These are two explanations for the low pay in broadcasting. If the excess supply argument holds, the higher pay earned by entry-level hires at daily newspapers compared to broadcasting should result from differences in the supply of trained graduates. If supply is not the determinant of salaries, but rather the perceived attractiveness of broadcasting, then supply should be unrelated to salary. It is possible that both supply and the attractiveness of broadcast jobs work together to hold down wages in broadcasting. If supply is comparable for newspapers and broadcasting, the observed differences in wages may be explained as a "compensating wage differential." If supply is greater for broadcasting than for newspapers, both supply and compensating differentials may be at work.

Data allowing for a comparison of the supply and demand for entry level jobs in broadcast news versus the daily newspaper industry were obtained for the first time in 1991. Stone incorporated items dealing with hiring practices in his annual survey of news directors of television and radio stations. Similar items had been included in the 1991 survey of daily newspaper editors conducted for the Dow Jones Newspaper Fund. The 1991 newspaper survey, was, in turn, a replication of a study conducted by the Newspaper Fund at irregular intervals beginning in 1970. These surveys provide parallel data on demand for labour. Data on supply can be inferred from the 1991 Annual Survey of Journalism and Mass Communication Graduates.

In the broadcast news survey, questionnaires were mailed in the summer of 1991 to all 960 non-satellite commercial television stations in the United States and a probability sample of 810 commercial radio stations drawn from the population of 6,600 stations. Joint AM-FM news operations were counted as a single station. After two mailings, responses were received from 506 television stations (53 per cent) and 315 of the radio stations (39 per cent). News operations existed at 412 of the responding television stations and 275 of the responding radio stations. Only broadcast stations with a news operation were used in these analyses. Editors at 1,590 daily newspapers in the United States were sent a questionnaire in January of 1991. After two mailings, 704

(44 per cent) responded. The survey paralleled one conducted by the Newspaper Fund in 1986 and dealt entirely with hiring practices.

In the broadcast survey, news directors were asked how many newsroom staff were hired in the past twelve months and how many of those were hired directly out of college. In the editor survey, respondents were asked to indicate how many persons were hired for the newsroom staff in 1990. Staff hires were broken down by position. In each case, the number of hires directly from college was determined.

The annual survey of graduates of U.S. journalism and mass communications programmes is conducted each year by the School of Journalism at The Ohio State University. A sample of schools is drawn from those listed in the Journalism Career and Scholarship Guide, published each year by the Dow Jones Newspaper Fund, and the Journalism and Mass Communication Directory, published annually by the Association for Education in Journalism and Mass Communication. To be included in the guide, the college or university must offer at least ten courses in news-editorial journalism including core courses, such as an introduction to the mass media and press law, as well as basic skills courses such as reporting and editing. Schools list themselves in the AEJMC Directory.

Administrators at the selected schools are asked to provide the names and addresses of their spring bachelor's and master's degree recipients. As the second step in the annual survey, a questionnaire is mailed in November or December to all spring graduates receiving either a bachelor's or a master's degree from the selected programmes. A second questionnaire is sent to non-respondents in January or February.

In the autumn of 1990, the survey was mailed to 5,002 individuals whose names and addresses were provided by the administrators of the eighty programmes sampled. A total of 2,948 respondents returned the questionnaires by the end of May of 1991. Of the returns, 2,596 were from students who reported they had actually completed their degrees during the April to July 1990 period. A total of 223 questionnaires were returned undelivered. Return rate computed as the number of questionnaires returned divided by the number mailed was 59 per cent. Return rate computed as the number returned divided by the number mailed minus the bad addresses was 62 per cent.

The graduate survey includes detailed questions on types of jobs sought and obtained by the respondents as well as type of curricular specialization. The data can be generalized to the population of graduates for that year, estimated by Becker to be approximately 33,300 bachelor's degree recipients and 2,700 master's degree recipients.

Becker reported that 57 per cent of the 1989-1990 graduates of journalism and mass communications programmes actually completed their studies in spring of that academic year, *i.e.*, spring of 1990. There is no reason to believe the graduates completing their studies at times other than spring would engage in different job hunting tactics or have different curricular specialization while in college.

A comparison of the schools in the OSU surveys and data obtained via a U.S. Department of Education census of four-year degree-granting institutions of higher education shows the appropriateness of the OSU data for this project. The Department of Education reported that 41 universities offered degrees in radio/television news broadcast in academic year 1990-91. All but 9 (78 per cent) are in the corresponding OSU survey. Of the 131 universities reporting degrees granted in radio/television (news broadcast and general), 93 (71 per cent) were included in the corresponding OSU survey. Of the 329 universities offering degrees in journalism/mass communi-cations, 260 (79 per cent) were included in that year's OSU survey.

In terms of degrees granted, however, the distortion is even smaller. Of the 6,641 degrees the Department of Education says were granted in radio/ television (news broadcast and general), all but 14.1 per cent were granted by schools included in the OSU surveys. Of the 12,173 degrees granted in journalism, all but 6.2 per cent were granted by schools included in the OSU surveys.

The methodology of the Department of Education census is distinct from the OSU methodology. A student receiving a degree from a journalism school would almost certainly be classified as receiving a journalism degree, though the student might well have specialized in broadcast journalism. The OSU Survey also includes data from schools not reporting communications degrees to the Department of Education. In sum, the OSU data allow for more precise designation of degrees granted by subfield of communication. The OSU Graduate Survey, based on reports of the graduates themselves, provides data not only on curricular specialization at the university but also types of work sought.

By combining the graduate data from the Annual Survey of Journalism and Mass Communication Graduates with the data on degrees granted, it is possible to make an estimate of the number of persons in the labour pool. This estimate can then be matched to the labour needs obtained from the news director and editor surveys.

Radio stations hired an estimated 5,444 persons for their news operations in 1990-91, 39.4 per cent of them from other radio stations. Another 34.0 per cent were hired directly from college. Of these college hires - or entry-level hires - 76.9 per cent had a journalism major, a little over half of them specializing in broadcast journalism. Some of these entry-level hires will have completed a master's degree; others will have earned a bachelor's degree. Becker projects that only 7 per cent of the journalism and mass communications degrees granted in 1989-90 were at the graduate level. The questions on hiring were less detailed (with less information obtained on the majors of the graduates), but the comparison shows that number of hires in radio has declined markedly from 1984 to 1990-91. The percentage of hires in radio coming directly from college, however, has increased about 11 per cent, a statistically significant change (at the.05 level). This offset a decline in radio hires from jobs outside broadcasting. Total radio news staffs were estimated at 19,700 in 1984 and 16,900 in 1991.

Television hired an estimated 5,069 persons for their news staffs in 1990-91, 64.9 per cent of them from other television stations. Television news directors report hiring 18.1 per cent of their 1990-91 employees directly from college. Of these, 91.1 per cent came from journalism and mass communications programmes. The 1990-91 television hires are an increase of just over 1,000 persons from the number hired in 1984. The percentage being hired directly out of college in 1990-91 is statistically comparable to 1984. Total television news workforce was 17,100 in 1984 and 23,100 in 1991.

Because of differential return rates by newspaper size in the 1990 survey of daily newspaper editors, the returns were weighted so as to accurately reflect the population of newspapers stratified by size. The sample data were then used to project the number of hires at the full population of daily newspapers. The daily newspaper industry hired an estimated 8,941 persons in 1990,55.0 per cent of them from other newspapers. The second largest group of hires came directly from college. These are entry-level hires. Of the daily newspaper hires directly from college, three-quarters came from journalism programmes. Just under 16 per cent of the new hires at daily newspapers in 1990 came from non-media jobs, and 7.1 per cent were hired away from other media. The 8,941 new hires for 1990 represent 15.7 per cent of the 56,900 newsroom employees estimated to be holding jobs in daily newspapers at the end of 1990.

The 1985 data have been weighted to reflect the population characteristics of 1990 so as to make the data sets comparable and correct for sampling bias in that earlier survey. Comparisons of the 1985 and 1990 surveys show the dramatic decline in hiring at daily newspapers during that period. The decline in hiring is accompanied by a decline (significant at the.05 level) in the percentage of hires coming directly from college, and, among the new hires, a slight (and statistically non-significant) decline in the percentage coming from journalism programmes. In actual numbers, there were 2,221 fewer hires directly from college in 1990 than in 1985, or a decline of 53.0 per cent.

Clearly, not all entry-level hires in radio, television, and daily newspapers come from journalism and mass communications programmes. The data presented here, as well as earlier research by Becker, Fruit and Caudill, Giles and Stone, indicate that the bulk of them do. Consequently, it is reasonable to turn to the Annual Survey of Journalism and Mass Communication Graduates for 1990 to estimate the supply of graduates for these jobs.

Respondents to the annual survey of graduates are asked if they had sought employment in radio, television, or daily newspapers since graduation. Among the 1990 bachelor's degree recipients, 18.0 per cent reported looking for a radio job, 25.7 per cent reported looking for a job in television, and 22.4 per cent sought daily newspaper positions. Based on the estimated 33,331 journalism bachelor's degrees granted that academic year, this would translate to 6,000 bachelor's degree recipients seeking work in radio, 8,566 seeking work in television, and 7,466 seeking work in daily newspapers. If master's degree recipients are added, the gross estimates are 6,090 in radio, 9,087 in television, and 8,239 in daily newspapers.

These estimates of the labour supply are gross in that they do not take into consideration the basic requirements of journalistic work in radio, television, and daily newspapers. A student with a degree in advertising and an internship with an advertising agency would not be qualified for the news positions of concern here. Qualification for the job has to do minimally with curricular specialization within journalism and mass communications, internships, and work for the appropriate campus medium.

In the view of news directors and editors, an applicant who has not learned the basics of writing and reporting for that medium is not qualified. Similarly, an applicant who has had an internship in the medium would be viewed as more qualified than one who has not. Work for the campus radio station would provide the applicant with more of the skills needed for radio work and more experience in the routines of that medium than a student without that experience. Students in television obtain relevant experience working for the campus television station; print students obtain their relevant experience with the campus newspaper.

5.2 per cent of the respondents in the graduate survey specialized in radio/television and sought a job in radio, 8.9 per cent of the graduates specialized in radio/television and sought a job in that medium, and 9.3 per cent specialized in print journalism and sought a job with daily newspapers.

The extra qualified graduates are those who did two of the following: specialized in the relevant curriculum, interned for the relevant medium, or worked for the relevant campus medium. The highly qualified graduates did all three. Only 648 graduates of 1989-90 would be labeled as highly qualified for jobs in radio, 1,008 would be considered highly qualified for television, and 1,619 would be highly qualified for daily newspapers. There were 3.29 persons seeking each of these jobs. The ratio of extra qualified persons to jobs available, however, was 1.17 to 1, while the ratio of highly qualified persons to jobs in radio news was 0.35 to 1.

For television, the ratio of persons seeking jobs to jobs available was 9.9 to 1. The ratio of extra qualified persons to jobs available was 3.8 to 1. The ratio of highly qualified entry-level applicants to jobs available was 1.1 to 1. For daily newspapers, the ratio of graduates seeking daily newspaper jobs to entry-level jobs available was 4.18 to 1. For extra qualified persons, the ratio was

2.06 to 1. For highly qualified persons, the ratio was 0.82 to 1. In sum, regardless of criterion used, television has an excess supply of applicants to entry-level job openings. At the gross level, this is nearly 10 persons for each job available. At the extra qualified level, the ratio is nearly 4 to 1. Neither of the other media enjoy this type of excess supply. In fact, when the OSU survey is compared to Department of Education data, all but 14.1 per cent of degrees granted in radio/television are included in the calculated labour supply for this study, compared to all but 6.2 per cent of journalism degrees.

Thus, the labour supply of radio/television graduates is probably even proportionately larger than the supply of journalism graduates. The data support the argument that television does not have to pay high wages because supply is outstripping demand.

For daily newspapers, there also is an excess supply of persons seeking jobs. That excess supply is 4 to 1 if job seekers are used as the criterion, and 2 to 1 if moderate qualifications are imposed.

If daily newspapers want the graduates who specialized in news-editorial journalism, had an internship with a newspaper, and worked for the campus paper, they will find that demand outstrips supply. This might explain the higher wages paid by daily newspapers in contrast to television news operations.

Radio presents a complicated picture. Wages in radio news were the lowest among the three employers examined here. Yet radio has the lowest ratios of supply to demand. There are three times as many jobs as highly qualified persons seeking them - using the criteria enumerated above.

The ratio of extra qualified persons to jobs available is close to 1 to 1. If radio reaches over to the television pool - as it may do over time - an even larger number of graduates is available. Many graduates may see radio as a steppingstone to television and readily make this transition.

It is also important to keep in mind that graduates with degrees in other fields compete with the graduates of journalism and mass communications programmes for entry-level jobs. Radio and daily newspapers report filling nearly 25 per cent of their entry-level jobs with these graduates.

That supply is almost limitless. Based on the data examined here, there is no evidence to support the argument that newspapers would have to pay higher salaries to compensate for the attractiveness of broadcasting. All three have adequate supplies of graduates. It does seem reasonable, however, that the gross excess supply in television serves to hold down salaries in the newsrooms.

THE IMPORTANCE OF COMMUNICATION SCHOLARS RESEARCHING THE INTERNET

Within the discipline, a handful of articles has addressed the importance of communication scholars studying the Internet. The reasons for study as well as the ways in which the Internet should be studied are varied. For example, in

1996, the Journal of Communication devoted the majority of its winter issue to "The Net." Within this issue, in a dialogue between Newhagen and Rafaeli, Rafeali pointed out that the development of the Internet, in part, is rooted in academe and, as such, "this alone behooves our involvement" in its study. Beyond this statement Rafeali suggested that researchers focus on what he called the "five defining qualities of communication" on the Internet which, although somewhat abstract, included "multimedia, hypertextuality, packet switching, synchronicity, and interactivity." Newhagen argued that communication researchers must take a more active role in understanding the Internet by first understanding computer architecture, an area often left to engineers. A bridge must be constructed between the worlds of communication and engineering so that communication researchers no longer find themselves in the position "where the engineers roll out a new technology, and we hold up numbers from 1 to 10, rating it."

Concerning the benefits of studying virtual reality, Biocca stated, "Communication researchers rarely have had the chance to observe the introduction, diffusion, and sociocultural presence of what may become the next dominant communication medium." However, he cautioned against viewing new communication technologies as a revolutionary by stating that many "new" technologies build upon, and borrow from, existing ones.

As such, researchers are likely to start out using existing theories and methods to study a new technology. He suggested focusing on questions such as the shape the medium is taking, and how the medium shapes and is shaped by the user-areas well suited to communication research. In a 1993 article, writing more broadly about humancomputer interface design, Biocca, as Newhagen was to do later in 1996, called for communication scholars to be more proactive in researching computer-mediated communication (CMC) by taking part in the design and development of new communication technologies. Although, both of Biocca's articles were written just prior to the Internet's widespread public diffusion, his ideas, as if in anticipation of its introduction, are very applicable to the Internet and have been echoed in the later writing of Newhagen and Rafaeli.

Other communication scholars assuming the importance of studying the Internet have suggested additional approaches to its study. December argued for the need to define specific units of analysis for Internet research that would act as guideposts for researchers, helping to facilitate cross study comparisons.

These four units were defined as media space, media class, media object, and media instance. He also proposed a definition of Internet-based computer-mediated communication as that which involves information exchange that takes place on the global, cooperative collection of networks using the TCP/IP protocol suite and the client-server model for data communication. Messages may undergo a range of time and distribution manipulations and encode a variety of media types. The resulting information content exchanged can involve a wide range of symbols people use for communication.

As such, he argued that the Internet is not a single medium but is instead made up of several media. Additionally, he cautioned that researchers studying on-line services such as Prodigy or America OnLine (AOL) should be aware that they were not actually conducting Internet-based research because these access providers offer proprietary services not available on the Internet.

While this caveat is technically correct, it is perhaps overly restrictive. In addition to offering proprietary services to its users, on-line vendors such as AOL also function as Internet Service Providers (ISPs), allowing for communications to be exchanged via the global network. In contrast to December, Morris and Ogan viewed the Internet as a single flexible mass medium capable of the synchronous and asynchronous transmission of text, audio, and video communication.They argued that the Internet provides the opportunity for communication researchers to rethink rather than abandon traditional views on mass media and to adopt a more flexible perspective on communication models.

Additionally, they suggested that researchers study the Internet using a variety of existing frameworks, such as network analysis, and theories, such as social presence. In summary, these scholars essentially argue that communication in relation to other disciplines should be a leader, if not the leader, in researching the Internet because it is a communication phenomenon.

Communication scholars need to be proactive and creative in their research designs in order to reach this goal. To do this, they must possess a thorough understanding of how the technology works by taking an active role in the design and evaluation of future Internet applications.

RATIONALE

Knowledge of the extent to which Internet-related topics have been addressed and what methods of enquiry have been applied can assist communication researchers in placing their work within a broader range of studies. This information also identifies over- and under-emphasized topics and methods.

Lastly, knowledge of the degree to which the Internet is represented within a discipline can provide researchers with a sense of the area's development and relative importance to the field as a whole. It is not uncommon for communication researchers to analyse articles within an individual journal or a range of journals in order to assess the status of the discipline as a whole with respect to a particular issue.

Examples of these studies include analyzing the frequency with which qualitative research is published, investigating the content and quality of published content analyses, and assessing the status of published mass communication articles by women across eight journals. Continuing this type of enquiry, this study examines the publication history of Internet research among five leading journals in the field.

JOURNAL SELECTION CRITERIA

While acknowledging the presence of newer electronic Internet and new technology-specific publications such as Internet Research and Journal of Computer-Mediated Communication, this study purposely focuses on mainstream, established communication journals. The reasons for this emphasis are threefold.

First, and most obvious, the Internet is a channel for communication and as such it falls within the realm for study by communication researchers and, in turn, publication in our leading, established communication journals. Second, established journals-those in existence for a period of decades-have the distinct advantage of having built both a reputation and a following over time. These journals are widely read within the discipline, contributing to scholars' perceptions of and currency with changes in the field. A third reason, closely related to the second, is that established journals can be viewed as historical records that document the field's evolution. Ideally, these journals reflect trends in the development of a discipline and the segments of society with which it deals as accurately as possible for the benefit of current and future scholars.

Selection of the five journals examined in this study employed two criteria: previous research identifying leading journals in the field and the reputation of Social Sciences Abstracts as a valid resource for communication research. In a content analysis of women's published research in mass communication, Dupagne, Potter, and Cooper identified eight leading communication journals, defined according to high circulation counts and low acceptance rates.

The journals identified in their study included: Communication Monographs, Communication Research, Critical Studies in Mass Communication, Human Communication Research, Journal of Broadcasting and Electronic Media, Journal of Communication, Journalism Quarterly, and Quarterly Journal of Speech.

These journals functioned as a starting point for this study; however, application of the second criterion, communication research indexed in Social Sciences Abstracts, resulted in the omission of four titles from the original list. The decision to further limit the journals examined was based on a twofold rationale. First, electronic databases are increasingly used by scholars to conduct literature searches because of their ease of use and convenience in comparison to print indexes. Within the vast realm of electronic indexes available for searching, Social Sciences Abstracts is a widely used leading index published by the highly reputable indexing service, H. W. Wilson Company. Second, subject-specific indexes, such as Social Sciences Abstracts, are typically more useful to and more likely to be used by scholars than general indexes, such as Expanded Academic Index, because they cover indexed journals in more detail, are more likely to index all articles in a journal rather than a chosen few, and they provide longer, more detailed abstracts.

By restricting the focus to leading communication journals indexed in Social Sciences Abstracts, this study attempts to take into consideration a broader view concerning how scholars in other disciplines might perceive the role of our discipline in the area of Internet research based on the presence of communication journal articles contained in the index. With the application of this second criterion, the final list of journals examined in this study include: Communication Research, Human Communication Research, Journal of Broadcasting and Electronic Media, Journal of Communication, and Journalism and Mass Communication Quarterly. Measures. This study uses December's definition of Internet-based communication but with a slightly more liberal view on what constituted Internet-based communication.

An article was considered Internetbased if it focused on computer-mediated communication technologies requiring access to an ISP, including services such as AOL or Prodigy, or closely simulated an Internet-based communication environment (*e.g.*, intranets, e-mail exchange between AOL members). This definition broadly included the Internet in general, intranets, World Wide Web (WWW), e-mail, mailing lists, bulletin boards, newsgroups, chat, virtual reality games such as multi-user domains (MUDs), and video/audio/text computer conferencing. From the interfaces specified above, it can be seen that in most instances Internet access was necessary for communication to occur. As with any area of research, certain information is useful in providing scholars with an overall sense of an area's progress or current status. For the purpose of this study, the concept of current status is operationalized into nine measures-author name, authorship, author rank, affiliation, topic, interface, method, total number of Internet-based articles per issue, and total number of research articles per issue. Identification of an area's primary researchers provides scholars with a sense of which perspectives may be dominant in an area of study. While quantity of publication by an author does not necessarily equate with quality of research, it can provide scholars, especially those new to an area, with a starting point in the literature. The same can be said for the order of authorship on an article.

Distinguishing between primary and secondary authors can indicate, but not necessarily guarantee, which researchers are initiating studies, taking primary responsibility for the studies, and acting as primary contacts or "experts" in an area. Knowledge of which universities or organizations are conducting research in a particular area is beneficial for those interested in matters such as networking, educational, and employment opportunities.

The rank (*e.g.*, faculty, staff, student) of an author provides information on the diversity or homogeneity of the contributors to an area of research. This study attempts to answer two basic questions. First, what is the frequency and pattern, if any, of published Internet-based research articles in five of the leading communication journals? Second, what do the contents of these articles reveal about the status of Internet research within and outside of the communication discipline?

UNIT OF ANALYSIS

The unit of analysis for this study was the scholarly communication research article that focused on Internet-based communication. This included "research in brief" articles but excluded editorials, rejoinders, and book reviews. Coders primarily read titles and abstracts to determine if an article fit this study's definition of Internetbased research. In instances where article titles and abstracts did not provide sufficient information, coders skimmed the articles for details.

POPULATION DATA

All research articles were examined in four major communication journals between the years 1994-1999. Because frequency of publication over time was one question asked by this study, population data were used instead of sample data in an effort to obtain a more accurate depiction of publishing trends across time by these journals.

The four journals selected for the main study included Communication Research, Human Communication Research, Journal of Broadcasting and Electronic Media, and Journal of Communication. A fifth journal, Journalism fa Mass Communication Quarterly, was selected for a pilot study to test the codebook. To identify leading communication journals publishing Internet-related articles, a basic keyword search was conducted using the term "Internet" in the Social Sciences Abstracts electronic database; four journals were consistently referenced in the search results and thus selected for closer examination. One limitation of this selection process concerns the exclusion of some communication journal titles from the Social Sciences Abstracts index. However, this limitation was considered acceptable given the broader focus of the study discussed earlier.

Despite this limitation, the five journals selected for this study are examples of the mainstream publication outlets available through most of the field's major associations: the Association for Education in Journalism and Mass Communication, Broadcast Education Association, and International Communication Association. The starting year for the study, 1994, was selected because, based on the Social Sciences Abstracts search results, in general, Internet publications did not begin to increase until that point in time. The first recorded Internet article in the database occurred in 1992; one article was referenced in 1993. However, in each year thereafter, the number of articles increased steadily. This pattern is consistent with the growing popularity of the Internet with the general public in the United States. The communication journals selected for study during this time frame contained a total of 961 research articles (323 from the pilot study and 638 from the main study). Each article was examined to determine if it met the definition of Internet-based research. Those articles that qualified were then coded.

OPERATIONAL DEFINITIONS

To answer the questions proposed in this study, nine measures were recorded for each Internet-based research article: author name, authorship, author rank, affiliation, topic, interface, method, total number of Internet-based articles per issue, and total number of research articles per issue. For each article the last name and initials of all authors were recorded.

Authorship was coded as primary (first author) or secondary (all additional authors). The rank of each author was coded as faculty, student, staff (university affiliated, non-faculty/non-student employees), government employee, business employee, or other. Author affiliation was recorded as the name of the university or organization with which the author was identified at the time of publication.

Rather than attempt to anticipate the range in subject matter, article topic was recorded as open text by each coder and then later grouped into six broad categories: access, adoption/diffusion, policy, research/theory, social interaction, and other. Interface, the application used to communicate via a computer, was divided into eight categories: World Wide Web, e-mail, mailing lists/newsgroups/ bulletin boards, chat rooms, virtual reality game sites (*e.g.*, MUDs, MOOs), video/audio/text-based conferencing, Internet in general (no specific interface identified), and other (coders recorded the specific interface).

Method of enquiry was coded as policy study, critique/essay (non-policy studies), interview/case study, content analysis (qualitative and quantitative), experiment, survey, other (coders recorded the specific method) and combination for multiple methods used within a single study (each method was recorded and then weighted). Lastly, for each journal issue, coders recorded the total number of Internet-based articles and overall total number of research articles.

CODING PROCEDURES

The author and another communication researcher acted as coders. The codebook was created by the author and reviewed for clarity by the second coder. A pilot test to check for intercoder reliability was conducted on all issues of Journalism and Mass Communication Quarterly, 1994-1999, resulting in a 100 per cent overlap of 323 articles. Discrepancies in coding were discussed, and slight modifications for the purpose of clarification were made to the codebook before proceeding to the four journals selected for the main study.

Reliabilities for the number of Internet-based research articles and total number of articles for the pilot test were at the acceptable levels allowing for the inclusion of these articles in the study, under separate reporting. Intercoder reliability for the main study was calculated using a 20 per cent overlap. Issues for the reliability check were selected using a stratified random sample. The total overlap between the coders contained 128 articles.

INTERCODER RELIABILITY

For the main study, the level of agreement concerning which articles qualified as Internet-based research was 98.4 per cent. Percentages of agreement and Scott's pi corrections for chance (where applicable) were as follows for the measures: author name, 97.9 per cent; authorship, 97.9 per cent.96; author rank, 97.9 per cent.97; affiliation, 97.9 per cent; topic, 94.3 per cent; interface, 96.9 per cent.96; method, 97.7 per cent.97; and total number of research articles per issue, 96.9 per cent.

For the pilot study, percentage of agreement for Internet-based research articles was 84.6 per cent and 99.7 per cent for total number of articles per issue. Frequency analyses are reported for each measure. With the exception of overall trends in publishing, all other measures report data collected from the four journals in the main study. This is because intercoder reliability for the pilot study was only reached on the two measures: Internet-based articles per issue and total articles per issue.

TRENDS IN PUBLISHING

Of the 961 research articles analysed, 37 (3.9 per cent) were Internet-based. Among the four journals in the main study, 4.1 per cent (26 of 638 articles) were Internet-based. Trends in the publication of Internet-based articles across the five journals revealed no distinct pattern of increase, decrease, or stabilization during the six-year time period. This finding was also the case within each of the five journals.

Overall, the Journal of Communication (32 per cent) published Internet research articles the most frequently followed by Journalism and Mass Communication Quarterly (30 per cent), Journal of Broadcasting and Electronic Media (24 per cent), Human Communication Research (8 per cent), and Communication Research (6 per cent).

The percentage of published Internet-based research articles varied widely by year; however, a trend line reflecting a moving average suggests that the number of articles has increased over time.

TOPIC, INTERFACE, AND METHOD

Social interaction (31 per cent) was the topic most often researched. This was followed by research/theory (23 per cent); other (15 per cent), which included the topics of competition among local news web sites, digital art on the WWW, TV audience feedback via e-mail, and portrayals of the Internet in magazines; access (12 per cent) and adoption/diffusion (12 per cent); and policy issues (7 per cent).

The interface studied most often was the Internet in general (42 per cent) followed by mailing lists/newsgroups/bulletin boards (19 per cent), WWW (15 per cent), e-mail (12 per cent), and chat rooms (4 per cent), video/audio/text conferencing (4 per cent), and other (4 per cent) which included an Internet-based interactive health programme. The two most frequently used methods of enquiry were content analysis (27 per cent) and critique/essay (27 per cent).

These were followed by experiment (11 per cent) and survey (11 per cent), and, lastly, policy study (8 per cent), interview/case study (8 per cent), and combination (8 per cent), which included groupings such as network analysis and content analysis, and surveys and content analysis. The results of this study present a somewhat vague picture as to where this newest area of study is positioned within the selected journals.

In part, this is due to the low number of Internet articles available for examination and thus discussion. The results also indicate that scholars searching the Social Sciences Abstracts would find a scarcity of Internet-related research in our leading journals. It may be that the infrequent and uneven publication of Internet research in the journals examined is simply a typical reflection of any field's initial attempts to come to terms with a new area of study.

This finding suggests that Internet research is an area within the field that is clearly open for study. Within the four journals analysed, only two authors stood out in total number of publications potentially providing greater opportunity for other scholars to become better known through their research in comparison to more established areas in communication.

Not surprisingly, faculty are the dominant group publishing Internet research articles, but, again, because of the newness of the area student authors may have more opportunities to publish than in more established areas. While certain universities are represented more than others, it remains to be seen which programmes will eventually come to the fore regarding Internet-based communication research.

In the areas of topic, interface, and methods, similar opportunities for growth exist. However, as speculated by Biocca and Morris and Ogan, thus far, communication researchers primarily are using traditional methods to study the Internet (*e.g.*, content analysis, essays/critiques) with a few studies employing network analysis, as suggested by Morris and Ogan.

Additionally, research has tended to focus largely on the Internet in general, leaving specific interfaces such as mailing lists and e-mail in need of attention. Topics also seem to follow widely used categories (*e.g.*, adoption/diffusion, social interaction) in communication research. This trend may be useful for making comparisons across different types of media; however, it also risks overlooking effects that may be unique to the Internet.

The low number of Internet-based research articles (3.9 per cent) and the sporadic publication of the articles within the five communication journals examined may be attributed to several factors. To begin with, the Internet, despite nearly a three-decade history, is still a relatively new area of study. Although the World Wide Web, which helped make the Internet popular, became publicly available in 1992, it was not until 1995 that awareness of the Internet by the media and the general public began to increase.

With this increased awareness among the populace, researchers are realizing the importance of researching the Internet, but this can be a slow process. In 1995, Dennis Davis, the editor of Journal of Broadcasting and Electronic Media, wrote in his annual summary, "One of my editorial priorities is to increase the number of articles dealing with new technologies. To do this, the number of submissions will need to be increased. This past year 10 submissions (4.9 per cent) dealt with new industries or new technologies. Three times as many manuscripts dealt with existing industries (30 papers, 14.8 per cent). I would like to see a more even balance between submissions dealing with old and new industries."

To its credit, the Journal of Communication published a symposium on "The Net" in its 1996 winter issue. Factoring in the timeframe necessary for the review, decision, and printing process, the calls to action contained within this issue may partially explain the noticeable increase in the publication of articles during 1998. The drop off in 1999 may be a reflection of this cycle as well, or possibly a reflection of changes in editors' interests. Still, it seems clear that some of these journals are demonstrating a desire to publish Internet-based research articles; however, as Davis indicates, perhaps few studies are being submitted. Alternatively, it may be that a number of studies are being submitted; however, because of the relative newness of Internet-based research some of these studies may lack the theoretical grounding often desired in published works by our leading journals. A review of the literature reveals that communication researchers are attempting to unveil the parallels and distinctions between new and traditional technology theories and methodologies, but the research waters are still murky in this area.

Additionally, the emergence of new technology journals such as Internet Research and New Media and Society, may serve as alternative outlets for these studies, thus siphoning off submissions to the mainstream, established communication journals. As well, given the crossdisciplinary nature of the Internet (*e.g.*, computing, communication, human factors), depending on the topic, communication researchers may be submitting their works to journals in other fields. If this is the case, then the communication journals examined might more actively solicit Internet research submissions in an attempt to better represent the amount and type of research being conducted in this area. While this author does not advocate the lowering of acceptance standards for research articles, communication journals could potentially foster increased publication of Internet research, following the lead of the Journal of Communication, by dedicating issues to symposia on the topic.

These symposia could be viewed as debuts of Internet research that, while possibly less theoretically rigorous, would be considered valuable contributors to the development of future, more theoretically based studies. The main point to be emphasized is that the communication research community is widely dispersed across numerous universities and organizations worldwide.

Scholarly journals function, in part, as a communication link between researchers. Communication scholars interested in studying the Internet benefit most by knowing who else is researching in the area and what results have been found. Leading journals play an important role in conveying this information, but only if that information is being published. If it is the case, which remains to be seen, that Internet research is not being published because of a lack of strong theoretical foundations, then an important question needs to be addressed. Namely, how are scholars to build theory if they do not have access, which these journals can provide, to studies on which to build a foundation? The answer may lie in the emergence of topic-specific journals such as New Media and Society.

In 1996, Morris and Ogan, commenting on the Internet's growth (25 million at the time), asked, "Why, then, have communication researchers, historically concerned with exploring the effects of mass media, nearly ignored the Internet?" This is a question still in need of an answer, or possibly reformulation. We might also ask why our leading journals appear to be slow on the uptake.

Notably, Wartella and Reeves, in a 1985 study that examined historical trends in publishing about children and the media, observed "that the relationship between research activity and media popularity is not simultaneous." Their findings illustrated that research related to a communication technology (*e.g.*, film, radio, television) often lags behind the diffusion rate of the technology, a pattern confirmed in this study.

Nevertheless, Internet research appears to be an area of study with which communication researchers must become more comfortable and skilled at conducting. Unlike television, radio, or print media, the computer requires certain knowledge and skills to operate-and ultimately to study.

As Biocca and Newhagen and Rafaeli argue, communication scholars are being called upon to take a more active role in the understanding and design of new communication technologies. These challenges, as well as knowledge and skills requirements, may act as barriers for some researchers who are less technically oriented. This particular barrier may be offset over time as communication programmes develop tracks of study in new technologies on both the graduate and undergraduate levels that emphasize familiarity with and understanding of computer communication technologies.

Additionally, the Internet can simultaneously function as an interpersonal and mass channel for communication. This hybrid nature tends to blur the traditional lines used to distinguish different types of communication from one another. Is the Internet really a form of mass communication? Questions such as this one make it difficult for communication scholars to identify perspectives from which to study the Internet.

Finally, because Internet research is more or less in its infancy and as such lacks a strong history of research on which to build, communication researchers must be especially thoughtful about and creative in their approach to its study. They must also make the effort to network, outside of journal publications, with other Internet researchers to share research strategies and results.

Certainly, not every communication researcher is interested in studying the Internet nor, given the numerous areas available for study within the field, should it be the focus of every communication scholar or the sole topic of our leading publications. However, in general, to overlook the Internet as an area for study is to be remiss as a discipline.

Before concluding, two limitations must be addressed regarding the narrow focus of the research. First, the conclusions drawn from this study are primarily limited to the five journals examined.

It should be noted, though, that these journals have historically attempted to keep pace with changes in the discipline so that cautious speculations of a more general nature about the discipline's response to the Internet might be made. However, additional research examining a broader range of communication journals is necessary to confirm these speculations.

Second, the definition used to identify Internet-based research excluded articles examining computer-mediated communication more generally. Future studies may wish to examine this broader category of research as well. This study makes two primary contributions to the field. First, it informs communication scholars of the content and amount of published Internet research in leading journals that represent our research efforts both within and outside of the discipline. Second, it generates discussion concerning why the numbers are relatively low in light of earlier calls to action regarding the importance of studying the Internet. Both communication journals and communication scholars play important roles in determining where Internet research will be positioned within the discipline, as well as where the discipline will be placed relative to other fields investigating the technology.

Despite the small number of Internetbased articles published by five of our leading journals during the sixyear time period examined, communication scholars studying the Internet should be encouraged in that, overall, the number of articles published appears to be increasing.

However, to more accurately reflect the Internet's importance as a research topic within the discipline, it is hoped that the findings in this study will encourage communication scholars to submit more of their Internet-based research to our leading journals while current and future editors of these journals will be encouraged to include more of these articles in their publications. As a discipline we possess the potential be a leader in Internet research, and our core journals can, and should, reflect this potential not only to scholars within the field but also to the larger academic community.

THE SHIFTING AGENDA OF THE SOCIAL SCIENCES

At present, the study of mass communication and its influences on individuals and society is not at centre stage in the social and behavioural sciences. It was at an earlier time. After pioneering the investigation of the influences of mass communications, such fields as social psychology and sociology went on to pursue other agendas. To illustrate, between 1940 and the end of the 1950s, among the most respected media scholars were sociologists Lazarsfeld and Merton. Both of these world-class researchers made the study of mass media central to their discipline. Similarly, in social psychology, Hovland was conducting his classic experiments on communication and persuasion. During the 1960s, many psychologists were focusing intensely on the relation between television and violence. By the 1970s, however, their participation declined and their influence waned. Other kinds of scholars were undertaking media studies and distinguished sociologists and psycho-logists were no longer the central figures pushing forward the cutting edge.

That does not mean that research on mass communication ceased. For a time, the issue of violence and children continued to be almost a one-dimensional concern. What happened was that the social science agenda changed. For many in those disciplines, the level of importance assigned to the study of media effects was reduced by attention to other concerns.

As the late 1960s and early 1970s came, sociologists and psychologists turned to studies of deviant behaviour, such as the causes of the rising crime rate, youthful violence, drug use, the influences of the counterculture, the roots and consequences of social inequalities, such as racial and ethnic discrimination, and the unequal status of woman in society. The study of devip'ant behaviour and the problems of disadvantaged people have always been central in social science. Even many of the early studies of mass communications were conducted as a means of furthering these objectives. In other words, social scientists who had conducted media studies earlier returned to their traditional concerns, leaving basic research on the process and influences of mass communication to others.

THE LACK OF A PROGRAMMATIC APPROACH

Even during the golden age, when a series of well-known studies yielded significant theoretical advances, mass communication research was never conducted programmatically. With few exceptions, each study was a one-shot enterprise, done independently for its own sponsor's reasons. Such research sought short-term objectives that were deemed important at the time. There was no theoretical trail being followed, or accumulative refinement of concepts leading from the results of one study to the design of the next. In contrast, programmatic research and concept refinement is often the case in the physical and biological sciences, where one investigator's results yield insights or theoretical advances that open pathways taken by subsequent researchers. Even today, mass communication research seldom follows a programmatic approach, holding back the pace of theoretical development.

The lack of integration between studies is also reflected in the methodology employed in mass communication research. For example, concepts are often defined in a multiplicity of ways from one study to the next, with each researcher conceptualizing variables differently from the definitions of previous investigators. Such basic procedures as measurement, sample selection, and statistical analysis are conducted differently from one investigator to the next, even when researchers are studying essentially the same phenomena. Such a lack of methodological standardization makes it difficult to replicate studies of a particular process or effect, reducing the ability of investigators to accumulate evidence related to specific generalizations, hypotheses, or theories. It seems likely that this unintegrated approach will continue to be a handicap to the development of future milestones.

2

Sociological Theories of Mass Communication

INTRODUCTION

The sociological approach to communication theory· is based on the assumption that there exists a definite relationship between mass communication and social change. Some of the relevant theories that are discussed here try to provide answers to questions like these: Do mass media cultivate common beliefs about the world or set an agenda for people? How do people use media and why? Do media have control over audiences? And so on.

CULTIVATION THEORY

Cultivation theory is a social theory which examines the long-term effects of television. "The primary proposition of cultivation theory states that the more time people spend "living" in the television world, the more likely they are to believe social reality portrayed on television."

Developed by George Gerbner and Larry Gross of the University of Pennsylvania, cultivation theory derived from several large-scale research projects as part of an overall research project entitled 'Cultural Indicators'. The purpose of the Cultural Indicators project was to identify and track the 'cultivated' effects of television on viewers. They were "concerned with the effects of television programming (particularly violent programming) on the attitudes and behaviours of the American public."

Gerbner asserts that the overall concern about the effects of television on audiences stemmed from the unprecedented centrality of television in American culture. "The theory clearly posits that the cultivation effect occurs only after long-term, cumulative exposure to television. "He claimed that because TV contains so much violence, people who spend the most time in front of the tube develop an exaggerated belief in a mean and scary world." He posited that television as a mass medium of communication had formed in to a common symbolic environment that bound diverse communities together, socializing people into standardized roles and behaviours. "Today, the TV set is a key member of the household, with virtually unlimited access to every person in the family." He compared the power of television to the power of religion, saying that television was to modern society what religion once was in earlier times.

Cultivation Analysis is a positivistic theory, meaning it assumes the existence of objective reality and value-neutral research. A study conducted by Jennings Bryant and Dorina Miron, which surveyed almost 2,000 articles published in the three top mass communication journals since 1956, found that Cultivation Analysis was the third most frequently utilized theory, showing that it continues to be one of the most popular theories in mass communication research.

Background

"Gerbner attempted to devise a new, broad-based approach to the study of mass communication, one that focused on the process of mass communication itself." According to Miller, cultivation theory was not developed to study "targeted and specific effects (*e.g.*, that watching Superman will lead children to attempt to fly by jumping out the window) [but rather] in terms of the cumulative and overarching impact [television] has on the way we see the world in which we live". Hence the term 'Cultivation Analysis'. This theory has several assumptions, including:

- Television is essentially and fundamentally different from other forms of mass media: Gerbner, Gross, Morgan, and Signorielli argued that while religion or education had previously been greater influences on social trends, now "[t]elevision is the source of the most broadly shared images and messages in history... Television cultivates from infancy the very predispositions and preferences that used to be acquired from other primary sources... The repetitive pattern of television's mass-produced messages and images forms the mainstream of a common symbolic environment." Due to its accessibility and availability to the masses, television has become the "central cultural arm of our society."
- Television shapes the way our society thinks and relates: Gerbner and Gross write that "the substance of the consciousness cultivated by TV is not so much specific attitudes and opinions as more basic assumptions about the facts of life and standards of judgement on which conclusions are based." Simply put, the realities created by television are not based on real facts but on speculations. Gerbner observed that television reaches people, on average, more than seven hours a day. While watching, television offers "a centralized system of story-telling". Gerbner asserts that television's major cultural

function is to stabilize social patterns and to cultivate resistance to change. We live in terms of the stories we tell and television tells these stories through news, drama, and advertising to almost everybody most of the time.

- Television's effects are limited: Gerber's ice age analogy states that "just as an average temperature shift of a few degrees can lead to an ice age or the outcomes of elections can be determined by slight margins, so too can a relatively small but pervasive influence make a crucial difference. The size of an effect is far less critical than the direction of its steady contribution."

Definition

Cultivation theory in its most basic form, then, suggests that exposure to television, over time, subtly "cultivates" viewers' perceptions of reality. Gerbner and Gross say "television is a medium of the socialization of most people into standardized roles and behaviours. Its function is in a word, enculturation". Gerbner draws attention in his work to three entities—institutions, messages, and publics—which he seeks to analyse. Additionally, Gerbner was less concerned about the effect of cultivation on aggressive behaviour, and "more concerned that it affects viewers' beliefs about the world around them and the feelings connected to those beliefs."

MASS COMMUNICATION

Mass communication is the academic study of how individuals and entities relay information through mass media to large segments of the population at the same time. It is usually understood to relate to newspaper and magazine publishing, radio, television and film, as these are used both for disseminating news and for advertising.

Mass communication helps provide/interpret information, create social awareness, and educate the masses. Mass communication research includes most communication media institutions and processes such as, diffusion of information and media effects such as persuasion or manipulation of public opinion. In the United States for instance, several university departments were remodelled into schools or colleges of mass communication or "journalism and mass communication".

In addition to studying practical skills of journalism, public relations or advertising, they offer programmes on "mass communication" or "mass communication research." The latter is often the title given to doctoral studies in such schools, whether the focus of the student's research is journalism practice, history, law nor media effects. Departmental structures within such colleges may separate research and instruction in professional or technical aspects of mass communication. With the Internet's increased role in delivering news and information, mass communication studies and media organizations tend to focus on the convergence of publishing, broadcasting and digital communication. The academic mass communication discipline historically differs from media studies and communication studies programmes with roots in departments of theatre, film or speech, and with more interest in "qualitative", interpretive theory, critical or cultural approaches to communication study. In contrast, many mass communication programmes historically lean towards empirical analysis and quantitative research — from statistical content analysis of media messages to survey research, public opinion polling, and experimental research.

Although national standards for the study of interactive media have been present in the United Kingdom circa mid-nineties, course work in these areas tends to vary significantly from university to university. Graduates of Mass Communication programmes work in a variety of fields in traditional news media and publishing, advertising, public relations and research institutes. Such programmes are accredited by the Accrediting Council on Education in Journalism and Mass Communication.

The Association for Education in Journalism and Mass Communication is the major membership organization for academics in the field, offering regional and national conferences and refereed publications. The International Communication Association and National Communication Association (formerly the Speech Communication Association) includes divisions and publications that overlap with those of AEJMC, but AEJMC historically has stronger ties to the mass communication professions in the United States.

The disadvantages of mass communication are Media is subjected to physical, cultural and psychological barriers. It's difficult to obtain feedback from the masses.

MASS MEDIA AND SOCIETY

There has been enormous interest among social scientists to find out the effects of mass communication within society. This has resulted in a number of theories which essentially trace the relationship between mass communication and society.

However, no single integrated theory of communication has yet emerged which is universally accepted. We describe here some important theories of mass communication to help you to understanding how mass communication operates in society. Please note that early theories were based on assumptions that mass media have enormous and direct influence upon society. But later researches provide evidence against any direct cause and effect relationship between mass communication and society; rather they underline the importance of individual differences and personal influences on transmission, acceptance and retention of message. Sociological theories portrayed mass media as an outcome of changes' in society. There are other theories that express ideas on how the mass media ought' to or can be expected to operate under prevailing political and economic circumstances. Some of the important theories discussed here will provide you insights into the role of mass communication in society and the way in which an audience utilizes different mass media.

Mass media today are inextricable form of modern society. Without these media, society probably cannot conduct its affairs effectively. On their part, mass media, in a bid to serve the people, playa significant role in spreading new ideas, new forms of behaviour and information about a variety of products. Society, whether simple or complex, needs some communication system so that its various organizations may perform their designated functions. Mass media do what is demanded of them and while doing that the draw strength and support from society for their survival. This interdependence leads to some obvious questions, of causes and effects between mass media and society: What do mass media do for the society? What is the relationship between mass media and society? Are mass media the outcome of changes in society? Or do they simply constitute a response to certain demands?

HYPODERMIC OR BULLET THEORY

The hypodermic needle model (also known as the hypodermic-syringe model, transmission-belt model, or magic bullet theory) is a model of communications suggesting that an intended message is directly received and wholly accepted by the receiver. The model is rooted in 1930s behaviourism and is largely considered obsolete today.

The "Magic Bullet" or "Hypodermic Needle Theory" of direct influence effects was not as widely accepted by scholars as many books on mass communication indicate. The magic bullet theory was not based on empirical findings from research but rather on assumptions of the time about human nature. People were assumed to be "uniformly controlled by their biologically based 'instincts' and that they react more or less uniformly to whatever 'stimuli' came along".

The "Magic Bullet" theory graphically assumes that the media's message is a bullet fired from the "media gun" into the viewer's "head". Similarly, the "Hypodermic Needle Model" uses the same idea of the "shooting" paradigm. It suggests that the media injects its messages straight into the passive audience.

This passive audience is immediately affected by these messages. The public essentially cannot escape from the media's influence, and is therefore considered a "sitting duck". Both models suggest that the public is vulnerable to the messages shot at them because of the limited communication tools and the studies of the media's effects on the masses at the time.

Later Developments

The phrasing "hypodermic needle" is meant to give a mental image of the direct, strategic, and planned infusion of a message into an individual. But as research methodology became more highly developed, it became apparent that the media had selective influences on people.

The most famous incident often cited as an example for the hypodermic needle model was the 1938 broadcast of *The War of the Worlds* and the subsequent reaction of widespread panic among its American mass audience. However, this incident actually sparked the research movement, led by Paul Lazarsfeld and Herta Herzog, that would disprove the magic bullet or hypodermic needle theory, as Hadley Cantril managed to show that reactions to the broadcast were, in fact, diverse, and were largely determined by situational and attitudinal attributes of the listeners.

Lazarsfeld disproved the "Magic Bullet" theory and "Hypodermic Needle Model Theory" through elections studies in "The People's Choice". Lazarsfeld and colleagues executed the study by gathering research during the election of Franklin D. Roosevelt in 1940. The study was conducted to determine voting patterns and the relationship between the media and political power. Lazarsfeld discovered that the majority of the public remained unfazed by propaganda surrounding Roosevelt's campaign. Instead, interpersonal outlets proved more influential than the media. Therefore, Lazarsfeld concluded that the effects of the campaign were not all powerful to the point where they completely persuaded "helpless audiences", a claim that the Magic Bullet, Hypodermic Needle Model, and Lasswell asserted. These new findings also suggested that the public can select which messages affect and don't affect them.

Lazarsfeld's debunking of these models of communication provided the way for new ideas regarding the media's effects on the public. Lazarsfeld introduced the idea of the two step flow model of communication in 1944. Elihu Katz contributed to the model in 1955 through studies and publications. The two step flow model assumes that ideas flow from the mass media to opinion leaders and then to the greater public. They believed the message of the media to be transferred to the masses via this opinion leadership. Opinion leaders are categorized as individuals with the best understanding of media content and the most accessibility to the media as well. These leaders essentially take in the media's information, and explain and spread the media's messages to others.

Thus, the two step flow model and other communication theories suggest that the media does not directly have an influence on viewers anymore. Instead, interpersonal connections and even selective exposure play a larger role in influencing the public in the modern age.

DIFFERENTIAL PSYCHOLOGY

Differential psychology studies the ways in which individuals differ in their behaviour. This is distinguished from other aspects of psychology in that although psychology is ostensibly a study of individuals, modern psychologists often study groups or biological underpinnings of cognition.

For example, in evaluating the effectiveness of a new therapy, the mean performance of the therapy in one treatment group might be compared to the mean effectiveness of a placebo (or a well-known therapy) in a second, control group. In this context, differences between individuals in their reaction to the experimental and control manipulations are actually treated as errors rather than as interesting phenomena to study.

This is because psychological research depends upon statistical controls that are only defined upon groups of people. Individual difference psychologists usually express their interest in individuals while studying groups by seeking dimensions shared by all individuals but upon which individuals differ.

Importance of Individual Differences: Individual differences are essential whenever we wish to explain how individuals differ in their behaviour. In any study, significant variation exists between individuals. Reaction time, preferences, values, and health linked behaviours are just a few examples. Individual differences in factors such as personality, intelligence, memory, or physical factors such as body size, sex, age, and other factors can be studied and used in understanding this large source of variance. Importantly, individuals can also differ not only in their current state, but in the magnitude or even direction of response to a given stimulus. Such phenomena, often explained in terms of inverted-U response curves, place differential psychology at an important location in such endeavours as personalized medicine, in which diagnoses are customised for an individual's response profile.

Areas of Study: Individual differences research typically includes personality, motivation, intelligence, ability, IQ, interests, values, self-concept, self-efficacy, and self-esteem (to name just a few). There are few remaining "differential psychology" programmes in the United States, although research in this area is very active. Current researchers are found in a variety of applied and experimental programmes, including educational psychology, Industrial and organizational psychology, personality psychology, social psychology, and developmental psychology programmes, in the neo-Piagetian theories of cognitive development in particular.

TWO-STEP FLOW OF COMMUNICATION

The *two-step flow of communication* or *Multistep Flow Model*, says that most people form their opinions under the influence of opinion leaders, that in turn are influenced by the mass media. So according to this model, ideas flow from mass media to opinion leaders, and from them to a wider population.

Also known as the Multistep Flow Model is a theory based on a 1940s study on social influence that states that media effects are indirectly established through the personal influence of opinion leaders. The majority of people receive much of their information and are influenced by the media secondhand, through the personal influence of opinion leaders. The *Multistep Flow Model* says that most people form their opinions based on opinion leaders that influence the media. Opinion leaders are those initially exposed to a specific media content, and who interpret it based on their own opinion. They then begin to infiltrate these opinions through the general public who become "opinion followers". These "opinion leaders" gain their influence through more elite media as opposed to mainstream mass media. In this process, social influence is created and adjusted by the ideals and opinions of each specific "elite media" group, and by these media group's opposing ideals and opinions and in combination with popular mass media sources. Therefore, the leading influence in these opinions is primarily a social persuasion.

The two-step flow of communication model hypothesizes that ideas flow from mass media to opinion leaders, and from them to a wider population. It was first introduced by sociologist Paul Lazarsfeld *et al.* in 1944 and elaborated by Elihu Katz and Lazarsfeld in 1955 and subsequent publications. Lowery and DeFleur argue the book was much more than a simple research report: it was an effort to interpret the authors' research within a framework of conceptual schemes, theoretical issues, and research findings drawn broadly from the scientific study of small groups. Unlike the hypodermic needle model, which considers mass media effects to be direct, the two-step flow model stresses human agency.

According to Lazarsfeld and Katz, mass media information is channelled to the "masses" through opinion leadership. The people with most access to media, and having a more literate understanding of media content, explain and diffuse the content to others.

Based on the two-step flow hypothesis, the term "personal influence" came to illustrate the process intervening between the media's direct message and the audience's reaction to that message. Opinion leaders tend to be similar to those they influence—based on personality, interests, demographics, or socio-economic factors. These leaders tend to influence others to change their attitudes and behaviours. The two-step theory refined the ability to predict how media messages influence audience behaviour and explains why certain media campaigns do not alter audiences' attitudes. This hypothesis provided a basis for the multi-step flow theory of mass communication.

Lazarsfeld and Katz: Paul Lazarsfeld and Elihu Katz are considered to be the founders of functional theory and their book Personal Influence is considered to be the handbook to the theory.

Paul Felix Lazarsfeld: One of the first to embark on Communications research, was the first to introduce the difference between 'administrative research' and 'critical research' in regards to the media. Critical research he believed, criticizes the media institutions themselves for the perspective ways they serve dominant social groups. Critical research favours interperspective and inductive methods of enquiry. Lazarsfeld's study of the 1940 presidential election was published as The People's Choice. During the research revealed information about the psychological and social processes that influence voting decisions. The study also uncovered an influence process that Lazarsfeld called "opinion leadership." He concluded that there is a multistep flow of information from the mass media to persons who serve as opinion leaders which then is passed on to the general public. He called this communication process the "two-step flow of communication."

Elihu Katz: A professor in the School for Communication at the University of Pennsylvania collaborated in 1955 with Lazarsfeld, in research to observe the flow of influence at the intersections of mass and interpersonal communication and wrote their book Personal Influence Katz pursued Lazarfeld's research in a study of the flow of information. This is the basis of Personal Influence. Katz and Lazarsfeld concluded that:... the traditional image of the mass persuasion process must make room for 'people' as intervening factors between the stimuli of the media and resultant opinions, decisions, and actions."

PUBLISHED WORKS ON THE THEORY

The People's Choice: The presidential election 1940 questioned as to whether President Franklin Roosevelt would seek his third term in office. Funded by grants from the Rockefeller Foundation, Life magazine, and the pollster Elmo Roper, Columbia's Office of Radio Research conducted a new kind of study of voting. It was based on a panel study of 2,400 voters in Erie County, Ohio. Paul Lazarsfeld, Bernard Berelson, and Hazel Gaudet supervised 15 interviewers, who from May–October interviewed the strategically selected 2,400 members of the community several different times in order to document their decision making process during the campaign. They focused on what factors would influence their decisions as the campaign progressed. The People's Choice, a book based on this study presented the theory of "the two-step flow of communications," which later came to be associated with the so-called "limited effects model" of mass media: the idea that ideas often flow from radio and print to local "opinion leaders" who in turn pass them on to those with more limited political knowledge "opinion followers." The conclusion of the research explained that sometimes person to person communication can be more effective than traditional media mediums such as newspaper, TV, radio etc. This idea developed further in the book Personal Influence.

Personal Influence: In 1944, Paul Lazarsfeld contacted McFadden Publications in regards to his first book, The People's Choice. The two collaborated forming a mutually beneficial partnership in which Macfadden saw a way to financially profit from advertising to the female population and Lazarsfeld saw a way to gain more information on social influence. Out of this came the study conducted by the Bureau of Applied Social Research in which 800 female residents of Decatur, Illinois, where interviewed through panel interviews to discover what and who primarily influenced their decision making. Lazarsfeld worked with Robert Merton and thus hired C. Wright Mills to head the study. Another part of the research team, Thelma Ehrlich Anderson, trained local Decatur women to administer surveys to targeted women in town. By 1955. The Decatur study was published as part of Elihu Katz and Lazarsfeld's book Personal Influence. The book concluded that ultimately, face to face interaction is more influential than traditional media influence and thus confirmed the two-step flow model of communication.

Criticisms: The original two-step flow hypothesis—that ideas flow from the media to opinion leaders and then to less active sections of the population—has been criticized and negated by myriad consequent studies. Findings from Deutschmann and Danielson assert, "we would urge that the Katz-Lazarsfeld two-stage flow hypothesis, as a description of the initial information process, be applied to mass communication with caution". They find substantial evidence that initial mass media information flows directly to people on the whole and is not relayed by opinion leaders.

Furthermore, the two-step hypothesis does not adequately describe the flow of learning. Everett Rogers' "Diffusion of Innovations" cites one study in which two-thirds of respondents accredited their awareness to the mass media rather than face-to-face communication. Similarly, critics argue that most of Lazarsfeld's findings pertain to learning factors involved with general media habits rather than the learning of particular information. Both findings suggest a greater prevalence of a one-step flow of communication.

However, Lazarsfeld's two-step hypothesis is an adequate description to understand the media's influence on belief and behaviour. Troldahl finds that media exposure is a first step to introduce discussion, at which point opinion leaders initiate the second-step flow. These findings also realize opinion leaders decisive role in the balance theory, which suggests that people are motivated to keep consistency among their current beliefs and opinions. If a person is exposed to new observations that are inconsistent with present beliefs, he or she is thrown into imbalance. This person will then seek advice from their opinion leader, to provide them with additional cognitions to bring them back into balance.

MASS MEDIA EFFECTS AND SOCIETY

SEX AND VIOLENCE IN THE MEDIA

One of the more controversial areas of study of the media is what effect the media have on us. This is particularly timely as eyes are on Hollywood and the violent and sexy movies it makes.

Does all the sex in the media, particularly the movies and television, have anything to do with the sexual mores of society?

- How about violence in the media?
- Does it have a relationship with the increase in violence in our society?
- Does the media just mirror the sex and violence in society, or does it influence society? Remember the theme for this class that we discussed the first week.
- There have been countless studies trying to find out. Some of the most famous were the Payne.
- Studies in the late 1920s that looked at the impact of movie violence on children. And starting in the 1960s people started looking for a cause for the increase of violence in society.
- Violent crimes in this country were on the rise.
- We were at war.
- A president (John Kennedy) was assassinated.
- A presidential candidate (Bobby Kennedy) was assassinated.
- A civil right leader (Martin Luther King) was assassinated.

There was an attempt on the life of the Pope. There had to be a cause. Why the sudden increase? To some, the media especially television seemed a good candidate. After all, in the 1960s we had the first American generation raised on television. And if you looked at the fare on television, you saw all kinds of cop shoot-em-up shows. Movies, threatened with extinction thanks to television, had responded by including more violence and sex. A number of long-term studies were conducted to determine what, if any results, all that media violence was having on us. Four major results came from these studies. A fifth one has evolved over time.

Catharsis Theory

The first of these theories suggests that rather than be harmful violence in the media actually has a positive effect on society. The central assumption of the Catharsis Theory is that people, in course of daily life, build up frustrations. Vicarious participation in others' aggressions help release those tensions. In other words, every day our frustrations build up. Without a release valve we risk the chance of becoming violent, or at least aggressive. You do poorly on a test. You have to park to far away from the classroom. Some jerk cuts in front of you on the freeway. You get home and your significant other, or a child, starts demanding your attention. You snap back by yelling or hitting. That counts as violence as much as shooting someone. It is only a matter of degree. The Catharsis theorist would say that by watching violence in the media you release some of that tension and are less likely to be aggressive or violent. But can you say the same thing about sex in the media?

Aggressive Cues Theory

Then there is the opposite view, that violence DOES have an impact. Probably most prevalent of these theories is the Aggressive Cues Theory that has as its central assumption this: Exposure to aggressive stimuli will increase physiological and emotional arousal, which will increase the probability of violence. In other words, all that violence gets the adrenaline juices in us flowing and makes us more edgy, increasing the chance that we'll be more aggressive or more violent. Aggressive Cues theorists are quick to point out that watching violence does not mean we'll always be more aggressive or violent, but it increases the chances. And the way in which the violence is presented will have an impact on us, too. If we can relate to the protagonist committing the violence, or if the violence is presented in a justifiable way, we can be led to aggressive behaviour. If a bratty kid gets spanked in a media portrayal clearly an aggressive and violent act it sends a message that corporal punishment is acceptable under the right circumstances. If steelworkers see a show where steelworkers drink and brawl after work every day, they are more likely to accept that drinking and brawling are normal behaviour.

Observational Learning Theory

The Observational Learning theorist would take the Aggressive Cues theory a step further. This theory says that people can learn by observing aggression in media portrayals and, under some conditions, model its behaviour. If there are 50 ways to leave your lover, then there must be at least 49 ways to be violent or aggressive. And watching violent media portrayals will teach you new ways to be violent. Ever watch a whodunit, such as a Columbo episode, where you spot where the criminal makes the fatal mistake? Ever catch yourself saying, "If I ever committed a murder I would not make THAT mistake?" What? Are you suggesting there is a circumstance where you would kill someone? Or, how about this? Imagine walking down a dark alley and someone steps out in front of you and makes a threatening gesture. What would you do? Anyone think of some kung fu/karate moves you might make to defend yourself? That's a pretty aggressive/violent thought. And you learned it by watching a media portrayal.

So the Observational Learning theorist says that not only would the media violence increase the probability of the viewer committing an aggression or violence, it teaches the viewer how to do it. Does media mirror society or does it influence it? (The answer is both.) Further, the Observational Theorist hedges his bet by pointing out that you will not automatically go out and mimic the violent act, but you store the information away in your brain. Again, think about sex instead of violence. Does watching sexual portrayals teach you new ways to think about sex and perhaps engage in sexual acts? If you see that sleeping with someone on a first date is normal, after a while you start believing that everyone must be doing it, so you should, too.

Reinforcement Theory

One theory says that media violence decreases the probability of violence by the viewer. Two others say that it will increase the probability of violence. And then there is the Reinforcement Theory that debunks both. The central assumption of this theory is that media portrayals reinforce established behaviours viewers bring with them to the media situation. Violent portrayals will increase the likelihood of violent or aggressive behaviour for those who accept violence and aggression as normal. It will decrease the likelihood of aggression and violence for those brought up to believe that violence is bad. Violence merely reinforces prior beliefs. Instead of looking for blame in a violent media portrayal, the Reinforcement theorist would say that if you want to predict an outcome, look at the viewer's background. Look at the person's cultural norms and views of social roles. If person grows up in a crime-ridden neighbourhood, then violent portrayals are more likely to lead to violence.

Obviously, selective perception (go back to the communication lecture) is going on here. But the Reinforcement theorist would point out that there is going to be the exception to the rule. You are going to run across the gentle old man who everyone believed would never hurt a fly who whacks his family into a thousand pieces one day. Or you are going to find the gang member who one day recognizes the futility of violence and turns to the priesthood.

Cultivation Theory

A final theory on the effects of violence in the media has evolved out of more recent studies. It is the Cultivation Theory. Rather than predict that we will turn to or from violence, it looks at how we'll react to the violence. The central assumption of the theory is that in the symbolic world of media, particularly TV, shapes and maintains audience's conception of the real world In other words, the media, especially TV, creates fantasy world that is mean spirited and dangerous.

It also creates stereotypes of dominant/weak folk in society. For instance, imagine a bank robber who is big and mean. Is your imaginary bank robber of certain race? Are all people that look like this bank robber actually mean back robbers? Or how about this? You are starting to show some signs of age with gray hair and wrinkles around your eyes. If you are guy in the media, that is good. It shows a maturing. If you are woman, that is bad, it just shows that you are getting old and less vital. A male can be dominant and be looked up to. A woman who is dominant can be a bitch. All lawyers are crooks. All journalists are seedy (as in "The Front Page"). All media stereotypes! And the media tell us that it is a mean world out there. Driving freeways is unsafe because of driveby shootings and spectacular police car chases. Crime in the neighbourhood is rampant if you look at the nightly news. Some people who live vicariously through television feel it is unsafe to leave their home or apartment and become shut-ins.

PERSONAL FREEDOM AND A FREE SOCIETY

The freedom of a society, as I shall construe that, is closely tied to the personal freedom of the individual members of that society, understood in a certain way. A concern for personal freedom in some sense of the phrase is central to a number of evaluative stances in political philosophy.

Thus, on one account of it, anarchism involves "a concern for preserving individual freedom and a distaste for the coercive measures of governments...." A government coerces by "threatening to use force or impose punishments if a person does not follow its laws". Now, in what I take to be the central sense of the term, punishment requires a special standing or authority. As I understand it, to have the authority to punish is not necessarily to be justified in doing so, but it does away with a possible objection to its use by a given agent. It cannot be objected "It is not for you to do that."

Indeed, anarchism is often characterized in terms of distaste, not so much for the coercive measures governments take but rather for government itself. Here government is construed as a matter of the authority to command, to demand or insist on compliance when non-compliance is threatened, and, where appropriate, to punish. The problem of government is posed in terms of the loss of personal autonomy inherent in the authority of one person over another, whether they command, demand conformity, or punish. That is the tenor of the well-known brand of philosophical anarchism that was advocated by Robert Paul Wolff, for instance.

The anarchist's concern is often couched in terms of the authority of one person, or of a body of persons smaller than the society that is in question. I take it, meanwhile, that there can be whole societies-even societies reasonably thought of as political societies or polities-without such a ruling person or body. Even in such "acephalous" societies, there are issues of personal autonomy. Such societies are likely to have a variety of rules. Each member will then have the authority to insist on any other's conformity to a given rule and to rebuke any other for not conforming to it.

Evidently, I take it that one cannot rebuke someone without a special standing or authority. One can, of course, speak in a rebuking manner without such authority, just as one can speak in a demanding manner, without the authority actually to demand. Rebukes and demands may be unaccompanied by physical force or by threats that such force will be applied unless what is demanded is done. There is, nonetheless, something forceful about any rebuke, just as there is something forceful about demanding. Indeed, in The Concept of Law, Hart suggests that rebukes lie at the informal end of a spectrum at the formal end of which lie punishments imposed through due process of law.

Penal sanctions may sound-and may be-worse than informal demands and rebukes, but most people do not relish such forceful interventions from others. Most would prefer not to incur the reproofs of strangers, the rebukes of colleagues, or the reprimands of friends and intimates. Mill, the great philosophical champion of liberty, saw this clearly. And verbal chastisement can be the precursor of physical violence.

Suppose, now, that there is a rule in my society that women are not to contradict men. I know that if I, a woman, contradict a man on some point, the other members of my society have the authority to rebuke me for doing so. Accordingly, I may regularly decide not to make some point though I desire to do so. In other terms, my freedom is limited in an important way: there is something I want to do, but I risk an authoritative forceful negative response should I do it. The account of a society's freedom that I shall make use of in developing the negative argument reflects the idea that the standing threat of such a response is an important limitation on personal freedom. In speaking of a "threat" here I do not mean to imply that the response is imminent, or even probable, but rather that it is "in the cards." If someone has the standing to rebuke me for doing something, I know that, should he speak to me in a rebuking manner, I cannot dodge the issue by saying "It's none of your business." If he has the standing to rebuke me, it is his business.

I shall say that a given member, M1, of a society S, is personally free to perform a given action, A, in face of another member, M2, if and only if M1 is under no threat of an authoritative forceful negative reaction from M2 should M1 perform A or, indeed, should M1 propose to perform A. For the sake of brevity, I shall generally refer in what follows to being under no threat of a rebuke. It should be understood that all forms of authoritative forceful negative reaction are included under this heading.

Now, a given member, M1, of a society S, may be under a threat of rebuke from another member, M2, where these rebukes are not grounded in his membership in S as such. For instance, M1 promised M2, and no one else, that he would not do A. I am not concerned with such grounds here. The definition of personal freedom just given should be interpreted accordingly. What is at issue is rebukes whose ground is some aspect of the membership of M1 and M2 in society S.

I take it that a society itself can be "personally free" in the defined sense, insofar as it can be a member of a society of societies. Meanwhile, the type of societal freedom with which this essay is concerned relates to the personal freedom of a society's members as just defined. This might be referred to as the society's internal freedom. My focal case continues to be a society whose members are individual human beings as opposed to other societies.

I shall assume that, as a matter of definition, a society becomes less free as particular personal freedoms are subtracted from those its various members already have. This is clearly only a partial account of societal freedom. It concerns only a single condition under which a society can be said to become less free than it was. Nonetheless it is of interest to ask whether a society's relative freedom in the respect at issue is altered by one or another factor.

I shall not attempt to offer a full account of a free society. Given the notion of personal freedom with which I am operating, however, a plausible account will not allow that a society is free when its members have little personal freedom. Nor will it demand that a free society be maximally free, where a maximally free society is one in which, for any action whatever, each member of the society is personally free to perform that action in face of any other member. It may reasonably be questioned whether a maximally free society, as just defined, is possible. As will emerge, it can be argued that it is not, given what a society is.

A WISE SOCIETY

Some may be inclined to deny that there is such a thing as a society that is wise to any degree. They may point to the fact that wisdom involves or is closely connected to knowledge or, at least, good judgement and argue that a society is not the kind of thing that can be wise. Individual human beings can be wise but societies are not sufficiently like them for a wise society to be possible.

When it is presented, this argument may look plausible. Yet people regularly talk about a society's beliefs, judgements, decisions, and knowledge. Thus a particular society may be said to have made a wise (or unwise) decision, wrongly to consider itself superior to other societies, and so on.

When people talk about the belief of a society or other social group, they think of themselves as speaking literally rather than metaphorically. Rather than assuming that they are misguided, one might do well to consider what phenomenon on the ground, so to speak, they have in mind.

Perhaps because they think along the skeptical lines mentioned above, contemporary political philosophers have not paid attention to the idea of a wise society. Following John Rawls, they have considered the key quality of a good society to be its justice and focused on that.

In the Republic, Plato also focused on a society's justice. This did not lead him to neglect the idea of a wise society. Indeed, he thought of a society's wisdom as necessary to its justice. Notoriously, he did not think this way about its freedom. Plato does talk about freedom. His picture of what he called "democracy" in Book of the Republic is perhaps the closest to true anarchy-and maximal personal freedom-that one can imagine. It is not clear, indeed, how consistent a picture this is. There is some talk of "laws" and "courts" of law, yet-he says-one can do anything one pleases. Those condemned to death or exile walk about as if they are heroes and nobody cares.

This is not Plato's favored scenario. In the type of political society he favours, the laws are taken seriously. Most important for present purposes, the rulers are few in number and carefully selected and trained. Those with the right natural aptitudes go through the rigorous training necessary for one who loves wisdom-a philosopher-to reach his goal, knowledge of the Good.

Before the details of this training have been developed Plato considers what it is for a political society to be wise. What he says is open to different interpretations, and I shall not attempt carefully to probe it here. At a minimum, it seems fair to characterize his opinion as follows. The judgements of the rulers, in making rules and decisions for the society, must, in a phrase, track the Good.

I shall work with an account of a wise society that has something of the same spirit. I shall not require that such a society is ruled by a particular person or body of persons, however-let alone a body of persons trained from birth for the purpose. Thus I shall allow that in principle an acephalous society can be wise. I shall not attempt carefully to explore either the idea of wisdom in general or the idea of a wise society in particular. The account of the latter that I shall work with has something to be said for it, but it may well be that an alternative account is more plausible. I hope that my discussion will help to stimulate consideration of precisely this issue. In the meantime, it is important to see that on the account of a wise society proposed, the negative argument is sound. A wise society, on this account, is a society possessed of features that, whatever their relation to wisdom in particular, would appear to be desirable, all else being equal.

The working account I shall adopt appeals, simply, to a society's true value judgements, in particular those relating to the goodness and badness of human and societal features and actions. Such judgements may be very general-as in the judgement that wantonly destroying a human life is a very bad thing-or quite specific-as in the judgement that Hitler was an evil man. They may not lead to specific decisions or actions or they may. If one judges that wantonly destroying another's life is a very bad thing to do, for instance, one is likely to avoid such destruction.

A true value judgement evidently tracks the Good at least to some extent. It may be plausible to argue that if a value judgement fully tracks the Good it must not only be true but it must also have been made on good grounds. It is not, then, "fortuitously" true. That said, I focus here on the simpler condition. I shall assume that, by definition, the true value judgements of one who is wise will be relatively numerous.

This, along with the following points, is intended to apply both to individual human beings and to human societies. I shall assume one who is wise, as a matter of definition, does not make false judgements. If the truth on some matter of value is hard to discern, one who is wise will if necessary act on working assumptions understood to be such. These are relatively stringent conditions. They are not, however, as stringent as they might be. At the upper limit of wisdom, one would get everything right. I shall take the stated conditions to be both necessary and sufficient for one to be wise. I shall make the following comparative judgement about one who is wise on the above account. Any new true value judgement one makes in addition to those one has already made amounts, by definition, to an increase in one's wisdom. This is only intended to be a partial account of what makes for an increase in wisdom, but it suffices for presentation of the negative argument. It is now time to turn to the core of the negative argument. This is the pertinent account of what it is for a society to endorse a particular value judgement.

A SOCIETY'S VALUE JUDGEMENTS

I have elsewhere developed an account of what it is for a group to believe that such-and-such. I have also proposed a related account of what it is for a group to make a particular value judgement. Here I shall do little more than sketch the account, saying only what I take to be needed to make the negative argument. I proceed in terms of an illustrative value judgement, which may or may not be true: marriage is a valuable social institution. I shall refer to this judgement as V. Obviously any other particular judgement might stand in its stead.

According to my account of such matters, in terms that will be explained, a society judges that V if and only if its members are jointly committed to judge as a body that V. I have argued at length elsewhere that the concept of a joint commitment is a fundamental part of human life, embedded in many of those central concepts with which human beings approach their interactions with one another. I must now say something about what a joint commitment amounts to.

A joint commitment, as I understand it, is a commitment of two or more parties. It is not a combination of commitments, one of one party, one of another, and so on. Given their joint commitment, each party has sufficient reason to act accordingly, just as one has sufficient reason to act according to a personal decision one has made. As I understand the phrase, if one has sufficient reason to do something, then one is rationally required to do it, all else being equal.

Any joint commitment is a joint commitment to "do" something as a body, in a broad sense of "do" that includes judging that V. To say that certain people are jointly committed to judge that V as a body means something like this. They are jointly committed as far as is possible together to constitute a single body-or person-that judges that V. I say more about this shortly. How do people become jointly committed? Failing special background understandings-in the basic case-a given joint commitment can only be created by all of the parties together. The same is true of its rescission. Here is a rough account of the conditions under which such a commitment is created in the basic case.

Each of the would-be parties must express his readiness to be jointly committed with the others in a particular way, and the fact that these expressions have taken place must be open to all or, in something like David Lewis's sense, common knowledge. Though I shall not attempt to elaborate on this point here, this account does not rule out joint commitments on a large scale. I take it that people can enter joint commitments in situations of strong pressure. Just as you can make a decision under pressure to do so, you can enter a joint commitment in such circumstances. To say that is not, of course, to contest the desirability of one's making decisions and entering joint commitments in the absence of such pressures.

Special background understandings allow for non-basic cases. Thus all of the members of a given population, large or small, may create an open-ended joint commitment such that one person or a smaller population of persons is in a position to create new joint commitments for the population as a whole. For example, the members of a labour union may jointly commit to conform as a body to any fiats issued by Jones under certain conditions. In that case when Jones issues a fiat under the relevant conditions, the union members are jointly committed to conform, as one, to that fiat. To keep things simple here, I am going to focus on societies where no such special background understandings prevail.

For the purposes of the negative argument the most important feature of a joint commitment is this. If I am jointly committed in some way with another person, I am answerable to him with respect to my proposed or actual non-conformity to the commitment. Not only do I owe him an explanation of any proposed or actual non-conformity, I also owe him actions that conform to the commitment. I owe these to him insofar as he participates in the joint commitment.

I have said that the negative argument is essentially conceptual rather than evaluative. The point just made may seem to refute that. However, it relates to what a joint commitment is, as opposed to its value or the value of any related actions.

One way of amplifying the point is as follows. There is a sense in which, by committing each party to act in certain ways, a joint commitment in and of itself creates in each party ownership of the actions in question. Being in the future, the actions are owned but not currently possessed: in that sense they are owed.

Evidently this puts each of the other parties in a special position in relation to me. If I propose not to perform an action the commitment requires, he has the standing or authority required in order that he demand it.

He can say, in effect, "Give me that! It's mine-qua party to the joint commitment!" He also has the standing to rebuke me. After the fact, he can say, in effect, "How could you not have given me that! It was mine!" Thus those who either propose to violate a standing joint commitment or who do violate one lay themselves open to the authoritative forceful negative reactions of the other parties.

So much, then, for the nature and implications of joint commitment. I turn now to the relationship of joint commitments to social groups. I have argued elsewhere that those who are jointly committed in some way constitute a social group in a central sense of the phrase. This accords with the rough characterization of a social group offered earlier in this chapter: its members are unified in such a way that they constitute more than a mere aggregate of persons.

Given this amplification, if certain persons are jointly committed to judge that V as a body then they constitute a social group. Indeed, they constitute a social group that judges that V. As I have argued elsewhere, to say that under these conditions people constitute a social group that judges that V answers to a standard everyday concept of a social group that judges that V.

In sum, the present account of a society's value judgement is not merely stipulative. It accords with entrenched, everyday understandings of the component ideas. On the account proposed, then, a society judges that V if and only if the members are jointly committed to judge that V as a body. That is, they are jointly committed as far as possible to constitute a single body that judges that V. How might this commitment be fulfilled?

When people are acting in conformity with the commitment, they might confidently state that V when talking to one another. They would refrain from calling V or obvious corollaries into question without preamble. In short, they would suggest by their actions and emotional expressions that V. They would refrain, therefore, from acting contrary to V and from reporting contrary actions with bravado.

Thus one would not say out loud, with an air of bravado "I've managed to avoid getting married again!" or, critically, "Marriage? That's for the birds!" I do not say that in order to act in conformity with the commitment people must personally judge that V. There are several reasons for this, but for now I simply state my understanding that a joint commitment to judge that V as a body does not require the parties personally to judge V. Should one judge that not-V, however, he is committed not to say this without preamble. Rather, he must say, for instance, "Personally, I don't think marriage is such a wonderful thing." This indicates that he is speaking not from the perspective of the group as a whole but from his personal perspective.

So much for the definitions and assumptions in terms of which I shall present the negative argument. They all have some plausibility, and it is worth considering what follows from them for the question: can a wise society be a free one? I am supposing that, by definition, a wise society endorses a fair number of true value judgements and eschews false ones, and that a new true value judgement added to its current stock of such judgements increases its wisdom. The negative argument can be put as follows.

Suppose that society S is wise. Suppose now that it adds a new true value judgement J to its current stock of true value judgements. By definition, it becomes wiser. Given the nature of societal value judgements in general, J provides the members of S, as such, with a ground for rebuking one another for a new range of possible actions, R. R includes speech acts as well as actions that do not involve speech. Thus S becomes less free.

A query may arise as to this conclusion. What if there was already a joint commitment in S-one distinct from that underlying S's new value judgement J-such that members of S have a ground for rebuking one another for the very same range of actions R covered in the case of J? Assuming for the sake of argument that this is possible, it is still fair to say that S becomes less free on making J, for now there is a new ground for rebukes in relation to R.

People can certainly have the standing to rebuke one another for performing a given action on more than one ground. Perhaps, for instance, several of us agreed not to do something, and I made a special promise to you that I would not do it. Then you can upbraid me both on the ground that we agreed not to do it and on the ground that you promised me not to do it. It seems fair to say, generally, that the more grounds for rebuke there are for one's performing a given action, the less free one is.

Now it is true, of course, that if S were to add a false value judgement to its current stock of value judgements, it would also become less free. The striking thing about the negative argument, however, is this: something that on the face of it is a bonus-S's increasing wisdom-turns out to have a specifiable cost-a corresponding loss in S's freedom. That assumes, of course, that a lessening of societal freedom, in and of itself, is a bad thing, while an increase in societal wisdom is a good thing. As said, at least on the face of it, this is so.

I should emphasize that the negative argument does not render problematic the idea that, all else being equal, it is better for a society to replace a false value judgement with a true one, if these are the alternatives. It implies, however, that it would make for more freedom in a society with a false value judgement if that judgement were simply abandoned-if the society were left with no view on the matter-rather than replaced by the corresponding true judgement. True judgements, just like false ones, reduce the freedom of society.

The negative argument raises or highlights several important questions. Before concluding I note and discuss a number of these without attempting fully to answer any. It may be proposed that the loss of personal freedom entailed by a wise society's increasing wisdom will make no practical difference if each member was happy to enter the relevant joint commitment. It may be added that it will matter even less if at the time they happily entered the joint commitment they personally endorsed the society's value judgement.

This seems not to be so. Suppose Qiong was happy to enter the joint commitment at issue in my focal example, personally believing that marriage was an excellent social institution. Suppose that through personal or vicarious experience she later changes her mind. Her change of mind is one thing; her society's change of mind is another. The joint commitment may still stand. She is then still subject to it.

At this point Qiong may well find none of her choices attractive. She can baldly make concordant statements she believes to be false and act in ways she takes to express a false value. She can cause herself to stand out from the crowd by saying, as the joint commitment permits," Personally, I think marriage as an institution is problematic." She can publicly violate the commitment and lay herself open to authoritative forceful responses. One may well shrink from any of these options, and from others that might be available-such as giving up one's membership in the society in question.

Knowing all this, one who is simply contemplating a personal change of mind may turn away from that option. Or the very movement towards such contemplation may itself be suppressed.

Note that Qiong's option of prefacing her antimarriage statement with" Personally" may do more than make her stand out from the crowd. (Some people might find that outcome relatively attractive.) Another possible outcome is likely to be less attractive. Though the joint commitment does not require her personally to endorse the value judgement in question, when she says or implies that she personally doesn't endorse it, she puts herself in a problematic position. People have reason to wonder if she can be relied upon to fulfill the commitment in the future. Might her contrary opinion not soon break out untrammeled? Might she be a spoiler? She may find herself shunned, though she did not violate the commitment.

In sum, even if each one of a number of people is happy to enter a given joint commitment, and each one's personal judgement at that point accords with the societal value judgement thus created, its providing a basis for rebuke makes a practical difference. It allows, in general terms, for a tension to arise between a given member's joint commitment, on the one hand, and his personal judgement on the other.

Some are inclined to think that if any human being violates a moral rule, any other human being has the standing to rebuke him for this. Moral rules, in turn, may be conceived of as existing independently of all actual societies, and as corresponding to the subset of true value judgements at issue in the present discussion. It may then be argued that the standing to rebuke another member of one's society that one gains from a new, true value judgement of that society does not make much practical difference to anyone's situation. Irrespective of our status as members of one or another society, we are all always open to rebukes from others for the violation of any moral rule. The fact that with an increase in a society's wisdom some people have a new ground for some such rebukes is of interest, to be sure.

However, it would not seem to make much difference from a practical point of view. I have argued elsewhere against the idea that human beings as such have the standing to rebuke one another for violations of moral rules. If they do not then the argument in the previous paragraph must be rejected: its central premise is false.

At the least, the truth of its central premise is not immediately obvious. Given that this is so, people who attempt to rebuke others" because what you are doing is morally wrong" may be given short shrift by those to whom they speak. These latter may simply, and sincerely, respond that" It's none of your business."

Thus even if rebukes were automatically in order by reason of the existence of moral rules as such, the practical impact of an increase in societal wisdom could be considerable." This runs counter to our values" may well be received as a more pertinent explanation of rebuke than" What you are doing is morally wrong."

Rather than attempting to curtail a society's wisdom-perhaps by making sure it does not address particular issues-is there a way of keeping its wisdom intact, and, indeed, increasing it, while reducing its impact on the society's members? The full spectrum of true value judgements may, indeed, include some that will lead a society that makes them to minimize the impact of its own value judgements.

I have in mind here value judgements associated with when and how to tell people off for violating a given joint commitment. It may be that it is best to start in a kind and non-forceful manner.

A maximally wise society, at least, will take this value judgement on board. It will then be incumbent upon its members to act appropriately if someone baldly says something contrary to a value judgement of the society. For instance, he might mildly observe "That's not a very democratic sentiment!" or "I'm surprised to hear someone from these parts saying that!" or "I take it that you are simply expressing your personal opinion?" If the person addressed answers the last question affirmatively, the joint commitments to which he and his interlocutor are parties will offer little basis for rebuke.

A society's embracing the value judgements currently under consideration-those advocating an initially kindly approachwill most likely reduce the frequency of rebukes. If a rebuke is considered acceptable in face of a recalcitrant interlocutor, however-one who will not say the expressed opinion is his personal one, or take it back in the light of gentle suggestion-they may well sometimes occur. Moreover, as all will understand, the members of the society will at all times have the standing to rebuke provided by the joint commitment that underlies any of that society's value judgements. Thus should one forego an initially kindly approach and immediately offer a rebuke, the person rebuked will not be able to respond, "It's none of your business." The parties, then, are still threatened with rebuke, in the sense in question here. What if forceful responses, though authoritative, never occurred? What might the effects of this be? How necessary to the very existence of a society's wisdom is the imposition, at least after gentler responses, of rebuke?

This question recalls Patrick Devlin's argument for the very strong thesis that a society risks disintegration if at least its core value judgements are not supported with the weight of the criminal law.

His idea was, roughly, that the very existence of the society depends on the persistence of those core judgements as its judgements.

If action contrary to those judgements was permitted by law, this would be liable to increase such action and would lead, eventually, to the demise of the society's value judgement as such.

The general question is: what is necessary to ensure that a given true societal value judgement will persist? I shall not attempt to answer this question here. That it can be raised suggests, at least, that there may be a cost to mitigating the effects of a society's wisdom to the point that even informal rebukes are disallowed. The cost in question is the loss of the society's wisdom.

EVALUATIVE QUESTIONS

Many evaluative questions arise. How good a thing is it that a society makes true value judgements as these have been understood here? Is it better, all things considered, that a society minimize its evaluative judgements or sticks only to certain areas of value judgement? Is a society that is good overall one that looks the other way as far as values, or some kinds of value, are concerned-irrespective of its capacity to get things right? If so, why is that? Personal freedom is likely to be invoked at this point. Invocation alone, however, is not enough. Given that a diminution in personal freedom is always a loss, how is it to be weighed against an increase in the wisdom of a given society? All else being equal, is it indeed better for a society to make a true value judgement rather than no judgement on the topic or a false one? These questions are important and timely. They press us to think further about the wisdom of a society, its implications and its value.

CRITICISMS OF CULTIVATION THEORY

Scholars think that cultivation research focuses more on the effects rather than who or what is being influenced. Jennings Bryant agrees and says that the research to date has more to do with the 'why's' and 'how's' of a theory as opposed to gathering normative data as to the 'what's', 'who's', and 'where's'." Critics have faulted the logical consistency of cultivation analysis, noting that the methods employed by cultivation analysis researchers do not match the conceptual reach of the theory. The research supporting this theory uses social scientific methods that are typically used with limited effects findings. Another possibility is that the relationship between TV viewing and fear of crime is like the relationship between a runny nose and a sore throat. Neither one causes the other—they are both caused by something else.

" Many also question the breadth of Gerbner's research. When using the Cultural Indicators strategy, Gerbner separated his research into three parts. The second part focused on the effects of media when looking at gender, race/ ethnicity, and occupation. Michael Hughes writes about this process that "it does not seem reasonable that these three variables exhaust the possibilities of variables available...which may be responsible for spurious relationships between television watching and the dependent variables in the Gerbner at al. analysis" Also, the variables Gerbner did choose can also play a factor in the amount of time a person has available to watch TV.

For example, a person who works part-time is likely to have more time on their hands than someone who works a fifty-hour workweek. Just based on this example alone, one can see how correlating these variables specifically to the way a person views violence in the world can be problematic. Another piece of evidence that comes from Daniel Chandler is that "those who live in high-crime areas are more likely to stay at home and watch television and also to believe that they have a greater chance of being attacked than are those in low-crime areas." He claims as well, "when the viewer has some direct lived experience of the subject matter this may tend to reduce any cultivation effect." So, if an individual identifies with the media's message, they are less likely to let it affect their beliefs. This is probably due to the fact that they already have their own opinion on the matter.

Gerbner is also criticized for the fact that he "lumped together" all forms of violence; he did not split up the different types of television programmes. Chandler argues, "different genres—even different programmes—contribute to the shaping of different realities, but cultivation analysis assumes too much homogeneity in television programmes" This point is addressed by Horace Newcomb who argues that violence is not presented as uniformly on television as the theory assumes; therefore, television cannot be responsible for cultivating the same sense of reality for all viewers. When considering different programmes that are on television, it makes sense that scholars would criticize Gerbner's lack of categories. For example, Saturday morning cartoon "play" violence is in combination with a murder on *Law and Order*. This does not seem to logically fuse together. Morgan and Shanahan understand this dispute, but they contend "that people (especially heavy viewers) do not watch isolated genres only, and that any "impact" of individual programme types should be considered in the context of the overall viewing experience."

Chandler maintains, "Cultivation theory focuses on the amount of television viewing or 'exposure', and does not allow for differences in the ways in which viewers interpret television realities." This interpretation can vary from innocent viewing to getting ideas for carrying out an act of violence. There should be a way to continue research into this area of study. Cultivation analysis has also been criticized by humanists for examining such a large cultural question. Because the theory discusses cultural effects, many humanists feel offended, thinking that their field has been misinterpreted. Horace Newcomb writes "More than any other research effort in the area of television studies the work of Gerbner and Gross and their associates sits squarely at the juncture of the social sciences and the humanities."

The theory has also received criticism for ignoring other issues such as the perceived realism of the televised content, which could be essential in explaining people's understanding of reality. Wilson, Martins, and Markse argue that attention to television might be more important to cultivating perceptions than only the amount of television viewing. In addition, C. R. Berger writes that because the theory ignores cognitive processes, such as attention or rational thinking style, it is less useful than desired.

Lastly, it is argued that there is no evident correlation in the research. "Critics are quick to point out that the correlation between TV viewing and fear of criminal victimization can be interpreted plausibly in more than one way. The correlation could indicate, as Gerber contended, that TV viewing cultivates or causes fear of crime. But it could make just as much sense to interpret the relationship the other way—fear of crime cause people to watch more TV. After all, most TV shows depict a just world in which the bad guys get caught in the end."

THE FUTURE OF CULTIVATION THEORY

Nielsen informed the general public that "television viewing had reached an all-time high" in November 2009. With this new age of technology, we have access to television at our fingertips at almost every moment of the day. A variety of studies expanded cultivation research into new areas, or updated areas of earlier work to reflect notable changes in media messages. " The introduction of the Internet has multiplied our viewing capabilities and we can be more selective than ever.

Hulu, YouTube, TiVo, On Demand, and other computer-mediated technologies are making this process affordable, quick, and easy. We should, therefore, be looking at the cultivation theory with even more respect. In the same breath though, we should be focusing on the cultivation theory in other forms of media. The Internet plays a huge role in our communication and the way we, as Americans, receive information. Those who study the cultivation theory should consider extending it to various other media outlets. So far, Cultivation Analysis has been applied to other forms of media, including video games. A longitudinal, controlled experiment conducted by Dmitri Williams, in 2006, examined the presence of cultivation effects in the playing of an online game. Over the course of playing the video game for one month, participants changed their perceptions of real world dangers. However, these dangers only corresponded to events and situations present in the game world, not other real-world crimes.

AGENDA-SETTING THEORY

Agenda-setting theory describes the "ability [of the news media] to influence the salience of topics on the public agenda." That is, if a news item is covered frequently and prominently the audience will regard the issue as more important. Agenda-setting theory was formally developed by Dr. Max McCombs and Dr. Donald Shaw in a study on the 1968 presidential election. In the 1968 "Chapel Hill study," McCombs and Shaw demonstrated a strong correlation ($r > .9$) between what 100 residents of Chapel Hill, North Carolina thought was the most important election issue and what the local and national news media reported was the most important issue. By comparing the salience of issues in news content with the public's perceptions of the most important election issue, McCombs and Shaw were able to determine the degree to which the media determines public opinion. Since the 1968 study, published in a 1972 edition of Public Opinion Quarterly, more than 400 studies have been published on the agenda-setting function of the mass media, and the theory continues to be regarded as relevant.

FUTURE OF AGENDA-SETTING THEORY

As a result in the changes in technology, there have been major changes in the ways in which people receive their news. Newspapers, broadcast television, and terrestrial radio are all examples of "vertical media" which is rapidly declining.

Now the more common form of media is "horizontal media." The main differences are that it is more specialized and people pay premiums for this type of media. Horizontal media includes cable television and satellite radio as well as other media that is paid for. Horizontal and vertical media intersect in virtual brand communities, or the Internet. This is because the Internet is free like vertical media but serves specialized interest groups like horizontal media. Now people seek news in different ways, the media and its agenda have had to adapt. Although the major tenets of agenda setting theory have maintained their importance with the changes of new media, an aspect of agenda setting theory has changed. This change is known as Agenda Melding which focuses "on the personal agendas of individuals vis-à-vis their community and group affiliations

". This means that individuals join groups and blend their agendas with the agendas of the group. Then groups and communities represent a "collected agenda of issues" and "one joins a group by adopting an agenda." On the other hand, agenda setting defines groups as "collections of people based on some shared values, attitudes, or opinions" that individuals join. This is different from traditional agenda setting because according to Shaw *et al.* individuals join groups in order to avoid social dissonance and isolation that is also known as "need for orientation ". Therefore in the past in order to belong people would learn and adopt the agenda of the group. Now with the ease of access to media, people form their own agendas and then find groups that have similar agendas that they agree with. The advances in technology have made agenda melding easy for people to develop because there is a wide range of groups and individual agendas. The Internet makes it possible for people all around the globe to find others with similar agendas and collaborate with them. In the past agenda setting was limited to general topics and it was geographically bound because travel was limited.

Criticisms:

- Agenda setting is an inherently causal theory, but few studies establish the hypothesized temporal order (the media should set the public's agenda).
- The measurement of the dependent variable was originally conceptualized as the public's perceived issue "salience," but subsequent studies have conceptualized the dependent variable as awareness, attention, or concern, leading to differing outcomes.
- Studies tend to aggregate media content categories and public responses into very broad categories, resulting in inflated correlation coefficients.

USES AND GRATIFICATIONS THEORY

Uses and Gratifications Theory (UGT) is an approach to understanding why and how people actively seek out specific media to satisfy specific needs. UGT is an audience-centred approach to understanding mass communication. Divergent from other media effect theories who question "what media do to people?", UGT focuses on "what people do with media?" This Communication theory is positivistic in its approach, based in the socio-psychological communication tradition, and focuses on communication at the mass media scale. The driving question of UGT is: *Why* do people use media and what do they use them for? UGT discusses how users deliberately choose media that will satisfy given needs and allow one to enhance knowledge, relaxation, social interactions/companionship, diversion, or escape.

It assumes that audience members are not passive consumers of media. Rather, the audience has power over their media consumption and assumes an active role in interpreting and integrating media into their own lives. Unlike other theoretical perspectives, UGT holds that audiences are responsible for choosing media to meet their desires and needs to achieve gratification. This theory would then imply that the media compete against other information sources for viewers' gratification.

UGT has a heuristic value today because it gives communication scholars a "perspective through which a number of ideas and theories about media choice, consumption, and even impact can be viewed."

Criticism

The data behind the theory is hard to extrapolate and at times is not found. How each audience, individual and group perceives a given media outlet is extremely difficult to gauge. A main argument lies in how the media, producers and editors want the material to be interpreted. News reports on a rising restaurant could be seen as a threat to local establishments but was intended as a positive note to how well the community is doing. Morley says that "creators of media content have a preferred reading that they would like the audience to take out of the text. However, the audience might reject it, or negotiate some comprise interpretation between what they think and what they text is saying, or contest what the text says with some alternative interpretation". The biggest issue for the Uses and Gratifications Theory is its being non-theoretical, vague in key concepts, and nothing more than a data-collecting strategy. Using this sociologically-based theory has little to no link to the benefit of psychology due to its weakness in operational definitions and weak analytical mode. It also is focused too narrowly on the individual and neglects the social structure and place of the media in that structure.

Due to the individualistic nature of Uses and Gratification theory, it is difficult to take the information that is collected in studies. Most research relies on pure recollection of memory rather than data. This makes self-reports complicated and immeasurable.

The Uses and Gratifications theory has been denounced by media hegemony advocates who say it goes too far in claiming that people are free to choose the media and the interpretations they desire. Audiences interpret the media in their own terms and any debate for or against this can be argued, and depending on the circumstances, won by either side. Each individuals' actions and effects on those actions will depend solely on the situation. The Uses and Gratifications theory does not properly account for these natural occurrences but does hold a valid argument that each individual has unique uses to which the media attempts to meet their gratifications.

Theorist Explanation

"The nature of the theory underlying Uses and Gratifications research is not totally clear". This makes the line between gratification and satisfaction blurred, calling into question whether or not we only seek what we desire or actually enjoy it.

"Practitioners of Uses and Gratifications research have been criticized for a formidable array of shortcomings in their outlook — they are taxed for being crassly atheoretical, perversely eclectic, ensnared in the pitfalls of functionalism and for flirting with the positions at odds with their functionalist origins".

The Active Audience

Jay Blumler presented a number of interesting points, as to why Uses and Gratifications cannot measure an active audience. He stated, "The issue to be considered here is whether what has been thought about Uses and Gratifications Theory has been an article of faith and if it could now be converted into an empirical question such as: How to measure an active audience?" Blumler then offered suggestions about the kinds of activity the audiences were engaging with in the different types of media.

- *Utility:* "Using the media to accomplish specific tasks"
- *Intentionality:* "Occurs when people's prior motive determine use of media"
- *Selectivity:* "Audience members' use of media reflect their existing interests"
- *Imperviousness to Influence:* "Refers to audience members' constructing their own meaning from media content".

25 years later, in 1972, Blumler, McQuail and Brown extended Lasswell's four groups. These included four primary factors for which one may use the media:

- *Diversion*: Escape from routine and problems; an emotional release,
- *Personal Relationships*: Social utility of information in conversation; substitution of media for companionship,
- *Personal Identity or Individual Psychology*: Value reinforcement or reassurance; self-understanding, reality exploration,
- *Surveillance*: Information about factors which might affect one or will help one do or accomplish something.

Katz, Gurevitch and Haas saw mass media as a means by which individuals connect or disconnect themselves with others. They developed 35 needs taken from the largely speculative literature on the social and psychological functions of the mass media and put them into five categories:

- *Cognitive Needs*: Acquiring information, knowledge and understanding,
- *Media Examples*: Television (news), video (how-to), movies (documentaries or based on history),
- *Affective Needs*: Emotion, pleasure, feelings,
- *Media Examples*: Movies, television (soap operas, sitcoms),

- *Personal Integrative Needs*: Credibility, stability, status,
- *Media Examples*: Video,
- *Social Integrative Needs*: Family and friends,
- *Media Examples*: Internet (e-mail, instant messaging, chat rooms, social media),
- *Tension Release Needs*: Escape and diversion,
- *Media Examples*: Television, movies, video, radio, internet.

Dependency Theory

Dependency theory is a body of social science theories predicated on the notion that resources flow from a "periphery" of poor and underdeveloped states to a "core" of wealthy states, enriching the latter at the expense of the former. It is a central contention of dependency theory that poor states are impoverished and rich ones enriched by the way poor states are integrated into the "world system."

The theory arose as a reaction to modernization theory, an earlier theory of development which held that all societies progress through similar stages of development, that today's underdeveloped areas are thus in a similar situation to that of today's developed areas at some time in the past, and that therefore the task in helping the underdeveloped areas out of poverty is to accelerate them along this supposed common path of development, by various means such as investment, technology transfers, and closer integration into the world market. Dependency theory rejected this view, arguing that underdeveloped countries are not merely primitive versions of developed countries, but have unique features and structures of their own; and, importantly, are in the situation of being the weaker members in a world market economy.

The premises of dependency theory are that:

- Poor nations provide natural resources, cheap labour, a destination for obsolete technology, and markets for developed nations, without which the latter could not have the standard of living they enjoy.
- Wealthy nations actively perpetuate a state of dependence by various means. This influence may be multifaceted, involving economics, media control, politics, banking and finance, education, culture, sport, and all aspects of human resource development (including recruitment and training of workers).
- Wealthy nations actively counter attempts by dependent nations to resist their influences by means of economic sanctions and/or the use of military force.

Dependency theory states that the poverty of the countries in the periphery is not because they are not integrated into the world system, or not 'fully' integrated as is often argued by free market economists, but because of *how* they are integrated into the system. This introduces a paradoxical effect, in that although both the first and third-world countries are benefitting, the poorer side is being locked into detrimental economic position. They rely on the rich for the little work that is available to them, yet this causes a barrier from the nation growing independently. In a future perspective, such nations have no opportunity to improve their quality of life. It is classified under the sociological theories of mass communication.

NORMATIVE THEORIES OF MASS MEDIA

Normative theories explain how the media 'ought to' or can be 'expected to' operate under the prevailing set of political-economic circumstances. Since each society controls its mass media in accordance with its policies and needs, it formulates its own separate press theory. Therefore, each theory is connected with the kind of political system in which the society has to conduct its socio-economic political affairs. Siebert et al., in 1956, mentioned four theories, based on classification of the world's national media systems into four categories. Denis McQuail, in the 1980s, considered it appropriate to add two more theories to the original set of four. He concedes that these theories "may not correspond to complete media systems" but "they have now become part of the discussion of press theory and provide some of the principles for current media policy and practice".

AUTHORITARIAN THEORY

According to this theory, mass media, though not under the direct control of the State, had to follow its bidding. Under an Authoritarian approach in Western Europe, freedom of thought was jealously guarded by a few people (ruling classes), who were concerned with the emergence of a new middle class and were worried about the effects of printed matter on their thought process. Steps were taken to control the freedom of expression. The result was advocacy of complete dictatorship.

The theory promoted zealous obedience to a hierarchical superior and reliance on threat and punishment to those who did not follow the censorship rules or did not respect authority. Censorship of the press was justified on the ground that the State always took precedence over the individual's right to freedom of expression.

This theory stemmed from the authoritarian philosophy of Plato (407–327 B.C), who thought that the State was safe only in the hands of a few wise men. Thomas Hobbes (1588–1679), a British academician, argued that the power to maintain order was sovereign and individual objections were to be ignored. Engel, a German thinker further reinforced the theory by stating that freedom came into its supreme right only under Authoritarianism.

The world has been witness to authoritarian means of control over media by both dictatorial and democratic governments.

LIBERTARIANISM OR FREE PRESS THEORY

This movement is based on the right of an individual, and advocates absence of restraint. The basis of this theory dates back to 17th century England when the printing press made it possible to print several copies of a book or pamphlet at cheap rates. The State was thought of as a major source of interference on the rights of an individual and his property. Libertarians regarded taxation as institutional theft. Popular will (vox populi) was granted precedence over the power of State.

Advocates of this theory were Lao Tzu, an early 16th century philosopher, John Locke of Great Britain in the 17th century, John Milton, the epic poet (*"Aeropagitica"*) and John Stuart Mill, an essayist (*"On Liberty"*). Milton in *Aeropagitica* in 1644, referred to a self righting process if free expression is permitted "let truth and falsehood grapple." In 1789, the French, in their Declaration Of The Rights Of Man, wrote *"Every citizen may speak, write and publish freely."* Out of such doctrines came the idea of a "free marketplace of ideas." George Orwell defined libertarianism as "allowing people to say things you do not want to hear". Libertarians argued that the press should be seen as the *Fourth Estate* reflecting public opinion. What the theory offers, in sum, is power without social responsibility.

SOCIAL RESPONSIBILITY THEORY OF MEDIA

Virulent critics of the Free Press Theory were Wilbur Schramm, Siebert and Theodore Paterson. In their book *Four Theories Of Press*, they stated "pure libertarianism is antiquated, outdated and obsolete." They advocated the need for its replacement by the Social Responsibility theory. This theory can be said to have been initiated in the United States by the Commission of The Freedom Of Press, 1949.

The commission found that the free market approach to press freedom had only increased the power of a single class and has not served the interests of the less well-off classes. The emergence of radio, TV and film suggested the need for some means of accountability. Thus the theory advocated some obligation on the part of the media to society. A judicial mix of self regulation and state regulation and high professional standards were imperative.

Social Responsibility theory thus became the modern variation in which the duty to one's conscience was the primary basis of the right of free expression.

Soviet Media/Communist Theory: This theory is derived from the ideologies of Marx and Engel that "the ideas of the ruling classes are the ruling ideas". It was thought that the entire mass media was saturated with bourgeois ideology. Lenin thought of private ownership as being incompatible with freedom of press and that modern technological means of information must be controlled for enjoying effective freedom of press.

The theory advocated that the sole purpose of mass media was to educate the great masses of workers and not to give out information. The public was encouraged to give feedback as it was the only way the media would be able to cater to its interests.

Two more theories were later added as the "four theories of the press" were not fully applicable to the non-aligned countries of Asia, Africa and Latin America, who were committed to social and economic development on their own terms. The two theories were:

DEVELOPMENT COMMUNICATION THEORY

The underlying fact behind the genesis of this theory was that there can be no development without communication. Under the four classical theories, capitalism was legitimized, but under the Development communication theory, or Development Support Communication as it is otherwise called, the media undertook the role of carrying out positive developmental programmes, accepting restrictions and instructions from the State. The media subordinated themselves to political, economic, social and cultural needs. Hence the stress on "development communication" and "development journalism". There was tacit support from the UNESCO for this theory. The weakness of this theory is that "development" is often equated with government propaganda.

DEMOCRATIZATION/DEMOCRATIC PARTICIPANT MEDIA THEORY

This theory vehemently opposes the commercialization of modern media and its top-down non-participant character. The need for access and right to communicate is stressed. Bureaucratic control of media is decried.

SOCIAL RESPONSIBILITY OF MEDIA

An important consideration in doing ethnographic research in the study of new electronic media is the social presence attributes of the technology itself.

Short, Williams, and Christie were apparently the first researchers to conceptualize the construct they called social presence, which they defined as being a quality of the communications medium itself.

As they elaborated, social presence "varies between different media... affects the nature of the interaction... and interacts with the purpose of the interaction to influence the medium chosen by the individual who wishes to communicate".

Media perceived as high in social presence are generally judged (on Semantic Differential Scales) by users as warm, personal, sensitive, and, sociable; those low in social presence as cold, impersonal, insensitive, and unsociable. Chief among the reasons for differentiating media in their degree of social presence is the medium's ability to restrict stimulus-conveying information. More specifically, media that are less able to convey non-verbal elements are more likely to be judged as being low in social presence.

In another sense, social presence is the degree to which a medium is perceived as conveying the "presence" of the communicating participants; it is dependent not only on the words involved in the communication but on the full range of verbal and non-verbal cues, and the communication context.

Thus CMC technologies typically would be judged lower in social presence than face-to-face communication (FTF) because of the lower bandwidth of information conveyed by the former (vis-a-vis verbal and non-verbal messages).

This notion of the bandwidth of the medium is closely related to media richness, a construct developed by Daft and Lengel. Rice describes the term as the:

Extent to which media are able to bridge different frames of reference, make issues less ambiguous, or provide opportunities for learning in a given time interval, based on the medium's capacity for immediate feedback, the number of cues and senses involved, personalization, and language variety. The essential underlying element in both of these notions is that a good match between the medium's characteristics (high in social presence or media richness) and the intent of the communication activity (getting to know someone, strategic decision making) should lead to higher performance and satisfaction.

The importance of all of this to ethnographic research is, how can one adequately do participatory research with media that are judged low in social presence or media richness?

Stated another way, how will the ethnographic researcher be able to make adequate sense out of communication that restricts important cues such as non-verbal behaviours? in their study of e-mail in organizations, Garton and Wellman have discussed the consequences of e-mail's exclusion of non-verbal cues: E-mail does not supply non-verbal interactional cues to group members, such as eye contact, gestures, nodding approval, frowning, or hesitating before replying.

There are no contextual cues, either: Participants cannot use seating arrangements to identify coalitions and cleavages, or choose meeting sites to identify the importance of sponsorship of meetings. Because e-mail users typically are identified by name only, people are not constantly reminded of the social roles cues others have beyond the narrow confines of the task group.

Users may not be aware of another group member's gender, race, expertise, or organizational position. One approach to this dilemma is to take account of the ways participants do compensate at times for the restricted bandwidth of the medium by providing clarifying cues in their messages.

Social role cues can be transmitted in e-mail (either implicitly or explicitly) by adding status information to their "signatures," by their writing style, or by forwarding communications to (or from) important persons.

Baym also found the standard components of Usenet posts for a soap opera news group—*e.g.*, "from" line, "subject" line, "organization" line (site of message's origin), and the quotation system, in addition to signatures—to provide subtle contextualizing cues about the sender's interests and status.

Other examples of clarifying cues are:

- Emotions used to pictorialize emotional states (*e.g.*, the computer "smiley face"),
- Meta-messages included to communicate physical states (*e.g.*, using " " to designate jocularity),
- Acronyms used to designate degree of emotion (*e.g.*, "FOTFL" to represent "failing on the floor laughing," or a greater degree of merriment beyond a mere smile or grin).'

As Walther, Anderson, and Park noted in their meta-analysis of computer mediated interaction, the interpersonal effects expected to accrue rapidly in face-to-face interactions can (and do) occur in CIVIC, but these interpersonal cues require extended time interactions.

That is, interactional, contextual, and social cues that provide immediate feedback in FTF communication have to be stated explicitly in CIVIC and require more time to develop. Deep knowledge of an organizational culture may also enhance the participants' hermeneutic ability to embellish an e-mail with meaning.

Of course, social cues do more than merely clarify or boost informational richness in FTF or CMC encounters; they also mark a person's identity (*e.g.*, gender, age, ethnic, class, sexual, cultural, occupational, etc.) as being of a certain moral or political character. Gender norms, for example, are a powerful means of designating the inappropriate or disvalued behaviours of men and women in specific contexts and vary widely from ideologically dominant expressions to the communication contexts and media of subaltern groups.

Thus, women ethnographers learn very quickly how their bodies—not only skin colour and body shape, but also aspects of clothing, adornment, hair style, and facial, gestural, and speech styles—affect the way they are perceived in the field, and the roles and motives attributed to them.

Embodiment in all of its forms is not a condition that can be controlled independently or somehow neutralized. Rather, it is through the ethnographic body performing with other cultural members that one learns the schemes of cultural valuation. Practical problems of "fitting in" are of a piece with issues of acculturation which are enormously important to understanding the scene being studied.

In CMC environments, where perceptions of identity derive almost totally from what and how one writes, the notion of representational reality collapses and the ambiguity of action becomes foregrounded. Multiple identities are tried on, and specific traits or behaviours may be expressed more boldly in the widespread use of aliases, aptonyms, and role-playing domains in which players build characters for themselves. By detaching self-expression from the politics of the body, CMC liberates its users from certain kinds of discriminatory practice and promotes a low-risk, often playful, exploration of skill sets.

Certainly, the texts one writes may unwittingly leak signs of personal identity which could be attributed by readers to the author's embodied self.

As long as there are other users supervising the actors and the threads of their discourse, standards of plausibility, coherence, and trustworthiness will still apply to the textual contributions. Ultimately, the CMC ethnographer should be prepared to confront the ambiguity of identity performance as a central fact of virtual life, worthy of study on its own terms.

Concerns about testing the informational richness, or the authenticity, of virtual action against criteria of embodied action may be much less important to the project of ethnography than issues of how computing worlds are socially constructed, what recognizably human purposes they serve, and how they relate to a range of other "possibility spaces." Reduced social presence also affects the way in which researchers enter virtual scenes. Interaction management seems to function similarly in FTF and CMC in the opening and closing phases of encounters, but in CMC the choice of names and the use of attention-getting strategies are critical decisions.

The risks of field entry may be lessened by learning the norms of such strategies in advance. Thus the "outsider" designation one usually expects in the first stages of an FTF project may be less of a problem in entering a virtual space once the right level of competence has been gained via observation.

On the other hand, veteran members often do not suffer novices gladly, and the ethnographer may need to ask for the cooperation of the group (or its influential members) in order to be heard, or to engage them in directed queries or tasks. Researchers face subtle differences in the social makeup and interactional preferences of virtual scenes, which may require them to devise different strategies for entry and field positioning than in FTF situations.

SOCIAL STRATEGIES

Matters of self-presentation and scope of action are critical to the relations built among researchers, the virtual "places" populating the Internet, and the cultural membership. Correll, for example, was able to convey the location, look, and meanings of the "furniture" of the Lesbian Cafe mostly from her observations of electronic postings, but also from interviews. Compared to Leal's analysis of the relation of TV sets to the domestic material culture in working-class Brazilian homes, the mise-en-scene of the Cafe is not nearly as dense, tactile, and sensuous.

Despite this possibly unfair comparison, "the sense of a common reality [in the Lesbian Cafe] was used by patrons much like physical settings are used by co-present conversationalists—as a source of mutually relevant topics". Like the dialogue one hears in a radio play, conversationalists in the Lesbian Cafe must include many more references in their ordinary talk to objects, the current status of the objects, and the presence or absence of people in and around those objects in order to maintain orientation and sustain a convincing sense of as-if reality. The lean exposition Correll offers would likely be unacceptable in other forms of ethnographic work, but it turns out to be the one that matters to the women who "drink" and socialize there.

Media ethnographers begin their on-line presence in a variety of ways. One mode used by some is that of the unknown, unobtrusive observer. Over a three-year period, Harrington and Bielby collected and printed messages posted on two soap opera BBS's by subscribers to two commercial on-line computer services. They do not report interactions of any kind between themselves and the posters.

Presumably, the computer services were not notified of the initiation of the research activity, nor were the BBS system operators. Interestingly, while the authors appear unconcerned about their own lurker posture, they note the suspicion held by many of the BBS users that their conversations were being overheard by "industry insiders". Scodari also relies on transcripts of fan BBS discourse in interpreting critical reactions to changes in the soap, Another World, although she aligns her own interests much more closely with the fans she quotes than Harrington and Bielby.

Open participation characterizes the approach of several other studies and more closely resembles normative field practice. Baym started as an unabashed soap fan and news group contributor and found it easy to continue openly as an analyst of the group:

My position in the [rec.arts.arts.soaps, or r.a.t.s., newsgroup] is that of a participant at least as much as a researcher. As a long-time fan of soap operas, I was thrilled to discover this group. It was only after I had been reading daily and participating regularly for a year that I began to write about it. As the work has evolved, I have shared its progress with the group members and found them exceedingly supportive and helpful. They have acted as research participants as well as subjects and have treated me more as an ambassador than a researcher.

The confidence each party had in the other paved the way for Baym to obtain other forms of data besides the news group's messages, especially electronic mail correspondence with several participants and responses to open-ended questions she posted to r.a.t.s. Similarly, Correll's membership in the Lesbian Cafe, and the approval she got from the bar's founder, assisted her in posting queries and interviewing several of the patrons both by e-mail and in person. Some researchers actually run the facilities that enable computer users to "find" the research project. In an early study, Myers operated a university

BBS for two months and set up a number of networked research tools in order to investigate the perceived social context of CMC: on-line surveys, a focus group, and a role-playing game.

More recently, Lindlof et al. launched a Web home page for X-Men fans that offered graphic content (thus participating in the X-Men array of more than 60 Internet locations), links to other X-Men sites, a survey to capture data, and a solicitation for dialogues with on-line X-Men users and page producers.

Like the Baym and Correll studies, the research purpose was stated openly in order to invite cooperation; however, its sudden appearance and the research team's initial contacts with users were sometimes met with suspicion, critique (of their knowledge of X-Men), and humorous skepticism.

It became clear that the World Wide Web page of hypertext URLS's (Uniform Resource Locator) that linked to other pages related to the X-Men topic constituted the study's "gatekeeper" in the traditional sense of enabling an initial contact. The study also hints at the possibilities of participatory design in which ethnographers may act as the interpreters of diverse voices, usage interests, and aesthetic tastes in the design of networked systems.

A final strategy for consideration moves the researcher physically alongside the user in order to "read" his or her real-time decision making and styles of engagement. The user's dyadic interplay with a computer forms a focal interest, but included in this arena would be the material context of computing (*e.g.*, its location in a room, the CD-ROM's on hand), the institutional culture (*e.g.*, considering open viewing of sex sites as sexual harassment), interpersonal resources or constraints (*e.g.*, informal rules for sharing URL's), and the specific reality of what it means to "do computing" that these signify for users.

Models for this approach exist in the literature on social television viewing and family computer usage. However, since Internet usage is typically a solitary venture, the more promising route would seem to lie in some version of the "shopping with consumers" protocol from the field of consumer behaviour.

Accompanying users on their way through the kinetic pathways of virtual space and eliciting talk on a wide range of subjects, either retrospectively or on-the-spot, enables the researcher to understand the more embodied dimensions of CMC. In effect, the researcher shadows the user's on-site computing. The advantages of the approach are its close proximity to the user and setting, and the ability to comprehend computing performance as an activity that has a rich, localized back stage—that is, as more than lines of type scrolling down a screen.

In ethnographies of embodied social scenes, the researcher must continually negotiate with the culture membership and convince them of the value of the study and the reasonableness of the person doing the research. It is not unusual for ethnographers to have to adjust their persona somewhat differently as they pass through a scene, or disclose different versions of the project, since the members of a group often relate asymmetrically or even conflictively to each other.

CMC ethnographies, as we have shown, also involve some degree of negotiation when anonymous observation is not the method of access. Virtual spaces offer a limited window in which to explain one's purpose, and electronic text is not the most suitable medium for engaging in a sensitive interaction.

Trust tends to be a heightened concern where entry and exit and unbridled information disclosure are easily accomplished. Mistakes, once made, can have disastrous results, and be very hard to rectify. Institutional principles for informed consent are now being formulated for research on the World Wide Web, but it will take longer for ethnographers themselves to develop a consensus around protocols for responsible virtual space entry and ways to insure the fair treatment of those they study without compromising very seriously the conduct of enquiry.

TECHNICAL UTILITIES

In this section, we discuss the use of technical utilities for accomplishing research tasks. Some computer systems allow asynchronous communication interactions to be studied either by saving the individual messages, or archiving all postings for later perusal. Most of these have been around for some time. The ones we discuss here are electronic mail, news groups over Usenet, and list servers. Electronic mail is asynchronous (users generally are not communicating in realtime), quick (in terms of transmission and reply), text-based, and configured for dyadic or multiple connections (can be sent one-to-one, one-to-many, or many-to-many). Moreover, e-mail can be stored and manipulated. As Garton and Wellman noted in a recent review:

E-mail can be stored in external memory for future retrieval, searching, editing, and forwarding to others. People can edit their own or other's messages to change their meaning. The historical record of interaction may be used for surveillance of individual and group interactions, to review past decisions (as Oliver North belatedly learned), and to bring new members up to date.

What makes this modality particularly suitable for ethnographic research are its personal-contact and archival functions.

For example, in his 9-month participant-observation study of "Zytech," a computer systems firm, Workman utilized e-mail in the following ways:

- Being placed on the company's various distribution lists, which on a daily basis delivered internal documents, minutes of meetings, meeting agendas, and announcements;
- Scheduling interviews;
- Accessing hundreds of BBS's, including Zytech correspondence going back several years;

- Communicating with informants, including follow-ups to FTF interviews.

Though the staggered progress of e-mail interviewing does not promote the same qualities of rapport or spontaneity as personal interviews, it does permit a more elastic time frame for both interviewer and participant to think carefully about the meanings of questions and replies.

In another organizational study, special software was used to automatically save the headers (but not the message content) of all departmental e-mail to a designated file whenever a user read or transmitted a message, yielding a non-reactive means of learning who communicates with whom, when, and about what.

For ethnographic purposes, the value of this procedure lies in its capacity to augment such methods as interviews or on-site observation.

However, the ability to retrieve and store this information without the users' permission (or below their conscious awareness, even when permission is granted) carries the potential for ethical abuse at worst, and suspicion on the part of participants at best. Usenet is a protocol that describes how groups of messages can be stored on and sent between computers, many of which lay outside of the Internet. In actuality, Usenet forms a "virtual forum" for the electronic community that is divided into a plethora of news groups dedicated to varied areas of interest. News group articles are read and written through programmes called newsreaders that keep track of articles that have been read, allow users to edit what has been read, and enable readers to reply to previously posted messages in the aforementioned study, Baym reported her participant-observation of a news group made up of soap opera aficionados.

Even though some Usenet sites can archive messages off-line, Baym herself saved the messages posted on the r.a.t.s group while she was an active member. Even working with a medium often described as low in social presence or media richness, she was able to develop a "thick" description of the personalities of this community based on features of their postings:

- Signature files (files automatically attached to postings containing identifying information about the sender),
- Humour in the messages,
- Self-disclosure,
- Comments made about personal lives.

By capitalizing on the features of Usenet news groups, variations of focus group interviewing become possible. During a two-month period of operating a public BBS, Myers set up a computer-mediated focus group "to determine what motivated frequent and active BBS use". As an alternative to a simple discussion, a focus group consisting of a theoretically interesting set of users could work on a virtual task. MacGregor and Morrison describe an editing-group protocol in which groups of people were given the opportunity to re-edit existing news reports (including video footage) in order to produce a more "ideal" version, thereby enabling them to understand viewers' journalistic values more concretely.

It is not difficult to see how this task could be adapted to computer news groups and the multimedia capabilities of high-end work stations, although techniques for training and monitoring the users in their editing-group activities would need to be developed.

Listserv groups (managed by listserver software) are similar to news groups in that they are discussion groups, but they operate in a completely different way by using the Internet e-mail system to exchange messages. Once a person subscribes to a Listserv group (or Listproc group, as they are called on networks other than the early Bitnet), their name is added to a mailing list that receives postings from everyone else subscribed to the list.

Many listservers offer features that allow users to search and retrieve files that are archived, and search the archives using keyword searches. Thus, anyone from a remote site can access archived messages for study from the host computer.

This capability raises interesting ethical issues: How does one receive consent to study the stored communications of users of a particular listserver? Is open access to a person's communications implied in the use of this service? Are the archived files considered the property of the individual subscribers, or are they "owned" in some form of fiduciary relationship by the listserv operator? Because the Internet has developed so rapidly, many such legal and ethical questions have yet to be resolved. The CMC technologies mentioned above have been in place for a while and are generally well known to most researchers. Most of the communication from these sources is asynchronous, *i.e.*, it is archived for later review and becomes an excellent database.

However some of the newer systems allow for the actual observation of synchronous, or real-time, communication behaviour. It is to these we now turn.

Some of the more recent real-time technologies are:

- Internet Relay Chat (IRC) systems, or" chat lines";
- The entire gamut of multiple-user technologies, *e.g.*, MUDs (Multiple User Domains, formerly known as Multiple User Dungeons), MOOs (MUD Object-Oriented), and MUSHes (Multi-User Shared Hallucination);
- Groupware,
- Desktop videoconferencing over the Internet. All of these systems operate synchronously and as such more approximate face-to-face communication.

Internet Relay Chat (IRC) is a multi-user synchronous communication capability available worldwide to users with Internet accessibility.

These real time" chat lines" provide for mutithreaded conversations from more than two users in something very similar to an" electronic cocktail party". In these" chat rooms" users are able to don bogus" personas" (false identities) and communicate with interactants from all over the globe. These chat lines are very popular on commercial services like America Online and are now available through various web browsers (*e.g.*, students can" chat" with the president of a university via its Web site).

One step up from IRC is a whole family of computer programmes that allow more than just written conversation in real time. These are multi-user programmes that, in addition to providing text, allow the additional depiction of a physical environment. Multiple User programmes are designed to offer a pseudo-physical dimension via its object orientation. In MOOs, for examples, individuals" virtually" move through" rooms," interact with virtual" objects" such as chairs, doors, and the like, and have virtual conversations with others. As Reid has remarked, in MUDs," text replaces gesture and has even become gesture itself".

A third, more recent technology is found in a generation of software called" groupware." Unlike MUDs, MOOs, MUSHes, MUCKs, and the like that are used more for entertainment and amusement, groupware is being developed mainly for business and professional uses.

Most of the newer groupware programmes use Web-based technology and allow not only for sharing e-mail but for conducting synchronous multiuser conferencing. The promise for ethnographers in this technology lies in the" common thread" that runs through all these programmes--*i.e.*," the construction of shared memory" and recording of group discussions.

In essence, groupware allows for observing the" virtual office," *i.e.*, electronic mail, conferencing, scheduling, shared documents, electronic" whiteboards," and so on, and recording these interactions. All of this can function in real time or be archived for later study.

Appearing now on the horizon is the capability to use the desktop computer for real time videoconferencing. Using fairly inexpensive video cameras attached to desktop computers, and software such as CU-SeeMe technology, mediated FTF interactions are now available for study. As soon as compression capabilities for full-motion video are perfected, these dispersed FTF interactions, mediated by the computer, can be recorded and used in data analysis.

When considering all these new technologies, the type of research done may have to be dictated by the characteristics of the medium. That is, for asynchronous media, the type of research conducted would be more akin to that for studying other forms of written communication, while synchronous media enable types of research more equivalent to naturalistic observation--*i.e.*, observing the unfolding of communicative events in real time. It was inevitable that interpretive analysts would turn their attention to the profusion of common culture now moving through the Internet. Forms of ethnographic enquiry are being applied to many of the events that occur in virtual space, although questions remain about how well these approaches engage CMC phenomena. One such question is the appropriateness of" community" as a conceptual device. The conventional idea of community as a stable locus for the practice of ritual, custom, and moral obligation applies to cyberspace groups, albeit in the context of a shifting sense of commitment.

When members can easily come and go, when many" members" do not even post, and when identities cannot be verified beyond the current situation, the power of a community ethos may be weakened considerably. The structural properties of the Internet also raise questions about how far a user community extends. For example, can any array of Web sites found by a search term be considered a" community," and if not, what criteria do we use for including a site in the community set?

Finally, what is the relationship of computer-mediated action to local social networks? It has been suggested, for example, that the growing reliance on computer technology for communicating with distant others may undermine the vitality of public life in so-called real communities or play a role in their economic and social fragmentation. Answers to these and other important issues about virtual community await further and more inventive empirical studies.

If there is one theme that runs through the differences between FTF (embodied) and CIVIC (virtual) ethnography, it is the problem of participation. CIVIC ethnography moves us into questions of what it means to engage in and explain" experience" without being co-present with others. Screen-life is a social sphere of its own with vocabularies, motives, and expectations that increasingly re-interpret the meanings of off-screen-life (*e.g.*, mail becoming known as" snail mail").

Objectifications of life in the screen world are also a part of that world. Computer users do act as textual performers and analysts, and knowingly comment on the skills of other text-makers. The use of symbolic codes like" FOTFL" and the real-time deployment of a character in a MUD are operations that create the affect of participation for users, and it would be unusual for ethnographers; not to consider their situated usage.

However, the sites of semiotic action in CMC are not the texts, but the persons who produce them. The text-threads from a Usenet news group or a stack of e-mail messages exnominate the moments in which they were created and read, and the influences of local institutions on their users' action are seldom seen in the messages themselves. In the years ahead, ethnographers will be struggling with basic questions of what it means to" participate" in simulated worlds as well as with developing tactical ways to participate as researchers. Closely related to the problem of participation are issues of trust and ethical conduct to which we have alluded at various points in this chapter. These issues assume even more importance than usual in research practice due to the greater potential for engaging in covert surveillance of CIVIC social life and the still-unsettled distinctions between" public" and" private" behaviour across the range of cyberspace contexts. The problem of the stable identifiability of persons who post in Usenet news groups, respond by e-mail, or visit a Web site may also confound the principle of informed consent as a precondition for engaging a human subject's participation. Generally, there is little debate about the need to provide as much disclosure as possible about research procedures to those who are asked to participate, and to shelter them from the possible harmful consequences of participation and subsequent publication.

However, as King notes, extremely wide ranges of" group accessibility" and" perceived privacy" exist on the Internet. The highest accessibility characterizes those public BBS groups that are unmoderated and unregulated, while the least accessible community is" a private, closed e-mail group where the subscription address is not published and there are enforced requirements to join". Perceived privacy varies in terms of both the sensitivity of the information (in which, for example, a substance abuse support group would seek a very high level of privacy) and the need to disseminate information to the widest possible client group (the National Communication Association's CRTNET would seek a low measure of privacy).

Yet a great many Internet conversations can in fact be monitored with relative ease, which complicates the understanding of what is permissible to study and whether observation is truly" covert" if no barriers are erected to keep one from observing.

Of course, it probably does matter to many virtual groups whether it is a naive visitor who is stopping briefly at their fora, or a person whose goal is to cast a long-term, analytic eye on their activities and publish the result. The conventional view holds that any research of on-line participants should" strive to obtain some degree of informed consent whenever possible.... Most importantly, researchers should negotiate their entry into electronic communities, beginning with the `owner' of the discussion, if one exists".

Preserving the dignity and empowerment of the persons being studied, even if their" real" identities and locations are unknown, demands that the researcher take steps to explain all of the elements of the study that may bear on their decision to participate voluntarily. Taking a different view, Jones argues that the highly elusive, evanescent presence and essentially unknowable identity of most of the subjects in cylberspace obviates the need in most cases for pursuing consent formally:" If the research does not involve identifiable subjects, there is no risk to subjects, and therefore the protection of these rights and interests no longer applies". Jones goes on to argue that the strict application of conventional human subject protections would be especially detrimental to the study of cyberspace, which exists as an arena in which individuals can enjoy the freedom of withholding, revealing, and even fabricating information about themselves.

Somewhere between these positions is King, who states that" the perceived level of privacy with which most members of cyberspace forums post notes is the level that researchers are obligated to protect". At the stage of publication, she advocates the removal from messages of all headers, signatures, references to the name and type of the group (e-mail, Usenet news group, etc.), and references to any person's name or pseudo-name. It may be that the evolving use of networked systems will alter the customs and arguments for what constitutes" privacy" and" autonomy," in turn informing the ethical practice of ethnography. Finally, the implications of computer networks for the construction of the research text are of great importance. One can adapt the same hypermedia programming tools used in other scholarly efforts to the production of ethnographies that would in turn be fully compatible with the World Wide Web's system architecture. An example of such an effort is the Survivors of the Shoah Visual History Foundation, which has set out to videotape oral histories of all living Holocaust survivors and digitize them in hypermedia format along with maps, documents, photos, and written texts of the interviews.

The files, perhaps numbering 150,000 by the end of the decade, will be fully cross-referenced and accessible for on-line searches by key words. Similarly, ethnographies of CMC culture can be envisioned which would provide the discursive threads that underpin an analysis, along with field notes, full-text interviews, generations of Web page design, graphic material, and URL's to the ethnographic sites themselves and related research projects. Presumably the author would also be" available" in a rather immediate sense to readers via the research text's Web site or e-mail. What distinguishes an archive a reader can navigate at will from a research text is that the latter usually embodies arguments, claims, and evidence in a style conventionalized within the discipline. While readers have always had non-linear access to a text, it is the linear narrative designed by the author that academic communities recognize as the only one subject to critique.

The capabilities of hypermedia threaten this formulation of the research product and the concept of authorial control that stands behind it.

If readings of an ethnography are neither the ones an author intended nor the ones deemed important or legitimate by a discipline, then its use-value becomes as widely distributed among communities of practical interest as the Internet itself. The move to modular, multi-threaded (but not necessarily plotless) research texts not only reduces the researcher's story to the stature of one among a potentially limitless number, it also accelerates the epistemological decentering of enquiry that began with the challenge to objectivist ethnography nearly twenty years ago.

3

New Media: Technology for Social Change

INTRODUCTION

Social Movement Media has a rich and storied history that has changed at a rapid rate since New Media became widely used. The Zapatista Army of National Liberation of Chiapas, Mexico were the first major movement to make widely recognized and effective use of New Media for communiques and organizing in 1994. Since then, New Media has been used extensively by social movements to educate, organize, share cultural products of movements, communicate, coalition build, and more. The WTO Ministerial Conference of 1999 protest activity was another landmark in the use of New Media as a tool for social change. The WTO protests used media to organize the original action, communicate with and educate participants, and was used an alternative media source.

The Indymedia movement also developed out of this action, and has been a great tool in the democratization of information, which is another widely discussed aspect of new media movement. Some scholars even view this democratization as an indication of the creation of a "radical, socio-technical paradigm to challenge the dominant, neo-liberal and technologically determinist model of information and communication technologies." A less radical view along these same lines is that people are taking advantage of the internet to produce a grassroots globalization, one that is anti-neo-liberal and centered on people rather than the flow of capital. Of course, some are also stepchild of the role of New Media in Social Movements. Many scholars point out unequal access to new media as a hindrance to broad-based movements, sometimes even oppressing some within a movement. Others are stepchild about how democratic or useful it really is for social movements, even for those with access. There are also many New Media components that activists cite as tools for change that have not been widely discussed as such by academics.

New Media has also found a use with less radical social movements such as the Free Hugs Campaign. Using web sites, blogs, and online videos to demonstrate the effectiveness of the movement itself. Along with this example the use of high volume blogs has allowed numerous views and practices to be more widespread and gain more public attention. Another example is the on-going Free Tibet Campaign, which has been seen on numerous web sites as well as having a slight tie-in with the band Gorillaz in their Gorillaz Bitez clip featuring the lead singer 2D sitting with protesters at a Free Tibet protest. Another social change seen coming from New Media is trends in fashion and the emergence of subcultures such as Text Speak, Cyberpunk, and various others.

NATIONAL SECURITY

New Media has also recently become of interest to the global espionage community as it is easily accessible electronically in database format and can therefore be quickly retrieved and reverse engineered by national governments. Particularly of interest to the espionage community are facebook and twitter, two sites where individuals freely divulge personal information that can then be sifted through and archived for the automatic creation of dossiers on both people of interest and the average citizen.

INTERACTIVITY AND NEW MEDIA

Interactivity has become a key term for number of new media use options evolving from the rapid dissemination of Internet access point, the digitalization of the media, and media convergence. In 1984, Rice defined the new media as communication technologies that enable or facilitate user-to-user interactivity and interactivity between user and information. Such as Internet replaces the "one-to-many" model of traditional mass communication with the possibility of a "many-to-many" web of communication. Any individual with the appropriate technology can now produce his or her online media and include images, text, and sound about whatever he or she chooses. So the new media with technology convergence shifts the model of mass communication, and radically shapes the ways we interact and communicate with one another. Vin Crosbie described three communications media in "What is new media?". He saw Interpersonal media as "one to one", Mass media as "one to many" and, finally New Media as Individuation Media or "many to many".

When we think of interactivity and its meaning, we assume that it is only prominent in the conversational dynamics of individuals who are face-to-face. This restriction of opinion does not allow us to see its existence in mediated communication forums. Interactivity is present in some programming work, such as video games. It's also viable in the operation of traditional media. In the mid 1990s, filmmakers started using inexpensive digital cameras to create films. It was also the time when moving image technology had developed, which was able to be viewed on computer desktops in full motion. This development of new media technology was a new method for artists to share their work and interact with the big world. Other settings of interactivity include radio and television talk shows, letters to the editor, listener participation in such programmes, and computer and technological programming. Interactive new media has become a true benefit to every one because people can express their artwork in more than one way with the technology that we have today and there is no longer a limit to what we can do with our creativity.

Interactivity can be considered as a central concept in understanding new media, but different media forms possess different degree of interactivity, even some forms of digitized and converged media are not in fact interactive at all. Tony Feldman considers digital satellite television as an example of a new media technology that uses digital compression to dramatically increase the number of television channels that can be delivered, and which changes the nature of what can be offered through the service, but does not transform the experience of television from the user's point of view, as it lacks a more fully interactive dimension. It remains the case that interactivity is not an inherent characteristic of all new media technologies, unlike digitization and convergence.

Terry Flew (2005) argues that "the global interactive games industry is large and growing, and is at the forefront of many of the most significant innovations in new media" (Flew 2005). Interactivity is prominent in these online computer games such as *World of Warcraft*, *The Sims Online* and *Second Life*. These games, developments of "new media", allow for users to establish relationships and experience a sense of belonging, despite temporal and spatial boundaries. These games can be used as an escape or to act out a desired life. Will Wright, creator of *The Sims*, "is fascinated by the way gamers have become so attached to his invention-with some even living their lives through it". New media have created virtual realities that are becoming mere extensions of the world we live in. With the creation of Second Life people have even more control over this virtual world where anything that a participant can think of in their mind can become a reality in Second Life.

New Media changes continuously due to the fact that it is constantly modified and redefined by the interaction between the creative use of the masses, emerging technology, cultural changes, etc.

THE INDUSTRY

The new media industry shares an open association with many market segments in areas such as software/video game design, television, radio, and particularly movies, advertising and marketing, which seeks to gain from the advantages of two-way dialogue with consumers primarily through the internet. The advertising industry has capitalized on the proliferation of new media with large agencies running multi-million dollar interactive advertising subsidiaries. Interactive web sites and kiosks have become popular. In a number of cases advertising agencies have also set up new divisions to study new media. Public relations firms are taking advantage of the opportunities in new media through interactive PR practices.

CREATIVE SERVICES

Creative services are a subsector of the creative industries, a part of the economy that creates wealth by offering creativity for hire to other businesses. Examples include:

- Design and production agencies.
  - Studios
  - Software development firms
  - Temp agency.
- Marketing firms.
  - Public relations agencies
  - Advertising agencies
  - Promotional agencies
  - Branding agencies.
- Entertainment Industries.
  - Talent agency
  - Guilds.

Like lawyers and accountants in the professional services sector, creative services firms sell a specialised technical service to satisfy the needs of companies that do not have this expertise themselves.

ENTERTAINMENT AND FINE ARTS

In addition, multimedia is heavily used in the entertainment industry, especially to develop special effects in movies and animations. Multimedia games are a popular pastime and are software programmes available either as CD-ROMs or online. Some video games also use multimedia features. Multimedia applications that allow users to actively participate instead of just sitting by as passive recipients of information are called *Interactive Multimedia*.

In the Arts there are multimedia artists, whose minds are able to blend techniques using different media that in some way incorporates interaction with the viewer. One of the most relevant could be Peter Greenaway who is melding Cinema with Opera and all sorts of digital media. Another approach entails the creation of multimedia that can be displayed in a traditional fine arts arena, such as an art gallery. Although multimedia display material may be volatile, the survivability of the content is as strong as any traditional media. Digital recording material may be just as durable and infinitely reproducible with perfect copies every time.

SPECIAL EFFECT

The illusions used in the film, television, theater, or entertainment industries to simulate the imagined events in a story are traditionally called special effects.

Special effects are traditionally divided into the categories of optical effects and mechanical effects. With the emergence of digital film-making tools a greater distinction between special effects and visual effects has been recognized, with "visual effects" referring to digital post-production and "special effects" referring to on-set mechanical effects and in-camera optical effects.

Optical effects (also called photographic effects), are techniques in which images or film frames are created photographically, either "in-camera" using multiple exposure, mattes, or the Schüfftan process, or in post-production processes using an optical printer. An optical effect might be used to place actors or sets against a different background.

Mechanical effects (also called practical or physical effects), are usually accomplished during the live-action shooting. This includes the use of mechanized props, scenery, scale models, pyrotechnics and Atmospheric Effects: creating physical wind, rain, fog, snow, clouds etc. Making a car appear to drive by itself, or blowing up a building are examples of mechanical effects. Mechanical effects are often incorporated into set design and makeup. For example, a set may be built with break-away doors or walls, or prosthetic makeup can be used to make an actor look like a monster.

Since the 1990s, computer generated imagery (CGI) has come to the forefront of special effects technologies. CGI gives film-makers greater control, and allows many effects to be accomplished more safely and convincingly – and even, as technology marches on, at lower costs. As a result, many optical and mechanical effects techniques have been superseded by CGI.

MASS MEDIA AND SOCIETY

COMMUNICATION IN INDIA: HISTORICAL PERSPECTIVES

Communication, as it is known today, has originated and evolved in the West, particularly in the United States of America. With the development of technologies, the communication methods also developed. The methods became complex and sophisticated.

But the concept of 'communication' has been with us since the creation of man. The methods and the process differs from region to region, country to country. Even now, with the idea of 'global village' becoming a reality, we differ as far as methods and process of communication are concerned. The Upanishads, the Gita, the Sangeet Ratnakara, the Natya Shastra, Manu Smriti, Sanskrit literature, works on Vaishnavism, Bhakti, the medieval saints and Sufism did communicate and are still communicating valuable thoughts to us on the subject.

We need to study these materials to find out the methods and process of communication prevailing at that time. You must be aware of various seminars and workshops being conducted to formulate a policy regarding satellite communication. Some experts say as a result of exposures to foreign television programmes, our values and culture may be damaged beyond repair. The negative influence of such telecasts may prove detrimental to the development of the nation.

Religion and Philosophy: Some scholars say that the Indian tradition has hardly any thoughts on communications. Those who grant such thoughts have a negative view on the issue. 'Communication' has been a word coined in the recent past to explain a particular area of study. Therefore, in our ancient literature this view was not dealt with separately. But, a lot has been said about the process and methods of communication in our literature. Communication does not exist in a vacuum. Communication is an integral part of our social-political and cultural life. It was as important then as it is now. It worked according to the social and cultural norms. At present, we must ensure that it works as per the socio-cultural ethos of our nation. Otherwise the fabric of the nation may be disturbed.

Mysticism and Intrapersonal Communication: Our way of life is influenced by religion and various philosophical teachings. As a God fearing people we have found various ways to worship the almighty Profound thoughts and philosophies took birth from those way of worship. Mysticism is one such way. Mysticism has given birth to a new method of communicating one's deep realization and understanding of God and the universe. Mysticism is centred on oneself.

It is a process by which one plunges into the deepest core of one's heart or self. A profound communication takes place in one's innermost. This communication process can be termed as interpersonal communication with oneself. Mira Bai and Kabir communicated so much in a very easy way because their realization was clear. We have not explored this mystical process. This mystical approach possibly can help us to communicate with our people more effectively.

Interpersonal Communication enriched interpersonal communication. This area of Communication has not been sufficiently explored. Some enthusiastic communication professionals take a parochial view and try desperately to invent a communication theory or a model which existed in the ancient times. Having discussed the importance of interpersonal and interpersonal communication, we shall discuss the importance of Indian philosophy in Communication. We come to know about the process of communication in ancient India through treatises on the arts, religion and mysticism. We can also go through Sanskrit, Persian, Urdu and Hindi sources. Accounts of Vedanta, Bhakti, Vaishnavism and Sufism speak volumes of communication. To be effective in our communication we should be able to establish their relevance to the people of modern India. This Indian orientation will help us to recast and reform the whole outlook towards communication concepts norms, and beliefs. We ought to turn to the Indian philosophical tradition which has tremendous intellectual and spiritual resources and can easily supply us with a basic framework for a creative and relevant communication process, The impact of this heritage has been felt through the ages and its richness and universality has been acknowledged by the world. Since the present communication concept and discipline has developed in the west, we do gel carried away by its Western perception and hence become ineffective in the Indian situation. It is therefore, necessary that we ground ourselves firmly in our culture, beliefs and ethos. We need not copy the western models blindly. And thus consequently suffer the loss of inspiration.

INDIAN HERITAGE AND COMMUNICATION VALUES

In India, communication is inextricably linked with philosophy and religion. Sarvapalli Radhakrishnan says, "the pursuit of philosophy is deemed a religious vocation. Therefore, in order to come to terms with the cultural ideal that animates Indian society, we need to examine, brief though they may be, the outlines of Indian philosophy". The Upanishads call attention to the value of the knowledge (Vidya) of ultimate (Satya) as a means of liberation (Moksha). The Upanishads, greatly emphasize the need to look inward for a clearer understanding of reality. The basic tenet of the Upanishads is the need to acquire self-knowledge and thereby liberate oneself from worldly bandages.

Jain and Buddhist Values: With the passage of time, a number of non-Vedic philosophical traditions sprang up. The Charvakas placed heavy emphasis on the material world and discarded all notions of transcendentality. Jainism was another tradition of philosophy which was non-Vedic in character. It maintained that both the animate and the inanimate world were eternal and independent. Therefore one has to be tolerant to all that exists on earth. Buddhism, another non-Vedic philosophy constituted a powerful reaction against the ritualism that characterized the Vedas and the transcendentalism that was associated with the Upanishads. The individual, according to Buddhism, should diligently work out his salvation, from pain and suffering.

Indian Schools of Philosophy: Later Indian Philosophy began to move further and further away from the original ways of thinking and, indeed, split into different and competing systems. Although these systems do not by any means constitute mutually exclusive categories they display sufficient variation for each to warrant on autonomous conceptual status. Of these, there are six that deserve close attention. They are the Nyaya; Vaisesika; Sankhya; Yoga; Mimamsa; Vedanta and Advaita. These schools, too, contributed to the formation of the Indian tradition. The Indian schools of philosophy originated from the Vedas; two schools are Vedic the Mimamsa and the Vedanta; the four—

Samkhya, Yoga, Vaisesika, and Nyaya-have their base in the Vedas. Therefore, these six schools are classed as Vedic or Astika. The two schools of Buddhism and Jainism are called Nastika as they do not accept Vedic authority. These eight schools are products of the great thought that characterized the post-Vedic age.

Each school of philosophy is called a Darsana, meaning a view or a vision of the truth, The aims and aspirations of life are not only the pursuit of material gains (Artha) and pleasure (Kam) but also virtue and morality which chasten life (Dharma) and spiritual enlightenment and freedom (Moksa). Each school is associated with a sage (Rishi) as its first promulgator—Samkhya with Kapila, Yoga with Paanjali, Vaisesika with Kanada, Nayaya with Gautama Mimamsa with Jaimini and Vedanta with Badarayana-Vyasa. Because of their mutual relationship, these six schools fall into three groups of allied systems, Samanatantras. Samkhya and Yoga go together; the philosophical framework of Sarnkhya is accepted by Yoga with the addition of God as the omniscient first Teacher. The specialty of Yoga is the practical aspect of the methods of mental control by which the philosophical ideal of the Samkhya, namely, the isolation (Kaivalya) of the Spirit from Matter is achieved. But Yoga as a Sadham or preparatory discipline and means came to be accepted by all schools. Today, it has, with the help of science, andown in' strength and gained a world-wide vogue. The vaisesika doctrines form the basis of Nyaya, both being schools of realism and pluralism.

The Mimamsa and Vedanta go together because of their common Vedic basis but otherwise they differ fundamentally. The former is concerned with Karma and Dharma the performance of ordained duty, but the latter to the opposite of Karma, namely, renunciation from activity; according to Vedanta, knowledge (Jnana) is the means of salvation (Moksa). Mimamsa is thus related to the Karma-Kanda (Samhita and the Brahmna portion of the Vedas), and Vedanta to the Upanishads. The Mimamsa also made a valuable contribution to the science of interpreting texts; it came to be known therefore as Vakya sastra (the rules of constructing a sentence). But what do all these mean to us today. Our tradition, philosophy culture, and religion are not dead. We still practice our ancient religion. We do study our ancient philosophy and theology. Our beliefs are largely based on Karma and Dharma. Therefore, these things have meaning in our day to day life. The words coined in various philosophical and theological books are still being used by us to convey the same meaning. Thus, to communicate meaningfully, we must be well grounded in this rich heritage. But a little caution-we must not be so heavily grounded in these, so as not to be able to fly and explore the richness of clear blue sky.

IMPLICATIONS FOR AN INDIAN PERSPECTIVE OF COMMUNICATION

What implications does this survey of Indian philosophy have for communication theory? On tile basis of these philosophical tenets, we can construct a workable model of communication for the Indian situation. This may differ substantially from models found the Western countries. Each culture may have models of communication of its own. What is essential is that any communication model must be based on a cultural context. Otherwise the meaning conveyed may differ from the intended meaning to be conveyed in a communication.

Many times, we may fail to communicate if we do not take this cultural context into consideration. In India generally the primary focus of interest in communication is how does the receiver make sense of the stimuli that he receives so as to deepen his self-awareness. In the Western models, the basic questions that present themselves is how does the communicator affect/influence/manipulate the receiver and how does the communicator and receiver share information and enter into a two-way relationship. According to traditional Indian views, meaning should necessarily lead to self-awareness.

Hence the Indian definition of communication would be that it is an inward search for meaning—a process of intra-personal communication. In the West, communication is seen as the transference of meaning with the intention of influencing the receiver. But the ill India meaning brings enlightenment. Meaning, according to traditional Indian thought, was and as a process which leads to self-awareness, then to freedom, and finally to the truth. Mie, by freedom we mean the liberation of persons from ignorance from the illusion of the world, and the web of the artificial categories constructed all around us. Another significant point of divergence between the Indian and the Western ways is that the Indian way focuses attention on the intra-personal dimension as opposed to the interpersonal dimension.

In western ways, interpersonal communication leads to interpersonal communication, but in the Indian way interpersonal communications secondary to interpersonal communication. The Western way is an expression-oriented but the Indian way is interpretation oriented. The Indian way seems to suggest that what is important in human communication is to find out how a receiver makes sense of the verbal stimuli that arc received by him and engages in a search for meaning. This search is an inward one. The traditional authorities maintain that the reality is indeed within man. To know it is to be.

In other words, the distinction between the knower and the known narrows down considerably. The realization of truth is facilitated neither by language nor by logic and rationality. To know is to be; to know is to become aware of the artificial categorization imposed on the world by language and logic. It is only through an intuitive process that man will be able to lift himself out of the illusory world, which, according to the Indian viewpoint, is indeed the aim of communication. People may differ with this view. But we all must agree that in India realization dawns when we internalize the communication. It needs to be pointed out that one may not understand the current development in communication solely in the light of this model. We are living in a world where the borderlines between countries are disappearing very fast. We do know and feel at one with the happenings in other parts of the globe. We are passing through a phase of civilization which could be termed, at best, the transition, and 'chaotic' at worst.

SADHARANIKARAN: BASIS OF COMMUNICATION

Sadharanikaran, drawing from classical Hindu poetics, has been introduced into the modern communication discipline, essentially due to its qualification in this regard. The term has been an extensively used concept in Sanskrit and allied literary circles for explaining poetics, aesthetics and drama. It is rooted in Natyashastra of Bharata. There have been attempts to extend its history up to the Vedic period, but scholars widely believe that Bhattanayaka introduced the concept of sadharanikaran. He is credited for use of the term in his commentary on Natyashastra to explain the concept of rasa. The term sadharanikaran is derived from the Sanskrit word sadharan; and has been translated into English as "generalized presentation", "simplification", and "universalization".

This concept is bound with another concept, sahridayata, that is, a state of common orientation, commonality or oneness. Sadharanikaran is the attainment of sahridayata by communicating parties. When senders and receivers accomplish the process of sadharanikaran, they attain saharidayata and become sahridayas. In other words, communicating parties, for *e.g.*, actor and audience, become sahridayas when they are engaged in a communicative relation leading to the attainment saharidayata; and it is in this stage sadharanikaran is accomplished. Thus the essence of sadharanikaran is to achieve commonness or oneness among the people. In this light, the Latin word 'communism and its modern English version 'communication' come close to sadharanikaran. However, as Yadava puts it, "the characteristics and the philosophy behind Sadharanikaran are somewhat different from communication concept as developed in the Western societies".

MASS MEDIA AND MODERN SOCIETY

In political behaviour, opinion leading tends to correlate positively with status, whereas this is not the case in consumer behaviour. So for political behaviour, the general conclusion that the media merely fixes (confirms) people's opinion is not supported. Hovland, using experimental psychology, found significant effects of information on longer-term behaviour and attitudes, particularly in areas where most people have little direct experience (*e.g.* politics) and have a high degree of trust in the source (*e.g.* broadcasting). Since class has become a less reliable indicator of party (since the surveys of the

40s and 50s) the floating voter today is no longer the apathetic voter, but likely to be more well-informed than the consistent voter-and this mainly through the media.

There is also some very persuasive and empirical evidence suggesting that it is 'personal contact, not media persuasiveness' which counts. For example, Trenaman and McQuail (1961) found that 'don't knows' were less well informed than consistent voters, appearing uninterested, showing a general lack of information, and not just ignorance of particular policies or policies of one particular party. During the 1940 presidential election, a similar view was expressed by Katz and Lazarsfeld's theory of the two-step flow of communication, based on a study of electoral practices of the citizens of Erie County, Ohio. This examined the political propaganda prevalent in the media at the time during the campaign period to see whether it plays an integral role in influencing people's voting.

The results contradict this: Lazarsfeld et. al. (1944) find evidence for the Weberian theory of party, and identify certain factors, such as socio-economic circumstances, religious affiliation and area of residence, which together determine political orientation. The study claims that political propaganda serves to re-affirm the individual's pre-disposed orientation rather than to influence or change one's voting behaviour.

Thompson does not see 'mediated quasi-interaction' (the monological, mainly one-way communication of the mass media) as dominant, but rather as intermingling with traditional face-to-face interactions and mediated interactions (such as telephone conversations). Contrary to Habermas' pessimistic view, this allows both more information and discussion to come into the public domain (of mediated quasi-interaction) and more to be discussed within the private domain (since the media provides information individuals would not otherwise have access to).

FREE ENTERPRISE SOCIETY

Although a sizeable portion of mass media offerings-particularly news, commentaries, documentaries, and other informational programmes-deal with highly controversial subjects, the major portion of mass media offerings are designed to serve an entertainment function. These programmes tend to avoid controversial issues and reflect beliefs and values sanctified by mass audience. This course is followed by Television networks, whose investment and production costs are high. Jerry Mander's work has highlighted this particular outlook. According to him, the atomised individuals of mass society lose their souls to the phantom delights of the film, the soap opera, and the variety show.

They fall into a stupor; an apathetic hypnosis Lazarsfeld was to call the 'narcotizing dysfunction' of exposure to mass media. Individuals become 'irrational victims of false wants'-the wants which corporations have thrust upon them, and continue to thrust upon them, through both the advertising in the media (with its continual exhortation to consume) and through the individualist consumption culture it promulgates. Thus, according to the Frankfurt School, leisure has been industrialised. The production of culture had become standardised and dominated by the profit motive as in other industries. In a mass society leisure is constantly used to induce the appropriate values and motives in the public. The modern media train the young for consumption. 'Leisure had ceased to be the opposite of work, and had become a preparation for it.'

MASS MEDIA, MASS CULTURE AND ELITE

The relation of the mass media to contemporary popular culture is commonly conceived in terms of dissemination from the elite to the mass. There are periods when this process is reversed. During the 18th century it was the utmost chic for the aristocrats of the French Court to assume the guise of shepherds and peasants in their restive outings.

The long-term consequences of this are significant in conjunction with the continuing concentration of ownership and control of the media, leading to accusations of a 'media elite' having a form of 'cultural dictatorship'. Thus the continuing debate about the influence of 'media barons' such as Conrad Black and Rupert Murdoch. For example, the UK Observer reported the Murdoch-owned HarperCollins' refusal to publish Chris Patten's East and West, because of the former Hong Kong Governor's description of the Chinese leadership as "faceless Stalinists" possibly being damaging to Murdoch's Chinese broadcasting interests. In this case, the author was able to have the book accepted by another publisher, but this kind of censorship may point the way to the future. A related, but more insidious, form is that of self-censorship by members of the media in the interests of the owner, in the interests of their careers.

MASS MEDIA AND WOMEN'S STATUS IN RURAL INDIA

Cable and satellite television have grown rapidly throughout the developing world. The availability of cable and satellite television exposes viewers to new information about the outside world, which may affect individual attitudes and behaviours. This paper explores the effect of the introduction of cable television on gender attitudes in rural India. Using a three-year individual-level panel dataset, we find that the introduction of cable television is associated with improvements in women's status. We find significant increases in reported autonomy, decreases in the reported acceptability of beating and decreases in reported son preference.

We also find increases in female school enrolment and decreases in fertility (primarily via increased birth spacing). The effects are large, equivalent in some cases to about five years of education in the cross section, and move gender attitudes of individuals in rural areas much closer to those in urban areas. We argue that the results are not driven by pre-existing differential trends. These results have important policy implications, as India and other countries attempt to decrease bias against women. The growth of television in the developing world over the last two decades has been extraordinary. Estimates suggest that the number of television sets in Asia has increased more than six-fold, from 100 million to 650 million, since the 1980s (World Press Review, 2003). In China, television exposure grew from 18 million people in 1977 to 1 billion by 1995 (World Press Review, 2003). In more recent years, satellite and cable television availability has increased dramatically. Again, in China, the number of people with satellite access increased from just 270,000 in 1991 to 14 million by 2005.

Further, these numbers are likely to understate the change in the number of people for whom television is available, since a single television is often watched by many.

Beyond providing entertainment, television vastly increases both the availability of information about the outside world and exposure to other ways of life, particularly in otherwise isolated areas. Previous work has demonstrated that the information and exposure provided by television can change attitudes and behaviour. Gentzkow and Shapiro (2005) find effects of television viewership on attitudes in the Muslim world towards the West, and Della Vigna and Kaplan (2006) show large effects of the Fox News channel on voting patterns in the United States. In the developing world, Olken (2006) shows that television decreases participation in social organizations.

India has not been left out of the satellite revolution: a recent survey finds that 112 million households in India own a television, with 61 per cent of those homes having cable or satellite service (National Readership Studies Council 2006). This figure represents a doubling in cable access in just five years from a previous survey.

The study also find that in some states, the change has been even more dramatic; in the span of just 10-15 years since it first became available, cable or satellite penetration has reached an astonishing 60 per cent in states such as Tamil Nadu, even though the average income is below the World Bank poverty line of two dollars per person per day.

Most popular satellite television shows in India portray life in urban settings; further, a wide range of international programmes are now available. The increase in television exposure, therefore, is likely to dramatically change the available information about the outside world, especially in isolated rural areas. Indeed, anthropological case studies in India suggest that exposure to television in rural areas has an effect on behaviours as disparate as latrine building and fan usage.

In this chapter we explore the effect of the introduction of cable television in rural areas of India on a particular set of values and behaviours, namely attitudes towards and discrimination against women. Although issues of gender equity are important throughout much of the developing world, they are particularly salient in India. Sen (1992) argued that there were 41 million "missing women" in India women and girls who died prematurely due to mistreatment resulting in a dramatically male-biased population. The population bias towards men has only gotten worse in the last two decades, as sex-selective abortion has become more widely used to avoid female births. More broadly, girls in India are discriminated against in nutrition, medical care, vaccination and education. Even within India, gender inequality is significantly worse in rural than urban areas.

Given this, if satellite television increases the exposure of rural areas to urban attitudes and values, it is plausible that it could change some of these attitudes and behaviours. It is this possibility that we explore in this chapter. The analysis relies on a three-year panel dataset covering women in many Indian states between 2001 and 2003.

These years represent a time of rapid growth in rural cable access. During the panel, cable television was newly introduced in 21 of the 180 sample villages. Our empirical strategy relies on comparing changes in attitudes and behaviours between survey rounds across villages based on whether (and when) they added cable television.

Using these data, we find that cable television has large effects on attitudes and, to the extent we have information, behaviours. After cable is introduced to a village, women are less likely to report that domestic violence towards women is acceptable. They also report increased autonomy (for example, the ability to go out without permission and to participate in household decision-making). Women are less likely to report son preference (the desire to give birth to a boy rather than a girl). Turning to behaviours, we find increases in school enrolment for girls (but not boys), and decreases in fertility (which is often linked to female autonomy). These results are apparent when using regressions with individual fixed effects and when using a matching estimator.

In terms of magnitude, the introduction of cable television dramatically decreases the differences in attitudes and behaviours between urban and rural areas between 45 and 70 per cent of the difference disappears within two years of cable introduction in this sample.

The effect is also large relative to, for example, the effect of education on these attitudes and behaviours: introducing cable television is equivalent to roughly five years of female education in the cross section. These effects happen very quickly; the average village has cable for only 6-7 months before being surveyed again, which implies a rapid change in attitudes. However, this is consistent with existing work on the effects of media exposure, which typically find rapid changes (within a few months, in many cases) in behaviours like contraceptive use, pregnancy, latrine building and perception of own-village status. A central concern with the results is the possibility that trends in other variables (for example, income or "modernity") are driving both cable access and attitudes. We argue that this does not seem to the case. Changes in attitudes between the first two survey waves are not predictive of cable introduction between the second and third wave.

Further, among villages that add cable during the survey period, initial attitudes are not predictive of which year (2002 or 2003) they get access. It is difficult to identify the mechanism behind the effects in this paper precisely. However, we do find some suggestive evidence that the mechanism alluded to at the start of the paper {increased exposure to circumstances outside of the village {is operating. In particular, we find that the effects of cable are largest in areas with initially worse attitudes towards women, *i.e.*, those for whom cable is providing information most different from their current way of life. Although certainly not conclusive, this evidence is consistent with a model in which television changes the weight individuals put on the behaviours of their immediate peer group in forming their attitudes.

The results are potentially quite important for policy. Gender discrimination in India is a significant issue, and has been a consistent source of concern for policy makers and academics. A large literature in economics, sociology and anthropology has explored the underlying causes of discrimination against women in India, highlighting the dowry system, low levels of female education, and other socioeconomic factors as central factors.

Changing these underlying factors is difficult; introducing television, or reducing any barriers to its spread, may be less so. From the policy perspective, however, there are potential concerns about whether the changes in reported autonomy, beating attitudes, and son preference actually represent changes in behaviours, or just in reporting. For example, we may be concerned that exposure to television only changes what the respondent thinks the interviewer wants to hear about the acceptability of beating, but does not actually change how much beating is occurring. This concern is likely to be less relevant in the case of fertility or education; the former is directly verifiable based on the presence of a baby in the household, and the latter is listed as part of a household roster.

The fact that we find effects on these variables provides support for the argument that our results represent real changes in outcomes. Without directly observing people in their homes, however, it is difficult to conclusively separate changes in reporting from changes in behaviour. However, even if cable only changes what is reported, it still may represent progress: changing the perceived "correct" attitude seems like a necessary, if not sufficient, step towards changing outcomes.

HISTORY OF TELEVISION IN INDIA

State-run black and white television was introduced into India in 1959, but the take off was extremely slow for the first several decades by 1977, only around 600,000 sets had been sold. In 1982, however, the state-run broadcaster (Doordarshan) introduced colour television, which dramatically increased interest in, and viewership of, television. Even with colour, however, most programming remained either government-sponsored news or information about economic development. There were a few entertainment serials, which were watched with intensity. In the early 1990s CNN and STAR TV first introduced the possibility of access to non-government programming via satellite.

There was a large demand for this cable (satellite) television, which was, and continues to be, filled primarily by small entrepreneurs who buy a dish and a subscription and charge nearby homes to connect to it. This is especially true in rural villages, such as those in our sample. As we show in the data later, this means that cable access is more common in villages that are wealthier and have a higher population density, where more people can afford to pay for service and where it would therefore be more profitable to start a cable business.

However, dramatic declines in the prices of both the equipment and satellite service subscriptions (due in part to reduced tariffs and increased competition), coupled with income growth, have allowed cable to spread over time to more and more villages. In the 5 years from 2001 to 2006, about 30 million households, representing approximately 150 million individuals, added cable service (National Readership Studies Council 2006). And since television is often watched with family and friends by those without a television or cable, the growth in actual access or exposure to cable may have been even more dramatic.

The programme offerings on cable television are quite different than government programming. The most popular shows tend to be game shows and soap operas. As an example, among the most popular shows in both 2000 and 2007 (based on Indian Nielsen ratings) is "Kyunki Saas Bhi Kabhi Bahu Thi," (Because a Mother-in-Law was Once a Daughter-in-Law, Also) a show based around the life of a wealthy industrial family in the large city of Mumbai. As can be seen from the title, the main themes and plots of the show often revolve around issues of family and gender. Among satellite channels, STAR TV and Zee TV tend to dominate, although Sony, STAR PLUS and Sun TV are also represented among the top 20 shows. Viewership of the government channel, although relatively high among those who do not have cable, is extremely low among those who do (and limited largely to sporting events).

The introduction of television in general appears to have had large effects in Indian society.

In contrast to the West, television seems to be, in some cases, the primary medium by which people in rural villages in India get information about the outside world. For example, Johnson (2001) reports on a man in his 50's in a village in India who says that television is "the biggest thing to happen in our village, ever". He goes on to say that he learned about the value of electric fans (to deal with the heat) from television, and subsequently purchased one.

The same author quotes another man arguing that television is where they learned that their leaders were corrupt, and about using the court system to address grievances. On issues of gender specifically, television seems to have had a significant impact, since this is an area where the lives of rural viewers differ greatly from those depicted on most popular shows.

By virtue of the fact that the most popular Indian serials take place in urban settings, women depicted on these shows are typically much more emancipated than rural women. For example, many women on popular serials work outside the home, run businesses and control money.

In addition, they are typically more educated and have fewer children than their rural counterparts. Further, in many cases there is access to Western television, with its accompanying depiction of life in which women are much more emancipated. Based on anthropological reports, this seems to have affected attitudes within India. Scrase (2002) reports that several of his respondents thought television might lead women to question their social position and might help the cause of female advancement.

Another woman reports that, because of television, men and women are able to open up a lot more." Johnson (2001) quotes a number of respondents describing changes in gender roles as a result of television.

One man notes, "Since TV has come to our village, women are doing less work than before. They only want to watch TV. So we [men] have to do more work. Many times I help my wife clean the house."

Although television overall seems to have had large effects, cable television in particular may be even more significant. This is both because it dramatically increases television viewership, and because the content is very different (again, since popular serials mostly feature urban life).

Scrase (2002) reports on respondents who note that prior to cable there was almost no entertainment, and very little current affairs, whereas the offerings on cable were broad. There is also a broader literature on the effects of television exposure on gender issues in other countries. Many studies find effects on a variety of outcomes: for example, eating disorders in Fiji, sex role stereotypes in Minnesota and perceptions of women's rights in Chicago.

Telenovelas in Brazil have provided a fruitful context for studying the effects of television. For example, based on ethnographic research, La Pastina (2004) argues that exposure to telenovelas provides women (in particular) with alternative models of what role they might play in society. Pace (1993) describes the effect of television introduction in Brazil on a small, isolated, Amazon community, arguing that the introduction of television changed the framework of social interactions, increased general world knowledge and changed people's perceptions about the status of their village in the wider world.

Kottak (1990) reports on similar data from isolated areas in Brazil, and argues that the introduction of television affects (among other things) views on gender, moving individuals in these areas towards having more liberal views on the role of women in both the workplace and in relationships. Interestingly, the studies in Brazil also suggest that the patterns of television viewing shortly after it is first introduced may be quite different than what is seen later on. The evidence suggests that in the first years after introduction, interactions with the television are more intense, with the television drawing more focus (both at an individual level, and community-wide). It is during this early period that Kottak (1990) and others argue that television is at its most influential.

Most of the villages in our analysis are at this early stage of television exposure, suggesting this may be an ideal period to look for effects. The evidence described above, of course, is drawn primarily from interviews and case studies, and obviously does not reflect a random sample of these populations. Nevertheless, the overall impression given by the anthropology and sociology literature is that the introduction of television had widespread effects on society, and that gender issues are a particular focal point. Our data and setting provide an opportunity to test this hypothesis more rigorously.

SOCIAL MOVEMENTS, THE INTERNET, AND THE PRESS

Establishing a presence over the Internet, it is believed, will be one of the key factors that contribute to a social movement or contentious group rising to prominence. The Internet has been used with equal vigour by the right and left, and Internet skill is now considered integral to political communication among progressive intellectuals, students, and activists.

Mainstream media, meanwhile, are seen as becoming less approachable because of emerging ideologies and exigencies. As an alternative, the Internet is celebrated for contributing to political normalization, democratic pluralism, the development of a democratic media politics by the establishment of alternative media, and "the cyber-diffusion of contention."

Does the power of the Internet as a political and communication tool, then, circumvent the relevance of the mainstream mass media?

Research and practice suggest not, pointing out that mainstream media, in fact, gain particular importance in the "network information politics" of transnational advocacy networks. Network activists cultivate credibility with the press and package their information in a timely and dramatic way to draw press attention. Even groups that circumvent a focus on garnering mainstream media attention do sometimes provide hypertext links and information as press releases on their Web sites.24 The Zapatista movement in Mexico used the Internet for everything from voting in plebiscites by participants from forty-seven countries, to drawing in the mainstream media to create awareness and outrage worldwide.

For a journalist seeking information on today's social protests, protest groups' Web sites present complex debates, research papers, rationales, and contact details, all of which may be expected to make the movement, its contexts, and its participants more accessible to journalists than ever before.

Studies on journalists' Internet use in the United States26 have chronicled the rapid increase in Internet use by journalists and the gradual shifts in attitude towards such use-journalists are using the Web for researching stories, finding new sources, receiving press releases and information, updating breaking news, interviewing sources, and engaging in dialogue with readers. Literature is now emerging on the nebulous relationship between bloggers and journalists and journalist-bloggers. A next step in research into Internet use might involve how such use plays out in the final product of the journalist-the media story-and the decisions that surround it. The two practices of sourcing/attribution and framing, in particular, are significant to this study for two reasons. First, as the literature review above shows, these two practices involve location of power in a given story. Sourcing/attribution determines who gets a "voice," and whose interpretation of events gets reported in mainstream media. Framing, especially thematic framing, gives "context." In one recent study, television journalists covering breast cancer appeared to have increased their use of thematic frames and their discussion of research developments across time, but did not change other practices, such as the dominant citation of medical doctors as sources.

Most important, reporters today, as compared to reporters thirty years ago, can access material online and possibly provide a thematic, contextualized story on their own terms. So, did access to the Internet in 1999 enable reporters to expand their sourcing and/or provide greater thematic framing in their coverage as compared to reporters in 1967?

As evident from the literature, research into the relationship between movements and the media, and the role of the Internet in this relationship, stands at a juncture that is both exciting and undecided. An earlier study on the WTO protests points to the need to develop a new theory of media, political elites and social movement relations. Drawing on the literature and theory presented above, and using the case of social protest coverage as a lens to study this relationship, the following research questions were developed:

- *RQ1:* Was there a significant difference in sourcing and attribution between press coverage of the Vietnam anti-war protests (March on the Pentagon) in Washington, D.C., in October 1967 and the anti-WTO protests in Seattle in November-December 1999?

- *RQ2:* Was there a significant difference in "framing" between press coverage of the anti-Vietnam war protests (March on the Pentagon) in Washington, D.C., in October 1967 and the anti-WTO protests in Seattle in NovemberDecember 1999?
- *RQ3:* Does the Internet appear to have made an impact on the sourcing and attribution in press coverage of the antiWTO protests?
- *RQ4:* Does the Internet appear to have made an impact on the "framing" in the press coverage of the anti-WTO protests?

METHOD

Content Analysis. This content analysis compares the coverage of two separate movements. The longitudinal design compares not one publication's coverage with another's, but the totality of coverage given to one movement by a set of publications with that given to another by the same (or similar) set of publications. For this, coverage of the anti-WTO (World Trade Organization) protests in Seattle is compared with pre-Internet protest coverage given to the Vietnam anti-war protests.

The Vietnam anti-war protests, in particular "The March on the Pentagon" on October 21 and 22, 1967, in Washington, D.C., provide a good comparison for study with the anti-WTO protests labeled "The Battle for Seattle," held between November 30 and December 3,1999, in Seattle.

In both cases, these protests (a) came relatively early in the movement through coalition-building and mobilization; (b) used similar protest repertoires such as celebrity speakers, banners, slogans, and costumes; (c) involved some violence; (d) attracted police force; and (e) were relatively sudden, which gave the media little time to plan their sourcing/attribution, or frames for coverage. Even though the two protests are separated in time and in journalistic advancement, this very separation, in fact, provides the opportunity to study whether the manner of journalistic coverage stayed static.

The Sample: Newspapers and Magazines. The publications were chosen to represent national as well as local coverage and newspaper as well as magazine coverage. This was essential to tap into source use by local as well as national journalists, and episodic as well as "thematic" frames, the latter being more likely to appear in magazine coverage.

Three weeks' coverage was picked from each newspaper. The universe of coverage was examined, *i.e.*, the entire newspaper was scanned for relevant coverage. The newspapers were from October 15 through November 4, 1967, for the Vietnam anti-war protests, and from November 23 through December 13, 1999, for the anti-WTO protests. This comprises coverage from the week before the protests, the week during the protests, and the week after the protest.

For The March on the Pentagon, the national newspaper studied was the New York Times, considered the newspaper of record even in the 1960s. The local newspaper was the Washington Post, which serves as the local newspaper for Washington, D.C.

For the Seattle Protests, the national newspaper was the New York Times, again, and the local newspaper was the Seattle Times. This, of course, raises the question of comparability between the Washington Post and the Seattle Times. However, during both protests, these publications were the local, big-city publications for the venues where the protests were situated. Moreover, the sourcing and framing practices of these two publications have been studied together and comparatively in the past, with researchers noting similarities between the two publications' coverage decisions.30

The sample for the newspapers was collected from the Lexis Nexis Academic database. The magazines sampled for both protests were three issues each of Time and Newsweek: the weeks before, during, and after the protests. The sample produced a total of 444 stories.

Of the 444 stories analysed, 232 were anti-Vietnam war protest coverage and 212 were anti-WTO protest coverage. A total of 330 of these were news stories and 114 were editorials. In the case of the anti-Vietnam war protest coverage, the local newspaper, the Washington Post, carried 106 stories, while the New York Times carried 109. Time provided three stories and Newsweek 14. In the WTO coverage, the Seattle Times carried a total of 152 stories while the New York Times, the national newspaper, had 47.

Time magazine had 5 stories during the three weeks' issues examined, while Newsweek had 8 stories during this same period. In the total coverage of both protests, a total of 3,752 sources were used, with 39 per cent as Official (Govt. and Trade) sources, 15 per cent as Authoritative (Govt. and Trade) sources, 25 per cent as Official (Protester) sources, 17 per cent as Authoritative (Protester) sources, and 4 per cent as Unknown Protester sources.

Analysis of Variance was used to see whether there were any significant differences between the anti-WTO coverage and Vietnam antiwar coverage on the "sourcing" and "framing" elements.

The five dependent variables (DVs) measuring sourcing patterns, Official (Govt. and Trade) sources, Authoritative (Govt. and Trade) sources, Official (Protester) sources, Authoritative (Protester) sources, and Unknown Protester, were studied with a univariate analysis. The two variables measuring framing patterns, "Frame of the Story," and "Valence of the story," were subjected to a chi-square test.

- RQ1 asked whether there was a significant difference in sourcing and attribution between press coverage of the Vietnam anti-war protests in Washington, D.C., in October 1967 and the anti-WTO protests in Seattle in November-December 1999. Anti-WTO protest coverage used significantly more official sources than the Vietnam anti-war protest coverage. The anti-WTO protest coverage also used significantly more authoritative sources than the Vietnam antiwar protest coverage.

No significant difference was found, however, in the use of official (protester) sources between the anti-WTO protest coverage and the Vietnam anti-war protest coverage. Similarly, no significant difference was found in the use of authoritative (protester) sources between the antiWTO protest coverage and the Vietnam anti-war protest coverage.

Finally, no significant difference was found in the use of "unknown protester" sources between the anti-WTO protest coverage and the Vietnam anti-war protest coverage.

- RQ2 asked whether a significant difference existed in "framing" between press coverage of the Vietnam anti-war protests and the antiglobalization protests in Seattle. The two variables that measured the framing patterns in the coverage, "Frame of the Story" and "Valence of the Story," showed no significant difference between the coverage given to the two protests. For "Frame of the Story," the anti-WTO protest coverage had 63 stories with a thematic frame, 103 with an episodic frame, and 46 stories in which the frame was mixed. The Vietnam anti-war coverage had 56 stories with a thematic frame, 138 stories with an episodic frame, and 38 stories with a mixed frame.

For the "Valence of the Story," the anti-WTO protest coverage had 42 stories with Valences supportive of protesters, 57 stories with Valences supportive of government/trade (the target of the protesters), and 103 stories in which the Valences were neutral. The Vietnam anti-war coverage had 65 stories in which the Valences were supportive of protesters, 58 in which the Valence were supportive of the target, and 109 in which the Valences were neutral.

- RQ3 and RQ4 enquired into the Internet's influence in the sourcing and framing of coverage of WTO protest. However, these data showed limited use of the Internet by journalists. The number of stories identifying an Internet role was very small and therefore not viable for statistical analysis. For a sample of the size picked for this study, the lack of an Internet focus or role is in itself quite revealing.

DISCUSSION

Clearly, the most significant finding of this research is that journalists today seem to be citing official and authoritative sources more than journalists did in the 1960s, at least as far as protest coverage is concerned. These findings acquire even more significance in helping understand present-day journalism's treatment of social movements and social protest, for two reasons. First, it can be argued that from what we know about the Vietnam war and its key players, sources like the U.S. president and the U.S. administration, in particular, were unquestionably more indispensable to war coverage than they would be to coverage of the anti-WTO protest, given the considerations of nationalism and national security.

Therefore, journalists could be expected to approach those sources substantially more often for coverage of a war than for coverage of free-versus-fair trade issues. The exact opposite seemed to be the case.

Second, it is important to note one fact about the particular Vietnam anti-war protest sampled in this study-The March on the Pentagon. It took place in October 1967, which is noted by political scientists and media scholars as being before public opinion turned against the war. This should be considered in the context of analyses of the mass media's role in the Vietnam war era.

While it was once popularly believed that the mass media were pivotal in turning public opinion against the war, mass media scholars later argued that the media at first ignored opposition to the war and, after the My Lai massacre and the Tet offensive in 1968 and 1969, respectively, merely followed public opinion when it became too large to ignore.

So, during the coverage of The March on the Pentagon in 1967, the credibility of official sources was not already an issue for journalists, at least not as much as after 1968. One could, therefore, expect greater reliance at the time on official sources.

Vietnam era journalists like Walter Cronkite and David Brinkley have, in hindsight, explained this reliance as resulting from the lack of official dissent. Brinkley, who is noted as critiquing America's role in the Vietnam war as early as in 1963, has said, "I don't think that many people did disagree (with America's role in the war). And those that did, didn't want to go public."

In the case of the anti-WTO protests in 1999, however, national security was not an issue; journalists did not need to index announcements or decisions from government administration.

The increase in reliance on official sources in the WTO protests over the Vietnam antiwar protests, then, signifies a growing and almost reflexive dependence on "the official" as the dominant and primary source.

One example of this was the quoting of a public speech by President Bill Clinton, who had arrived in Seattle for the WTO meetings.

The Seattle Times led its report with: "President Clinton today referred to the 'interesting hoopla' surrounding the WTO protests, condemning people who came to Seattle to 'break windows, hurt small businesses and stop people from going to meetings to have their say.'"

However, even when there was no press conference or speech mandating coverage (for instance in a multi-part, serialized news analysis by the New York

Times), stories were focused overwhelmingly on reactions from official and authoritative sources (city officials, merchants, WTO delegates, international governments) with little or no perspectives from protesters. This intensification of reliance on official sources, in particular, indicates that journalists today, more than in the sixties.

It is important to acknowledge, however, that journalistic reliance on official sources during the WTO protests may be explained by the fact that the target for these protests was a more diverse group of institutions, albeit one that included government and trade sources. Journalists may not have been questioning the credibility of these official sources as much as in the case of The March on the Pentagon, where the target was clearly the government and military.

The findings also showed, however, that the significantly greater dependence on official and authoritative sources from within the establishment is not matched by a corresponding increase in sourcing and attribution of official and authoritative sources from the other side of the issue. The New York Times series discussed above is also a good example of this.

Similarly, journalists today are no more willing to quote "unknown protesters," *i.e.*, street protesters who are not protest leaders or officials of protest organizations and are not sought out for their "quote-worthiness." This is consistent with the literature on social protest coverage over the decades: journalists feature unusual participants but ignore the rank-and-file demonstrators.

Next, the lack of a change in the frames given to the two protests further indicates that coverage of social protest does, in fact, follow a pattern.

Journalists have traditionally been criticized for favoring episodic over thematic frames, using their own frames and filters to the detriment of the movement message, and rarely exposing casual readers and viewers to the rationale behind the movements' arguments.

Such a continued prevalence of thematic stories using episodic frames with a negative valence, citing "quote-worthy" protesters and employing descriptions of colour, costumes, and mayhem, is typified in the words of journalist Kenneth Klee in the Newsweek cover story titled "Seattle Under Seige," on December 13, 1999: " The protests drew an equally wide array of groups, from stilt walkers to beefy Teamster mechanics to a guy in a get-up that made him look like J.P. Morgan with a sinister mosquito beak. Where was he from? 'Planet Earth.'"

This also serves as an example of episodic coverage prevailing despite a thematic format-this was a "news feature" magazine article, where thematic discussions are better facilitated than in news reports in daily newspapers.

A social movement like the anti-globalization movement, which is relatively new, with diverse and dispersed issues, is more challenging for a reader/ audience member to immediately recognize.

For media coverage to form public opinion on it, more thematic coverage may in fact be necessary. To have it played out in the mainstream media as episodic news of "disorder" and "deviance," increasing the media's reliance on sources such as the police, fire officials, owners of damaged property, and other such official sources once again points to a pattern of protest coverage with templates of delegitimization built into reporters' coverage decisions. This brings the discussion to the other key focus of this study, the role of the Internet. While the findings above are consistent with the literature on the coverage of social protest, and contribute to that literature some contemporary and comparative perspective, the limited use of the Web by journalists speaks to the continued discounting of protester sources.

Given the multiple points of access to the movement's discussions available via the Internet, journalists could actually have moved beyond reliance on (and suspicion about, and ethical concern with using) protester press releases, meetings, or other material.

This apparent non-impact of the Internet on protest coverage is consistent with the literature, particularly a 1994 study on journalists' Internet use, which found that "the forms of information retrieval may be different, but the same organizational power structures, sources, and news frames are still evident."

In the context of the celebration over the networking power of Internet-mounted social protests, however, this becomes even more revealing. One study using in-depth interviews with journalists who covered the anti-WTO protests has found that journalists did refer to the Internet but, ultimately, not only relied on old patterns of protest coverage but also used the Internet predominantly for the same sources that they would have referred to anyway, albeit offline.

We cannot conclude, however, that all journalists all the time are dismissive or resistant to accessing protest sources over the Internet or directing their readers/audiences to information and debates available on Web sites.

For one thing, 1999 was really only the beginning of the Web age, which can explain the limited Internet role in WTO coverage. While protesters were using the Web in new and creative ways to mobilize, journalists were still acquiring the skills and the savvy to use the Web without compromising credibility.

This study, therefore, may be viewed as a foundation for the systematic and continued analysis of journalists' use of the Web and Internet in providing voice and context to stories such as social protest, civil action, and people's movements. Obviously, this content analysis did not sample online media to determine what was there in 1999.

This was because the content analysis was designed to compare periods-the antiWTO protests with the Vietnam anti-war protests. The Vietnam anti-war protests, of course, were not covered online. Future research, therefore, might involve a study of online coverage using the same modes of analysis (*i.e.*, sourcing and framing) to explore journalists' use of the Internet and their distribution of Web site information and hypermedia links within their stories; studies of hyperlinking by online journalists are now emerging.

Future research should include not only quantitative analyses but also qualitative analyses, through in-depth interviews and surveys, with journalists who covered the anti-WTO protests and other protests (such as the protests against the war in Iraq, especially since these grew out of the anti-globalization protests with some of the same groups and, indeed, the same Web sites), to enquire into the reality and reasons for the choices journalists made in their sourcing, framing, and Internet use.

It is possible, for instance, that these journalists did, in fact, use online resources but did not cite them in the stories, thereby making them invisible to a content analysis.

It becomes important to acknowledge here that this study is an attempt to track early impact and use of the Internet by journalists. While network activists were early adopters of the Web for coalition building and mobilizing for the WTO protests, journalists in 1999 were likely resistant to using the Web and the Internet as overt, attributable sources of information.

This suspicion about the credibility of the Web is one possible explanation for the fact that journalists were more likely to write stories about activists' use of the Web/Internet than they were to use these technologies themselves.

Moreover, in 1999 journalists also viewed these information technologies as emerging competition to their own role as sources of information. This study's focus, therefore, is situated in the early era of somewhat "tentative" Internet use in the newsroom.

It is this very vantage point, however, that makes this study intriguing as a backdrop against which to track emerging information-gathering practices in the newsroom. Documenting the use of the Internet during its early years might provide insights into its current and future use.

For instance, much is likely to have changed between 1999 and the present in terms of journalists' reception of information from alternative voices over the Internet, such as blogs.

One significant question to ask would be: In their use of the Internet, have journalists begun using Web sites, blogs, or people cited on these, as primary sources? Some new studies have suggested that even though some journalists stay resistant to using Internet technologies, and report skepticism of social movements' Web sites, they do seem receptive to corporate and public relations organizations' Web sites, and even interact online with these organizations. One study has shown that even bloggers continue to work within existing discourses about the war in Iraq, primarily employing pro-war and anti-war frames. To summarize, this chapter's findings on how journalists use the Internet, and its disuse for certain types of coverage, points even more strongly to what scholars have called a selection bias. It also alerts us to the need to study patterns of "gatekeeping" in journalists' use of the Internet. This study contributes to the study of the sociology of news production in an Internet age, as well as the reception of new social movements by the press. Other studies on the political communication strategies of social movements, particularly during social protests, may help build a body of theory for the study of Internet-age social protest and press coverage.

In recent years, anabolic steroid use among professional athletes has received significant coverage in print and broadcast media. As an example, when the late baseball player Ken Caminiti told Sports Illustrated in 2002 that about half of all major league players use steroids to enhance athletic performance, mainstream sports journalists and government officials demanded that professional baseball institute drug testing procedures, which it did in August of that year.

More recently, in March 2005, a veritable all-star team of current and former players testified before the Committee on Government Reform in the U.S. House of Representatives about continued steroid use in professional baseball.1 Following that hearing, the committee called on officials from the National Football League, and in subsequent months, a separate committee heard from officials representing professional basketball, hockey and soccer.

Steroid use, in sum, has emerged and remained on the policy making agenda, if only as a consequence of political opportunism (*i.e.*, the chance for elected officials to help "clean up" professional sports) stemming, in part, from dramatic media reports.

Because adolescents frequently idolize professional athletes, whom they observe earning millions of dollars and living glamorous lifestyles, they might be inclined to experiment with the drugs professionals have been known to use.

Through mass communication, they also may develop inaccurate perceptions of health risks, as well as perceptions of normalcy about drug use in sports. Drawing on data gathered by the Inter-University Consortium for Political and Social Research (ICPSR) at the University of Michigan in 2003, this chapter explores attitudes of high school seniors towards the use of anabolic steroids, with specific emphasis on the potential effects of mass communication in helping to shape those attitudes.

The 2003 Youth Risk Behaviour Surveillance System, administered by the Centers for Disease Control and Prevention, found that 6.8 per cent of adolescent males and 5.3 per cent of adolescent females had experimented anabolic steroids at some point in their lifetime. Yet, while scholars have examined relationships between exposure to mass communication and attitudes towards alcohol, cigarettes, and illicit drugs, very few studies have included the use of steroids, and none have focused solely on that subject.

Studies that have examined relationships between exposure to mass communication and attitudes of adolescents have focused largely on perceptions of ideal body image. Generally, where young women often develop unrealistic expectations of how thin they should be, young men often develop unrealistic expectations of how muscular they should appear.

With respect to mass communication, young women observe emaciated models on the covers of magazines such as Cosmopolitan and Glamour, while young men often peruse the photographs in Muscle and Fitness and Flex. Members of both sexes often seek to emulate those they observe in glossy magazines-or in other venues of pop culture. Movies feature hypermuscular action stars, and television offers sporting events, as well as pseudo-sporting events such as professional wrestling, almost non-stop. In recent years, many participants in "legitimate" sports have joined their wrestling counterparts in appearing somewhat cartoonish relative to the average person.

Apropos to cartoons, the physical dimensions of both Barbie and G.I. Joe have become more unrealistic in recent years, with Hasbro even introducing the extraordinarily muscular G.I. Joe Extreme. As Luciano (2001) observes, "If the original G.I. Joe had been life-size, he would have had a thirty-two-inch waist, forty-four-inch chest, and twelve-inch biceps; his successor would flaunt thirtytwo-inch biceps, dimensions that even Arnold Schwarzenegger wouldn't be able to attain".

Adolescent males enter puberty, then, having been inundated throughout childhood with unrealistic, yet idealized, versions of physical size. Given the pressures of adolescence (*i.e.*, fitting in with others, but at the same time, seeking to develop a unique identity), some young men may seek to appear "untouchable" when it comes to muscularity. A substantial portion of these individuals actually may not participate in competitive sports, nor seek to participate; they merely want to appear as muscular as possible and are willing to take their chances with anabolic steroids in pursuing that look.

Thus, in conceptualizing the problem of steroid use by adolescents, one must appreciate that even at a relatively young age, individuals may have very different reasons for using steroids. One young athlete may seek to earn a college scholarship, while another may seek to develop a physique that he believes his peers will admire.

Additionally, contrary to what one might intuit, steroid use is increasing fastest among young women-not young men-with increased muscle tone a primary motivator. As more young women participate in both recreational and competitive sports, and as universities continue to expand scholarship opportunities for female athletes, steroid use will likely hold steady, if not increase, in that demographic.

In sum, whether adolescents of either sex obtain steroids from an Internet source, from a friend at the gym, from a visit to Tijuana, Mexico, or even from a physician, large amounts of these drugs are available for those who seek to try them. The challenge for the present study is to identify quantitative relationships among (a) key demographics, (b) participation in athletics, and (c) exposure to mass communication, and attitudes towards anabolic steroids. Ideally, such relationships will shed light on how the perceptions of adolescents may be shaped by mediated sources of information, which may then lead to behaviours such as experimentation.

The following section describes the theoretical framework guiding quantitative analyses used in this study, as well as a brief review of the socio-historical context in which data were gathered by the ICPSR.

As a theory of mass communication, agenda setting asserts that while media may not tell us exactly what to think, they frequently tell us what to think about, when the issues at hand do not otherwise obtrude into our lives. As an example, while media need not tell us to consider war or the price of gasoline, they might tell us to consider an issue such as performance enhancing drug use in professional sports. As an extension of that theory, second level agenda setting asserts that the attributes of issues emphasized in media reports can affect how we think about those issues.

Where agenda setting tends to focus on objects, McCombs and Reynolds explain, second level agenda setting considers the characteristics, or attributes, of those objects. Thus, in reports about anabolic steroids, foci might include health risks, illicit use among professional athletes for performance gain, policy enactments, rule violations, or availability of the drugs, among other emphases.

The fact that data used in the current study were gathered in 2003 makes a review of emphases observed in 2002 especially relevant.

In 2002, a retired major league baseball player and former MVP named Ken Caminiti told Sports Illustrated in a highly publicized exposé that about half of all professional baseball players use anabolic steroids to enhance performance. As Denham reported, mainstream sports journalists responded in large numbers to the revelation (or allegation), demanding that major league baseball do something about drug use. Members of Congress also took an interest, calling on professional baseball to include a drug-testing programme as part of collective bargaining talks that year.

About three months after the Sports Illustrated article appeared, and following a barrage by other media outlets, an agreement reached between players and owners in August 2002 included the introduction of drug testing.

When the ICPSR gathered its data in 2003, it appears likely that high school seniors who attended to sporting news in 2002 and into the new year would have been exposed to considerable criticism of not only professional baseball, but all sports from which reports of performance enhancing drug use emerged. Large media companies tend to support dominant social norms, values, and ideals, and they do so by expressing support for fair play as well as advocating penalties for those who break the rules. In recent years, athletes have broken the rules in sport by using the likes of amphetamines and steroids to enhance performance.

Thus, in the context of the present study, one might expect heavy media reliers to (a) estimate higher levels of steroid use in professional sports and (b) express more negative attitudes about the use of steroids to enhance performance, following a year in which sports journalists pulled few punches in blasting professional baseball and other sports affected by drug use.

Yet, in theorizing about the relationships between mass communication and adolescent attitudes towards anabolic steroids, one might expect athletic participation to be a significant predictor in statistical equations as well, perhaps controlling the effects of other variables.

Athletes may be more likely to get the "scoop" on steroids from other athletes, as opposed to media sources, and through social learning, or emulating the behaviours of those they admire, they may perceive a "need" to meet other athletes on the same figurative playing field.

In short, steroid use may be viewed by even the youngest of athletes as merely a part of modern-day competition. Shildrick (2002) has written on factors associated with the "normalization" of illicit drug use among young people, and while the author concluded that normalization theory presents an overly simplistic explanation of illicit drug use, peers nevertheless stand to influence risky behaviours. Ultimately, with demographic controls and athletic participation in the equation, the present study advances the following hypotheses:

- *H1:* A significant relationship will emerge between exposure to mass communication and estimated use of illicit drugs by professional athletes, with higher media reliers expressing higher estimates.
- *H2:* A significant relationship will emerge between exposure to mass communication and attitudes towards the use of anabolic steroids, with higher media reliers expressing more negative attitudes.

In addition to asking high school seniors to estimate the prevalence of drug use in professional sports and to express their attitudes towards such use, the ICPSR also asked students to estimate the amount of self-inflicted harm that steroid users cause themselves. To this end, Denham conducted a content analysis that may shed light on the relationship between exposure to mass communication and assessment of health risk.

THE DOMINANT FOUR THEORIES OF THE PRESS

The seminal work Four Theories of the Press established the dominant paradigm in analyzing global media systems and, in particular, in assessing levels of press freedom in countries and regions throughout the world. Other theories on press systems followed, such as development journalism in developing countries, revolutionary media, and democratic-participant media. However, the newer theories were mostly complementary to the established four theories of the press.

Of the four theories, "the authoritarian system has been most pervasive both historically and geographically," according to Siebert. The goal of the media under such a system was to support and advance the policies of the government so that it could achieve its objectives.

Werner J. Severin and James W. Tankard, Jr. in summarizing the major characteristics of the four theories wrote that the authoritarian concept was based on the sixteenth and seventeenth century English history and philosophy of the absolute power of the monarch.

Contrary to the authoritarian theory, libertarian theory held that man was rational and an end in himself. The happiness and the well-being of the individual was the goal of society. The social responsibility theory was an outgrowth of the libertarian theory and was first developed in the twentieth century United States by the Commission on Freedom of the Press, which emphasized social responsibility of the press.

The last of the four theories was the Soviet communist theory, which was based on Marxist ideology and value of unity - unity of the working class and unity of the Party. For the sake of unity, there should be only one right position and only one truth, the absolute truth. Under the Soviet system, the government had a division of censorship.

CRITICISM OF THE FOUR THEORIES

Dominant as the four theories have been, there is no lack of criticism of them. Critical of the social responsibility theory, John C. Merrill, who strongly argued for the independence of individual journalists in his writings, asked his students: Who should be the authority in defining what responsible journalism is? Shouldn't journalists themselves be allowed to make that judgement?

The most comprehensive criticism of the four theories came almost forty years after the theories were first published. In "Last Rights: Revisiting Four Theories of the Press," published in 1995 and written by a group of media scholars from the same school where the four theories originated, the authors found the overall theoretical framework of the four theories flawed.

The book, edited by John C. Nerone, pointed out that the four theories were not value-free despite their valuefree appearance. The theories were based on a pro-capitalist bias and were the products of capitalism and of the Cold War era. Because of such bias, the authors contended that while the four theories were critical of the Soviet communist media, they ignored the concerns of the libertarian media, especially the concentration of media ownership.

The authors argued that the theories focused only on the political control of the media, state power, but were silent on other kinds of power and restraint on the media. For example, the theories only discussed media's political freedom, not economic freedom from the market forces and ownership ties. Another problem with the theories, the authors argued, was that it allowed only two media environments - libertarian and authoritarian - the other two being only the derivatives of the free and the controlled media environments. The book also listed "internal inconsistencies and inadequacies" among the four theories.

In a study examining the press systems in China and Japan, Betty H. Winfield et al. found that Western scholarship on press systems tended to disregard the cultures, philosophies, and traditions that distinguish Asian mass media. She said studies such as the four theories of the press keep a Western emphasis while ignoring political foundations and beliefs in Asian societies.

Shelton A. Gunaratne conducted research on West-centrism in communication theories. He believed that the four theories "ignored the dynamic diversity inherent in complex dissipative social systems" and found them "static" and "deontic".

WESTERN PRESS THEORIES VERSUS EASTERN PRESS SYSTEMS

In an attempt to research and categorize press systems in Asian countries, Jiafei Yin found major difficulties or misfits in trying to pigeonhole Asian media systems according to the four press theories, which were developed by Western media scholars and were based on Western philosophies and the analysis of Western history, politics, and culture. The following section discusses why the dominant press theories could not satisfactorily describe the realities of media in Asia.

THE "LIBERTARIAN PRESS" IN ASIA

SELF-CENSORSHIP IN THE ASIAN PRESS

The Japanese press is considered the liveliest in East Asia and was ranked the freest in Asia by the Freedom House for 2005. Reporters Without Borders gave Japan the second-highest ranking in Asia in press freedom after South Korea for its 2005 report.

Japan's press industry is the largest in the world. It has five national daily newspapers, each claiming a circulation in the millions. That compares with the top two dailies in the United States -USA Today and The Wall Street Journal - each of which has a circulation of around 2 million.

Yomiuri Shimbun, the paper with the largest circulation in the world, has a circulation of 14 million. Asahi Shimbun has a circulation of 12 million. These two Japanese national dailies are the only two newspapers in the world with a circulation surpassing 10 million. The circulations of the other three range from 2.7 million to 5.6 million.

Japanese journalists are well trained and well informed. They have to study for months to pass rigorous exams to even get hired. The exam includes a ninety-minute general intelligence test, a ninety-minute writing test, and a ninety-minute foreign language proficiency test, usually in English, Spanish, French, or Chinese.

Even if a candidate gets good scores, he or she has to pass three to four interviews. Special schools help prepare university students and graduates for the test. But Japanese journalists may find their training and skills wasted under a press club system.

To understand the nature of the Japanese press system, the economic system in Japan has to be examined first. Democracy describes Japan's political system, but freewheeling capitalism is out of the question in Japan although, theoretically speaking, Japan practices free market capitalism. The Japanese economy has thrived and become a dominant force in the global economy under state-guided capitalism. Instead of regulating the industry, the government helps the industry to grow and compete on the global market. Government and big corporations in Japan are partners in nation building. Political freedom and rights do not translate into economic liberalism in Japan, which has much to do with the Japanese culture, or the Asian culture.

In Asian societies, especially those under the influence of Confucian thought, the strength of a country is regarded as more important than the profitability of a company, and the well-being of a family is more important than individual rights and freedom.

For a country like Japan with limited arable land and scarce resources, the survival and prosperity of the nation take priority in national life. The royal family and often the government are symbols of the nation, and they command respect. Such a cultural tradition contradicts the Western concept of media as a watchdog and the ultimate goal of libertarian philosophies - man as an end in himself. In Japan, media keep cozy relations with the government and the big industries through the press club system, or "information cartels," which comprise press clubs, industry associations, and media conglomerates, which Freeman calls "the unholy trinity." The press clubs channel information from government offices to media organizations.

Such a club system discourages independent reporting and thoroughness in journalistic investigations and results in "uniformity of content" and "pro-establishment style of journalism". The information cartels ensure no competition among media outlets and no scoops. In Asian societies, the motto promoted is not Darwin's "survival of the fittest," but the survival of all, which may explain why in many Asian countries, such as Japan, China, and Singapore, comparative advertising is banned.

The club system works well for the Japanese press, which profits from large circulations, high advertising revenue, and exclusive information access from the government. But it is a system designed by the industry to serve media companies' economic interests, a system that has frequently led the press to support state goals.

It is in this sense that the media can be understood as collaborators with the state in the management of society, Freeman said. Such a system discourages investigative reporting and places a premium on relying on official sources rather than alternative information. It interferes with the public's right to receive relevant information in a timely manner.

As a result, all the high-profile political scandals that emerged in the first half of 2002 were not uncovered by the vernacular dailies, but by the non-mainstream weeklies. Because of its less than rigorous reporting, the Japanese press fails to act as a watchdog of the government and is called a lapdog, which was blamed for failing to keep the public informed of the irregularities within the financial industry and the corruption within the government. When the Asian financial crash hit Japan in 1997, the magnitude of the crisis took the public by surprise.

An in-depth analysis of the Japanese press system makes it clear that the ideas available at the "marketplace of ideas" are rather limited. Free competition that is at the very core of the libertarian theory is stifled under the press club system, which also bars reporters from foreign and non-mainstream media outlets from attending exclusive press briefings and getting official press releases.

While government control of the press in Japan is not a major issue, control by professional associations and the media organizations themselves is still very effective and produces the same result of a less informed public. The reason why the Freedom House rated the Japanese press as the freest in Asia may be because of the fact that the Japanese government seldom takes direct actions against the press or journalists. In Japan, there is hardly such need, as the press polices itself rather diligently.

Like Japan, South Korea is a newspaper-rich country. South Koreans get their news primarily from daily newspapers. The country has ten national dailies, which are in circulation wars in the millions. In addition, there are 100 free dailies, 314 specialized dailies, 1,999 weeklies, 2,319 monthlies, and 1,245 other periodicals. All newspapers print forty-eight to fifty-six pages for advertising space. In South Korea, each household subscribes to two or three national papers and one local paper, a dream for newspaper owners in any country.

For 2005, the Freedom House rated the press in South Korea "free." And the Reporters Without Borders described the South Korean press as opposite of that of North Korea: "diverse, privately owned and critical of the government". South Korea is a relatively new democracy. After decades of fighting for democracy, South Koreans started to enjoy their political rights in 1987 when a civilian government was sworn in after a general election.

But until Kim Dae Jung, a freedom fighter and folk hero, became president in 1998, the newly found press freedom in South Korea had been contained by its press club system like Japan's, by the common economic interests of the government and big business in South Korea, including the media, and by the influence of Confucian values.

South Korean industries, like those of Japan, used to be guided and supported by the government. The press in South Korea has allied itself with the government and big businesses and is widely seen as "pro-business," "pro-government," and "conservative". Chong-Hyuk Kim, a reporter for the Joong Ang Ilbo in South Korea, told a Freedom Forum panel that South Korea's ostensibly democratic government barred publishing the size of foreign reserves and foreign debt. He said, "It has become traditional practice between government and media in South Korea not to report critical and important information.

The government insisted if that kind of information were revealed, it would be harmful to national security and the national reputation. The media accepted that kind of assertion". The result of such secrecy was the unexpected Asian financial crash in 1997, which hit the South Korean economy hard and caught its people unprepared.

A reader of the Chosun Ilbo, one of the largest papers in the country, wrote: "Korean journalism still is a superficial observer of the events and does not carry a torch for the righteous social and ethical standards in a rapidly transforming materialistic society. It still is timid and not impartial and indifferent to power politics".

The press system in South Korea had many similarities with that of Japan until Kim Dae Jung became president in 1998. Since then the South Korean press has started to develop in a new direction, and the press club system is being phased out. Press freedom in South Korea improved noticeably during the tenure of Kim, when the press became more aggressive in covering the government and more vocal in criticizing government policies. But the unprecedented press freedom in Korean history under Kirn's government was overshadowed by government's crackdown on the major papers with charges of tax evasion in 2001.

Press freedom is still fragile in South Korea, and its press system is in a transitional stage. It remains to be seen if the South Korean press is finally breaking away from self-censorship or if it still wants to maintain good relations with the government and big businesses by avoiding coverage of critical issues. Self-censorship is not only a major issue in Japan and South Korea but also a major concern in Hong Kong and Thailand. The media in Hong Kong and Thailand are in a category of their own. They are among the freest in Asia when they resort to sensationalism to survive the intense competition. In Hong Kong, tabloids represent the mainstream press. Practice of yellow journalism, including sensationalized reporting, price wars, and stealing talent from competitors, reached its climax in 1995 and again in 1997. In both Hong Kong and Thailand, the press exercises a high degree of freedom when it is dealing with non-political topics, but starts to be cautious when news stories concern politics, the government, or the royal family.

Before Hong Kong was returned to China, many of the newspapers in the former British colony were pro-British. Since the sovereignty changed hands, more papers are now pro-Beijing. Self-censorship is considered a major concern and the main threat to an independent and free press in Hong Kong despite a great deal of aggressive reporting.

Part of the problem of press self-censorship was due to the fact that after Hong Kong was returned to China, the ownership of some of the major newspapers changed hands, including the South China Morning Post. The new press owners have investments on the Chinese mainland and do not want to offend the officials in Beijing.

BBC News introduced the media in Hong Kong as editorially dynamic, free, and diverse, but it cited increasing self-censorship and pressures on editorial policies. In Hong Kong, direct government intervention of the press is minimal. However, pressure from the central government in Beijing and new owners of the press makes many editors and reporters wary of how to handle sensitive information or topics.

A public opinion poll found that 48 per cent of the people in Hong Kong believed the local news media practiced self-censorship. The study showed that 62 per cent believed the local news media had qualms when criticizing the central government, while only 34 per cent believed it had concerns in criticizing the local government. "The number of respondents who said the media practices self-censorship has significantly increased, mainly because they think the media has become apprehensive when criticizing the central government," a survey organizer said.

Newspapers in Hong Kong adopted specific strategies in the politics of self-censorship. Francis L. F. Lee and Angel M. Y. Lin argued that in transitional societies such as Hong Kong when political pressure on the press is added to a commercial media system and a professional journalistic culture, the politics of self-censorship often becomes a strategic contest between the media and political actors.

The Ming Pao daily constructed the debate as a factional rivalry in order to position itself as an arbitrator, according to Lee and Lin. In contrast, the popular Apple Daily presented the story as a sovereign people's fight against a powerful entity, which was much more critical towards the central government. "Nevertheless, it also appropriated the dominant discourse, constructed internal contradictions, and decentralized the Chinese central government to smooth out the radicalism of its criticisms".

Jasper Decker, a former staff member at the South China Morning Post, also observed less obvious characteristics of self-censorship, such as the tone and attitude in news stories concerning China. Reporting became less aggressive. Management emphasized the virtues of writing to allow readers to read between the lines. In 1997, the New York Times noted that Ming Pao had "reduced the space given to columnists critical of China and has toned down its previously aggressive reporting of China".

Other newspapers avoided devoting space to politically sensitive topics by assigning their reporters to cover other, non-controversial topics. A content analysis of 1997 editorials of major newspapers in Hong Kong found that 56.2 per cent of the editorials addressed local issues in Hong Kong, while only 8 per cent of the editorials discussed issues in China and 7.6 per cent dealt with topics related to the ties between Hong Kong and China.

Self-censorship was an issue even before 1997. Jim Sciutto, a former Hong Kong journalist, claimed, "Self-censorship is nearly epidemic in Hong Kong, affecting the entire media hierarchy from publishers to beat reporters. A free Hong Kong press is already eroding."

In a 1990 survey of Hong Kong journalists, 5 per cent admitted fear of criticizing China in their work, and 54 per cent believed that their fellow journalists felt the same way. The anxiety was not alleviated in the following six years as a similar survey in 1996 found that one in every four journalists expressed concerns over criticizing China.

As much of the self-censorship in Hong Kong was the result of pressure from newspaper editors and owners, some local journalists and researchers argued that it was censorship, not self-censorship on the part of the reporters. Carol Lai, a former chairwoman of the Hong Kong Journalist Association, believed that the influence of editors might have impacted journalists' writing more than any threats from the government.

She believed most of the reporters wanted integrity in their reporting, tried to report accurately and objectively and seldom censored themselves. Some editors, however, watered down criticism or killed stories they deemed offensive. Media owners and editors censored their reporters in the hope of preventing interference from the central government so they could keep their papers in business.

Others might wish to expand their investment on the mainland. The Hong Kong Journalist Association noted that the South Chin Morning Post had reduced and diluted its coverage of China since Robert Kuok became an owner in 1993. "In Hong Kong, pro-Beijing forces don't fight the media, they buy it".

In order to be successful, the media in Hong Kong have learned to remain apolitical. Since the late 1960s, major newspapers in Hong Kong have become increasingly less partisan and have avoided taking less popular stand on issues, and instead, have focused more on the market and middle-class liberalism in order to increase profits. Self-censorship in Hong Kong prompted one Hong Kong journalist to compare Hong Kong tycoons, who toned down their coverage of China, with mainland media outlets, which became more aggressive in their reporting as they sought market share. In the near future, Hong Kong may have to learn a thing or two from the mainland press when it comes to press freedom, according to Mark Simon of the Apple Daily.

In Southeast Asia, the Thai press enjoys a considerable degree of freedom. Its 1997 constitution protects media freedom, freedom of expression, and access to information. Even under the media-unfriendly prime minister Thaksin Shinawatra the media were free to criticize government policies and cover cases of corruption and human rights abuses, but journalists tended to exercise self-censorship regarding the military, the monarchy, the judiciary, and other sensitive issues.

Press freedom is deep-rooted in the Thai culture. However, the tradition of self-censorship in Thailand is as long as its history of a free press. Despite the freedom they enjoyed in the 1980s, Thai editorial writers and reporters censored themselves, mindful that there were unwritten government rules regarding the coverage of the monarchy, government affairs, internal security matters, and Thailand's international image.

"Self-censorship is probably a perfect form of political control. Politicians in power don't have to risk creating public ire by openly bullying the media. Media proprietors and journalists know exactly what the 'invisible rules' are". The degree of press freedom and selfcensorship in Thailand is often dependent on the kind of government that is in power. The Thai government under Prime Minister Thaksin provided a telling example.

Since Thaksin came to power, the majority of media outlets were forced into submission. Some journalists lamented that truly independent journalists were now "a rare and endangered species" as too many members of the media were influenced by the lure of political favour, or in fear of political power. The government rewarded media outlets supportive of its policies through the allocation of advertising by telecommunications firms and state enterprises, which resulted in an increasing level of self-censorship. More sophisticated media outlets included mild criticism of the government in their coverage but avoided more serious issues or pursuing issues further.

In such a media environment, anyone in the broadcast media speaking more than "30 per cent of the truth" could get into trouble. The media were thus forced into three categories - government partisans, government mouthpieces, and those that engage in self-censorship.

Most mainstream newspapers were won over by the government either through friendly persuasions sweetened with advertising deals or through political pressure, and all television stations were pressured into practicing self-censorship in covering the government.

Using sharper words, The Nation wrote, "...the majority of those who own media outlets sense Thaksin's political invincibility and are prostituting themselves voluntarily. The broadcast media are the most obvious, acting in collusion with the government.... Nowadays, broadcasters are considered strategic partners with the government. Lump-sum financial rewards have made parts of the media into circus dogs that are ready to do summersaults."

The print media were no exception, the article said. Publishers were more willing to follow the government line to ensure their business future. Self-censorship was increasingly becoming the normal code of conduct for editors and journalists under Thaksin.

Under a climate of fear and self-censorship within the media community, the Thai media have morphed into the "custodian of the government". In one particular case, the owner of the newsmagazine, Siamrath, exercised self-censorship by canceling the distribution of 30,000 copies of an issue that contained reports critical of the government. In another case, the management of the Bangkok Post removed its editor Veera Prateepchaikul for "irritating" the prime minister by using the word "arrogance".

Concerned over the retreat of press freedom, The Nation argued, "The professional integrity of the media should never be conditional on the political power or popularity of a leader, much less his power of patronage to throw financial benefits their way".

Two recent court rulings upheld the constitutional rights to freedom of expression in the country, one vindicating former iTV journalists, who were dismissed for refusing to compromise their professional integrity, and the other in favour of media-freedom advocate Supinya Klangnarong and the Thai Post, who were sued for defamation.

Also in 2006, all the free TV channels covered the anti-Thaksin activities, with the exception of only one channel. That was unprecedented under the government of Thaksin. The Freedom House can rate the Thai press as "free," such as in 2002, or "partly free" since 2003. But it is certainly a different kind of free press even though its self-censorship practices are much less systematic than Japan's.

SELF-CENSORSHIP VERSUS SOCIAL RESPONSIBILITY THEORY

There are fundamental differences between press self-censorship in Asia and the Western social responsibility press theory. First, as discussed earlier, the social responsibility theory derived from the libertarian theory, which emphasizes the freedom of the press and pluralism in the marketplace of ideas. Therefore, the basis of the social responsibility theory is still press freedom, even when the press is urged to use that freedom responsibly.

Press self-censorship in Asia, however, is based either on control by the press clubs in the case of Japan and, formerly, South Korea or on fear of government retribution in the case of Hong Kong and Thailand. In either case, freedom of the press is being severely curtailed. Second, the goal of the Hutchins report, A Free and Responsible Press, is to recommend ways in which a free press can better serve the society at large.

The report proposed five standards in improving the quality of news reporting, including the comprehensive coverage of news events to ensure its accuracy, representation of different demographic groups in society in news reports, and the provision of service to all the constituencies of society. But the primary goal of press self-censorship in Asia is for self-preservation. It is to protect the business interests of the press rather than to better serve the public. Newspapers in these Asian countries are highly profitable; thus, the management does not want to offend the government or big business.

Third, ideally speaking, if the social responsibility press theory is implemented in the newsroom, the result will be a better-informed public and a more ethical and responsible press, whereas press self-censorship in Asia can only result in uniform content, suppressed information, and a poorly informed public. If the ultimate goal of the press in these Asian societies is the pursuit of profits, it will be difficult for the press to be socially responsible or professionally ethical.

THE "AUTHORITARIAN PRESS" IN ASIA - THE INFLUENCE OF CONFUCIANISM

The press in Singapore and Malaysia is often regarded as the prototype of authoritarian press in Asia. In both countries, the means to control the press are very similar to those used in sixteenth or seventeenth century England, including government censorship, suspension of license, legal actions against the press, and even shutdown of the offending publications.

But that is where similarities with Western authori-tarianism end. The authoritarian press theory was based on the historical analysis of sixteenth and seventeenth century England while the authoritarian press in Singapore and Malaysia is shaped more by the Asian cultural tradition and the practical needs of the countries' geo-political realities.

While government authority came more from the absolute power of the monarchy in sixteenth and seventeenth century England, in Asian societies, especially in Singapore, which is under the heavy influence of Confucius's teachings, governments regard themselves both as parents and as rulers, which helps explain why even gum chewing and flushing toilets are regulated. According to the Confucian hierarchical order of political system, government is the paternalistic figure of the land.

"The ruler is the wind. People are the grass. When the wind blows, the grass is sure to bend," Confucius said. But Confucius was also a philosopher. He said, "Authority springs from morality, not force". He believed that people should accept authority, but authority must be just. Confucius asked: "When government leads by the right example, who dares to go astray?" In contrast, authoritarian theory does not address the quality of a government or the morality of the rulers.

Singapore is a society where a no-non-sense government promotes Confucian values of education, hard work and clear moral principles. The Singaporean government is one of the very few in Asia where corruption is rare. The government is as clean as the streets in Singapore, which is often considered the cleanest city in the world. The government in Singapore prides itself on its system of meritocracy and efficiency.

Different views are tolerated to a certain extent, but if the press publishes articles the government takes offence to, the government pursues the press relentlessly all the way to the court, which often has a chilling effect on the press. Confucianism extols cooperative and harmonious relations, which are what the Singaporean government hopes to cultivate both at home and abroad.

The government keeps a watchful eye on the press for any stories that address race relations, religion, or problems in neighbouring countries. Such stories are banned in the Singaporean press because of the mixed racial and religious makeup of its population and its often-sensitive relations with its neighbours.

Violence and chaos caused by racial and religious differences in neighbouring countries put the Singaporean government on high alert. Former Prime Minister Lee Kuan Yew said that any journalist who did not support Singapore-Malaysia relations would be sent to jail.

Malaysia has many similarities with its neighbour, Singapore, in its treatment of the press, as the two countries were once merged into one for a brief period in their history. Both governments are unequivocal promoters of" Asian values" and loud critics of Western culture.

Asian values in Malaysia include emphasis on the social role of the press, which is for development, and on morality, which in part might have resulted from the Islamic influence in the country.

Confucian influences are not as heavy in Malaysia as in Singapore, where Chinese account for about 75 per cent of the population. In Malaysia, Muslims make up about half of the population. Malaysian leaders, especially former Prime Minister Mahathir, have the government-knows-best attitude.

The government has set the goal of making Malaysia a developed country by the year 2020, and it wants the press to help in that endeavor, which means highlighting government development plans, promoting racial and religious harmony by suppressing coverage of racial and religious issues, and controlling Western influences by limiting overseas TV programming to 30 per cent. While the Singaporean government is often criticized for trying to silence dissent and punish the press for negative coverage, the government in Malaysia has promoted positive press coverage on such topics as" Asian values" and national development. In some aspects, Malaysian media seem to border on the communist system not only in promoting positive news coverage, but also in media ownership. Party press sets the trend in Malaysia, where political parties own major stocks in media agencies. The ruling political party UMNO owns media giants the New Straits Times and Utusan Malaysia.

The Chinese and Indian parties in the country also have acquired major stocks in media agencies that cater to their ethnic groups.

The government has a direct stake in the media too by owning the national news agency, Bernama, which has the right to distribute foreign news reports. Under authoritarian rule, governments do not own the media; they punish the media when they are not happy with the coverage. One salient feature of the authoritarian press system is government's various ways of punishing and controlling the press when the press is defiant.

Even though the Malaysian government punishes occasional rebellious papers, the Malaysian press, especially the mainstream press, mostly saves the government's wrath through compliance with very restrictive press laws.

The Printing Presses and Publications Act of 1984 gives the minister of home affairs the power to revoke publishing licenses without judicial review. As a result, the Malaysian mainstream press has become so tame that its credibility has been questioned. Zaharom Nain wrote,"... The Malaysian mainstream media - the press and broadcasting - have never aspired to be the guardians of the freedom of speech." "... The mainstream newspapers'failure to be a credible source of information is a reflection of a journalist's failure in performing her duties professionally," a member of the National Union of Journalists said. The inaction of the press against government suppression of press freedom came under fire too." The credibility of Malaysian journalists has been damaged as much by dilution of professional standards and ethics as by passivity in tackling legal and administrative restrictions".

4

Mass Communication and Media Research

INTRODUCTION

The character and directions of academic enquiry are ever-changing. Old subjects evolve, their influence waxes and wanes; new subjects emerge. All as the result of many Media and Mass Communication Research different intellectual and social processes on different levels – national, regional and international. The field of Media and Communication is a relative young discipline; many of us have first-hand experience of its gestation and birth. The study of media and mass communication has evolved steadily since the 1950s. Changes in contemporary political systems, the cross-fertilization or conflict of different cultures, the development of social institutions and organizations, not to mention new information technologies, have influenced the development of the discipline significantly.

The number of scholars in the field of Media and Communication Research has increased dramatically during the last decade, and some excellent research communities have been created. But, there are aspects that arouse some critical reflections – most of which concern whether and to what extent the work in our field raises relevant questions about the relations between media and society.

An attunement of research to the agendas – and even the interests – of new systems of public grants, external financiers and, furthermore, new structures for higher education has thrust scientific enquiry into a period of change. Research tends to be more administrative, and short-term perspectives prevail at the expense of the long-term accumulation of knowledge. Too little time is devoted to academic debate and critique; there is no "career value" in such undertakings. The leeway for independence and the freedom to utter unpleasant truths have diminished – perhaps not formally, but de facto.

The pressures at play in this overall trend may well have more far-reaching consequences for a relatively "new" field of research like Media and Communication than in older and more established disciplines.

THE EMERGENCE OF THE DISCIPLINE IN THE NORDIC COUNTRIES

Modern Media and Communication Research has its roots in a variety of disciplines: Political Science, Economics, Sociology, Psychology, History, Literature and Linguistics. Within these fields, questions relating to mass media had tended to be marginalised. Serious gaps in knowledge had opened concerning how the external manifestations of media and communication related to their inner life, and to the place the institutions occupy in our societies and cultures. This, just as television was becoming an ubiquitous household fixture and computers had started their conquest. The frustration relating to these 'white spots on the map' spurred the creation of the discipline of Media and Communication Research on eminently interdisciplinary foundations. Behind the urge to create a specialised discipline was the desire to strengthen the field through the elaboration of shared concepts, theoretical starting points and methods.

Some of the scholars who were active in the 1970s and 1980s – today we call them pioneers – worked hard to establish Media and Communication as a discipline in its own right. Among the pioneer generation were researchers like Svennik Hotter and Hedge Stubby in Norway; Karl-Erik Rosengren, Kettle Nowak, Olof Holden, Stir Hadenius and Lennart Weibull in Sweden; and Frands Mortensen, Erik Nordahl Svendsen and Karen Siune in Denmark. All were aided and abetted from time to time by Kaarle Nordenstreng in Finland, where Journalism and Mass Communication had been an academic discipline since the 1940s.

Many of these researchers also founded training programmes for journalists and information officers in an era when demand for professionals in these areas skyrocketed. Other main actors were the national associations of media researchers, all of which were formed towards the end of the 1970s. These may be seen as an outgrowth of Nordic collaboration, which has a history of some 30-40 years, having first been manifested in a pan-Nordic conference for media and communication research held in 1973 at the Ovogeneses outside Oslo. That same year saw the decision to establish a Nordic documentation center for media and communication research, NORDICOM. Clearly, Nordic collaboration in the area was a chief preprequisite to the development of the discipline in the Nordic countries. This Nordic base provided, and continues to provide, a much more conducive platform for research than any of the five countries alone can offer.

Nordic research collaboration also benefited from Nordic researchers' active involvement in the IAMCR/AIERI (International Association for Mass Communication Research) and its regularly recurring conferences in the1970s. Nearly all the so-called pioneers were present in Leipzig in 1974, which marked a definite step in the history of the Association. And then there was

Leicester 1976, Warsaw 1978... It is no mere coincidence that the Swedish association was formed on the way home from Leicester, and the Norwegian association at the conference in Warsaw. In retrospect it is interesting to see how several different factors, especially regional and international processes, coalesced to make an extraordinary national expansion possible. Still, without the entrepreneurial efforts of individual researchers it would not have happened.

And then...?

In the Nordic region, research and education in Media and Communication were finally unified in the late 1980s and early 1990s. The process took place more or less simultaneously, in a variety of academic departments, some in the Social Sciences, others in the Humanities. This was the case in Denmark, Norway and Sweden. The exception was Finland, as earlier mentioned, where Journalism and Mass Communication, and Communication Studies, respectively, had been independent and well-established disciplines for many years.

Viewed in historical perspective, media researchers in the Social Sciences and media researchers in the Humanities for many years kept their distance from one another in terms of theory and methodology. In the Humanities, the focus has often rested on the meaning of human expression from the perspective of Linguistics, Philosophy, the Arts and Literature. The social scientists have, for their part, occupied themselves more with the media institutions and their relations with other institutions, particularly those having to do with democracy, and the effects and comprehension of mediated messages. Whereas methodology has long been a pivotal concern within the Social Sciences, it has been relatively peripheral in the Humanities. For many years, a 'front line' ran through the Nordic research community, dividing those who applied quantitative methods from those who used qualitative.

New disciplines like Media and Communication Research find themselves in something of a dilemma. On the one hand, they seek to develop a discipline that merits national and international recognition; on the other, they want to remain open and non-doctrinaire in their relations with neighbouring disciplines. Often, however, the institutionalisation of a research field, particularly in its early phases, implies a risk of a block in communication with other disciplines – which occurred in the case of Media and Communication Research. The developmental phase coincided, what is more, with a new direction in work in the Humanities known as 'the cultural turn'.

The 'cultural turn' represented a development that brought social scientists and their colleagues in the Humanities closer. Scholars in the field increasingly trained their focus on the roles media play in cultural processes, on the media's potential to create meaning in a broader sense, and on the adaptation of media messages to modes of understanding commonly applied to cultural phenomena. Nowadays it is no longer always easy to tell the difference between work in the two traditions.

The concept of *text* became central in almost every sense of the word. We may speak of a process of hybridization in some regions of the field. The 'cultural turn' has had a far stronger impact on media studies than on many other fields. The outcome, however, has not been greater unity of focus, but rather the opposite, and in retrospect we may ask: In an era when issues relating to the power and morality of media institutions were more urgently important than ever before, where were the social scientists – why were they so quiet? Was it because they were busy pursuing consensus in the field, or was it because of 'marketisation'? Or, were they simply totally absorbed in the Zeitgeist?

For a young discipline in which most researchers nowadays have their background solely in Media and Communication Research and where contacts with early media research and work in neighbouring disciplines are few, "trends" can have an exceedingly strong impact and may lead to widespread conformism. Some critics have lamented the lack of historical perspectives in much of contemporary Media and Communication Research. The wheel has been re-invented, time and again. Researchers tend to develop a nose for trends and for what is politically correct. In this way it is entirely possible for a field of research to be characterised at once by conformism and multidisciplinarity or, perhaps more aptly, eclecticism.

Media and communication researchers borrow theories, perspectives and methods from other disciplines. Many doctoral dissertations of recent vintage refer – often without much reflection – to a handful of theories garnered from more general cultural and social theory. The works take their inspiration from one, often even several methodologies, without pausing to consider that methods, too, are founded on basic assumptions about the nature of the object to be explored. (Hotter 2006) Scholars in our field have always borrowed and will surely continue to borrow, due to the nature of the phenomena they concern themselves with. Borrowing in itself should not disqualify us from making the occasional contribution to the development of theory and methodology in other disciplines, but the record to date shows remarkably few such contributions. What is more, we find that issues relating to the media are today being studied in many different disciplines, independent of what has been done, or is being done by researchers in Media and Communication.

Media and Communication is variegated in the extreme, and few syntheses embrace the field as a whole. The field is broad, specialities are many, with new ones appearing from time to time. Indeed, the field can give the impression of incoherence. Specialisation, which is not always solidly founded in theory or methodology, may cause the field to disintegrate into small groups, each a discursive community unto itself. Members' credibility within the community increases, all the while their work is marginalised in relation to the research community at large.

The burgeoning flora of journals these days mirrors the situation. Commercial publishing houses have caught the scent and flocked to the arena. New research specialities are carved out and new journal titles started up all the time. As a consequence, there is a risk that our field may become 'balkanized' to an even greater extent. Furthermore, the rapid increase in seeming diversity may well – as in many other cases of rapid expansion – result in redundant and repetitive publication. Which, in turn, implies a risk that perceptions of academic standards will continue to vary, and with them the quality of published work. Variation in standards is not to be confused with a healthy variety of interests, points of departure, concepts and methods, without which the discipline cannot thrive. Theoretical and methodological pluralism needs to be deliberately cultivated, and this requires competitive interaction between qualitative research environments.

The frantic hunt for research funding, increasing pressures to publish in international journals, and far-reaching specialisation – on a market that has become increasingly trend-sensitive – are not unrelated. Thought, reconsideration, and reflection are scarce in day-to-day academic life. Monographs, as demanding of the scholar's time and effort as they are important to our science, are not profitable ventures.

Specialisation with studies of high quality is not a problem in itself, but it can be problematic unless accompanied by enquiry on a systems level. Without these latter studies, we have no knowledge of the whole to which we can relate the various parts. There is a risk that extreme specialisation may lose its fertility for lack of impulses and an inability to formulate new problems of relevance. Today, there is not much in the way of a media philosophy that can unite findings and theories. The lack of such a philosophy can hamper progress in our field. Media and communication researchers face some real challenges today. In the world of multilevel governance with private and public actors media landscapes and media cultures are undergoing fundamental and far-reaching metamorphoses. Not to mention the ramifications of phenomena like ICT, media convergence and global media structures.

How to bridge the digital – or more correctly – the knowledge divide is a topic of considerable attention even for media researchers. The main question is the gap between north and south. The gap between the rich and poor still prevails as a result of disparities in access to resources, knowledge and technology, especially in rural areas. But, the divide is also reproduced within virtually every country of the world and often reflects other gaps – those between income groups, the sexes and ethnic groups.

We need to better understand how media and communication may be used, both as tools and as a way of articulating processes of development and social change, improving everyday lives and empowering people to influence their own lives and those of their fellow community members (Hemer and

Tufte 2005). In this digital age it is easy to marginalize traditional media as radio, newspapers, journals and books, and fail to confront critical issues such as the lack of media freedom in many parts of the world, the rising global concentration of private media ownership, the absence of media legislation and the challenges facing public service media.

We also have reason to ask questions about media with a focus on gender and the gender order. The media mirror reality, yes, but they also contribute to constructing hegemonic definitions that all too frequently are depicted as self-evident – as natural, all-pervasive and invisible as the air we breathe.

The research community also bears a responsibility for the cultivation of media and information literacy in society at large. A precondition for a good layman's understanding of the media is new knowledge and the communication of that knowledge. *Media literacy* means understanding how mass media work, how they create reality and produce meaning, how the media are organized, and knowing how to use them wisely. Proponents of media literacy view greater knowledge of the media and communication in society as contributing to participation, active citizenship, development and life-long learning.

With the growing convergence of radio, TV and computer technologies, including the emergence of various hybrids and specializations, we see how a variety of electronic media, information and communication is gradually becoming common goods.

Interactive media like the Internet also imply invitations to risky behaviour in connection with media use. The time for simple media effects approaches has passed. Instead, the issues of media content and media use need to be contextualised in a multifactor, risk-based framework as concluded by several researchers (Hargrave and Livingstone 2006). Traditional media literacy is no longer sufficient.

There is a need to develop new skills and competencies that render users and consumers 'information literate". Media literacy has tended to focus on cultural expression and has a critical dimension that information literacy lacks. Recently, however, information literacy is increasingly connected to issues of democracy and active citizenship. There is a need to bring the two forms of literacy together.

TIME TO REGAIN THE INITIATIVE – NATIONALLY, REGIONALLY AND INTERNATIONALLY

In our attempts to comprehend and explain contemporary reality we sometimes find the tools at our disposal too mechanical, too blunt and unidimensional. It has proved easier to ask *what* and *how* than to ask *why*. How, then, can Media and Communication Research meet these challenges? We need a good dose of critical self-examination, where we consider the relevance of the questions we formulate, where we are more judicious in our choice of theoretical perspectives and more conscious of the ontological and epistemological underpinnings of the methods at hand, and where we evaluate the validity of our findings and the conclusions we draw from them (Hotter 2006). And, we definitely need more collaboration – within our field and with other disciplines.

We need to learn more from one other, to share knowledge and context. Collaboration between disciplines and collaboration across national frontiers, with the aim of enriching the research environment, is vital to the development of fruitful discursive communities. Research communities themselves need to create platforms to achieve long-term goals through national, regional and international collaboration.

Internationalization is both enriching and necessary in the multicultural and global world of today as it is with regard to scholars' interest in broader, more all-inclusive paradigms.

We need comparative studies in order to shed light on important issues. We have to build on past work but break new ground. We need fresh, unexpected ingests and new comparative research questions. We need to develop analytical frameworks that will guide comparative analysis of media systems. Without comparative studies we run an obvious risk that certain factors will grow out of proportion. And we have to be able to point to possible areas and strategies for future research.

But, we also have to maintain and further develop national and regional collaboration, not least as a means to ensure that internationalization does not take place at the expense of knowledge about, and reflection on, scholars' own societies and cultures. Fruitful national and regional dialogues are a great boon in international exchanges and vice versa.

The overall objective must be to enable our research field to answer questions about the role of media with regard to the distribution of power and influence in our societies, in addition to questions relating to media content and the role of media in everyday life. We should not lose sight of the fact that, *power, identity* and *inequality* are still concepts of vital relevance in media and communication research (Holding 2005). The outcome of this process will depend on our degree of involvement in discourses outside our institutions and closest circles.

It is time to regain the initiative – nationally, regionally and internationally. And, we must dare to do more. That is, enter a new phase in the development of our knowledge about media and communication, where we raise our level of ambition so that the diversity and richness of Media and Communication Research as a field may bear fruit and inspire other disciplines. So that we, in an age when the media are among the strongest influences in our societies, do not by default leave science-based media philosophy and media criticism to others.

MASS COMMUNICATION RESEARCH TRENDS

Scholars of mass communication-and indeed other fields-seem always to be interested in knowing research trends in their areas. Which methods are used most and least often? Which areas have been more or less studied? Which statistics are most and least in use? How does funding for research compare with that of other fields, and what kinds of studies are more or less likely to receive funding? Studies published in journals provide a good, but not entirely comprehensive, data source to answer these questions. Each year hundreds of articles on a wide range of topics are published in academic communication journals.

Viewing this literature from a distance, one can discern larger patterns and. trends in mass communication research. Knowing them can help researchers and students identify areas of strength and weakness, and of abundance and scarcity, in the research. Scholars may tackle topics that a meta-analysis shows have been ignored or they may refine a method to avoid problems identified in an analysis of dozens or even hundreds of individual studies.

One problem with generalizing from published journal articles to the whole mass communication field is that books, monographs, book chapters, and convention papers are excluded. Despite this drawback, many researchers argue that journal articles are a barometer of research trends1 and reflect the evolution of communication research. For most mass communication scholars, journal articles are the main channel for reporting current research after convention and conference papers.

Several systematic reviews or meta-analyses of mass communication journal articles have already been carried out, especially in the 1970s and 1990s. This monitoring has been important in a field that changes rapidly, but many of these studies have been limited in scope. Some have analysed only one topic or one journal.

The present thematic meta-analysis is wider in scope to provide a larger and more representative picture of recent research trends in mass communication. This study analyses ten major mass communication journals during the decades of the 1980s and 1990s.

These journals were chosen based on circulation, acceptance rate, and blind review process as the most widely read and highly esteemed in the mass communication field. The twenty-year time period covered by this present study was chosen to provide a long enough span to observe trends and also because the last decade has not yet been examined in detail. This time period also enables us to evaluate predictions made by previous meta-analyses about the future of mass communication research, if one keeps in mind that our findings are limited to the major journals of our field, publications whose focus most likely changes more slowly than conference papers, newer journals, and possibly books and book chapters.

META-ANALYSES OF MASS COMMUNICATION RESEARCH

Previous meta-analyses of mass communication research have focused on the following topics. Qualitative versus Quantitative Methods, The emphasis on qualitative and quantitative research in mass communication journals has interested many researchers and scholars in general. Some studies have examined changes in methodology over time. Each has found an increase in the use of quantitative research.

Cooper, Potter, and Dupagne investigated the assumption that the amount of qualitative research has increased during the past decades. They studied eight journals during the 1965-1989 period. A systematic interval of three years was used to choose the sample from a population of twenty-five years. They did not find an expected increase in qualitative research. Instead, they found that qualitative research was actually more common in the late 1960s, but in the 1970s and 1980s quantitative research far exceeded it.

They argued that this finding did not mean that qualitative research was losing favour with researchers, but rather that the journals sampled might not have been ones that qualitative mass media researchers sought out, considering that many of the high circulation journals were still heavily quantitative in orientation during this time period.

Weaver, surveying trends in the field, urged more studies that combine qualitative and quantitative methods. Previous research has shown that very few such studies have been published.

In those studies that combined more than one method, the combinations tended to be quantitative. Weaver argued that there was an increase in research combining the two approaches in the 1980s. This trend was expected to continue. But subsequent studies have shown that qualitative research has not increased, at least not in high circulation communication journals. Their primary focus is still quantitative research, even though more researchers continue to attest to the larger role that qualitative research should be playing.

THEORETICAL FRAMEWORKS

Several reviews of mass communication research have focused on whether there was an explicit theoretical framework evident in the articles. Riffe and Freitag found that only a fourth of the articles employing content analysis included an explicit theoretical framework, and fewer than half of them had clearly stated hypotheses or research questions that guided the analysis. Overall, research in mass communication has been found lacking in theoretical development by this and other reviews.

MEDIUM

Print media have been the focus of many research studies. Weaver and Gray found that 56 per cent of the articles between 1955 and 1974 in Journalism

Quarterly dealt with print media. Electronic media or a combination of electronic and print media constituted 26 per cent.

They attributed this dominance to numerous historical articles on newspapers, magazines, and books. Other studies have also demonstrated the dominance of research on print media in mass communication journals. But these results were derived from only one journal-Journalism Quarterly. Since then the journal has widened its scope, and in 1995 it changed its name to Journalism and Mass Communication Quarterly.

One might ask today whether studies of print media still dominate. Television is the medium with the highest exposure among most groups in society. It is only logical that it will receive attention in proportion to its reach in society. There are newly discovered areas in television research that have drawn increased interest. In the past, visual aspects of television have not received a great deal of attention.

Television has mostly been studied in terms of its verbal messages (for theoretical and methodological reasons), but now there is an increased interest in studying visual images and how they interact with the verbal content of television to affect the audience. The Internet does not seem to have dethroned television yet as a focus for research, although there are increasing numbers of communication studies about the Internet.

FUNDING

Mass communication research has traditionally received less frequent funding than any of the other social sciences, according to studies by Weaver and Gray, and Zhi and Swiencicki. Weaver and Gray, studying the period from 1954 to 1978, found only one-fourth of the mass communication studies reported in Journalism Quarterly and Public Opinion Quarterly acknowledged funding, while the average funding rate for journals from the three disciplines of psychology, sociology, and political science was 55 per cent. Zhu and Swiencicki studied the 1983-1993 period for these two journals plus Journal of Communication, Journal of Broadcasting and Electronic Media, Critical Studies in Mass Communication, and Communication Research.

They found only 22 per cent of the sampled articles reported funding compared to 56 per cent in the other disciplines. In their analysis of two major journals from 1954 to 1978, Weaver and Gray found that research funding was evenly balanced among university, government, and private sources. This present study checks on this balance during the 1980s and 1990s.

METHOD

The objective of this present study is to investigate trends in published mass communication research during the decades of the 1980s and 1990s in ten major journals. We were particularly interested in the use of qualitative and quantitative methods, the presence of theoretical frameworks, the medium (or media) being studied, and acknowledgment of funding (its presence or lack of, and sources of).

SAMPLE

As mentioned earlier, many meta-analyses have focused on single journals, but generalizing from one journal to most journals in the field is questionable. Studying more than one journal allows for wider generalization. We have analysed mass communication research published in the twenty years between 1980 and 1999 in ten major mass communication journals in the United States. We have excluded book reviews, essays, and commentaries as well as articles not dealing with mass communication. "Research-in-brief" articles also were not included.

Major mass communication journals were defined as those that have a circulation of more than 1,500, employ a blind review process, and have a typical acceptance rate under 20 per cent. Based on these criteria, the selection was made from The Iowa Guide. Four of these journals-Journalism and Mass Communication Quarterly, Journal of Communication, Journal of Broadcasting and Electronic Media, and Critical Studies in Mass Communication-are the official publications on mass communication research of four major professional societies.

We realise that the results of this study are influenced by the sample used. From the outset, for example, excluding "research in brief" meant that a certain line of research published in the selected journals was not included in our sample. We excluded these reports because they rarely included information on many of our key variables. The choice of "major" or "big" journals also restricts the kind of research we analysed, but we thought that studying the more general and larger circulation journals (as opposed to the more narrowly focused and smaller circulation publications) would be the most representative of mass communication research since these journals likely reach more scholars in the field than the newer journals. The fact remains that our findings can only be generalized to these journals and that different results would be likely from a wider selection of journals and publications than we analysed.

For each journal, one issue was selected randomly to represent each year. Thus there are a total of 196 issues analysed in this study. A table of random numbers was used to make the issue selection for each journal. A range was set (from 1 to 4 if the journal was quarterly, or 1 to 6 if it was bi-monthly). A random starting point was chosen, and then the researchers moved down the table taking the first number that fell within the range. Twenty numbers were selected for each journal, each representing a year. A total of 889 research articles related to mass communication published in the ten journals between January 1980 and December 1999 were included in this analysis.

CODING INSTRUMENT

Variables coded for each article included the general method of research (qualitative, quantitative, or a mix of both), the data gathering procedure (survey, content analysis, etc.), the theory behind the study (if any), the source of funding, and the time period from which data were gathered. If the method by which the results were determined involved numerical or counting procedures and statistics were used to report data, the chapter was classified as quantitative. Quantitative research included mostly content analyses, surveys, and experiments.

Qualitative research involves being closely involved with the subjects to increase depth of understanding. It does not convert what is observed into numerical form in order to perform mathematical procedures. It often includes focus groups, direct observation, in-depth interviews, and case studies, as well as legal, policy, and historical research. If more than one data gathering procedure was used, the method was coded as a mixture of quantitative if all the methods were quantitative, a mixture of qualitative if all the methods were qualitative, or a combination of both qualitative and quantitative when both kinds of methods were used. For example, a survey in addition to in-depth interviews would be coded as a combination of qualitative and quantitative methods.

We also coded the communication medium studied. An article was classified as print if it dealt exclusively with print media (newspapers, magazines, trade journals). It was considered broadcast if it dealt with television and/or radio. When print and broadcast were both studied, the article was coded as a combination. Studies of the Internet were coded separately. Some studies that did not mention any particular medium were coded as "media in general." Finally, an "others" option included other mass media studies too infrequent to have their own categories. These included videotext, cinema, wire services, public relations, and video games, as well as non-media studies (such as studies of mass communication students or faculty). Theory was among the most difficult variables to code. We specifically looked for any theory mentioned. When no theory was specifically mentioned, we re-examined whether any theory was strongly implied but fell short of being mentioned. When more than one theory was mentioned, the dominant one was coded. When more than one seemed dominant, the first one mentioned was coded.

Funding source options included university, government, and private. More than one funding source could be checked for a single article; the category "combination" was included to be used for this situation. The funding status and funding source were coded based on the acknowledgment made by the author(s) in the text, footnotes, or the endnotes.

Study length was coded as an interval variable. It was later receded for ease of analysis. The categories created were (1) less than three months, (2) from more than three months to one year and (3) more than one year.

DATA COLLECTION

One mass communication doctoral student did the coding. An intercoder reliability test of a sample of 26 articles using Krippendorf's alpha showed 78 per cent agreement. The lowest agreement was over data gathering method (65 per cent) and the highest agreement was over the theory mentioned (100 per cent).

STATISTICS

Considering the exploratory nature of this study, the statistical significance level was set at.05 to minimize Type II errors (overlooking real relationships). The statistic most employed was the difference of proportions test, mainly to examine whether the changes over the decades were significant or not. These tests are usually two-tailed.

FINDINGS

Methods. It has been widely asserted and assumed that qualitative methods have re-emerged in mass communication research. This assumption is evident in U.S. mass communication programmes where the number of courses in qualitative methodologies appears to be growing. Contrary to expectations, however, qualitative research was not given as much attention as quantitative research in the 1980s in the 8 journals studied by Cooper, Potter, and Dupagne. They speculated that these journals might have been biased against publishing qualitative research, and that such research might have been published in other journals that were more qualitatively oriented. But their analysis included most of the leading journals with the largest circulations in the field. A reanalysis of the 1980s using our 10 journals (7 of which overlapped with those analysed by Cooper, Potter, and Dupagne), and an analysis of the 1990s, confirms their findings. The use of qualitative methods did not increase significantly during the twenty-year period we analysed. There was a slight increase of 4 per cent from the early 1980s to the late1990s. Even in the 1990s, non-qualitative studies clearly dominated in the 10 mass communication journals we analysed. Incorporating 1970s data from Cooper, Potter, and Dupagne, the gap between qualitative and quantitative research seems to have increased from the 1970s to the 1980s and then leveled off in the 1990s. The use of both methods jointly in single studies has been rare, especially in the 1980s and 1990s.

Experiments ranked third, nearly doubling in frequency from the early 1980s to the late 1990s. One reason that these three methods are used the most may be related to funding, considering that studies employing quantitative methods are more likely to have received funding than those not using such methods. Increased use of experiments is consistent with the rise of the cognitive approach that uses experiments as the main method of data gathering and also with an increase in funding of experimental research.

USE OF THEORY

The use of theory was not common, even for articles using quantitative methods. Of the 889 studies only 39 per cent referred to a theory (30.5 per cent specifically mentioned and 8.7 per cent implied). Most of these theories were cited in quantitative studies, especially surveys.

The theories most frequently mentioned were ones relating to uses and effects of media, and also that only three theories (Information Processing, Uses and Gratifications, and Media Construction of Social Reality) were cited in 10 per cent or more of the studies.

MEDIUM

The traditional broadcast and print media were most likely to be studied in leading mass communication research journals during the last two decades. Studies on broadcast exceeded studies on print in both decades. The overall difference of 13.5 per cent between the two areas is statistically significant.

Although we are now in the age of the Internet and the World Wide Web, this was not yet reflected in mass communication research published in major journals in the 1990s.

There was a slight increase from the 1980s to almost 7 per cent in the late 1990s, but overall studies about the Internet constituted only 2 per cent of all the articles we analysed. Almost all of these studies appeared in the1990s, when the Internet began to be considered a mass medium.

Broadcast research exceeded print research in all the five-year intervals studied. When broadcast research increased, print research decreased, and vice versa. Looking only at the first and last time periods, it is clear that broadcast research decreased about 10 per cent while print research remained at the same level.

The decrease in broadcast research seemed to be due mainly to an increase in research on the Internet and other media, and non-media studies.

FUNDING

For the two decades combined, only 254 or slightly more than one-fourth (28.6 per cent) of the published studies we analysed acknowledged receipt of financial support from an intramural or extramural source.

Weaver and Gray, studying funding between 1954 and 1978, found a similar pattern: only 26 per cent of their studies mentioned a funding source. This funding rate is also roughly comparable to the one found by Zhu and Swiencicki who studied mass communication research funding from 1983 to 1993. Overall, 22 per cent of their studies were funded. A clear trend can be detected from our data.

There has been a gradual decrease over the years in frequency of funding. While 36.2 per cent of all studies were funded in 1980-1984, this decreased significantly to 23.8 per cent in 1995-1999. Funding in the early 1980s for published studies was nearly evenly split between university, government, and private sources with no one source dominating, similar to Weaver and Gray's findings for the 1950s, 60s and 70s. They regarded this diversity in funding sources as healthy. But towards the late 1980s and early 1990s, we found government funding decreased proportionally with a small rebound in the late 1990s.

Private funding increased slightly in the late 1980s, but decreased notably in the 1990s, especially in the last half of the decade.

University funding increased steadily during the 1980s and 1990s, becoming by far the dominant funding source in the 1990s. The dominance in university funding can be regarded as a positive development because of the freedom of enquiry usually supported by academic institutions, but as Weaver noted, the relatively low level of funding provided by universities as compared with government and private sources also restricts the kind of research that can be done. We found no correlation between funding and the time period covered by a study. In other words, there was no significant difference in proportion of funded studies by time span of the study (less than three months, from three months to one year, or more than one year). But there was definitely a greater tendency for quantitative studies to receive funding.

DISCUSSION

This study sought to analyse and update trends in mass communication research published in ten leading journals during the past two decades, with special attention to whether the debate over approaches has resulted in changes in methods used, which media are most and least studied, how theory-guided the research is, which theories are most often relied upon, and whether funding levels and sources have changed.

One notable finding is the lack of any increase in qualitative research articles in the journals sampled and the continued emphasis on the funding of quantitative studies.

The reasons why qualitative research is not more prominent in major journals could be further investigated. Is this due to the perceived orientation of these journals or to the actual orientation of these journals? In other words, is there a "bias" among the major journal editors in favour of quantitative research or do qualitative researchers not submit to these journals because of a perceived bias, page length restrictions, or other reasons? These questions could be further examined in surveys of journal editors and qualitative researchers.

One of the limits of our findings is that using the article as the unit of analysis does not account for the space devoted to such articles. Qualitative research generally requires more pages to report than does quantitative. Thus we would expect journals that carry fewer articles to publish relatively more qualitative research per issue.

In the six journals with lower article frequency (they carried 12 per cent of total articles analysed), both methods of research are represented equally, while in the four journals with higher article frequency (they accounted for 88 per cent of the sampled articles) qualitative methods are significantly less likely to be used, confirming our expectation.

Because our sample of articles came mainly from the four journals that averaged more than three articles per issue, these articles are most likely to be shorter and thus to employ quantitative methods. These findings confirm the dominance of the quantitative social science research approach in major mass communication journals in the last two decades of the Twentieth Century. However, these generalizations can be applied only to the ten journals studied here.

Our findings may create the impression that relatively little qualitative research is conducted in the mass communication field, but it seems likely that more qualitative research is published in other more specialized (and lower circulation) journals, book chapters, monographs, and books. Our sample of journals did not include many of the journals that qualitative researchers typically read and publish in, although it did include some, such as Critical Studies in Mass Communication and Journalism and Mass Communication Monographs.

Another major finding of this analysis is the dominance of mass communication studies focused on traditional broadcast and print media, especially television, and newspapers. Will these media continue to dominate research as we enter further into the "Internet age"?

So far there has been only a slight decrease in traditional media research and a slight increase in mass communication research about the Internet. Some of the reasons may be the difficulty of conducting Internet studies, the slow acceptance of the Internet as a mass medium, the failure of the Internet to replace traditional media, and its fairly limited reach. Yet more research on new media is expected in the coming years, at least more than was evident in our sample of articles.

One indication of this is a recent analysis by Kim and Weaver of the index of Communication Abstracts from 1995 through 1999. This abstracting service includes studies broadly related to communication from more than 200 journals, as well as reports and books.

Kim and Weaver found that Internet-related publications increased rapidly from only ten in 1995 to 188 in 1999, an increase from 0.7 per cent to 9.5 per cent. In addition, some new online journals have emerged, such as Convergence and the Web Journal of Mass Communication Research, and much research about the Internet is published in such journals as Journal of Computer Mediated

Communication and New Media and Society. Theoretical development is probably the main consideration in evaluating the disciplinary status of the field. As our field grows in scope and complexity, the pressure for theoretical integration increases. It seems that scholars in the field should be developing and testing theories to explain the process and effects of mass communication. However, that was not widely evident in our sample.

Overall only 39 per cent of the studies referred to any theory, and most of these references were to previously existing theories. DeFleur's analysis of the state of theory building seems to apply to our results. Most of the articles we analysed seemed to be one-shot studies without a theoretical trail. This information is not news to mass communication researchers. A 1991 survey of major scholars in the field of communication revealed that only 37 per cent of them thought theoretical development of the field was either good or very good.

Funding is of central importance to any field of research. However, the data we have about funding for mass communication research is limited, as few studies have empirically investigated this issue, which almost all communication scholars must face. While mass communication has been growing in terms of more and new media channels, a larger labour force, and more colleges offering mass communication education, there has been no corresponding increase in the proportion of funded research. This study finds that overall funding for mass communication remains low; there has been a steady decline in proportions of funded research from the early 1980s to the late 1990s, at least that research published in major journals analysed in this study.

In addition, a balance between university, government, and private funding sources was no longer evident in the 1990s, when the university became the main source of funding. This has one advantage: unlike government and private sectors, the university typically does not have an agenda favoring one sort of research more than another. Thus, theoretical as well as applied research can be pursued, but university funding tends to be lower in actual dollars than that from private and government sources. The decline of government support for mass communication studies may be due to government funding agencies not recognizing mass communication as an academic discipline. Mass communication scholars have a long way to go before being fully recognized by funding sources within the government. The decline in private funding is harder to explain. The increase in university funding may imply that within the university, mass communication is becoming more accepted as a legitimate field. More systematic investigation as to the cause of the changes in funding patterns would be useful.

Contrary to Berelson's 1959 declaration that the field of mass communication research was "withering away,"51 the field has actually grown and blossomed in the five decades that have followed. This is apparent from the proliferation of communication schools, doctoral programmes, associations and divisions in the associations, graduate student enrollment, journals, and books.

In spite of such growth, the findings of this review of mass communication research published in ten leading journals suggest considerable stability in methods, media, and funding patterns during the 1980s and 1990s, as compared with the previous two or three decades. There were some changes in methods and in the theories most and least studied, but the general picture was one of more stability than change, at least in these major journals.

It must be remembered, however, that this observation does not include the dozens of conference papers, books, book chapters, and articles in newer, less widely circulated journals. There seems to be much change already going on in the mass communication field, but not yet in the major journals of the field.

Depending on one's view of the value of continuity and change, this can be interpreted as positive or negative. It does seem likely, however, given the dramatic changes in communication media and scholarship during the past decade, that research in the major journals in mass communication will also change in the coming decade.

This study examined one issue from each of the twenty years of investigation for each of the ten journals selected. Thus while this research of mass communication research trends is one of the most ambitious so far in terms of population studied and variables examined, we are aware that the sample may be skewed in favour of quantitative research. A larger sample that includes different journals and books (and even conference research papers) would likely yield different results. We leave that formidable task to others to explore.

SHAPES OF MASS MEDIA

Broadcast: Television and radio programmes are distributed through radio broadcasting in excess of frequency bands that are highly regulated by the Federal Communications Commission. Such regulation comprises determination of the width of the bands, range, licensing, kinds of receivers and transmitters used, and acceptable content.

Cable programmes are often broadcast simultaneously with radio and television programmes, but have a more limited audience. By coding signals and having a cable converter box in houses, cable also enables subscription-based channels and pay-per-view services.

A broadcasting organisation may broadcast many programmes at the similar time, through many channels (frequencies), for instance BBC One and Two. On the other hand, two or more organisations may share a channel and each use it throughout a fixed part of the day. Digital radio and digital television may also transmit multiplexed programming, with many channels compressed into one ensemble.

When broadcasting is done via the Internet the term web casting is often used. In 2004 a new phenomenon occurred when a number of technologies combined to produce pod casting. Pod casting is an asynchronous broadcast/narrowcast medium, with one of the main proponents being Adam Curry and his associates the Pod show.

Film: 'Film' encompasses motion pictures as individual projects, as well as the field in common. The name comes from the photographic film (also described film stock), historically the primary medium for recording, and displaying motion pictures. Several other conditions exist—*motion pictures* (or presently *pictures* and "picture"), *the silver screen*, *photoplays*, *the cinema*, *picture shows*, *flicks*—and commonly *movies*.

Films are produced by recording people and objects with cameras, or by creating them by animation techniques and/or special effects. They comprise a series of individual frames, but when these images are shown rapidly in succession, the illusion of motion is given to the viewer. Flickering flanked by frames is not seen due to an effect recognized as persistence of vision—whereby the eye retains a visual image for a fraction of a second after the source has been removed. Also of relevance is what causes the perception of motion; a psychological effect recognized as beta movement.

Film is measured by several to be a significant art form; films entertain, educate, enlighten, and inspire audiences. Any film can become a worldwide attraction, especially with the addition of dubbing or subtitles that translate the film message. Films are also relics created by specific cultures, which reflect those cultures, and, in turn, affect them.

Video Games: A video game is a computer-controlled game where a video display such as a monitor or television is the primary feedback device. The term "computer game" also comprises games which display only text (and which can so theoretically be played on a teletypewriter) or which use other methods, such as sound or vibration, as their primary feedback device, but there are extremely few new games in these categories. There always necessity also be some sort of input device, usually in the form of button/joystick combinations (on arcade games), a keyboard and mouse/trackball combination (computer games), or a controller (console games), or a combination of any of the above. Also, more esoteric devices have been used for input. Usually there are rules and goals, but in more open-ended games the player may be free to do whatever they like within the confines of the virtual universe.

In general usage, a "computer game", or a "PC game" refers to a game that is played on a personal computer. "Console game" refers to one that is played on a device specifically intended for the use of such, while interfacing with an average television set. "Arcade game" refers to a game intended to be played in an establishment in which patrons pay to play on a per-use foundation. "Video game" (or "videogame") has evolved into a catchall phrase that encompasses the aforementioned beside with any game made for any other device, including, but not limited to, mobile phones, PDAs, advanced calculators, etc.

Audio Recording and Reproduction: Sound recording and reproduction is the electrical or mechanical re-creation and/or amplification of sound, often as music. This involves the use of audio equipment such as microphones, recording devices, and loudspeakers. From early beginnings with the invention of the phonograph by purely mechanical techniques, the field has advanced with the invention of electrical recording, the mass manufacture of the 78 record, the magnetic wire recorder followed by the tape recorder, the vinyl LP record. The invention of the compact cassette in the 1960s, followed by Sony's Walkman, gave a major boost to the mass sharing of music recordings, and the invention of digital recording and the compact disc in 1983 brought huge improvements in ruggedness and quality. The mainly recent growths have been in digital audio players.

An album is a collection of related audio recordings, released jointly to the public, usually commercially. The term record album originated from the information that 78 RPM Phonograph disc records were kept jointly in a book resembling a photo album. The first collection of records to be described an "album" was Tchaikovsky's *Nutcracker Suite*, release in April 1909 as a four-disc set by Odeon records. It retailed for 16 shillings—in relation to the £15 in contemporary currency.

A music video (also promo) is a short film or video that accompanies a complete piece of music, mainly commonly a song. Contemporary music videos were primarily made and used as a marketing device planned to promote the sale of music recordings. Although the origins of music videos go back much further, they came into their own in the 1980s, when Music Television's format was based on them. In the 1980s, the term "rock video" was often used to describe this form of entertainment, although the term has fallen into disuse.

Music videos can accommodate all styles of filmmaking, including animation, live action films, documentaries, and non-narrative, abstract film.

Internet: The Internet (also recognized basically as "the Net" or less precisely as "the Web") is a more interactive medium of mass media, and can be briefly described as "a network of networks". Specifically, it is the worldwide, publicly accessible network of interconnected computer networks that transmit data by packet switching by the average Internet Protocol (IP). It consists of millions of smaller domestic, academic, business, and governmental networks, which jointly carry several information and services, such as e-mail, online chat, file transfer, and the interlinked web pages and other documents of the World Wide Web.

Contrary to some general usage, the Internet and the World Wide Web are not synonymous: the Internet is the system of interconnected *computer networks*, connected by copper wires, fibre-optic cables, wireless connections, etc.; the Web is the contents, or the interconnected *documents*, connected by hyperlinks and URLs.

Towards the end of the 20th century, the advent of the World Wide Web marked the first era in which mainly individuals could have a means of exposure on a level comparable to that of mass media. Anyone with a web location has the potential to address a global audience, although serving to high stages of web traffic is still relatively expensive. It is possible that the rise of peer-to-peer technologies may have begun the procedure of creation the cost of bandwidth manageable. Although a vast amount of information, imagery, and commentary (*i.e.*, "content") has been made accessible, it is often hard to determine the authenticity and reliability of information contained in web pages (in several cases, self-published). The invention of the Internet has also allowed breaking news stories to reach approximately the globe within minutes. This rapid growth of instantaneous, decentralized communication is often deemed likely to change mass media and its connection to society.

"Cross-media" means the thought of distributing the similar message through dissimilar media channels. A similar thought is expressed in the news industry as "convergence". Several authors understand cross-media publishing to be the skill to publish in both print and on the web without manual conversion effort. A rising number of wireless devices with mutually incompatible data and screen formats create it even more hard to achieve the objective "make once, publish several".

The Internet is quickly becoming the centre of mass media. Everything is becoming accessible via the internet. Instead of picking up a newspaper, or watching the 10 o'clock news, people can log onto the internet to get the news they want, when they want it. For instance, several workers listen to the radio through the Internet while sitting at their desk.

Even the education system relies on the Internet. Teachers can get in touch with the whole class by sending one e-mail. They may have web pages where students can get another copy of the class outline or assignments. Some classes have class blogs in which students are required to post weekly, with students graded on their contributions.

Blogs (Web Logs): Blogging, too, has become a pervasive form of media. A blog is a web site, usually maintained by an individual, with regular entries of commentary, descriptions of events, or interactive media such as images or video. Entries are commonly displayed in reverse chronological order, with mainly recent posts shown on top. Several blogs give commentary or news on a scrupulous subject; others function as more personal online diaries. A typical blog combines text, images and other graphics, and links to other blogs, web pages, and related media. The skill for readers to leave comments in an interactive format is a significant part of several blogs. Mainly blogs are primarily textual, although some focus on art (art log), photographs (photo log), sketchblog, videos (vlog), music (MP3 blog), audio (pod casting) are part of a wider network of social media. Microblogging is another kind of blogging which consists of blogs with extremely short posts.

RSS Feeds: RSS is a format for syndicating news and the content of news-like sites, including major news sites like Wired, news-oriented society sites like Slashdot, and personal blogs. It is a family of Web feed formats used to publish regularly updated content such as blog entries, news headlines, and pod casts. An RSS document (which is described a "feed" or "web feed" or "channel") contains either a summary of content from an associated web location or the full text. RSS creates it possible for people to stay up with web sites in an automated manner that can be piped into special programmes or filtered displays.

Pod Cast: A pod cast is a series of digital-media files which are distributed in excess of the Internet by syndication feeds for playback on portable media players and computers. The term pod cast, like broadcast, can refer either to the series of content itself or to the method by which it is syndicated; the latter is also described pod casting. The host or author of a pod cast is often described a pod caster.

Mobile: Mobile phones were introduced in Japan in 1979 but became a mass media only in 1998 when the first downloadable ringing tones were introduced in Finland. Soon mainly shapes of media content were introduced on mobile phones, and today the total value of media consumed on mobile towers in excess of that of internet content, and was worth in excess of 31 billion dollars in 2007. The mobile media content comprises in excess of 8 billion dollars worth of mobile music (ringing tones, ring back tones, true tones, MP3 files, karaoke, music videos, music streaming services, etc.); in excess of 5 billion dollars worth of mobile gaming; and several news, entertainment and advertising services. In Japan mobile phone books are so popular that five of the ten best-selling printed books were originally released as mobile phone books.

Similar to the internet, mobile is also an interactive media, but has distant wider reach, with 3.3 billion mobile phone users at the end of 2007 to 1.3 billion internet users. Like e-mail on the internet, the top application on mobile is also a personal messaging service, but SMS text messaging is used by in excess of 2.4 billion people.

Practically all internet services and applications exist or have similar cousins on mobile, from search to multiplayer games to virtual worlds to blogs. Mobile has many unique benefits which several mobile media pundits claim create mobile a more powerful media than either TV or the internet, starting with mobile being permanently accepted and always linked. Mobile has the best audience accuracy and is the only mass media with a built-in payment channel accessible to every user without any credit cards or PayPal accounts or even an age limit. Mobile is often described the 7th Mass Medium and either the fourth screen (if counting cinema, TV and PC screens) or the third screen (counting only TV and PC).

Print Media

Book: A book is a collection of sheets of paper, parchment or other material with a piece of text written on them, bound jointly beside one edge within covers. A book is also a literary work or a main division of such a work. A book produced in electronic format is recognized as an e-book.

Magazine: A magazine is a periodical publication containing a diversity of articles, usually financed by advertising and/or purchase by readers.

Magazines are typically published weekly, biweekly, monthly, bimonthly, or quarterly, with a date on the cover that is in advance of the date it is actually published. They are often printed in colour on coated paper, and are bound with a soft cover.

Magazines fall into two broad categories: consumer magazines and business magazines. In practice, magazines are a subset of periodicals, separate from those periodicals produced by scientific, artistic, academic or special interest publishers which are subscription-only, more expensive, narrowly limited in circulation, and often have little or no advertising.

Magazines can be classified as:

- Common interest magazines (*e.g.*, Frontline, India Today, The Week, The Sunday Times, etc.),
- Special interest magazines (women's, sports, business, scuba diving, etc.).

Newspaper: A newspaper is a publication containing news and information and advertising, usually printed on low-cost paper described newsprint. It may be common or special interest, mainly often published daily or weekly. The first printed newspaper was published in 1605, and the form has thrived even in the face of competition from technologies such as radio and television. Recent growths on the Internet are posing major threats to its business model, though. Paid circulation is declining in mainly countries, and advertising revenue, which creates up the bulk of a newspaper's income, is shifting from print to online; some commentators, nevertheless, point out that historically new media such as radio and television did not entirely supplant existing.

Outdoor Media: Outdoor media is a form of mass media which comprises billboards, signs, placards placed inside and outside of commercial structures/ objects like shops/buses, flying billboards (signs in tow of airplanes), blimps, and skywriting. Several commercial advertisers use this form of mass media when advertising in sports stadiums. Tobacco and alcohol manufacturers used billboards and other outdoor media extensively. In a 1994 Chicago-based revise,

Diana Hackbarth and her colleagues revealed how tobacco- and alcohol-based billboards were concentrated in poor neighbourhoods. In other urban centres, alcohol and tobacco billboards were much more concentrated in African-American neighbourhoods than in white neighbourhoods.

Purposes: Mass media encompasses much more than presently news, although it is sometimes misunderstood in this method. It can be used for several purposes:

- Advocacy, both for business and social concerns. This can contain advertising, marketing, propaganda, public dealings, and political communication.
- Entertainment, traditionally through performances of acting, music, sports, and TV shows beside with light reading; since the late 20th century also through video and computer games.
- Public service announcements and emergency alerts (that can be used as political device to communicate propaganda to the public).

MASS MEDIA

The mass media are diversified media technologies that are planned to reach a big audience by mass communication. Broadcast media (also recognized as electronic media) transmit their information electronically and comprise television, radio, film, movies, CDs, DVDs, and other devices such as cameras and video consoles. Alternatively, print media use a physical substance as a means of sending their information, such as a newspaper, magazines, comics, books, brochures, newsletters, leaflets, and pamphlets. The organizations that manage these technologies, such as television stations or publishing companies, are also recognized as the mass media. Internet media is able to achieve mass media status in its own right, due to the several mass media services it gives, such as e-mail, web sites, Internet, and television. For this cause, several mass media outlets have an attendance on the web, by such things as having TV ads that link to a web site, or having games in their sites to entice gamers to visit their web site. In this method, they can utilize the easy accessibility that the Internet has, and the outreach that Internet affords, as information can easily be broadcast to several dissimilar regions of the world simultaneously and cost-efficiently. Outdoor media is a form of mass media that comprises billboards, signs, placards placed inside and outside of commercial structures and objects like shops and buses, flying billboards (signs in tow of airplanes), blimps, and skywriting. Public speaking and event organizing can also be measured as shapes of mass media.

Issues with Definition: In the late 20th Century, mass media could be classified into eight mass media industries: books, newspapers, magazines, recordings, radio, movies, television, and the internet. With the explosion of digital communication technology in the late 20th and early 21st centuries, the question of what shapes of media should be classified as "mass media" has become more prominent. For instance, it is controversial whether to contain cell phones, video games, and computer games (such as MMORPGs) in the definition. In the 2000s, a classification described the "seven mass media" became popular. In order of introduction, they are:

1. Print (books, pamphlets, newspapers, magazines, etc.) from the late 15th century,
2. Recordings (gramophone records, magnetic tapes, cassettes, cartridges, CDs, DVDs) from the late 19th century,
3. Cinema from in relation to the 1900,
4. Radio from in relation to the 1910,
5. Television from in relation to the 1950,
6. Internet from in relation to the 1990,
7. Mobile phones from in relation to the 2000.

Each mass media has its own content kinds, its own creative artists and technicians, and its own business models. For instance, the Internet comprises web sites, blogs, pod casts, and several other technologies built on top of the common sharing network. The sixth and seventh media, internet and mobile, are often described collectively as digital media; and the fourth and fifth, radio and TV, as broadcast media. Some argue that video games have urbanized into a separate mass form of media.

While a telephone is a two method communication device, mass media refers to medium which can communicate a message to a big group, often simultaneously. Though, contemporary cell phones are no longer a single use device. Mainly cell phones are equipped with internet access and capable of connecting to the web which itself a mass medium. A question arises of whether this creates cell phones a mass medium or basically a device used to access a mass medium (the internet). There is currently a system where marketers and advertisers are able to tap into satellites, and broadcast commercials and advertisements directly to cell phones, unsolicited by the phone's user. This transmission of mass advertising to millions of people is a form of mass communication.

Video games may also be evolving into a mass medium. Video games convey the similar messages and ideologies to all their users. Users sometimes share the experience with each other by playing online. Excluding the internet though, it is questionable whether players of video games are sharing a general experience when they play the game separately. It is possible to talk about in great detail the events of a video game with a friend you have never played with because the experience was identical to you both. The question is if this is then a form of mass communication.

Massively multiplayer online role-playing games (MMORPGs) such as Run escape give a general gaming experience to millions of users throughout the globe. It is arguable that the users are getting the similar message, *i.e.*, the game is mass communicating the similar messages to the several players.

Features: Five features of mass communication have been recognized by Cambridge University's John Thompson:

- "[C]omprises both technological and institutional methods of manufacture and sharing" This is apparent throughout the history of the media, from print to the Internet, each appropriate for commercial utility.
- Involves the "commodification of symbolic shapes", as the manufacture of materials relies on its skill to manufacture and sell big quantities of the work. Presently as radio stations rely on its time sold to advertisements, newspapers rely for the similar reasons on its space.
- "[S]eparate contexts flanked by the manufacture and reception of information"
- Its "reach to those 'distant removed' in time and space, in comparison to the producers".
- "[I]nformation sharing" - a "one to several" form of communication, whereby products are mass produced and disseminated to a great quantity of audiences.

Mass vs. Mainstream: "Mass media" is sometimes used as a synonym for "mainstream media", which is distinguished from alternative media by the content and point of view. Alternative media are also "mass media" outlets in the sense of by technology capable of reaching several people, even if the audience is often smaller than the mainstream. In general usage, the term "mass" denotes not that a given number of individuals receives the products, but rather that the products are accessible in principle to a plurality of recipients.

Mass vs. Local: Mass media is distinguished from local media by the notion that whilst the former aims to reach a extremely big market such as the whole population of a country, the latter broadcasts to a much smaller population and area, and usually focuses on local news rather than global events. A third kind of media, speciality media, gives for specific demographics, such as speciality channels on TV (sports channels, porn channels, etc.).

These definitions are not set in stone, and it is possible for a media outlet to be promoted in status from a local media outlet to a global media outlet. Some local media, which takes an interest in state or provincial news, can rise to prominence due to their investigative journalism, and to the local region's preference of updates in national politics rather than local news. The Guardian, formerly recognized as the Manchester Guardian is an instance of one such media outlet. Once a local daily newspaper, The Guardian is currently a nationally respected paper.

METACOMMUNICATIVE COMPETENCE

Metacommunicative competence is the ability to intervene (in a guiding or constructively controlling way) within difficult conversations and to correct communication problems by utilizing the different ways of practical communication:

- *Verbal communication*: By words or their meaning
- *Paraverbal communication*: Loudness of speaking, manner of speaking, when keeping silent, meaning of interrupting or interfering the conversation
- *Non-verbal communication*: Body language (facial expression, eye contact, gestures), messages without words
- *Extraverbal communication*: Time, place, context, orientation towards target groups, tactile (feeling by touching) and olfactory (smelling) aspects.

Within the metacommunicative competence the aforementioned ways of communication can be used in a balanced and therefore credible, authentic way as well as simultaneously observed (Meta-analysis), if necessary corrected and adapted to an evolvement, a new influence or a new situation.

When metacommunicating, you are trying to constructively control situation. Within metacommunicative competence you are trying to find a way of analysing conversations to avoid and correct problems. Many author's have come up with theories that help to do the same things and correct communication problems, such as David Morley's, "Communication", A revised vocabulary of culture and society.

In Morley's essay he states that, "Communication refers to the activity of imparting, or transmitting messages containing, information, ideas, or knowledge is known as interpersonal communication or the idea of conversation." This relates back to metacommunication because you need to be able to anaylaze the content of the communication process. When communicating we have two models we use. These models are called standard or transmission and constructionist. It's easier to think of these models like the standard or transmission, just sending and receiving messages, and constructionist, as the screening process, how you communicate is actually determining what the message is. When metacommunicating you are basically using the constructionist model of communication, the screening process, to screen out all the messages that could possibly be conveyed during communication and using that to figure out what the message being conveyed to you actually is. In Daniel Chandler's essay, "The Transmission Model of Communication", he states "that there is no allowance for interpretation, differing purposes, unequal power relations, and situational context", In reality there must always be room for this and within metacommunicative competence, you learn how and when this can be a really effective way to do so.

SEMIOTICS

Semiotics, also called semiotic studies or semiology, is the study of sign processes (semiosis), or signification and communication, signs and symbols, and is usually divided into three branches:

- *Semantics:* Relation between signs and the things to which they refer; their *denotata*
- *Syntactics:* Relations among signs in formal structures
- *Pragmatics:* Relation between signs and their effects on those (people) who use them

Semiotics is frequently seen as having important anthropological dimensions; for example, Umberto Eco proposes that every cultural phenomenon can be studied as communication. However, some semioticians focus on the logical dimensions of the science.

They examine areas belonging also to the natural sciences – such as how organisms make predictions about, and adapt to, their semiotic niche in the world. In general, semiotic theories take *signs* or sign systems as their object of study: the communication of information in living organisms is covered in biosemiotics or zoosemiosis.

Syntactics is the branch of semiotics that deals with the formal properties of signs and symbols. More precisely, syntactics deals with the "rules that govern how words are combined to form phrases and sentences." Charles Morris adds that semantics deals with the relation of signs to their designata and the objects which they may or do denote; and, pragmatics deals with the biotic aspects of semiosis, that is, with all the psychological, biological, and sociological phenomena which occur in the functioning of signs.

TERMINOLOGY

The term, which was spelled *semiotics* (Greek: *semeiotikos*, an interpreter of signs), was first used in English by Henry Stubbes (1670) in a very precise sense to denote the branch of medical science relating to the interpretation of signs.

All that can fall within the compass of human understanding, being either, first, the nature of things, as they are in themselves, their relations, and their manner of operation: or, secondly, that which man himself ought to do, as a rational and voluntary agent, for the attainment of any end, especially happiness: or, thirdly, the ways and means whereby the knowledge of both the one and the other of these is attained and communicated; I think science may be divided properly into these three sorts.—*Locke, 1823/1963.*

Locke then elaborates on the nature of this third category, naming it (*Semeiotike*) and explaining it as "the doctrine of signs" in the following terms: Nor is there any thing to be relied upon in Physick, but an exact knowledge of medicinal physiology (founded on observation, not principles), semiotics, method of curing, and tried (not excogitated, not commanding) medicines. In the nineteenth century, Charles Sanders Peirce defined what he termed "semiotic" (which he sometimes spelt as "semeiotic") as the "quasi-necessary, or formal doctrine of signs", which abstracts "what must be the characters of all signs used by...an intelligence capable of learning by experience", and which is philosophical logic pursued in terms of signs and sign processes. Charles Morris followed Peirce in using the term "semiotic" and in extending the discipline beyond human communication to animal learning and use of signals.

Ferdinand de Saussure, however, viewed the most important area within semiotics as belonging to the social sciences: It is... possible to conceive of a science which studies the role of signs as part of social life. It would form part of social psychology, and hence of general psychology. We shall call it semiology (from the Greek someone, 'sign'). It would investigate the nature of signs and the laws governing them. Since it does not yet exist, one cannot say for certain that it will exist. But it has a right to exist, a place ready for it in advance. Linguistics is only one branch of this general science.

FORMULATIONS

Semioticians classify signs or sign systems in relation to the way they are transmitted. This process of carrying meaning depends on the use of codes that may be the individual sounds or letters that humans use to form words, the body movements they make to show attitude or emotion, or even something as general as the clothes they wear. To coin a word to refer to a *thing*, the community must agree on a simple meaning (a denotative meaning) within their language. But that word can transmit that meaning only within the language's grammatical structures and codes. Codes also represent the values of the culture, and are able to add new shades of connotation to every aspect of life.

To explain the relationship between semiotics and communication studies, communication is defined as the process of transferring data from a source to a receiver.

Hence, communication theorists construct models based on codes, media, and contexts to explain the biology, psychology, and mechanics involved. Both disciplines also recognize that the technical process cannot be separated from the fact that the receiver must decode the data, *i.e.*, be able to distinguish the data as salient and make meaning out of it.

This implies that there is a necessary overlap between semiotics and communication. Indeed, many of the concepts are shared, although in each field the emphasis is different. In *Messages and Meanings: An Introduction to Semiotics*, Marcel Danesi (1994) suggested that semioticians' priorities were to study signification first and communication second. A more extreme view is offered by Jean-Jacques Nattiez (1987; trans. 1990), who, as a musicologist, considered the theoretical study of communication irrelevant to his application of semiotics. Semiotics differs from linguistics in that it generalizes the definition of a sign to encompass signs in any medium or sensory modality. Thus it broadens the range of sign systems and sign relations, and extends the definition of language in what amounts to its widest analogical or metaphorical sense. Peirce's definition of the term "semiotic" as the study of necessary features of signs also has the effect of distinguishing the discipline from linguistics as the study of contingent features that the world's languages happen to have acquired in the course of human evolution.

Perhaps more difficult is the distinction between semiotics and the philosophy of language. In a sense, the difference is a difference of traditions more than a difference of subjects. Different authors have called themselves "philosopher of language" or "semiotician". This difference does *not* match the separation between analytic and continental philosophy. On a closer look, there may be found some differences regarding subjects. Philosophy of language pays more attention to natural languages or to languages in general, while semiotics is deeply concerned about non-linguistic signification. Philosophy of language also bears a stronger connection to linguistics, while semiotics is closer to some of the humanities (including literary theory) and to cultural anthropology.

COMMUNICATION THEORY FRAMEWORK

It is helpful to examine communication and communication theory through one of the following viewpoints:

- Mechanistic: This view considers communication as a perfect transaction of a message from the sender to the receiver.
- Psychological: This view considers communication as the act of sending a message to a receiver, and the feelings and thoughts of the receiver upon interpreting the message.
- Social Constructionist (Symbolic Interactionist): This view considers communication to be the product of the interactsnts sharing and creating meaning. The Constructionist View can also be defined as, how you say something determines what the message is. The Constructionist View assumes that "truth" and "ideas" are constructed or invented through the social process of communication. Robert T. Craig saw the Constructionist View or the constitutive view as it's called in his article, as "...an ongoing process that symbolically forms and re-forms our personal identities." The other view of communication, the Transmission Model, sees communication as robotic and computer-like. The Transmission Model sees communication as a way of sending or receiving messages and the

perfection of that. But, the Constructionist View sees communications as, "...in human life, info does not behave as simply as bits in an electronic stream. In human life, information flow is far more like an electric current running from one landmine to another". The Constructionist View is a more realistic view of communication because it involves the interacting of human beings and the free sharing of thoughts and ideas. Daniel Chandler looks to prove that the Transmission Model is a lesser way of communicating by saying "The transmission model is not merely a gross over-simplification but a dangerously misleading representation of the nature of human communication". Humans do not communicate simply as computers or robots so that's why it's essential to truly understand the Constructionist View of Communication well. We do not simply send facts and data to one another, but we take facts and data and they acquire meaning through the process of communication, or through interaction with others.

- Systemic: This view considers communication to be the new messages created via "through-put", or what happens as the message is being interpreted and re-interpreted as it travels through people.
- Critical: This view considers communication as a source of power and oppression of individuals and social groups.

Inspection of a particular theory on this level will provide a framework on the nature of communication as seen within the confines of that theory.

Theories can also be studied and organized according to the ontological, epistemological, and axiological framework imposed by the theorist.

Ontology essentially poses the question of what, exactly, it is the theorist is examining. One must consider the very nature of reality. The answer usually falls in one of three realms depending on whether the theorist sees the phenomena through the lens of a realist, nominalist, or social constructionist.

Realist perspective views the world objectively, believing that there is a world outside of our own experience and cognitions. Nominalists see the world subjectively, claiming that everything outside of one's cognitions is simply names and labels. Social constructionists straddle the fence between objective and subjective reality, claiming that reality is what we create together.

Epistemology is an examination of how the theorist studies the chosen phenomena. In studying epistemology, particularly from a positivist perspective, objective knowledge is said to be the result of a systematic look at the causal relationships of phenomena. This knowledge is usually attained through use of the scientific method.

Scholars often think that empirical evidence collected in an objective manner is most likely to reflect truth in the findings. Theories of this ilk are usually created to predict a phenomenon. Subjective theory holds that understanding is based on situated knowledge, typically found using interpretative methodology such as ethnography and also interviews. Subjective theories are typically developed to explain or understand phenomena in the social world.

Axiology is concerned with what values drive a theorist to develop a theory. Theorists must be mindful of potential biases so that they will not influence or skew their findings.

MAPPING THE THEORETICAL LANDSCAPE

A discipline gets defined in large part by its theoretical structure. Communication studies often borrow theories from other social sciences. This theoretical variation makes it difficult to come to terms with the field as a whole. That said, some common taxonomies exist that serve to divide up the range of communication research. Two common mappings involve contexts and assumptions.

CONTEXTS

Many authors and researchers divide communication by what they sometimes called "contexts" or "levels", but which more often represent institutional histories. The study of communication in the US, while occurring within departments of psychology, sociology, linguistics, and anthropology (among others), generally developed from schools of rhetoric and from schools of journalism. While many of these have become "departments of communication", they often retain their historical roots, adhering largely to theories from speech communication in the former case, and from mass media in the latter.

The great divide between speech communication and mass communication becomes complicated by a number of smaller sub-areas of communication research, including intercultural and international communication, small group communication, communication technology, policy and legal studies of communication, telecommunication, and work done under a variety of other labels. Some of these departments take a largely social-scientific perspective, others tend more heavily towards the humanities, and still others gear themselves more towards production and professional preparation. These "levels" of communication provide some way of grouping communication theories, but inevitably, some theories and concepts leak from one area to another, or fail to find a home at all.

FUNCTIONS OF THE MASS MEDIA

Though there are two main functions of mass communication, which are overt and latent functions of communication, six specific functions of the mass media could be identified here.

These are:

1. Surveiance of the environment. This is the collection and distribution of information within and outside a particular environment. The information flow is necessary for unity and coherence if we live in the society of collectivity;
2. Correlation of parts of the society. This includes the interpretation of the information, the prescription of conduct and, the comment on social value;
3. Transmission of social heritage. By communicating information through the mass media we are transmitting social and cultural values, which aim at sustaining the society;
4. Educating the masses. Education on the policies of governments and on the rights and responsibilities could be carried out through the mass media.
5. Entertainment function. The mass media also entertain the public by providing emotional relaxation, intrinsic and cultural enjoyment (*i.e.* provision of momentary escape from problems) and killing boredom; and
6. Mobilization function. This function of the mass media is very important to developing communities everywhere. It seeks to bring the people together and helps to advance national development.

It could be seen from the foregoing functions that the mass media provide information and education, personal identity, entertainment and most importantly integration and social interaction by giving insight into the circumstances of others as well as by helping with the development of social empathy.

DANGER

The advent of press freedom has given rise to unprecedented abuse of the mass media by unscrupulous mass communicators and authoritarian leaders in society. There is proliferation of community newspapers and FM radio stations in Ghana and the Ghanaian communities around the world. There is also access to internet and the SIL forum on the popular ghanaweb site which bring Ghanaians together everyday by the magic of the electronic media. While this development should be welcomed and appreciated in the light of healthy competition among ethnic media practitioners there is also the inherent danger of dividing and destroying the very communities these mass communicators seek to help develop!

The path of sycophancy, bootlicking, blackmailing of individuals and arrogance of political affiliation lies close to the good functions of the mass media discussed above and must be avoided if the role of the media in our community development is to be made meaningful.

SUGGESTIONS

The mass media must serve essential functions in the society by accepting and fulfilling certain obligations to the society. These obligations are mainly to be met by setting high professional standards of informativeness, truth, accuracy, objectivity and balance. In accepting and applying these obligations the elements of the mass media should be self-regulating within the framework of law and established institutions. They should therefore avoid whatever might lead to crime, violence or civil disorder or give offence to any group of people in the society because of their faith or ethnicity. The media as a whole should be pluralistic and reflect the diversity of their society by giving access to various points of views and to rights of reply.

THE MASS MEDIA IN INDIA

Mass media in India, especially news media, are undergoing significant changes in the current liberalised environment. To understand these changes, it is useful to examine the road traversed so far. This requires looking at media in two phases of India's history - pre-colonial and post-colonial. Each medium has taken its own evolutionary path.

Compared with many other developing countries, the Indian press has flourished since independence and exercises a large degree of independence. In 2001, India had 45,974 newspapers, including 5364 daily newspapers published in over 100 languages. The largest number of newspapers were published in Hindi (20,589), followed by English (7,596), Marathi (2,943), Urdu (2,906), Bengali (2,741), Gujarati (2,215), Tamil (2,119), Kannada (1,816), Malayalam(1,505) and Telugu (1,289). The Hindi daily press has a circulation of over 23 million copies, followed by English with over 8 million copies. There are several major publishing groups in India, the most prominent among them being the Times of India Group, the Indian Express Group, the Hindustan Times Group, The Hindu group, the Anandabazar Patrika Group, the MalayalaManorama Group (Malayala Manorama is the largest circulated daily newspaper in India), the Sahara group, the Bhaskar group, and the Jagran group. India has more than forty domestic news agencies. The Express News Service, the Press Trust of India, and the United News of India are among the major news agencies.

Colonial Journalism

William Bolts, an ex-employee of the British East India Company attempted to start the first newspaper in India in 1776. Bolts had to beat a retreat under the disapproving gaze of the Court of Directors of the Company.

Bengal

The *Hickey's Bengal Gazette or the Calcutta General Advertiser* was started by James Augustus Hickey in 1780. The *Gazette*, a two-sheet newspaper, specialised in writing on the private lives of the Sahibs of the Company. He dared even to mount scurrillious attacks on the Governor-General, Warren Hastings', wife, which soon landed "the late printer to the Honourable Company" in trouble.

Hickey was sentenced to a 4 months jail term and ₹.500 fine, which did not deter him. After a bitter attack on the Governor-General and the Chief Justice, Hickey was sentenced to one year in prison and fined ₹.5,000, which finally drove him to penury. These were the first tentative steps of journalism in India.

Calcutta

B.Messink and Peter Reed were pliant publishers of the *India Gazette*, unlike their infamous predecessor. The colonial establishment started the *Calcutta Gazette*. It was followed by another private initiative the *Bengal Journal*. The *Oriental Magazine of Calcutta Amusement*, a monthly magazine made it four weekly newspapers and one monthly magazine published from Calcutta, now Kolkata.

Madras (Chennai)

The *Madras Courier* was started in 1785 in the southern stronghold of Madras, which is now called Chennai. Richard Johnson, its founder, was a government printer. Madras got its second newspaper when, in 1791, Hugh Boyd, who was the editor of the *Courier* quit and founded the *Hurkaru*. Tragically for the paper, it ceased publication when Boyd died within a year of its founding.

It was only in 1795 that competitors to the *Courier* emerged with the founding of the *Madras Gazette* followed by the *India Herald*. The latter was an "unauthorised" publication, which led to the deportation of its founder Humphreys. The *Madras Courier* was designated the purveyor of official information in the Presidency. In 1878, The Hindu was founded, and played a vital role in promoting the cause of Indian independence from the colonial yoke. It's founder, Kasturi Ranga Iyengar, was a lawyer, and his son, K Srinivasan assumed editorship of this pioneering newspaper during for the first half of the 20th century. Today this paper enjoys the highest circulation in South India, and is among the top five nationally.

Bombay

Bombay, now Mumbai, surprisingly was a late starter - *The Bombay Herald* came into existence in 1789. Significantly, a year later a paper called the *Courier* started carrying advertisements in Gujarati. The first media merger of sorts: The *Bombay Gazette*, which was started in 1791, merged with the

Bombay Herald the following year. Like the *Madras Courier*, this new entity was recognised as the publication to carry "official notifications and advertisements". 'A Chronicle of Media and the State', by Jeebesh Bagchi in the *Sarai Reader 2001* is a handy timeline on the role of the state in the development of media in India for more than a century. Bagchi divides the timeline into three 'ages'. The Age of Formulation, which starts with the Indian Telegraph Act in 1885 and ends with the Report of the Sub-Committee on Communication, National Planning Committee in 1948.

Post Colonial Journalism

The Age of Consolidation that follows stretches from 1951, with the extension of the Indian Telegraph Act to the whole of India and ends with the promulgation of the "Indecent Representation of Women (Prohibition) Act" in 1985. The current age is the Age of Uncertainty, which began in 1989 with the introduction of the Prasar Bharati (Broadcasting Corporation of India) Bill.

Two News Agencies

Press Trust of India (PTI) and United News of India (UNI) are the two primary Indian news agencies. The former was formed after the it took over the operations of the Associated Press of India and the Indian operations of Reuters soon after independence on August 27, 1947. PTI is a non-profit cooperative of the Indian newspapers. UNI began its operations on March 21, 1961, though it was registered as a company in 1959 itself.

Popular Publications in Urban India

- *Malayala Manorama* (Malayalam daily).
- *Mathrubhumi* ([2] daily).
- *Madhyamam* (Leading Malayalam daily from Calicut)([3] daily).
- *Dainik Jagran* (Hindi daily) 19.2 million readers (IRS 2005).
- *The Times of India* (English daily) 7.05 million readers (IRS 2005).
- *Amar Ujala* (Hindi daily).
- *Anandabazar patrika* (Bengali daily).
- *Lokmat* (Hindi daily).
- *India Today* (weekly; Hindi edition most popular).
- *Sambhaav* (Gujarati daily).
- *Gujarat Samachar* (Gujarati daily).
- Daily Thanthi (Tamil daily with 14 editions and a circulation of 790,900).

Popular English Dailies in Urban India

- The Times of India.
- Hindustan Times.

- The Hindu.
- The Telegraph.
- Deccan Chronicle.
- The Asian Age.
- The Economic Times.
- The New Indian Express.
- Mid-Day.
- Deccan Herald.
- Indian Express.
- India today.
- Outlook.
- India's Wine Publication.

Television in India

A huge industry by itself, the Indian silver screen has thousands of programmes in all the states of India. The small screen has produced numerous celebrities of their own kind some even attaining national fame.TV soaps are extremely popular with housewives as well as working women. Some small time actors have made it big in Bollywood.

Indian television started off in 1959 in New Delhi with tests for educational telecasts. Indian small screen programming started off in the early 1980s. At that time there was only one national channel Doordarshan, which was government owned. The Ramayana and Mahabharat was the first major television series produced. This serial notched up the world record in viewer ship numbers for a single programme. By the late 1980s more and more people started to own television sets. Though there was a single channel, television programming had reached saturation. Hence the government opened up another channel which had part national programming and part regional. This channel was known as DD 2 later DD Metro. Both channels were broadcasted terrestrially. Interestingly the Government of India required Licenses that TV owners needed to acquire during the initial years of the spread of Television (including the 1970s). A seemingly authoratarian, but obviously poorly thought out scheme that died a silent death and almost surely had no meaningful purpose while it lasted.

Television in India has been in existence for nigh on four decades. For the first 17 years, it spread haltingly and transmission was mainly in black and white. The thinkers and policy makers of the country, which had just been liberated from centuries of colonial rule, frowned upon television, looking on at it as a luxury Indians could do without. In 1955 a Cabinet decision was taken disallowing any foreign investments in print media which has since been followed religiously for nearly 45 years. Sales of TV sets, as reflected by licences issued to buyers were just 676,615 until 1977. Television has come to the forefront only in the past 21 years and more so in the past 13. There were initially two ignition points: the first in the eighties when colour TV was introduced by state-owned broadcaster Doordarshan (DD) timed with the 1982 Asian Games which India hosted. It then proceeded to install transmitters nationwide rapidly for terrestrial broadcasting. In this period no private enterprise was allowed to set up TV stations or to transmit TV signals. The second spark came in the early nineties with the broadcast of satellite TV by foreign programmers like CNN followed by Star TV and a little later by domestic channels such as Zee TV and Sun TV into Indian homes. Prior to this, Indian viewers had to make do with DD's chosen fare which was dull, non-commercial in nature, directed towardsonly education and socio-economic development.

Entertainment programmes were few and far between. And when the solitary few soaps like Hum Log (1984), and mythological dramas: Ramayan (1987-88) and Mahabharat (1988-89) were televised, millions of viewers stayed glued to their sets When, urban Indians learnt that it was possible to watch the Gulf War on television, they rushed out and bought dishes for their homes. Others turned entrepreneurs and started offering the signal to their neighbours by flinging cable over treetops and verandahs. From the large metros satellite TV delivered via cable moved into smaller towns, spurring the purchase of TV sets and even the upgradation from black and white to colour TVs. DD responded to this satellite TV invasion by launching an entertainment and commercially driven channel and introduced entertainment programming on its terrestrial network. This again fuelled the purchase of sets in the hinterlands where cable TV was not available.

The initial success of the channels had a snowball effect: more foreign programmers and Indian entrepreneurs flagged off their own versions. From two channels prior to 1991, Indian viewers were exposed to more than 50 channels by 1996. Software producers emerged to cater to the programming boom almost overnight. Some talent came from the film industry, some from advertising and some from journalism.

More and more people set up networks until there was a time in 1995-96 when an estimated 60,000 cable operators were existing in the country. Some of them had subscriber bases as low as 50 to as high as in the thousands. Most of the networks could relay just 6 to 14 channels as higher channel relaying capacity required heavy investments, which cable operators were loathe to make. American and European cable networks evinced interest, as well as large Indian business groups, who set up sophisticated headends capable of delivering more than 30 channels.

These multi-system operators (MSOs) started buying up local networks or franchising cable TV feeds to the smaller operators for a fee. This phenomenon led to resistance from smaller cable operators who joined forces and started functioning as MSOs. The net outcome was that the number of cable operators in the country has fallen to 30,000. The rash of players who rushed to set up satellite channels discovered that advertising revenue was not large enough to support them. This led to a shakeout. At least half a dozen either folded up or aborted the high-flying plans they had drawn up, and started operating in a restricted manner. Some of them converted their channels into basic subscription services charging cable operators a carriage fee.

Foreign cable TV MSOs discovered that the cable TV market was too disorganised for them to operate in and at least three of them decided to postpone their plans and got out of the market.. The government started taxing cable operators in a bid to generate revenue. The rates varied in the 26 states that go to form India and ranged from 35 per cent upwards. The authorities moved in to regulate the business and a Cable TV Act was passed in 1995. The apex court in the country, the Supreme Court, passed a judgement that the air waves are not the property of the Indian government and any Indian citizen wanting to use them should be allowed to do so. The government reacted by making efforts to get some regulation in place by setting up committees to suggest what the broadcasting law of India should be, as the sector was still being governed by laws which were passed in 19th century India.

A broadcasting bill was drawn up in 1997 and introduced in parliament. But it was not passed into an Act. State-owned telecaster Doordarshan and radiocaster All India Radio were brought under a holding company called the Prasar Bharati under an act that had been gathering dust for seven years, the Prasar Bharati Act, 1990. The Act served to give autonomy to the broadcasters as their management was left to a supervisory board consisting of retired professionals and bureaucrats. A committee headed by a senior Congress (I) politician Sharad Pawar and consisting of other politicians and industrialist was set up to review the contents of the Broadcasting Bill. It held discussions with industry, politicians, and consumers and a report was even drawn up.

But the United Front government fell and since then the report and the Bill have been consigned to the dustbin. But before that it issued a ban on the sale of Ku-band dishes and on digital direct-to-home Ku-band broadcasting, which the Rupert Murdoch-owned News Television was threatening to start in India. ISkyB, the Murdoch DTH venture, has since been wallowing in quicksand and in recent times has even shed a lot of employees. But News Corp has been running a C-band DTH venture in the country which has around 20,000 subscribers. In 1999, a BJP-led government has been threatening to once again allow DTH Ku-band broadcasting and it has been talking of dismantling the Prasar Bharati and once again reverting Doordarshan's and All India Radio's control back in the government's hands. Some things change only to remain the same.

Cable Television

In 1992, the government liberated its markets, opening them up to cable television. Five new channels belonging to the Hong Kong based STAR TV gave Indians a fresh breath of life. MTV, Star Plus, BBC, Prime Sports and STAR Chinese Channel were the 5 channels. Zee TV was the first private owned Indian channel to broadcast over cable. A few years later CNN, Discovery Channel, National Geographic Channel made its foray into India. Star expanded its bouquet introducing Star World, Star Sports, ESPN and Star Gold. Regional channels flourished along with a multitude of Hindi channels and a few English channels. By 2001 HBO and History Channel were the other international channels to enter India. By 2001-2003, other international channels such as Nickelodeon, Cartoon Network, VH1, Disney and Toon Disney came into foray. In 2003 news channels started to boom.

PUBLIC OPINION RESEARCH IN COMMUNICATION AND PUBLIC RELATIONS

The importance of sound and significant Public Relations research to the management of all organizations is greater today than it has been in the past. Top executives are spending many hours studying how public attitudes towards their industries may affect their future operations, or turn into opportunities in terms of the market place and their growth. The focus of opinion research and Public Relations research has been changing from the study of traditional publics to a greater attention to the study of "issues", and how best to make an impact on public attitudes for their benefit. The tools of public relation research may not have undergone much change in the past decade. But there is an all round effort to bring timely and actionable processed data into the hands of decision-makers quickly and effectively. Public Relations research serves these three functions:

- Most frequently, it may simply confirm assumptions and hunches about the state of public opinion on an issue, or a company. This is a highly useful kind of back-up function, in many ways analogous to the use of quality control systems in the manufacturing end of a business.
- A second role of research is to clarify questions on which limited information is available, or on which apparently contradictory data are to be found. Research can help sort out what people really mean and when they say they like or dislike an organization—the reasons they cite for these feelings, and even the origin of the feelings.
- Research re-orients our thinking and conceptualization of Public Relations problems. It helps us to define and focus on our objectives and target group, and in assigning priorities to Public Relations problems and Public Relations actions.

There are many research techniques available for conducting Public Relations and public opinion research. A very old and still useful method is to carry a content analysis of how an issue or a problem is treated in the press, published data, and the like. Such desk research gives a pretty fair measure of the salience of the problem and often useful hints as to which aspect of it seem to be arousing the greatest public interest. For many people, Public Relations research is synonymous with public opinion surveys, and their various market research and survey techniques, each of which has its merits and its limitations. Properly used, these different techniques can complement one another and produce a mosaic of data giving new insights into long-standing problems. Another form of opinion research, which is a useful tool for Public Relations professionals is depth survey. This is nothing more than an effort to let the public tell the researcher how it views the Public Relations programmes. In these surveys the researcher carefully avoids imposing his point of view on the respondent. Depth studies are useful in the early stages of programme in giving clues to the perimeters of a problem. They can also provide some really valuable themes for the Public Relations campaign. Good research takes time. And if undertaken must not be unnecessarily hurried, even if the findings are required in a hurry. It must take its own course with all the procedures completed fully and the analysis of data done properly to throw up the required leads to evolve the Public Relations strategy and programme.

Managing Effectiveness: The secret of managing effectiveness lies in "how to do it", or the methodology of doing things. Success in communication results out of managing four important steps:

- Right selection;
- Right motivation;
- Right evaluation;
- Training and development.

Selecting the right message, the right target group, and the right media is the first step. Motivating your target group to perceive and then act as you want them to be the next. Having done that, evaluating what has been achieved, what has not been achieved, and what needs to be done further is vital. This may be part of the programme undertaken, but must be planned beforehand. Feedback in communication is crucial—there should be one-way communication if one needs success.

With all this, admen, publicity men, and Public Relations men (and in all three cases women too) must be constantly trained to be professionals in the techniques, thin-inputs and the final execution of programmes and campaigns. Training should be an ongoing process, and not something which is done only when the going is tough, or when there is an acute need for qualified people. Because of the link of advertising with marketing, a number of training programmes-in-company and external are available to advertising people. But in the field of publicity and Public Relations, there exists a big vacuum, which must be filled up in the coming years-especially when Public Relations is becoming more and more important in business and industry.

SOCIAL MARKETING IN PUBLIC RELATIONS

Public Relations professionals in increasing numbers have begun to realize that social causes can benefit tremendously from the Public Relations way of marketing, thinking the planning. This is known as 'social marketing'. The term 'social marketing' has been defined as the 'design, implementation and control of programmes, calculated to influence the acceptability of social ideas and involving considerations of product planning, pricing, packaging, communication, distribution and marketing research'. In short, it means 'the application of marketing techniques in moulding public opinion for or against a social issue, or 'selling' an idea to serve a social cause, or wherever specific public or social programmes and campaigns require significant changes in the attitudes and behaviour on the part of the relevant "publics". The most successful example of employing marketing techniques for popularizing a public programme in India has been the Nirodh commercial distribution, drawing on the marketing skills of a number of large consumer goods companies. Similarly, there have been several social advertisement campaigns, like the Bombay Municipal Corporation campaign on water conservation, or Indian Oil's "Save Oil" campaign, or Hyderabad Municipal Corporation's "Keep Your City Beautiful" campaign. Let us take a practical example.

Business houses design products and services in terms of the needs and wants of target groups of consumers. Similarly, in social marketing, target audiences must be studied and appropriate "products or services" designed by the organization, so that the target audiences find it desirable to accept the product or service. Thus, if the National Savings Organization wants income-earners to save by buying Saving Certificates, which in the long run will help to curb inflation in the country, many types of "schemes" can be designed to contribute to this social objective.

For instance, instead of cash incentives for buying consumer products, wholesalers, dealers and even retailers may be given Savings Certificates, or coupons-for buying a certain volume of a product or products, a Savings Certificates worth a fixed sum is given to the buyer. Many such "products" can be designed to achieve the social objective of developing the saving habit. Thus in social marketing, the Public Relations men can view it as a marketing problem requiring the designing of the "right product or service", offered at the "right place", at the "right price or effort" to the "right consumer or target audience" with the support of the "right promotion". However, it must be added that such an approach may not guarantee total success, but it does offer a systematic framework for planning the social efforts.

5

Journalism and Mass Communication

DEPENDABLE JOURNALISM

The news director of a television station in a mid-to-large market area explained why he denied my request to accompany his reporters as they gathered news. I would unobtrusively observe and occasionally ask journalists to explain strategies. He said he tells all his reporters to imagine that when their story comes up in the newscast, he is handing them a certain number of viewers. He cupped two big hands together as if to hold the audience. "When their story is done I want them all back. The last thing I want them thinking about are news values." The news director added that this wasn't his idea. He only wanted to keep his job. "In this business," he explained, "you have to think with a cash register in your head."

In that newsroom, and in four other local television newsrooms I observed, journalists--from reporters and videographers to news directors-were much more decision takers than decision makers. Their autonomy was bounded by three universal commands: Do whatever it takes to maximize audience; minimize cost; don't embarrass big advertisers or the owners' other interests. Only after satisfying these demands were reporters and editors free to practice journalism as they saw fit. As a consequence, content was designed more to sell than inform. Abbreviated reports of simple, visual, emotional, and obvious events displaced explanations of complex, significant, and underlying issues.

Contrast the freedom of action in these newsrooms--which now supply most Americans with their news--with the expectations of journalism's national codes of ethics. Most codes imply that the journalist is a "professional" free of any obligations except responsibility to enlighten the public. And so they place full moral responsibility for news on the shoulders of individual practitioners. The American Society of Newspaper Editors Statement of Principles, for example, holds that:

The primary purpose of gathering and distributing news and opinion is to serve the general welfare by informing the people and enabling them to make judgements on the issues of the time. Newspapermen and women who abuse the power of their professional role for selfish motives or unworthy purposes are faithless to that public trust. No mention is made of executives of parent corporations with "cash registers in their heads" who might bend journalists to the wills of major investors, sponsors, and powerful sources.

This chapter argues that contemporary national codes of ethics are based more on the fantasy that journalists control what becomes news than the reality of control by owners. In fact, a long accretion of journalistic autonomy has stalled and appears to be eroding as corporations providing news seek to maximize return to shareholders. Journalism's national ethics codes, then become less relevant to practitioners and deceive the public by deflecting criticism from owners onto their employees.

The codes also are unethical themselves to the extent that journalists become decision takers rather than decision makers. We need a more realistic code that recognizes those who wield power and assigns them appropriate responsibility. The argument begins with an analysis of journalism's moral blueprints.

It compares their language to the research literature of reporter and editor autonomy, including recent court cases and surveys of American journalists in print and broadcast media. It concludes with a proposal for a "structural" framework for journalism ethics that takes into account the growing influence of forces outside the newsroom, such as the executives of corporations that own news media, the interests of corporate "siblings," and the markets for investors, advertisers, sources, and consumers.

ANALYZING CODES OF ETHICS

Although the question of who journalists are is not addressed in national codes, this analysis will count managers who supervise newsroom employees, but not those in other departments. And it includes all news department employees. In newspapers, everyone from the executive editor to contract or freelance reporters and photographers is considered a journalist. In television, everyone working in the news department--from president of the news division at the network and news director at a local station--down to production assistant is included.

Of the four most widely cited codes--enacted by the Society of Professional Journalists, the American Society of Newspaper Editors, the Associated Press Managing Editors, and the Radio/Television News Directors Association--three begin with plausible and lofty language about the role of journalism in a democratic society. The Code of Ethics of the Society of Professional Journalists, for example, begins: "Members of the Society... believe that public enlightenment is the forerunner of justice and the foundation of democracy. The duty of the journalist is to further those ends by seeking truth". Each code then lists more specific do's and don'ts intended to realise these broad goals.

The oldest of American journalism's codes, written by the American Society of Newspaper Editors in 1922 and most recently revised in 1975, aims all of its moral injunctions at individual "practitioners," "journalists," and "newspaper men and women." No others are mentioned. Further, the code is cast as a covenant between two parties only, intended to "preserve, protect and strengthen the bond of trust and respect between American journalists and the American people".

The newest code, updated by the Society of Professional Journalists in September 1996, also places responsibility for news solely and directly on journalists. No other actors are assigned moral duties. The code is divided into four sets of moral commands, each of which begins with the phrase, "Journalists should."

The third such injunction says "Journalists should be free of obligation to any interest other than the public's right to know". That heading obliges journalists to "refuse gifts, fees, free travel and special treatment, shun secondary employment, political involvement, public office and service in community organizations" that might conflict with objective reporting. All of these lie within the control of the individual journalist.

He or she must give up some personal benefit to avoid an ethical breach. But parallel with these individual-level injunctions are others in which it is not the journalist's self-interest that must be restrained but that of the corporate or other owner. For example, journalists are obliged to "deny favored treatment to advertisers and special interests and resist their pressure to influence news coverage." Here journalists are asked to decide when the owning corporation must deny itself benefits, such as revenues from advertisers, to avoid an ethical breach. By making no distinction between individual and corporate levels of obligation, the code implies that journalists have this authority.

The Radio/Television News Directors Association code begins: "The responsibility of radio and television journalists is to gather and report information of importance and interest to the public accurately, honestly, and impartially". It contains 10 references to individual broadcast journalists and one to the "broadcasting industry." No other actors are mentioned.

The Associated Press Managing Editors' code, revised in 1995, departs from the others in naming an institution, "the newspaper," as the principal subject of moral injunctions. It commands that "the newspaper should report the news without regard for its own interests, mindful of the need to disclose potential conflicts. It should not give favored news treatment to advertisers or special-interest groups". This language reduces the asymmetry of a subordinate class of employees--journalists--making decisions for the corporation that owns the newspaper. But it may not achieve parity.

For newspapers (and television stations) which are part of larger corporations, the subordinate local unit is still being asked to decide an issue that affects the bottom-line of the parent corporation. Given the hierarchical structure of conglomerate corporations, it is more likely that parent corporations will impose policies on their subsidiaries than the reverse. Corporate financial pressures on subordinate firms have occurred despite the protests of the most influential editors. Gene Roberts resigned as executive editor of the Philadelphia Enquirer rather than accept continuing cuts in resources for reporting. Under Roberts the Enquirer won 17 Pulitzer prizes. The corporation applying the pressure was the chain with perhaps the nation's highest reputation for quality, Knight-Ridder.

Common to each of these four national ethics codes is the notion that journalists--individually or in the aggregate--are, or should be, free of business-related constraints imposed by those who pay them and distribute their work. In fact, the obligations are reversed. Corporations employing journalists are expected to conform to the demands of this special class of workers.

Such an arrangement reverses the usual direction of corporate authority. It deprives owners of their traditional right to use their assets as they see fit. Since the First Amendment's guarantee of press freedom has been interpreted as a privilege of the owner and not of the employees or of the community, this reversal might be seen as obstructing the spirit of the First Amendment. Before going any further, we should ask whether this unusual arrangement of employees making decisions for owners actually exists.

Historical evidence indicates that American journalists have been bowing to the demands of owners since the marriage of the steam engine and the printing press gave birth to news as an industry in the 1800s. According to Bates: Will Irwin, Upton Sinclair, George Seldes, Morris Ernst, Oswald Garrison Villard, Leo Rosten, and Robert Lasch all had analysed how profit-seeking interfered with truth-seeking in the press; so had several critics of the 19th century.

The tension between the owner's business interests and journalism was one of the primary reasons Pulitzer proposed professionalizing journalism through higher education at the turn of the 20th century. This struggle was also the centerpiece of the Hutchins Commission's critique of the news at mid century: "The press is... caught between its desire to please and extend its audience and its desire to give a picture of events and people as they really are". Several media historians have noted an accretion of authority for journalists beginning with the waning of the "Yellow Press" at the turn of the 20th century. They note that journalists have become much better educated and compensated than the "ink-stained wretches" of earlier periods of American journalism.

Indeed, two recent court decisions--one each in print and broadcast news--have re-evaluated the U.S. Department of Labor's 50-year-old classification of journalism as a trade protected by wage and hour laws. In December 1994, a federal court judge ruled that former Washington Post reporter Thomas

Sherwood was exercising professional prerogatives and receiving a professional level of pay. In April 1996, a federal court of appeals ruled that writers, editors, and producers at NBC News must be classified as "artistic professionals".

The Sherwood case bears directly on journalistic autonomy. In her opinion Judge Norma Johnson noted: Sherwood's job... required him to originate story ideas, piece together seemingly unrelated facts, analyse facts and circumstances, and present news stories in an engaging style. The Court further finds that Sherwood's fact-gathering involved more than passively writing down what others told him. He was required to cultivate sources, utilize his imagination and other skills in seeking information, and continuously develop his finely tuned interviewing skills.

While the evidence that Sherwood was a smart and highly skilled reporter is undeniable, the judge passed over how much the journalist's exercise of authority required permission. The evidence also showed Sherwood's choice of topic and story angle, his choice of sources, his handling of quotes, and the time he had to cultivate sources and write stories all were subject to approval by his superiors. Sherwood worked not within a structure of collegial control but within a hierarchy.

Not even the Post's newsroom meets the standards of autonomy in journalism's national ethics codes. Even at a paper such as the Washington Post, by reputation a paper where reporters have unusual freedom, editors were not elected by their peers, but appointed from above. The most influential manager was selected by business persons outside the newsroom.

Similarly, the resources available to the newsroom were determined not by a committee of journalists but by the parent corporation's board of directors. Were Rupert Murdoch to buy the Post (God forbid!), he could change the operation of the newsroom as quickly as he did when he took over Britain's best-selling newspaper The Sun in 1974 and switched its orientation from labour to conservative.

As owner, Murdoch could dismiss any journalist disagreeing with his notion of news without any hearing or professional due process. And Murdoch could violate journalism's codes of ethics without fear of sanction because none contains enforcement language. The First Amendment would protect Murdoch from any government response.

Not even the Post's newsroom meets the standards of autonomy in journalism's national ethics codes. Like many educated and skilled whitecollar employees, these journalists enjoy some authority over their work product. They are not assembly-line workers. But their autonomy is clearly bounded by corporate superiors, not by allegiance to peer standards.

Ironically, during the same half century journalists were gaining those responsibilities Judge Johnson noted, scholars studying the question of who has influence over the news were locating control over the news further and further from reporters and editors. The notion of journalists as arbiters of news was implied in the famous "gatekeeper" study conducted by White. But the 1950s were only half over when Breed contradicted the notion at least of reporter autonomy with his classic survey of 120 journalists at northeastern newspapers. He described a newsroom culture established by management that--usually subtly--enforced management's orientation towards news. The reporters' choice was to go along or get out.

From the 1970s into the early 1980s researchers such as Epstein in network television, Sigal, Sigalman, and Fishman in newspapers, Powers and Bantz, McCorkle, and Baade in local television, Tuchman across several media, and Hirsch reanalyzing White early data, documented that newsroom routines-established more by their employers than by journalists--dictated news content and practice. In the mid- 1980s Altschull argued that news has always been advertisers. Turow conceptualized journalists as holding only one of 13 power roles that determine media content. Bagdikian located most of the power to shape news well above the newsroom in corporate boardrooms. Soloski argued that professionalism is a widely shared myth in American newsrooms that is manipulated by managers to control news work.

In the 1990s Auletta, Squires, and Underwood described the economic rationalization of network television and newspaper newsrooms in response to profit pressures from owners and the stock market. McQuail proposed an array of social forces outside the newsroom as the determiner of news. Shoemaker and Reese offered a five-level analysis in which owners of media firms exerted the greatest control. McManus theorized that news results from an elaborate compromise among powerful market-driven influences outside the newsroom.

Similarly, scholars who analysed the application of journalism ethics in newsrooms found that journalists are more often the object than the subject of codes. Davenport randomly surveyed 100 newspaper managing editors and an equal number of local television news directors. Eighty per cent of respondents who had written codes said they were imposed on the newsroom by managers with little rank-and-file discussion.

In a review of research, Boeyink found that ethics codes were effective only when publishers decided they were important. Beam surveyed 300 top editors at 60 newspapers of varying sizes. He found that professional autonomy makes more sense considered as an organization level, rather than individual level, variable. Writing about reporters in the American news industry, Fink concluded: "Either you and the hand that feeds you agree on ethics in reporting or writing, or you (not your editor) will be a very unhappy employee--or unemployed".

RECENT TRENDS IN JOURNALISTIC AUTONOMY

Random surveys, each of more than a thousand U.S. journalists, conducted every 10 years since the early 1970s suggest that journalism's century-long ascent towards professionalism has stalled and may, in fact, be reversing. The newsroom surveys show a strong trend towards declining journalistic autonomy. Weaver and Wilhoit, who conducted the last two surveys, wrote:

Compared to the early 1970s, journalists in the 1982 sample reported a significant decline in their freedom to decide news story emphasis and editing. The 1992 interviews suggest that newsroom autonomy has diminished further, and at a startling pace. For the first time in three decades, barely half of reporters see themselves [with] the newsroom clout of their predecessors. And the lessening autonomy is occurring at a time when many in the workforce--who entered the profession during a tide of heavy hiring of young staff in the late 1970s and early 1980s--have been in the newsroom long enough to have established their authority.

Four of five journalists laid the loss of autonomy to profit-driven management decisions as well as pressure from government, advertisers, or a hostile public. A comment the researchers deemed typical read: "There is increasing pressure from large corporations, including my own, for bottom-line profit and gains at the expense of long-term quality". By contrast, only 8 per cent said they were hindered by professional standards of ethics, good taste, or objectivity.

Other surveys show a similar trend. A 1993 Associated Press Managing Editors survey of 627 newspaper journalists showed rising discontent from a survey 8 years earlier, particularly among the young, minorities, and best educated. Almost half the journalists with graduate degrees counted themselves dissatisfied enough to want to leave their jobs. "About half of these dissatisfied journalists say they do not have sufficient autonomy on the job," the report said, "they lack resources to do their jobs properly and they are not very impressed with the quality of their newspapers".

A 1995 Associated Press Managing Editors study of newsroom managers also showed less autonomy and greater stress than a similar survey in 1983. "Fully 66 per cent of responding editors said their news hole was reduced in the past year. Half reported losing news staffers who were not replaced. Eighty per cent reported that 'there is more work than I can complete in a normal day'". All of these limitations were imposed from above the newsroom.

Summing up these changes for newspapers in an article titled "The Thrill is Gone," Stepp concluded: "In the age-old battle between the editorial side and the business side, the editorialists have lost the upper hand". In local television--the part of the news industry growing A fundamental principle of ethics is that those with greatest power bear the greatest moral accountability.

Fastest over the past several decades in employment, consumer loyalty, and influence over news practice--the outlook for journalistic autonomy is more dismal still. According to Fink, "In television sheer perversity is at work-a sort of Gresham's Law of Journalism: poor quality, low-cost entertainment shows drive out high quality, high-cost news programming". If these assessments are accurate, journalists are more decision takers than decision makers. While they cannot disavow responsibility for their actions so long as they retain the option to quit their jobs, their authority to produce high-quality ethical news reports is circumscribed, tightly for some, loosely for others. A fundamental principle of ethics is that those with the greatest power bear the greatest moral accountability. Journalism's ethical codes have it backward.

A recent text on media ethics concluded: "[I]t's futile to discuss... efforts by individuals to practice ethical journalism without examining the corporate profit motive and its impact on those efforts". Major American journalism ethics codes, however, not only fail to examine the corporate profit motive, most don't even recognize its existence. Difficult structural ethical questions lie at the heart of journalism conducted by profit-seeking businesses.

Particularly in the modern newsroom where barriers between the business side and the news side have been lowered or eliminated, journalism ethics must speak to potential conflicts of interest with powerful news-shapers outside the newsroom. Drawing on theoretical work by Turow, McQuail, and McManus, at least eight such powerful actors can be identified. In each case there should be both a prescription of an optimal relationship and an enforceable ethical proscription to protect the news department's interest in providing news that maximizes public understanding from the media firm's narrow self-interest in serving the following constituencies:

- Shareholders/Owners. If they seek maximum short-term returns on their investment, they may balk at spending what quality journalism requires.
- Rational advertisers seek the largest audience of potential customers in a context that both lends their claims credibility yet encourages consumption, all at the lowest cost. In contrast, quality journalism seeks the largest audience regardless of customer potential--wealth-and freedom from bias towards advertisers and the ethic of consumption.
- Sources may manipulate the supply of raw material for news in order to gain favorable exposure to their ideas and often themselves. In contrast, ethical journalism gathers information without fear or favour and without regard to the information subsidies of public relations.
- Consumers: More people may be attracted to entertainment information. Further, quality journalism that challenges popular myths and prejudices may drive away some consumers.
- Government: In an environment where parent conglomerates of media firms own companies affected by government regulation or government contracts, or simply by government spending, there may be pressure for biased news in return for favours.

- Parent corporations may exert pressure to report favorably or at least not initiate negative coverage of corporate siblings and their business interests.
- Media firms, represented by the newspaper publisher or TV station general manager or network CEO, may not allocate adequate resources to their news departments given the greater profitability of other choices, such as entertainment programming, or entertainment-oriented sections of a newspaper, or other business interests.
- Pressure groups including social institutions may exert influence on the newsroom for content that does not offend the group's sensibilities or that furthers its agenda. Quality journalism, however, is independent, acting in the best interest of the entire community.

The details of such a structural ethics of journalism are beyond the scope of this chapter. Fresh thinking about how to define, measure, and enforce a new moral code for news is urgently needed. Even the most modest proposal is likely to be highly controversial because structural ethics must negotiate the First Amendment, and more importantly, intrude on the "forbidden," realm of ownership prerogatives of private enterprises. My purpose here has been restricted to demonstrating that the current expressions of national codes of ethics ignore or gloss over the most serious moral issues in contemporary journalism. As long as they do, journalism's codes of ethics are themselves suspect ethically. At best, they are incomplete. At worst, they confuse and discourage needed reforms by permitting those who control the news to deflect criticism from themselves onto their employees.

In Britain, lone motherhood is not a neutral nor an apolitical status; it evokes strong moral evaluations and therefore easily becomes a political symbol. Although the historical status and treatment of British lone mothers has varied over time, they have almost continually been at the centre of public debates about the state of society in general, but more particularly of 'the family' and the role of women.

Most recently, political and media attention has focused on the doubling of the number of lone parent families in Britain over the past two decades (reaching around 20 per cent of all families with dependent children, over 90 per cent of whom are headed by a lone mother), on the growth of unmarried mothers as a proportion of all lone mothers, and on their increasing reliance on Income Support (the social assistance benefit) rather than on paid work.

Debate has centred around whether lone mothers prefer to live off the state, and may even be created by such policy 'cushioning', or whether they want to be 'self-sufficient' but cannot because welfare policies are unsupportive.

Arguably both views are wide of the mark; research reveals that lone mothers' moral views about 'good' mothering, and how this does or does not combine with paid work, is the crucial issue. Lone mothers received particularly damning attention at the hands of new right politicians and the popular media in 1993, in the context of the then Conservative government's 'back to basics' campaign. Indeed, 1993 has been dubbed 'The year of the lone mother'.

Lone mothers were depicted as a threat to the fabric of society, supposedly rearing delinquent children without the guidance of a proper father, and scrounging benefits and housing off the welfare state. Social policies were called for that would deal with this menace. Lone mothers received further attention in the media as a legitimate cause for social concern during 1996, again functioning as a sort of symbol as part of a national debate about 'moral values', as policies concerning divorce law reform and working mothers were debated.

And towards the end of 1997, lone mothers were once again in the political and media spotlight as a result of the New Labour government's social reforms. Here lone mothers functioned as a symbol in the attempt to restructure social benefits towards welfare-to-work strategies.

Academics have played an important supporting role in media preoccupations with lone mothers. In particular, new right and revisionist/communitarian academics have gained space in the national media, and have propounded what Judith Stacey calls 'virtual social science'.

Here categorical assertion, anecdote and selective readings of 'facts' are posed as unbiased and fault-free authoritative research, in this case purportedly showing that lone mothers are formative members of a British 'underclass'. The US academic Charles Murray gained particular space in the press in the early-mid 1990s, with Cassandra-like statistical and rhetorical predictions that Britain was heading down the same slippery slope as the US, to extensive urban crime, drug use and disorder-where all this was the result of increasing 'illegitimate' births supported by the benefits system. The answer, in this view, is to stop 'supporting' lone motherhood through social policies and instead support the traditional married family.

Such negative portrayals of lone mothers have not gone unchallenged. Attempts have been made by voluntary pressure groups, such as the National Council for One Parent Families, and liberal left professionals and academics, as well as leading figures in the 'liberal' establishment, such as Church authorities, to reinsert a public image of lone mothers as 'normal' women who are doing their best in externally constrained and unfavourable circumstances. In this view, social policies should be enlarged to properly support such women in bringing up their children.

Consequently, mainstream political and media debates about lone mothers in Britain-and corresponding policy proposals-have become polarised between seeing lone mothers as a threat to society or as victims of social problems. Each of these positions, their propagation in the media, the role of academics within this, and the social policies that accompany them, is reviewed in more detail below: particular attention is focused on the ways in which the media have depicted black lone mothers.

But these polarised positions are not the only ways of understanding lone mothers' situation, or of framing the parameters for social policies in response. Indeed, other views may more accurately reflect how lone mothers themselves understand and experience their lives.

These alternative views of lone motherhood are also discussed albeit more briefly, because they have not gained wider legitimacy or currency in national media and political debates, nor influenced policy frameworks to any great extent. The propagation of particular media images of lone mothers and their accompaniment by recommendations for particular social policies, is posed rather simply above. Clearly, the media increasingly inform public understanding and comprehension of the social world, and play a role in placing issues on the political policy agenda-as this volume attests.

Nevertheless, the relationship between mainstream media presentations of lone motherhood and the actual or possible social policies that address their situation is not a relationship of simple stimulus-response.

As in other policy areas, this relationship is more complex, not least because government and political agendas influence and inform media coverage. It is perhaps more useful to see ideological issues lying at the root of both, which relate to shared social understandings about the relationship between individuals, states, markets and families, and to how 'explanations' are constructed in dominant western and academic categorical modes of thought.

REPRESENTATIONS OF LONE MOTHERS AS A SOCIAL THREAT

One perception of lone mothers expounded in mainstream political and media representations sees them as a social threat: both morally and financially. They are formative members of an underclass that has no interest in providing for itself in legitimate ways. This position links into the underclass theory that has developed in the USA in particular, but has been imported into, and gained influence in, Britain-although it also has its roots in a longstanding British 'social pathology' view of the poor.

This theory posits that, in spatially segregated areas, there is a developing class that has no stake in, and is hostile to, the social order. Lone mothers are seen as active agents in the creation of this underclass. In Britain, young single (that is, never-married) mothers have been focused on as the central culprits.

Lone mothers allegedly choose to have children outside wedlock to gain welfare and housing benefits, and then, supported by the state, they choose not to get a job. Their sons, assumed to be without male authority or roles, are said to drift into delinquency, crime and the drug culture, while their daughters learn and repeat the cycle of promiscuity and dependency. Popular media depictions of lone mothers as a social threat use emotional symbolism more fully than more 'respectable' academic tracts. Media reports, however, both draw on, and are sometimes written by, academics. The American new right/ republican academic Charles Murray has enjoyed particular prominence in the *Sunday Times,* to purvey his virtual social science.

Andrew Neil, when editor of this paper, claimed that he had introduced Murray to the British public and politicians, and sponsored his 'research' in Britain. During the early 1990s and especially in 1993, the *Sunday Times* and other right-wing broadsheets, along with the tabloid press, devoted considerable and regular editorial attention to stories about single mothers and the underclass. They also displayed some raw prejudice in doing so. An editorial in the *Sunday Times* for example argued that:

It is becoming increasingly clear to all but the most blinkered of social scientists that the disintegration of the nuclear family is the principal source of so much unrest and misery. The creation of an urban underclass, on the margins of society, but doing great damage to itself and the rest of us, is directly linked to the rapid rise in illegitimacy... It is not just a question of a few families without fathers; it is a matter of whole communities with barely a single worthwhile role model.

A headline in the same newspaper queried, 'Wedded to welfare-do they want to marry a man or the state?' The *Daily Mail,* with its ideological and political address to 'middle England', offered a similar viewpoint:

The Willenhall estate, on the outskirts of Coventry, houses a large number of single mothers. There are also a lot of young, single men, many living on the proceeds of either crime or benefit fraud and more or less attached to the young women... It is kept afloat by the niggardly (if costly) charity of the state and the local authority, that is to say the taxes paid by traditional two parent families.

The targeting of a particular public housing estate with a supposedly high proportion of young 'underclass' single mothers seems to be a virtual social science technique for delivering messages, and for concretising particular views, as used by Murray and journalists in the popular media. The flagship BBC television current affairs programme, *Panorama,* entitled 'Babies on benefit', broadcast on 20 September 1993, used a similar technique.

In this case it was the St Mellon's council estate in Wales that was portrayed as an underclass breeding ground. This estate had previously received critical attention from the then Conservative Secretary of State for Wales, John Redwood, in a speech arguing for policies that deterred young women from having babies outside marriage and supported by the tax payer. Indeed, the programme makers claimed that they were investigating his contentions. Both Redwood and the *Panorama* programme implied that St Mellon's was typical and could be extrapolated as representative of all lone mothers-despite more considered accounts revealing inaccuracies about the estate and lone mothers generally. Popular media presentations of lone mothers as a social threat link into a conservative new right political view of the state in society, where the welfare provision of housing, benefits and other social provision is castigated as encouraging state dependency, an underclass, and especially single (never-married) motherhood.

Peter Lilley's now infamous 'little list' speech at the 1993 Conservative Party conference, for example, alleged that single mothers were having children to secure welfare benefits and housing, while Stephen Green, Chair of the Conservative Family Campaign, argued that 'Putting girls into council flats and providing taxpayer funded child care is a policy from hell'.

But strands of an underclass discourse are also discernible in the communitarianism underlying the New Labour government's ideas about a 'stakeholder society'. The long-term unemployed, which includes lone mothers, are placed as 'socially excluded'; 'family values' are stressed as the key to a 'decent' and crime-free society, and an element of coercion is required to reintegrate the excluded back into society through paid work. New Labour's view that life in a married two-parent family is better for children and for social cohesion, most notably expounded by Tony Blair and Jack Straw, has been widely reported in the media since 1997.

Media, politicians and academics who promulgate this view of lone motherhood as a threat to society also campaign for social policies that do not reward or encourage such 'self-damaging conduct'.

Consequently, the New Labour government has implemented the previous new right Conservative government's proposal to remove the extra allowances available to (new) lone parents on both the universal child benefit payment and on targeted income-related benefits-with Harriet Harman (then Minister for Social Security and for Women) stating, 'Life is about work, not just about claiming benefit'. Other policy disincentives to lone motherhood advocated by those who hold a social threat view include restrictions on payments to lone mothers who have more children while receiving benefit (as is the practice in some American states). There are also suggestions that young single mothers on benefit should be placed in hostels where their sexual relations and children's upbringing can be supervised. This policy idea has been floated by the New Labour government, in linking hostels with job training-again revisiting proposals of the Conservative government. Encouragement and reward for traditional male breadwinner/female homemaker couples is also stressed by social threat advocates, with policy proposals to redress the supposed benefit bias towards lone, as opposed to married, parents (another reason given by New Labour for its lone parent benefit cuts). Other policy proposals include a tightening of the divorce law so that fewer lone mother families are created in the first place, as well as advocating 'moral' family and parenting education-the latter being the remit of the government's new National Family and Parenting Institute to be launched in April 1999.

Black Lone Mothers as a Social Threat

Until recently, 'race' and ethnicity were muted features of British social threat representations of lone motherhood. In the wake of the heightened media attention to lone mothers from 1993 onward, however, articles about black lone mothers began increasingly to be reported in the white-dominated media. Under the headline 'The ethnic timebomb', for example, the tabloid *Sunday Express* noted that more than 50 per cent of black families are headed by a lone mother and argued that, 'Almost six in ten black mothers are bringing up children on their own, urged on by the benefit system', implying a direct causal relationship between the incidence of black lone motherhood and the growing social security bill. Such claims ignore the fact that black lone mothers are more likely to be economically active and in full-time employment than their white counterparts; research suggests they also provide healthier lifestyles for their children. The *Sunday Express* article also raises the spectre of 'babyfathers' who-in newspaper accounts-father worryingly large numbers of children with multiple female partners.

Stories about 'babymothers' young black women who are presumed to have children by multiple male partners) also received considerable attention in the broadsheet press. Mainstream radio magazine programmes, such as BBC Radio 4's *The Locker Room* and *Women's Hour,* have also featured discussions about black lone motherhood and its social implications. Much of this coverage has echoed the ongoing debates in black media, especially the tabloid daily, *The Voice*-self-styled 'Britain's best black newspaper'-but there are significant differences between these stories as they are reported in the black press compared with their coverage in the white-dominated media.

First, there are no scare stories about social security bills. Second and importantly, there is a sense of debate in the black press, with the black readership responding to 'personal opinion' columns through the letters page. By contrast, coverage of black lone motherhood in the mainstream press tends to be devoid of vigorous questioning or alternatives, with a flat presentation suggesting that 'this is how it is' in the British black population. It is argued elsewhere that the emergence of a focus on black lone mothers in the British mainstream press is linked to the broader social threat concerns discussed above. It is suggested, moreover, that it is through such 'exotic' media explorations of black family life that white people vicariously play out their fears about social breakdown and relationships between men and women.

DYNAMIC TOUCHING OF MEDIA REPORTING

A somewhat different though complementary view of the phenomenon of popular-culture culpability is seen from the perspective of Shoemaker and Reese. Their approach examines how media content is influenced by factors in the context in which it is created.

Though one could view their theoretical perspective as examining media content as shaped by external social processes in a unidirectional (external forces lead to media content) manner, we argue that their theory can be expanded to examine the interrelated, multidirectional, dynamic relations between all elements-content, producers, public.

In Mediating the Message, Shoemaker and Reese identify five major spheres of influence on media content, from the most microscopic to the most macroscopic. We use these labels to identify sources of influence on the producers of news content as well as on the content itself. Though the labels are presented individually, we argue for their overlapping, multidirectional relationship with content as journalists go about the social practice of determining how to cover "the news." We introduce the levels of influence here briefly and will then apply them to each of the three events examined in this chapter.

The most microscopic level of influence on media content is the individual level, that is, the influence exerted by the individual reporter or columnist, the copy editor, and the editor-each person who has a hand in creating the news content. This can include deciding what constitutes news, selecting the angle of the story, writing the story, and editing it. Some of the factors that influence content decisions at the individual level are personal feelings, tastes and preferences, values, opinions, and the professional backgrounds and training of those directly involved in content decisions.

The media routines level focuses on the routines, or standard procedures, for gathering and disseminating news. Among the influences found at this level are news values-those characteristics that make an event newsworthy, such as deviance from the norm, sensationalism, prominence, proximity, timeliness, conflict or controversy, human interest, and impact on audience members or society as a whole.

Other media routines include objectivity, the five "Ws" (answering who, what, when, where, and why in every report), pack journalism, competition, reliance on other media for information or for whole stories, localism (getting the local angle on a story that takes place far away), simplicity (offering pat "answers" because complex situations are hard to explain and hard for readers to understand quickly), and over-reliance on a handful of sources.

The next level of influence, moving towards a more macroscopic perspective, is the organizational level. Analysis at the organizational level focuses on the impact of policies, managers, and owners of the organization in which the media content is produced. It is difficult to discuss influences at this level, as we do not know what went on in each newsroom during coverage of these three events. However, the opinions of upper management or concerns of those in the circulation or advertising-sales departments can influence coverage, as can organizational policies such as the degree of autonomy allowed to each reporter. The extramedia level has to do with elements and factors outside of the media organizations themselves, such as news sources, advertisers, government, interest groups, and the audience. This level includes actual, direct influences as well as the influence that news media personnel's perceptions of what these entities might do or how they might feel that also shape content. While influence of advertisers might weigh against extensive blaming of popular culture in news coverage, for example, pressure from some interest groups and activists, as well as governmental concern, could weigh towards the pursuit of this angle.

In terms of perceptions of audience preferences, some journalists may believe that audiences want to see and read about violence, sensationalism, scandal, and the lives of celebrities. This perception could have a profound impact, because giving the audiences "what they want" will presumably sell newspapers and space to advertisers. Thus, angles that have popular appeal may be advanced while more esoteric or abstract angles, such as the notion that society in general is responsible or that a complex nexus of forces are at fault, may take a back seat.

The notion of audience preference is also a cultural one. de Mooij argues the one such preference that is culturally bound is America's adherence to a cause-and-effect paradigm. She argues that it is a cultural norm in the United States to expect to have a logical explanation for any given event and that any event has concrete and measurable answers to the question of what caused it.

Journalists, if following this cultural norm or if presuming audiences follow it, may provide a concrete explanation rather than leave the tragedies unexplained. Subscribing to this cause-and-effect paradigm can be viewed as an individual influence on the part of reporters and editors, an extramedia influence that takes the shape of conceptions about audience preferences, or an ideological influence that entails broad-based cultural and societal beliefs.

The ideological level includes the influences that broad systems of beliefs and values have on the news-gathering process. Among the factors at play here are notions of "elite" and "popular" media, representations that define "mainstream" and "deviant" content, and the concept of hegemony. The latter suggests that entities enjoying political and economic power in existing societal structure will act in the interest of thwarting social change in order to protect their dominant status. We predict that these three case studies will show the use of defensive strategies when other media are, indeed, blamed.

Through the use of labels such as "tabloid," "paparazzi," and "trash TV" to draw theoretically distinct lines, journalists may construct readings of their own stories as the dominant discourse and those of "tabloid" media and "trash TV" as deviant. A subtext exists in this type of criticism that suggests a need to save people from their own tastes in media and popular culture. This is similar to the points raised by Bird and Jensen above, and is the central theoretical element of the study at hand. de Mooij's suggestion that as part of American culture, we-as members of society-need someone or something to blame whenever there is a tragedy, also has implications for hegemony and social order. In order for members of society to feel secure about the world around them, there has to be a rational cause, with a clearly identifiable source of blame, for each event. Thus, it is much more satisfying to place blame on a specific, tangible targetin this case, the non-elite media-rather than advancing the more unsettling notion that something is amiss in society at large.

The first case study involves the death of Princess Diana of Wales and the automobile accident that took her life and the lives of Dodi al Fayed and Henri Paul on August 31,1997. The accident occurred shortly after midnight in Paris when the Mercedes Benz in which the princess and her friend were travelling crashed in a tunnel near the Seine River. Dodi al Fayed and Henri Paul, the driver, were found dead at the scene. The princess died a few hours later of injuries she sustained in the crash.

The event was reported in newspapers around the world. The larger U.S. and U.K. newspapers gave extensive coverage to the event in the days following the crash. For example, on the first day of coverage The London Observer ran 28 articles, The New York Daily News ran 10 articles, and The Atlanta Journal and Constitution ran four articles.

This case study is based on analysis of those articles and others that were published in English-language newspapers from the day of the crash, August 31, 1997, through the day of Diana's funeral, September 6, 1997, when the focus of coverage shifted from the accident to the funeral. The articles were retrieved from the General News archive of LEXIS-NEXIS Academic Universe. In all, 507 stories were reviewed for relevant content, and those with relevant content were studied more closely.

Often, the first news reports of a tragic and unexpected event will present only the basic facts of the story, answering the fundamental journalistic questions of who was involved, what happened, when it happened, and where it happened, without speculation as to the causes of the event. It usually takes another day or more for the "how" and "why" questions to be answered.

However, this was not the case in the early reporting on Princess Diana's death. Answers to the "how" and "why" questions were included in the initial reports of the event because tabloid-press photographers were said to have been chasing the princess's car at the time of the accident.

Approximately 11 photographers, sources said, some on motorcycles and others in a car, set out after Diana and Dodi's Mercedes when it left the Ritz hotel in Paris. The photographers were apparently trying to get pictures that would confirm rumors of a romance between Diana and Dodi.

Several sources in the earliest stories claimed that the photographers caused the accident. Among them were Paris police, unspecified police, French journalists (their sources unnamed), a photographer for a London paper, Agence-France Presse (the French news agency), and British reporters.

No eyewitnesses to the crash were quoted in the early coverage-in other words, no source knew for certain that the photographers had actually caused the accident (and some sources even claimed that the car had lost the photographers). In spite of this, the idea that the photographers caused the accident became a part of every story reporting the facts of the event.

The Boston Heraldbegan an article by Joseph Mallia (Aug. 31,1997) with "Princess Diana and her companion Dodi Fayed were killed in a high-speed car crash early today in a tunnel near the Seine River in Paris, as their Mercedes was being pursued by photographers."

The Hindu of India began a story (no byline, Aug. 31) with "Britain's Princess Diana and her millionaire companion, Dodi El-Fayed, were killed in a car crash early on Sunday while being chased by photographers on motorcycles in a road tunnel in the French capital Paris." The third paragraph of an Associated Press story that ran in The Buffalo News on August 31 read "The crash happened shortly after midnight in a tunnel along the Seine River at the Pont de l'Aima bridge. It came as paparazzi-the commercial photographers who constantly tailed Dianafollowed her car, police said."

During the week after the fatal crash, when coverage of the event was at its most intense, nearly every article contained at least one source who blamed the producers of popular culture for Diana's death. Among these were family members and family representatives, dignitaries, ordinary citizens, and journalists themselves.

Other sources who blamed "the paparazzi," "the press," "the media," or "the tabloids" (sometimes including tabloid-style television shows) were an Arizona talk-radio host and many of his callers, Britons living in the United States (usually interviewed in pubs), un-named TV commentators, and David Perel, executive editor of the American tabloid The National Enquirer. Perel was quoted in several newspapers as saying that reckless action by the paparazzi probably caused the accident.

Some family members of the crash victims extended the blame to all photographers who pursue celebrities for photos to be printed in tabloid newspapers. Ellen Tumposky and Mike Claffey of The New York Daily News (Aug. 31) reported "The dead Egyptian playboy's father, Mohammed Al-Fayed, blamed the tragedy on the paparazzi, who were being held for questioning by Paris police. There is no doubt in Mr. Al-Fayed's mind that this tragedy would not have occurred but for the press photographers who have dogged and pursued Mr. Fayed and the princess for weeks,' a spokesman for the Egyptian billionaire said."

The Houston Chronicle (byline Houston Chronicle News Services, Aug. 31) reported "(Michael Gibbons), a spokesman for Buckingham Palace, noting that the incident occurred while the couple were being chased by photographers, said it was 'an accident waiting to happen.'... he repeated the palace's anger at the actions of photographers who pursue the royal family around the world." Other family members blamed not only tabloid-press photographers but also the editors and publishers of gossipy tabloid publications. The London Observer was one of the first to report a scathing statement from Diana's brother.

"This is not a time for recriminations," said Earl Spencer, "but I would say that I always believed the press would kill her in the end. But not even I could imagine that they would take such a direct hand in her death as seems to be the case. It would appear that every proprietor and editor of every publication that has paid for intrusive and exploitative photographs of her, encouraging greedy and ruthless individuals to risk everything in pursuit of Diana's image, have blood on their hands today."

None of the first-day stories reporting the reactions of world leaders and diplomats (such as President Clinton, the Singapore government, and the Pope) contained quotes that blamed popular culture. However, on the second day of coverage, several French government officials made statements blaming the paparazzi, as reported in The Hindu (by Vaiju Naravane, Sept. 1).

The president of the French Parliament, the former prime minister, Mr. Laurent Fabius... said that death precipitated by paparazzi proves that "photos, words and attitudes can also, in a certain sense, kill. These people must now face their responsibility."...The government's spokeswoman, Ms. Catherine Trautmann, who is also France's Culture Minister, was more vehement in her denunciation of the paparazzi. Princess Diana was the victim of the stubbornness of the press, she declared.

"The singlemindedness of the press had increased dramatically these past weeks... The circumstances of her death have thrown up questions about the functioning of this profession and above all of our society," Ms. Trautmann added. Among the stories that reported the reactions of ordinary citizens, most contained at least one source who blamed either the paparazzi who pursued the Mercedes or the press in general. Most of these "average-citizen" sources did not distinguish between the popular press and the elite press or their producers, nor did the reporters attempt to make any distinction for the sources. The blame laid by these sources was among the most vitriolic. The New York Daily News (article by Barbara Ross, Aug. 31) reported:

Britons in New York mixed their grief at Princess Diana's death with criticism of the press for its relentless pursuit of her.... Beverly Dorking, 25, of Leeds in northern England, said, "...she's been dogged and hounded by the media. They've been in her face since she was 19, and now they've taken away the world's most popular woman." Nicola Shigley, 24, of northern England, predicted a backlash against the media. She accused the media of spending "the last 10 years trying to put the woman to an end."

The San Diego Union-Tribune (article by Lillian Salazar Leopold, Aug. 31) reported "'The press has a lot to answer for,' said Mary Simpson, also of Liverpool. 'They hounded her to death. Literally, now.'"

The Seattle Times (article by Chris Solomon, Aug. 31) reported "Mitch Lease, 23...reflected bitterly on the circumstances of her death, a chase by photographers. I think the media should have given her a break a long time ago, and now they've killed her.'"

The London Observer (article by Roy Greenslade, Aug. 31) reported "In one bitter outburst on BBC TV, a woman demanded that a reporter and his cameraman slop filmmg. 'You've done this Io her,' she screamed. 'You're to blame. The media, the papers, all of you.'" Some articles blamed popular culture by quoting other publications and thereby demonstrating what seemed to be a world-wide consensus as to who was to blame for the tragedy. A London Observer article (byline: "foreign staff," Aug. 31) read:

The French newspaper Liberation gave over its whole front page to a picture of (Diana) with the headline, "One photo too many. "... Italy's La Stampa took up the same theme, stating tersely: "Dead for a photo".... Hong Kong newspapers agonised over their own home-grown paparazzi, with the Oriental Daily News recalling that a local pop singer, Leslie Cheung, had crashed his Porsche while being pursued by photographers.

It branded paparazzi as "criminals of a thousand years." The Daily Star, a Bangladesh newspaper, said that "Western press and society will need to embark on a long search of their souls to come to terms with the sense of guilt Diana's death must generate."

Alongside the just-the-facts stories and reaction stories were articles focused primarily on the causes of the accident. Many of these stories found some aspect of popular culture (either the photographers who chased Diana's car that night, tabloid-press photographers in general, tabloid newspapers, the editors and publishers of tabloid newspapers, or any member of the press who had purchased paparazzi photos) to be at fault. The tone of these articles was often angry and disgusted.

Earl Spencer's statement was used in several of these stories as a starting point for further discussion of the role of the paparazzi in Diana's death. Dave Walker, writing for TAe Arizona Republic (Sept. 1), began such a story by asking "Do the media have blood on their hands for the death of Princess Diana? That's what her brother, Earl Spencer, suggested in the aftermath of the car wreck..."

Walker went on to cite several sources who agreed with Spencer, including Dodi's father, Mohamed al Fayed, unnamed network television commentators, and Phoenix-area talk-radio host Charles Goyette, whom Walker quoted: "'The media are clearly to blame,' said Goyette, summing up the majority opinion among his callers. 'The consumers of this trash don't have the culpability, the media do.'"

An article in The Glasgow Herald (by Catherine Macleod, Sept. 1) quoted a source who followed Spencer's lead and blamed all the producers of tabloid newspapers: "...the Prince of Wales's biographer Jonathan Dimbleby said: 'It isn't only the reporters and photographers, it's those who hired them.' He added: 'It's the editors and proprietors who too often, offer glossy excuses about the public interest who need now to examine their consciences.'"

Some of the stories that discussed causes were actually editorials expressing the views of the writer or writers. For example, The London Observer (no by-line, Aug. 31) expressed the following opinion: "Anyone in the British Press who has bought and used the pictures snatched by paparazzi on so many previous utterly private occasions helped ensure that the ravening pack would be on the trail on Saturday night." Some of these articles were written in a narrative stylo, retelling the facts of the story dramatically while characterizing the photographers as degenerates. For example, Michael Daly of The New York Daily News (Aug. 31) wrote:

No matter how fast her car sped through the Paris night, the paparazzi on the motorbikes were sure to stay right behind her, for she was with the man said to be her lover.... The following Sunday, she was swarmed by those only interested in violating her private life.... They were still after the couple when she arrived in France.

The hounds kept baying, right up to early this morning, when motorcycles sped after Diana's car along the Seine. Her pursuers were right out of the 1961 movie "La Dolce Vita," in which a photographer named Paparazzo chases his prey on a motorscooter.... They chased the biggest score ever right to her death. The frenzy that began with "The Kiss" ended in two children being left without their mother.

Similarly, Luke Harding, Owen Bowcott, John Hooper, Paul Webster, Alex Bellos, Stephen Bates, and Chris Mihill of The London Observer (Aug. 31) wrote:

Even before Princess Diana and Dodi Fayed had strolled through the baroque central corridor of the Ritz hotel in Paris...the paparazzi were lurking in wait.... (Diana and Dodi's) presence was common knowledge among the small, ruthless, multilingual band of photographers who pursue her, very lucratively, for a living.... Around 7 p.m. on Saturday Diana left the Ritz in a chauffeur-driven car to do some shopping in the Champs Elysee. The press pack were, reportedly, in close pursuit....

Quite a few stories blamed "the press" in general or "the media" in general, not distinguishing the mainstream press from the tabloid press.

Among these were stories reporting that Diana herself had condemned the practices of the British press in an interview published in a French newspaper the week before the accident. J. Frank Lynch of The Atlanta Journal and Constitution (Aug. 31) reported "In Great Britain, 'the press is ferocious,"

Diana said in the article in the French daily Le Monde. 'It forgives nothing and is only hunting down mistakes. Each act is twisted; each gesture is criticized.'"

A number of stories about the causes of Diana's death divided the blame among several culprits. One of these culprits was Henri Paul, the driver of the Mercedes. On the first day of coverage, many articles noted that Paul had been driving at a speed well above the limit and that he lost control of the car, thus implying that the accident was at least partly his fault.

When the news of Paul's very high blood-alcohol level (which was more than three times the French legal limit) was released on day two, he became the target of finger-pointing in many more articles. However, none of the stories that blamed Paul let the producers of popular culture off the hook completely. An editorial in The Arizona Republic (no byline, Sept. 3) argued:

The swift and reckless rush to judgement, the desire to fix certain blame for the death of Diana, is also destructive and promises to leave victims. Misplaced blame might mask sorrow's pain, but it does not heal.

Diana Spencer, queen of celebrity, died from the impaired judgement of millions. We'll name a few. The paparazzi, a subset of photojournalists identified first and perhaps forever as the villains who ended the strange, fairy-tale existence of a lovely young woman, continue to receive disproportionate blame. Seven photographers face some type of charges related to the fatal crash.... So what of the judgement of those editors and publishers who buy sleaze and resell it under some loose definition of news? Impaired?

Morally warped? Yes.... And, so whal of the judgement of millions of readers who purchase the product now blamed for the death of a princess? Impaired? Warped? Yes.... However, in this tragedy, the person whose impaired judgement seems most responsible for the death of Princess Diana, is the man behind the wheel of the car carrying her and her boyfriend....

One of the few articles to seriously consider the culpability of Henri Paul was published by The Boston Globe (Sept. 1). (This story also contained several sources who blamed the paparazzi at the scene and the press in general.) Author Peter S. Canellos wrote:

Ralph Whitehead, a journalism professor at the University of Massachusetts, said all the hand-wringing over the misdeeds of media is "a momentary hysteria."

Unless proof emerges that paparazzi on motorcycles actually interfered with the progress of Diana's car, responsibility for the accident should rest with the driver, he said. The Mercedes limousine was traveling faster than 60 miles per hour-perhaps much faster-in a tunnel where the speed limit is 30, police said. The princess and her companion, Dodi Fayed, did not appear to be wearing seatbelts.

"What would Diana and the rest of the people in the car have lost if they'd been overtaken by photographers?" Whitehead said. "If you're a celebrity, you have a right to regard the paparazzi as a pain in the neck. But it's not the right response to put your life in jeopardy by speeding away."

For a few days, there was a bit of a tug of war between those sources representing the photographers (primarily their lawyers) and those representing the driver (the Fayed family and Paul's co-workers). Some of the stories printed on days two through seven offered opinions as to which party deserved more blame, while others blamed Western society as a whole for its fascination with celebrities.

In an article called "Time Has Come to Point Finger in Right Direction," Steve Wilson of The Arizona Republic (Sept. 3) wrote "I would like to interrupt all the finger-pointing in Princess Diana's death-do the paparazzi or the drunken driver deserve the most blame?-for this important message: It's the culture, stupid. Or more precisely, it's the stupid, celebrity-obsessed culture."

When the playwright Arnold Wesker spent several months at the offices of the *Sunday Times,* gathering background material for his drama *The Journalists,* he decided to produce an account of his observations. The resulting slim volume caused such offence to some of those he observed that its publication was held up for five years. This was his conclusion:

The journalist knows his world is among the least perfect of all imperfect worlds. Most are raring to get out and write books-the best of them do, frustrated by small canvases and the butterfly life of their hard earned thoughts and words. Wesker was not, suffice to say, overly impressed by what he found. Indeed, his book conveys a sense of bemusement that grown men (as national newspaper journalists in the main then were) could want to subject themselves to such demeaning work. More than a quarter of a century later, many people outside the media seem still to share that view. The industry has changed out of all recognition: relatively large numbers of journalists at all levels are women and not a few are black; and technological advance, long delayed while the trade unions remained strong, has transformed the job.

Yet the popular image of journalism appears often to remain that of the unscrupulous, dog-eat-dog press of 1920s Chicago, immortalised on stage and screen in *The Front Page*. There is undoubtedly a fear of the media, but above all there is a lack of understanding. And nowhere is that lack more evident than in the world of social policy.

NEW TREND USED FOR JOURNALISM

It is foolish, I believe, to reject the idea of a new direction for journalism. Some, like Merrill, fear that new direction will eliminate what tradition sees as the proper role of journalism, to be a fourth branch of government, a watchdog, to keep its eye on those who really wield power--the government, those who make law and those who enforce law; the corporations, the churches--and without fear or favour to report what they see. Objectivity simply does not exist. Even if it did exist, it would be wrong because objectivity always works on behalf of the status quo. It is true that the typical American journalist perceives this to be his highest calling: To get the facts and to lay out the facts for the reader, who may or may not act on those facts, as he or she sees fit. But objectivity is a mechanism for ensuring the status quo. It is an instrument to guarantee the preservation of institutions and the social order. It permits criticism of individuals but not of the fundamental system, political, economic, or social.

The state of impartiality is, in fact, defensive of the system. That in this model the press retains the potential to challenge the social order is the element that poses a threat to those who exercise power. Inasmuch as the press fails to live up to its potential, it is carrying out the political role that is desired of it by those in power. To the extent that the press endorses the idea that it is above politics it is serving the needs of power.

Isn't it the business of journalism to help the public understand? High up there among the reasons why I have been so murderously disappointed in today's press is, if you'll pardon the expression, its know-it-all-ness. The First Amendment was not written for the benefit of the press. It was written for the benefit of the people. Under the First Amendment, everybody has the right to be heard. It isn't only for people with the resources to own the newspapers and the broadcasting stations and the fibre-optic bitstreams.

Why are the media so unpopular? They always come in at the bottom in public opinion polls along with the politicians. I don't know all the reasons, but one of them, I'm sure, is their arrogance, their assumption outlined every day in the newspaper columns as well as on the Sunday TV shows where Sam Donaldson and George Will let us know every week how clever they are and how stupid we are.

When I was a journalist in my arrogant mode, I used to think down, too. In Washington, we always used to report movement: Who was up? Who was down? That's what the dumbbells wanted, we told each other. They didn't want to hear about issues, certainly not the complicated ones.... Well, don't let me go too far. We did do the complicated stories; we did try to report what the Hutchins Commission recommended, that is, the truth behind the facts. Some newspapers still do. Some TV reporters still do. But they are all losing ground--to tabloid papers and tabloid television. Or to USA Today and its many clones. Short and very spicy.

The Voice of Money

One of the ideas behind what we cheerfully speak of as the freest press in the world is that it gives voice to those among us who are the hardest to hear. Of course, I am talking about the poor, the homeless, the Black, the gay, the Native American.

Mainstream journalists need to listen to them, too. I think the Finnish Television Network did the right thing when its reporters went out into the community and asked ordinary people what they wanted to know more about. When they learned what it was, they went out and produced documentaries giving everybody a chance to be heard.

Unfortunately, it has dropped the programme. Even in Finland, I guess, it's very difficult to challenge the bottom line. But why not here? What have we got to lose, except--aha!--Money? It wins every time.

Giving up is not the answer. Money is for the most part indifferent to content. Audiences will likely be stimulated to pay attention to substantive news when they have participated in defining what it is. Definition is the key. Reporters can and should be devoting time to finding out what matters to audiences and then laying out the story for them with suggested solutions. This is what participatory journalism is all about. News is no longer defined in terms of the journalist's amorphous news judgement.

Permit me to raise yet another counter-cultural idea (I am using that phrase here to refer to something that runs counter to the standard culture of journalism). Is it in keeping with the idea of democracy for us to invoke the First Amendment just to avoid engaging a tough problem? Journalists could, with profit, devote more time to making our world a better place to live in than to roll eyeballs, scramble for high salaries, and insist rigidly on our rights under the First Amendment. Whatever we write or broadcast has consequences. Don't we have to pay attention to those consequences? We also have responsibilities, don't we?

Let me get into what I believe community journalism demands of journalists, certainly of reporters and editors; I hope we can include publishers and owners, but this means they must lower their financial expectations. Community journalism demands putting the public interest ahead of the maximization of profit. Think about that. But working stiffs, no matter how high, can't force this formula on the people or the corporations that pay their salaries. That's a weakness in community journalism.

Utopians hope that weakness will go away. In my new mood of guarded optimism (I love that phrase), I would like to try to persuade the bosses that by bringing the people into the process of journalism, they can continue to produce earnings while serving the needs of the people.

It isn't enough. The community journalist goes beyond the facts. Beyond them. I have come to respect the research and analytical insights of the English sociologist, John Burton, who wrote that if we are to have a stable society--and that means for the journalist, his or her boss, and all the people who live in the community--then everybody, all the people, all the social units, must have equal access to the community's resources and the skills they need if they are going to act within the rules of society. Those denied this kind of access, Burton said, will turn to "alienation behaviour". And that means going outside the norms of society to a life of what we, who have that access, call crime.

There is a special role for community journalists here, maybe the most important of all. They could become a third party to conflict. It's an idea that appeals to me, an idea that makes people in the media real mediators.

LET THE MEDIA PEOPLE MEDIATE

Best of all, however, the community journalist can and should bring the two sides together. Let the media people mediate. Most problems can be solved, or at least alleviated. Here is the classical third-party role. Study the background. Recognize that you can provide the data that shows the antagonists don't have to play the zero-sum game, where one wins and the other loses. The mediator finds the places where the antagonists are in agreement, no matter how small the area.

After all, most of us believe in our personal survival. And most of us believe in the survival of the community. That's a start. It may not be the journalist's job to bring the two sides together, but ask yourself: Who else is going to do it? You can be the *link* that facilitates communication and decision making by the actors. The journalist is not the one who comes up with a solution, but certainly a solution is what is meant to be the end product of the process.

This role is an extension of the First Amendment. It speaks not of our rights but of our responsibilities. It is the positive side of freedom. Why not be responsible to the community and for helping it solve its problems? There are risks. Very serious risks. That arrogance I have been talking about is one. We don't need journalists in the pulpit, but they can help the people in the pulpit, and that's no mean role to play. To carry this fearsome burden, reporters must be what they should be under any circumstances, well educated and learned in analysis. Here journalism really plays a part in what matters most and becomes a true fourth branch of government.

Journalistic objectivity and detachment may have been fine once upon a time, but that doesn't bring communities together. It may even drive them further apart. The apathy of the public is well known.

It is going to grow deeper and deeper if the public continues to see itself as separate and disconnected, uncared for and uncaring. People need to care if they are going to tune in to and read the news. An active community journalism has a chance to reverse that course.

When the United Nations *Human Development Report 1998* appeared, it revealed a somewhat damning picture of the UK as one of the most impoverished nations of the developed world: the UK was ranked fifteenth out of the seventeen countries included in the poverty index used by the report. In the UK one in seven of the population was below the poverty line, and the country contained about 30 per cent of Europe's children in poverty.

This was not the image conjured by the sparkling glitter of new Labour's 'cool Britannia', its millennium dome ascending symbolically skyward from reclaimed London mudflats, and consumer spending running riot on digital television sets in the homes of a population who were now all middle class.

Something was amiss, and as ever it was in the working and reworking of popular cultural narratives provided by the news media that explanations could be forged and framed. When the 'new Labour' government of Tony Blair came to power in 1997, one of its primary targets in the battle to 'modernise' the British state was the social security budget.

Social security minister Frank Field, with a reputation for an independent and tough approach in this area after an early career as a 'poverty lobbyist', and several years chairing the Commons Social Services Select Committee, was charged with 'thinking the unthinkable'.

But this task, as always, had to draw on public and deeply rooted mythology and understanding. In this chapter I briefly review how this process was worked out in the 1990s by examining news coverage of poverty and social security, and its consequences for public beliefs and policy.

SHIFTING GEAR IN THE RHETORICAL BATTLE

In earlier work I have argued that contemporary understanding of welfare is drawn from three roots-'efficiency, morality, and pathology: efficiency of the labour market and the economy; morality of the work ethic and self-sufficiency; and the pathology of individual inadequacy as the cause of poverty'.

These three vary in intensity as conditions change. With rising structural unemployment, awareness of and familiarity with the circumstances and causes of unemployment became more diffuse through the population. But the increasing moralism of work as the only route out of poverty, and as the best cure for residual idleness, increasingly formed the core of a hardening set of political axioms arguing that duties as much as rights were the key to modern citizenship. This rhetoric became pivotal to the Blairite agenda, and to the welfare reforms the new Labour government began to pursue in office.

Samuel Smiles was back in favour. While the worthy toiled, 'Most wretched and ignoble lot, indeed, is the lot of the idlers'.

The intense 'scroungerphobia' evident in both press and public attitudes in the 1970s abates somewhat in this later period. But the rhetoric and vocabulary are by now set. Drawing on this three-part framework, news about social security now becomes merely a variant on the earlier period.

Within that a predictable and familiar set of motifs recur. First, the economic burden posed by social security expenditure, a restraint on growth and a punitive impost on the hard-working tax paying majority. Second, the need for control and punishment for illicit dependency on benefits, and especially for fraud. Third, the clear and necessary boundary to be drawn between the deserving and undeserving poor, with single parents moving into greater prominence in the 1990s alongside the unemployed. Both receive vituperation as external to the social system, in association with the foreign or alien claimant. Fourth, the new moralism draws attention to the unduly pleasant 'lot of the idlers', when there is work to be done.

Tory Social Security Secretary Peter Lilley had the headline writers drooling in 1992 when yet another 'biggest crackdown ever against social security fraud' was launched at the party's annual conference. His gruesome adaptation of a Gilbert and Sullivan ditty ('I've got a little list/Of benefit offenders who I'll soon be rooting out/And who never would be missed…') had them rolling in the aisles and across the front pages.

As the *Mirror* warned of 'Dole scroungers facing new blitz', more simply in the *Daily Star* it was 'Stuff the spongers'. War was yet again declared on this outgroup of wasters, idlers, and loafers, a group set apart from the rest of society. The language of warfare underlines this imagery in two ways. First, battle is declared (as in the *Daily Mail* front-page spread, '£2bn blitz on dole cheats'.

Welfare claimants have endured more 'blitzes' than the Luftwaffe could ever have imagined possible. Second, readers are constantly reminded of their outgroup status by the recurrent and exemplary reporting of foreign spongers. In one brief period for example, from the *Mail* stable, we had 'A one man fraud factory', about a 'baby-faced 37-year-old' Nigerian who 'used Britain's benefits system like his own private bank' (*Mail on Sunday,* 21 September 1997); 'Thieving refugee sent benefit cash back home', about a Vietnamese caught shoplifting (*Daily Mail,* 25 July 1997); 'Irish fiddler takes British tax-payer for £1 million' (*Mail on Sunday,* 20 July 1997); 'First family of fraud' about a Pakistani family being tried for social security fraud in a Dutch court (*Daily Mail,* 20 April 1998); and an 'exclusive' exposé of the 'scandal of the illegal immigrant benefits industry' (*Daily Mail,* 30 June 1997).

Scorned for this scandalous exploitation of our softness and generosity as a nation, scroungers are as excoriated as other objects of social contempt, as hinted at by headlines like 'Fraud-busters make a dawn swoop on welfare scroungers', the comparison with drug dealers or child abusers not far from the surface.

Social security fraud, as I demonstrate below, remains a staple of reporting of the benefits system. Yet the arithmetic of this area of criminal activity remains riddled with anomalies. Calculations of annual fraud figures depend on presumptions that short-term fraud would have continued if undetected.

This indeterminacy gets played out in media reporting by the eternal refrain that '£1.4 bn benefit fraud is tip of iceberg' (*Daily Telegraph,* 10 July 1995). Dee Cook has carefully contrasted the policy and ideological response to social security fraud with tax evasion, which, as she points out, is equally a cost to the public purse resulting from criminal fraud. By 1995/96 the Department of

Social Security was undertaking over 10,000 prosecutions annually, compared with 192 by the Inland Revenue. In the same year, even assumed benefit 'savings' (which include payment 'irregularities') arising from this action amounted to £1.2 billion, compared with £5.2 billion actually accrued from imposing 'compliance' on would-be tax evaders.

Yet the latter remains veiled behind either total invisibility or humorous disregard for what is seen to be a victimless and innocent piece of mischief we would all engage in, given the opportunity.

Blurring the dividing line between welfare dependency and criminality fuels the sense that an unnecessary burden is being placed on the public purse by all this largesse. The day after disabled activists chained themselves to the railings at Number 10 in protest at threatened benefit cuts, that voice of middle England, the decade's most successful newspaper the *Daily Mail,* in its new conditional Blairite pose, argued that 'while those in genuine need will not be abandoned' the reforms would 'make sense of a welfare structure which creates a culture of dependency, fails to eradicate poverty, and yet imposes an ever-increasing burden on the economy'.

This was the welfare structure, as an earlier *Mail* lead article had pointed out, that 'has spawned a debilitating culture of welfare dependency, fecklessness, and fraud' (15 August 1997). The result, warned the *Sunday Times,* is that 'Benefit fraud is a way of life in Britain's sign-on society' (31 October 1993), a diagnosis echoed in the double page spread in the *Daily Mail* headed 'Sign up here for sick-note Britain' (14 April 1998).

This fecklessness arises from the alleged luxury of the lifestyles endowed by social security benefits, and from the indolence and ease with which the system is exploited. My clippings files bulge with annual examples of the, invariably misleading, summertime accounts of social security enriched holiday-makers. The *Daily Express* front-page lead 'Dole cheat's sun holiday' ('A dole cheat soaked up the Caribbean sunshine while still claiming benefit in Britain'), catches the flavour (16 August 1995).

But towering over all such narratives are those of the 'super-scroungers'. Among the more prominent such bogey figures recently was 47-year-old former pig worker and invalidity beneficiary Paul Booth, who in 1998 found himself getting more column inches than the resigning social security minister Frank Field. The *Daily Mirror* gave a double-page spread to Mr Booth and his two-family, eleven-children household (8 April 1998).

By the following week further investigation enabled the headline 'Scrounger and a liar' to be printed (14 April 1998). Not to be outdone the *Sun* topped its story with a mock-up medal, 'S.O.B.

Order of Scroungers of Britain', and invited its readers to submit details if they knew 'a bigger parasite than Paul Booth? We're looking for one to win our Scroungers of Britain gong' (8 April 1998). As the paper editorialised, 'Wasters like Booth are a huge millstone round our necks...layabouts who do nothing but breed should be cut off without a penny.' And it added archly, and none too elliptically, 'Perhaps we should cut something else off too'.

The same allusion had informed the paper's front-page lead a month earlier that 'Blair snips Jack the dads' as absentee dads were to find that 'Their pay packets or benefits will be slashed in a massive crackdown on scroungers and cheats'. The notion that social security was a drag of enormous proportions on the motor of economic growth had become prominent in political orthodoxy again by the advent of the new Labour government.

The 1998 Green Paper on Social Security in which Frank Field unveiled his unthinkable thoughts was rapidly distilled by the press into two congruent themes. First it was another 'War on cheats', in which 'Welfare cheats face spot fines' *(Express)* as the 'Shake-up in welfare hits the workshy' *(The Times)*.

To help this policy along the *Sun* invited us to 'Shop a bad dad-Field war on spongers who cost us a fortune'. In fact criticised from left and right the Green Paper soon saw its two principal begetters, Field and Social Services Secretary Harriet Harman, both out of office, victims of hubris and the charge that 'Ministers fire welfare blanks'.

But the central message of modern welfare reform was well and truly forged. In a forceful front-page spread the *Express* shows a bewhiskered Field as Moses coming down from the burning bush, tablets in hand, alongside the divine full page headline 'Thou shalt not shirk'. The second theme continued to be the welfare burden which made all this necessary. As the *Mail* had explained a year earlier, 'Labour's radical social security reformer Frank Field yesterday pledged to cut the Government's £90 billion a year welfare bill' ('Field sharpens the axe for a purge on welfare'-5 May 1997).

In fact, as many commentators have noted, UK welfare expenditure is relatively low by international standards. By 1995/96 UK expenditure on 'social protection' ranked ninth out of eleven in European comparisons, with only Italy and Portugal lower. Equally, as Hills points out, '...the UK is not a high tax country. Over the last twenty years the UK has moved from being slightly above the mid-point of the international range of tax as a share of national income to being clearly well below the international average'.

Nevertheless, the public rhetoric tells another story. Behind these 'unbearable' cost levels lies, of course, the excessive allocation of welfare generosity, not merely to too many recipients, but to quite clearly the wrong people. Maintaining a necessary cultural distinction between the deserving and undeserving poor remains one of the cardinal boundary sustaining functions of the public media, even though there are occasional shifts in the demographics of those two groups.

In the early 1990s, and occasionally thereafter, periodic out-bursts of puritanical outrage at single parents placed that large and rapidly growing group firmly in the firing line. Eventually the conclusion was clear: 'Lone parents are the biggest cheats: single mothers may be lying their way to £1 billion'. Not surprisingly, given both the popular and policy onslaught, we then find 'Fewer single mothers claiming benefit'. In contrast was the poignant tale of former legendary Liverpool soccer hard-man Tommy Smith, given a sympathetic treatment in his battle to regain his cancelled disability living allowance.

Equally sympathetic treatment is received by the 'genuinely' disabled, as in the case of an unambiguously 'deserving' woman whose plight was headlined in the *Sun* as 'No arms, no legs...but you're not disabled' (13 April 1998), in a story about a thalidomide victim whose Severe Disablement Allowance was stopped when the DSS found evidence of her selling puppies five years previously. By contrast our attention was drawn to the naivety and absurdity of Oxfam's venture into poverty in the UK. Real poverty is of course to be seen in the fly-encrusted faces of children lying helpless and starving on the dusty sun-baked ground of a far-away disaster zone.

As a *Daily Mail* feature, headlined 'Can you spot the difference', pointed out, 'generous people who wish to give to Oxfam are encouraged to do so by pictures of skeletal mothers and children in Africa'.

To help us understand the point, an accompanying photo of 'an African famine victim' is juxtaposed with a family snap of Paul Booth, the 'superscrounger', and his apparently rudely well-fed and voluminous family. This is not 'the poverty that means wearing rags or having no roof at night' (9 April 1998).

The durability of the deserving poor and the deeply-held foundational myths that sustain them enables a proud tradition of campaigning journalism to surface periodically.

In December 1997 the *Mail on Sunday* claimed a success in its 'campaign' on the much-maligned Benefits Integrity Project, with 'Benefits U-turn ends disabled mother's order' (28 December 1997) in a story about a woman crippled by multiple sclerosis whose Income Support had been withdrawn.

Even more emotively signalling a nostalgic search for its heroic campaigning past, the *Daily Mirror* produced a three-page 'Poverty-shock report' feature on the 'virus' which is 'spreading at an alarming rate... The name of this virus is poverty' (30 October 1998), with a two-column photo spread of a three-year-old girl clutching her doll in the bleak passage of a 'grim Liverpool estate'.

Only the relegation of the feature to pages 33-35 signalled a very different set of priorities from the barnstorming polemics of the *Mirror* under Bartholomew and Cudlipp half a century earlier.

Powerful myths about poverty, public expenditure, and the moral economy of welfare remain immovably planted at the core of public understanding of policies related to social security.

Since the 1980s some of these myths have been severely tested by changing economic conditions, yet their potency seems largely undiminished. These exemplars, however, should not disguise the very limited nature of news coverage of pertinent areas of public policy, and it is to that wider, and more calculated picture, that I now turn.

Small but Imperfectly Formed: a Measure of Social security News

To obtain a measure of social security coverage in the media this section extracts relevant data from a larger study of policy news undertaken at the Communication Research Centre at Loughborough University. The data summarised here cover all national UK news media throughout the year October 1996 to September 1997.

The first and most obvious finding is how little coverage social security gets. In that period there were just twenty-four stories primarily about social security on the BBC's main evening television bulletin, eleven on ITN, and in broadsheet newspapers not many more (twenty-six in the *Guardian,* twelve in *The Times*).

Social Security is not big news, even compared with other social policy areas such as education, housing and health. Health is by far the most regularly reported, even dwarfing education in a period when all the main parties were ostensibly committed to that field as a priority.

Social security, like other areas of social policy, is first and foremost about politics. Poverty, benefits, and welfare are refracted through the legislative cycle and the machinery of government, or at least that fraction of it which surfaces in media exposure.

During the same period the Prime Minister appeared in roughly 15 per cent of all such social security news items and other government ministers in 60 per cent. Claimants and non-political actors of any kind made up just 12 per cent of the total actors appearing in these stories.

When social security minister Frank Field published his Green Paper it received high-profile coverage, but nothing so extended and close focused as his ill-tempered resignation saga some weeks later. One facet of this less than comprehensive account of social security and poverty in the major news media is a diminishing attention to social policy news of any kind.

In recent years frequent charges of 'tabloidisation', not least from within journalism, have argued that the major news media, most especially broadcasting and the serious newspapers 'of record' had abandoned their traditional and honourable role of serving citizens with the essential diet of information required to perform their democratic role, and were instead moving to a more diverse and diverting fare with aspirations to entertain more than inform. I have examined the empirical foundation of this claim elsewhere. It shows a clear trend in both titles towards a much greater proportion of crime stories, and a rapidly diminishing proportion of both social policy stories and indeed of foreign news. With such a diminishing scope for news about poverty and social security it matters more than ever what aspects of these issues are given prominence or attention.

It is not altogether surprising, given the historic confusion in the British psyche between the iniquities of the criminally indigent and the lifestyles of the merely impoverished, that social security and crime news occupy close quarters in the journalistic corpus. In the period of our content analysis we examined both crime and social security stories.

Of all stories that were primarily about one or other of these topics, 27.1 per cent (in the tabloid press), 16.6 per cent (in the broadsheet press), and 11.7 per cent (in broadcast news) were about both-that is were about criminal activity associated with social security.

As I have noted above, it would be difficult to attribute this to the prevalence or scale of social security abuse, but it does certainly register a consistent association between the two areas of activity in the public mind, as we shall see shortly. My concern throughout this chapter has been, of course, primarily with the news media.

Nonetheless it would be remiss not to recognise that the welfare state in its various guises forms a luminous backcloth for the fictional lives of much popular drama, and no more so than in the working class sagas of the soap operas. In the lives and doings of these twenty-seven characters, and others like them, are embodied powerful and rich evocations of the understandings which imbue public perception of issues like social security. In *EastEnders,* for example, Irene (who claimed unemployment benefit despite living with her boyfriend Terry), fell foul of Susan (who also lives in the square but works for the Department of Social Security), leading to an inevitable showdown in the Queen Vic pub.

There can be little doubt, though evidence awaits, that in such constructions lie the source of much of the imagery and explication deployed by people in responding to news and experience of major social issues like poverty and social security.

Responding to the 'Wretched and Ignoble': Public attitudes

There is some evidence that public attitudes have, in recent years, softened and extended to suggest a broader understanding of the ways in which sections of the population are being cut adrift from 'comfortable Britain'. Despite that, the more severe responses which lie deep-rooted in our culture, and on which much of the media coverage illustrated here is based, seem entrenched. If anything the same surveys show that hostile attitudes to those who do not avoid dependency on the state have hardened. Although such attitudes soften in periods of recession, animosity to presumed fraudsters remains consistent, a pattern that offers circumstantial evidence, though no more, for a contrast between the fluctuating direct experience of people in the wider economy and their more constant exposure to the punitive odium attached to social security 'abuse' in the mainstream media.

The sturdy beggar and his cousins, the 'wretched and ignoble', live on in pre-millennial Britain. In the 1990s, theories popularised by writers like Charles Murray argued that a section of the population in the USA, and in other countries like it, notably in the UK, had become detached from the mainstream of society, primarily by virtue of its distinct culture.

What separated this group from the majority was its 'deplorable behaviour', making them a quite separate 'underclass'. The term, and the imagery and mythology on which it drew, became deeply rooted in the policy aspirations of social security reformers across the political spectrum.

It was, of course, but a renaming of that multitude whose 'vicious habits and destitute circumstances make it certain that... they must hunger and sin, sin and hunger' till death in the 'darkest England' where General William Booth took his Salvation Army a century ago.

While an alternative and more recent language of 'social exclusion' expressed the structural forces preventing the entry of large numbers into the benefits and delights of late-twentieth century society, both rhetorics established symbolic barriers between the consumers of the social security and benefits system and the larger majority whose labours and diligence provided that system's resources. The discursive battle to understand and encapsulate the mystery of severe and extensive poverty within the affluent communities of late-twentieth century society takes place in the pages of the daily press, and on the screens of the nation's living rooms, as much as on the floor of the House of Commons. That battle seems as flourishing and as critical as it was in General Booth's time, and no less is at stake.

6

Role of Journalism in Democracy

INTRODUCTION

In the 1920s, as modern journalism was just taking form, writer Walter Lippmann and American philosopher John Dewey debated over the role of journalism in a democracy. Their differing philosophies still characterize a debate about the role of journalism in society and the nation-state. Lippmann understood that journalism's role at the time was to act as a mediator or translator between the public and policy making elites. The journalist became the middleman. When elites spoke, journalists listened and recorded the information, distilled it, and passed it on to the public for their consumption. His reasoning behind this was that the public was not in a position to deconstruct the growing and complex flurry of information present in modern society, and so an intermediary was needed to filter news for the masses. Lippman put it this way: The public is not smart enough to understand complicated, political issues. Furthermore, the public was too consumed with their daily lives to care about complex public policy.

Therefore the public needed someone to interpret the decisions or concerns of the elite to make the information plain and simple. That was the role of journalists. Lippmann believed that the public would affect the decision-making of the elite with their vote. In the meantime, the elite (*i.e.* politicians, policy makers, bureaucrats, scientists, etc.) would keep the business of power running. In Lippman's world, the journalist's role was to inform the public of what the elites were doing. It was also to act as a watchdog over the elites, as the public had the final say with their votes. Effectively that kept the public at the bottom of the power chain, catching the flow of information that is handed down from experts/elites.

Dewey, on the other hand, believed the public was not only capable of understanding the issues created or responded to by the elite, it was in the public forum that decisions should be made after discussion and debate. When issues were thoroughly vetted, then the best ideas would bubble to the surface. Dewey believed journalists should do more than simply pass on information.

He believed they should weigh the consequences of the policies being enacted. Over time, his idea has been implemented in various degrees, and is more commonly known as "community journalism."

This concept of *community journalism* is at the centre of new developments in journalism. In this new paradigm, journalists are able to engage citizens and the experts/elites in the proposition and generation of content. It's important to note that while there is an assumption of equality, Dewey still celebrates expertise. Dewey believes the shared knowledge of many is far superior to a single individual's knowledge. Experts and scholars are welcome in Dewey's framework, but there is not the hierarchical structure present in Lippman's understanding of journalism and society. According to Dewey, conversation, debate, and dialogue lie at the heart of a democracy.

While Lippman's journalistic philosophy might be more acceptable to government leaders, Dewey's approach is a better description of how many journalists see their role in society, and, in turn, how much of society expects journalists to function. Americans, for example, may criticize some of the excesses committed by journalists, but they tend to expect journalists to serve as watchdogs on government, businesses and other actors, enabling people to make informed decisions on the issues of the time.

THE ELEMENTS OF JOURNALISM

According to *The Elements of Journalism*, a book by Bill Kovach and Tom Rosenstiel, there are nine elements of journalism. In order for a journalist to fulfil their duty of providing the people with the information they need to be free and self-governing. They must follow these guidelines:

1. Journalism's first obligation is to the truth.
2. Its first loyalty is to the citizens.
3. Its essence is discipline of verification.
4. Its practitioners must maintain an independence from those they cover.
5. It must serve as an independent monitor of power.
6. It must provide a forum for public criticism and compromise.
7. It must strive to make the significant interesting, and relevant.
8. It must keep the news comprehensive and proportional.
9. Its practitioners must be allowed to exercise their personal conscience.

In the April 2007 edition of the book, they have added one additional element, *the rights and responsibilities of citizens* to make it a total of ten elements of journalism.

PROFESSIONAL AND ETHICAL STANDARDS

In the UK, all newspapers are bound by the Code of Practice of the Press

Complaints Commission. This includes points like respecting people's privacy and ensuring accuracy. However, the Media Standards Trust has criticised the PCC, claiming it needs to be radically changed to secure public trust of newspapers. This is in stark contrast to the media climate prior to the 20th Century, where the media market was dominated by smaller newspapers and pamphleteers who usually had an overt and often radical agenda, with no presumption of balance or objectivity.

RECOGNITION OF EXCELLENCE IN JOURNALISM

There are several professional organizations, universities and foundations that recognize excellence in journalism in the USA. The Pulitzer Prize, administered by Columbia University in New York City, is awarded to newspapers, magazines and broadcast media for excellence in various kinds of journalism. The Columbia University Graduate School of Journalism gives the Alfred I. duPont-Columbia University Awards for excellence in radio and television journalism, and the Scripps Howard Foundation gives the National Journalism Awards in 17 categories. The Society of Professional Journalists gives the Sigma Delta Chi Award for journalism excellence. In the television industry, the National Academy of Television Arts and Sciences gives awards for excellence in television journalism.

FAILING TO UPHOLD STANDARDS

Such a code of conduct can, in the real world, be difficult to uphold consistently. Journalists who believe they are being fair or objective may give biased accounts—by reporting selectively, trusting too much to anecdote, or giving a partial explanation of actions. Even in routine reporting, bias can creep into a story through a reporter's choice of facts to summarize, or through failure to check enough sources, hear and report dissenting voices, or seek fresh perspectives.

A news organization's budget inevitably reflects decision-making about what news to cover, for what audience, and in what depth. Those decisions may reflect conscious or unconscious bias. When budgets are cut, editors may sacrifice reporters in distant news bureaus, reduce the number of staff assigned to low-income areas, or wipe entire communities from the publication's zone of interest.

Publishers, owners and other corporate executives, especially advertising sales executives, can try to use their powers over journalists to influence how news is reported and published. Journalists usually rely on top management to create and maintain a "firewall" between the news and other departments in a news organization to prevent undue influence on the news department. One journalism magazine, Columbia Journalism Review, has made it a practice to reveal examples of executives who try to influence news coverage, of executives who do not abuse their powers over journalists, and of journalists who resist such pressures. Self-censorship is a growing problem in journalism, particularly in covering countries that sharply restrict press freedom. As commercial pressure in the media marketplace grows, media organizations are loath to lose access to high-profile countries by producing unflattering stories. For example, CNN admitted that it had practiced self-censorship in covering the Saddam Hussein regime in Iraq in order to ensure continued access after the regime had thrown out other media. CNN correspondent Christiane Amanpour also complained of self-censorship during the invasion of Iraq due to the fear of alienating key audiences in the US. There are claims that the media are also avoiding covering stories about repression and human rights violations by the Israeli and Iranian regimes in order to maintain a presence in those countries.

REPORTING VERSUS EDITORIALIZING

Generally, publishers and consumers of journalism draw a distinction between reporting — "just the facts" — and opinion writing, often by restricting opinion columns to the editorial page and its facing or "op-ed" (opposite the editorials) page. Unsigned editorials are traditionally the official opinions of the paper's editorial board, while op-ed pages may be a mixture of syndicated columns and other contributions, frequently with some attempt to balance the voices across some political or social spectrum.

The distinction between reporting and opinion can break down. In the UK, the Press Complaints Commission states that "the Press, whilst free to be partisan, must distinguish clearly between comment, conjecture and fact" but some commentators have suggested there can sometimes be a blurring of opinion and fact. Complex stories often require summarizing and interpretation of facts, especially if there is limited time or space for a story. Stories involving great amounts of interpretation are often labelled "news analysis," but still run in a paper's news columns. The limited time for each story in a broadcast report rarely allows for such distinctions.

LEGAL STATUS

Journalists around the world often write about the governments in their nations, and those governments have widely varying policies and practices towards journalists, which control what they can research and write, and what press organizations can publish. Many Western governments guarantee the freedom of the press, and do relatively little to restrict press rights and freedoms, while other nations severely restrict what journalists can research and/or publish.

Journalists in many nations have enjoyed some privileges not enjoyed by members of the general public, including better access to public events, crime scenes and press conferences, and to extended interviews with public officials, celebrities and others in the public eye.

These privileges are available because of the perceived power of the press to turn public opinion for or against governments, their officials and policies, as well as the perception that the press often represents their consumers. These privileges extend from the legal rights of journalists but are not guaranteed by those rights. Sometimes government officials may attempt to punish individual journalists who irk them by denying them some of these privileges extended to other journalists.

Nations or jurisdictions that formally license journalists may confer special privileges and responsibilities along with those licenses, but in the United States the tradition of an independent press has avoided any imposition of government-controlled examinations or licensing. Some of the states have explicit shield laws that protect journalists from some forms of government enquiry, but those statutes' definitions of "journalist" were often based on access to printing presses and broadcast towers. A national shield law has been proposed.

In some nations, journalists are directly employed, controlled or censored by their governments. In other nations, governments who may claim to guarantee press rights actually intimidate journalists with threats of arrest, destruction or seizure of property (especially the means of production and dissemination of news content), torture or murder.

Journalists who elect to cover conflicts, whether wars between nations or insurgencies within nations, often give up any expectation of protection by government, if not giving up their rights to protection by government. Journalists who are captured or detained during a conflict are expected to be treated as civilians and to be released to their national government.

RIGHT TO PROTECT CONFIDENTIALITY OF SOURCES

The scope of rights granted to journalists varies from nation to nation; in the United Kingdom, for example, the government has had more legal rights to protect what it considers sensitive information, and to force journalists to reveal the sources of leaked information, than the United States. Other nations, particularly Zimbabwe and the People's Republic of China, have a reputation of persecuting journalists, both domestic and foreign.

In the United States, there has never been a right to protect sources in a federal court. Some states provide varying degrees of such protection. However, federal courts will refuse to force journalists to reveal sources, unless the information the court seeks is highly relevant to the case, and there's no other way to get it. Journalists, like all citizens, who refuse to testify even when ordered to can be found in contempt of court and fined or jailed.

RIGHT OF ACCESS

United States: In the United States, the Freedom of Information Act guarantees journalists the right to obtain copies of government documents, although the government has the right to black out some information from these documents. Other federal legislation also controls access to information.

Some states have more open policies for making information available, and some states have acted in the last decade to broaden those rights. New Jersey has updated and broadened its freedom of information legislation to better define what kinds of government documents can be withheld from public enquiry. Journalists in the state of Michigan have access to information based on the latest provisions from the state amended in 1996 PA 553 Office of the Michigan Attorney General.

Michigan's defined basic intent for the Freedom of Information Act (FIOA) is that it is an act that regulates and sets requirements for the disclosure of public records by all "public bodies" in the state.

The definition of a public body is any state officer, employee, agency, department, division, bureau, board, commission, council, authority, or other body in the executive branch of the state government (it does not however include the governor, or lieutenant governor. Other bodies included are school boards, or bodies created or funded by state or local authority. A public record is something that is written regarding the performance of a official function held by any of the previously named bodies.

Accessing information in the state of Michigan is available for records that are made public, which includes all records held by those named previously, but not those specifically marked as exceptions. Items that are commonly held as public record include meeting notes, voting records, and written statements. Records can be found and kept in a number of manners; anywhere from typewritten to handwritten, to printed, photographed, or even audio recording. Items as such are also allowed to be kept as public record in a combination of mediums per type of information.

Some information however, is not allowed to be public knowledge and is not available to look up as a public record. A public body may (but is not required to) withhold information from the public. Some items are exempt from the FOIA such as personal information about an individual that may be a clear invasion of privacy. Other information includes that which may impair an individual of having a fair trial, disclose the identity of a confidential source, information gathered during an investigation, or that which may put law enforcement personnel in danger.

Accessing public records in the state of Michigan is made possible via a request in writing to the FOIA coordinator of the public body. One may ask to inspect, copy, or receive a copy of a public record. An individual of any age can request this type of information. The only individuals not entitled to making requests as such are prisoners in state, county, or federal correctional facilities. It is also the responsibility of the public body to respond within five days of the request. There may be charges associated with copying, or providing the information requested. A denial may also be made by the public body in writing within the five day period, or within 15 business days if an extension is granted. If denied, the public body must provide a full explanation of the reason why the denial was made. A person does have the option to appeal a denial, or may take the request for disclosure to a circuit court.

If a court decides that a public body has violated the FOIA, it may grant the person looking for information, on top of providing the person with the information, hold the public body responsible for paying a $500 award to the individual looking for the information illegally denied.

Journalists can take this information in the State of Michigan and use it when looking up information that is pertinent to the topic under report or research and do so without violating privacy in order to justify stories or provide sources to enhance journalistic integrity.

India: In India, the Right to Information Act was passed in 2005, giving citizens the right to access state and national records.

France: In France, the freedom of press Act was passed in 1881, giving citizens the right to read and create any newspaper of his choice. In 1935, a new act was passed to protect the right of the journalist to work in good conditions, responding to the demand of the main journalist's Union, the 'Syndicat national des journalistes.

In 1971, two other unions, the Syndicat national des journalistes CGT, *and* Union syndicale des journalistes CFDT *signed the* charte de Munich*, a stylebook dedicated to protect the deontology and spirit of journalism on a broadbased attempt to boost it all over the world.*

JOURNALISTS HARASSMENT

In the summer of 1991, the St. Petersburg (Florida) Times broke a significant local story about charges of sexual harassment and sex discrimination at one of the city's larger employers. Women at the company charged that less qualified men were paid more, promoted sooner, and given better assignments. Subtle and even blatant sexual harassment was tolerated.

What made the story particularly significant was that the company in question was the St. Petersburg Times itself, and many of the women who had crowded into Chief Executive Andrew Barnes' office to voice their complaints were reporters, editors, and photographers. Some of the stories the women told Barnes in that meeting and in a written report would have competed for sheer rudeness with the comments Anita Hill claimed Supreme Court Justice Clarence Thomas had made to her. One man had said to a pregnant female staffer, "Your breasts are really getting huge." Another, a senior editor, had been talking with other editors about a company called TMS and the problems it was causing the newspaper. He turned to the female editor in the group and explained that TMS should "not be confused with PMS, which is worse for the company." The story attracted attention from other newspapers statewide, as well as national trade journals, and demonstrated that sexual harassment and sex discrimination are issues newspaper managers must be prepared to deal with within the newsroom, not just in stories about other organizations' problems.

The term "sexual harassment" is a relatively recent addition to our vocabulary. Psychologist Julia Wood suggests that such harassment has existed for most of history but remained unnamed; the absence of visibility, which resulted from the fact that harassment had no negative effects on the men who held power, made it difficult to recognize, think about, or stop.

Today courts have recognized two categories of sexual harassment, known as "quid pro quo" ("something for something") and "hostile environment" discrimination. The former refers to situations in which an individual promises a subordinate employee some sort of tangible job benefit, such as a raise, in exchange for sexual favours.

This category also likely would include more negatively stated interactions, such as a supervisor's threat that the victim will lose her job if she refuses the supervisor's request for sexual favours.

The latter, "hostile environment" discrimination, reflects circumstances in which an employee is subjected to a pattern of behaviour - such as unwanted sexual advances, degrading sexual comments about the employee, or similar problems- that interferes unreasonably with an employee's ability to perform his or her job or makes the workplace environment inhospitable, intimidating, or offensive. Many scholars argue that sexual harassment of women is widespread throughout academia and the workplace; however, a review of the communications and journalism literature suggests that relatively little research has been done on sexual harassment as a problem facing women journalists. Most earlier studies of women journalists focused almost entirely on sex discrimination and the likelihood of women achieving rank and pay equity with men. A review of that list also suggests that not much attention has been paid recently to studies of either discrimination against or harassment of women journalists.

One exception, the Associated Press Managing Editors Association harassment study in 1992, opened some eyes, according to Pam Johnson, managing editor of the Phoenix Gazette and chairwoman of the APME Newsroom Manage-ment Committee. Some of the major discoveries from the survey of 640 male and female journalists from nineteen U.S. newsrooms:

- Only 30 per cent of the respondents said their newspaper had clear guidelines for filing internal complaints about sexual harassment;

- 95 per cent of the victims of sexual harassment were women;
- 2 per cent of the men and 11 per cent of the women said sexual harassment or the fear of harassment had affected their daily work habits;

While the most prevalent form of harassment was annoying or degrading comments about sex, followed by offensive pictures or posters and annoying or degrading comments about women's bodies, the APME study found that women also reported having male associates grab their breasts and buttocks or make "jokes" to them about rape. Evidence of the female journalists' frustration came in the form of numerous vehement comments handwritten on the back of the survey form. Although most men surveyed tended to say there was no sexual harassment problem at their newspapers, women said it is a potential, if not specific, problem, and that it is neither reported nor punished in most instances.

Johnson, in writing about the study, observed: "Women in our newsrooms are impatient. They don't want to get ogled. They don't want to receive sex-related messages in their computers, they don't want to be put in the place of laughing off a sexual joke or challenging it and then having to pay for being forthright. And they definitely don't want to be fondled. But it's clear many feel vulnerable to any or all of these situations."

Flatow found that more than two-thirds of women working in the newsrooms of Indiana daily newspapers had indeed found themselves "vulnerable" to sexual harassment. In her survey of full-time editorial employees working at twenty-six Indiana dailies, Flatow found that 22.4 per cent of the women and 6.6 per cent of the men had experienced physical sexual harassment at some point during their careers. The same percentage of men, but nearly three times the percentage of women (61.8 per cent) reported experiencing verbal sexual harassment, and nearly a third of the women reported "non-verbal" sexual harassment.

One recent study of women journalists in Washington, D.C., showed that 60 per cent of the women accredited to the Capitol press gallery had been sexually harassed. The researchers, Katherine McAdams and Maurine Beasley, surveyed 273 women journalists and received responses from 37 per cent. Of those who responded, 80 per cent said they believe sexual harassment is a problem for women journalists. McAdams and Beasley argue that the issue of sexual harassment among women journalists needs to be investigated and brought into the open so that individual women no longer have to deal with the problem alone.

At the time of their study, Beasley and McAdams noted finding only one previous newsroom survey about sexual harassment. That study, conducted for the newspaper trade publication Newslnc., showed that 44 per cent of the 199 newsroom women surveyed had experienced sexual harassment on the job. That figure was twice the number of women in all fields reporting harassment in a 1991 Newsweek/Gallup Poll.

More recently, Bowen and Laurion studied sexual harassment among mass communication professionals. Among their sample of 52 female and 44 male respondents, the authors found that 32 per cent had experienced sexual harassment as students, 49 per cent had experienced sexual harassment as interns in a mass communication organization, and 65 per cent had experienced sexual harassment during their professional careers.

To most women, the importance of discovering the extent of sexual harassment among any group of women workers may seem obvious, and the threat of legal action by a harassed employee should be enough to get the attention of even the most old-fashioned newsroom managers. In addition, it seems particularly appropriate to examine sexual harassment among journalists because journalists have devoted considerable time in recent years to examining sexual harassment in other types of workplaces, including the federal government, the U.S. military services, and corporations. But the research also indicates that there are bottom-line considerations that make understanding and attempting to solve the problem of sexual harassment more pressing.

In short, the research indicates that sexual harassment has negative effects on women's work performance, as well as career advancement. In fact, the federal report Sexual Harassment in the Federal Government: An Update estimated that harassment cost the federal government $267 million over two years, including $76.3 million in lost individual productivity, and a recent analysis of sexual harassment in Fortune 500 companies concluded that sexual harassment costs each firm approximately $6.7 million annually.

Newspapers may not be able to figure the monetary costs of sexual harassment so conclusively, but there must be costs-in lost concentration on the stories, photos, or graphics assignments harassment victims would rather be working on. Indeed, many of Flatow's respondents reported that sexual harassment creates an environment of fear and intimidation at worst and even at best produces distractions that keep women from performing at the top of their ability.

Another major potential source of costs of which newspapers must be wary is lawsuits filed by women journalists who've been sexually harassed at work. Bunker concluded from a review of legal cases involving sexual harassment that media organizations should work to eliminate sexual harassment for their employees for selfish as well as noble reasons.

He noted that: "Media organizations, like other employers, are subject to strict liability for quid pro quo harassment by supervisors. In cases of hostile environment harassment, whether the harassment originates from supervisors, co-workers or non-employees, media organi-zations can be held vicariously liable if they know or should have known of the harassment and do not take immediate and effective steps to remedy it." Previous research and anecdotes like those reported by the female staffers of the St. Petersburg Times leave little doubt that sexual harassment is likely a problem for women newspaper journalists in the 1990s, despite all the effort those newspapers may put into coverage of and editorial outcry against sexual harassment in other fields. The study this paper discusses was designed to provide data about the extent and sources of sexual harassment that women journalists face. We hoped to address a number of research questions, including the following:

- What percentage of women have experienced sexual harassment during their careers as reporters, photographers, editors, and newspaper graphic artists?
- Who harasses women journalists- supervisors, peers, subordinates, news sources?
- What percentage of newspapers have written policy statements about sexual harassment, and to what extent are all employees aware of these policies?
- Are there personal or work environment charact-eristics that increase or decrease the likelihood that women will experience sexual harassment as journalists?
- What do women do about the instances of sexual harassment they encounter? Method

Female reporters, photographers, editors, and graphic artists were randomly selected for participation in the survey using a multilevel stratified sampling procedure. First, the researchers drew separate samples of small, medium, and large newspapers (seventy-two small, thirty-two medium, and sixteen large newspapers). We then contacted a newsroom manager (usually the managing editor) at each newspaper included in the samples and asked him or her to send us a list of all the female reporters, editors, photographers, and graphic artists on the newspaper's staff, including those working at bureaus.

After obtaining these lists, the lists were arranged in random order, and we then randomly selected names from the lists. This procedure ultimately produced a final sample of 208 women from small newspapers (daily circulation less than 25,000),184 women from mid-sized newspapers (daily circulation of 25,001-100,000) and 190 women from large newspapers (daily circulation greater than 100,000).

After all the names had been chosen, we sent each sample member a letter describing our project and requesting her cooperation. The letter also informed sample members that only female students or faculty members would be conducting the study interviews.

Interviewers first called each sample member to arrange an appropriate time and place to complete the interview; any woman who did not feel comfortable discussing the subject in her work environment was asked for a home telephone number and called at home. The first part of each interview was conducted using a computerassisted telephone interviewing programme; interviewers subsequently asked each participant for more details about her experiences, using a schedule of open-ended questions. The data from the interviews were analysed using SPSS for Windows.

Measures

Evaluation of Sexual Harassment as a Problem. For this section of the survey, respondents were told that "(f)or the purposes of the survey, sexual harassment is defined as any physical or verbal contacts that make the workplace inhospitable for women because of their gender." Each respondent then was asked to say whether, in her opinion, sexual harassment was "no problem at all, not much of a problem, somewhat of a problem, a significant problem, or a very serious problem" for women as newspaper reporters, editors, photographers, or graphic artists. Each respondent used the same scale to indicate how much of a problem sexual harassment had been for her personally in her own career as a journalist.

Experience with Sexual Harassment. Each respondent was asked how often she had been "subjected to sexual harassment that did not involve physical contact, such as inappropriate sexual comments, suggestions, or gestures" made to her or in her presence by the following types of individuals: supervisors or others in positions of authority at the newspaper, other coworkers at her same level, other coworkers at levels lower than hers, news sources, employees of news sources, or in any other professional setting.

For each potential source of harassment, the respondent was asked whether non-physical harassment had occurred never, rarely, sometimes, often, or nearly always/always.

The interviewers then used the same scale (never, rarely, etc.) and the same series of potential harassers (supervisors, same-level coworkers, etc.) to determine how often the respondent had been subjected to "physical sexual harassment - that is, unwanted physical contact."

Definitions of Sexual Harassment. The respondents were asked whether they strongly agreed, agreed, neither agreed nor disagreed, disagreed, or strongly disagreed that the following behaviours constituted sexual harassment:

- When a man frequently makes uninvited and unnecessary physical contact with a woman who works with him
- When a man tells sexual jokes to a woman who has never told the same kind of jokes to him
- When a man pressures a woman who works with him to go out on a date with him
- When a man frequently makes uninvited remarks that have sexual references or double meanings to a woman who works with him

- When a man flirts with a female coworker who has never flirted with him
- When a man displays sexually oriented pictures or calendars in places where women also work.

Sexual Harassment Policies. Respondents were asked whether their newspaper has a written policy statement dealing with sexual harassment. Those who said the newspaper had such a policy were asked: "Are all employees equally aware of this policy, are women more likely to be aware of it or are men more likely to be aware of the policy?"

Demographic and Work-Environmentlnformation. Each respondent was asked for her year of birth, marital status, job title, how many years she had worked as a journalist, how many people worked in the newsroom where she worked, what percentage of those people were women, whether her immediate supervisor was a man or a woman, and whether news employees at her newspaper were members of a union.

Results

Our goal had been to include about 100 women from each size of newspapers in the final survey, and we had anticipated that we would need approximately twice as many women in the initial sample to account for refusals to participate, ineligible respondents, and sample members who never could be reached. The most serious difficulty we encountered turned out to be contacting sample members, particularly those from the large and midsized newspapers, before they left their jobs, often for employment outside newspapers.

Once we had contacted sample members, refusals to participate in the survey were quite rare. Of the 582 women included in the original sample, we ultimately made some type of contact with 396, although in 85 cases, we only learned that the woman no longer worked at that newspaper. Of the 311 women our interviewers did speak with, only 33 refused to participate, for an unusually low refusal rate of 10.6 per cent. Eighty-four other women were contacted and agreed to participate, but could not be interviewed because of scheduling difficulties or some other problem.

Not surprisingly, the largest number of respondents were reporters (39 per cent). Eleven per cent of the respondents were copy editors, 15 per cent were section editors (*i.e.*, editors of features, business, or sports sections), and 4 per cent were city editors or assistant city editors.

Fourteen respondents (6.2 per cent) were news editors, and an equal number described themselves as editors. Six of the repondents (2.6 per cent) held managing editor or assistant managing editor positions, and another six were photographers. The remainder of the sample was graphic artists, photo editors, editorial writers or columnists, held some other position, or gave no title. The women ranged in age from 23 to 74, and their experience as journalists ran from less than one year to forty-five years. The smallest newsroom had only three employees; the largest an estimated 400 employees.

The percentage of newsroom employees who were women ranged from 4 to 90 per cent. About two-thirds (67 per cent) of the women had males as their immediate supervisors, about 31 per cent had female immediate supervisors, and five women reported having one or more supervisors of each gender. Nearly half of the women (47.6 per cent) were married.

The women were asked to indicate whether sexual harassment was no problem, not much of a problem, somewhat a problem, a significant problem, or a very serious problem for women journalists in general and in their own careers specifically. About 60 per cent of the women said sexual harassment is at least somewhat a problem for women as reporters, photographers, editors, and graphic artists, and more than one in 10 (11.5 per cent) said sexual harassment is a significant or very serious problem for women journalists.

Lower percentages reported having substantial trouble with sexual harassment in their own careers; nonetheless, more than one-third (36.1 per cent) said sexual harassment had been at least somewhat a problem for them personally, and 17 women (7.5 per cent) reported having had significant or serious problems with sexual harassment during their careers.

Cross-tabulation analysis determined that there was a significant relationship between beliefs about the seriousness of sexual harassment as a problem for women journalists and age. Older women (4174 years old) were three times as likely as the youngest women (23-30 years old) or the middle age group (31-40) to say that sexual harassment was no problem at all for women journalists.

Women in the 23-30 age group were twice as likely as those in the middle group and more than three times as likely as the oldest women to regard sexual harassment as a significant or very serious problem for women journalists. Women's ratings of sexual harassment as a problem for women journalists also were related to the percentage of women in their newsrooms.

Women working in newsrooms in which more than half of the employees were female were far more likely to say that sexual harassment was little or no problem for women journalists; these women were more than four times as likely as women in the least-female-populated newsrooms to say that sexual harassment was no problem at all for women journalists.

None of the demographic or work environment variables showed any significant relationship with women's views of sexual harassment as a problem in their own careers.

DEFINITIONS OF SEXUAL HARASSMENT

In addition to learning about the extent of physical and non-physical sexual harassment among women journalists, we also were interested in determining how women in the newsroom define sexual harassment. Thus, the women's responses to questions about whether a variety of types of behaviour constitute sexual harassment. Specifically, we asked the women to use a five-point scale to indicate the extent to which they would define it as sexual harassment if a man:

- Made repeated, unwanted physical contact with a female coworker,
- Told sexual jokes to a female coworker who had never told him similar jokes,
- Pressured a female coworker for a date,
- Repeatedly made remarks with sexual meanings or double entendres to a female coworker,
- Flirted with a female coworker who had not previously flirted with him,
- Displayed sexually oriented posters or calendars in areas where female coworkers would have to see them.

There was strong agreement that a man who makes repeated, unwanted physical contact with a female coworker is engaging in sexual harassment; 98.7 per cent of the women either agreed or strongly agreed with this statement. Almost as high a percentage (92.5 per cent) said pressuring a female coworker for a date constitutes sexual harassment, and 87.7 per cent either agreed or strongly agreed that making sexual comments or double entendres to a female coworker constituted sexual harassment. The great majority of respondents (86.3 per cent) also agreed or strongly agreed that displaying sexy posters or calendars was sexual harassment, and about 81 per cent agreed that telling sexual jokes to a female coworker who never had told the same kind of jokes to the man constituted harassment. The behaviour least likely to be defined as sexual harassment was flirting with a female coworker who hadn't flirted with the man before; 37.9 per cent of the respondents agreed or strongly agreed, but more than a third (33.9 per cent) disagreed or strongly disagreed.

Cross tabulations were conducted to determine whether demographic or newspaper characteristics (age, years of experience, circulation size) were related to respondents' likelihood of defining each of the behaviours as sexual harassment.

Age was significantly related to one measure - whether the respondent agreed that displaying sexually oriented pictures was sexual harassment; the oldest women (41-74 years old) were nearly twice as likely to strongly agree (59.3 per cent) as were the youngest group, 23- to 30year-olds (31.1 per cent). The relationship between age group and agreement that telling sexual jokes constituted harassment approached significance (p=.11), and the trend reflected the same pattern. Women in the oldest group were more likely than those in either of the two younger groups to agree that a man was sexually harassing a female coworker if he told sexual jokes when she never had told him the same kind of joke. The only other relationship that approached significance was between circulation size and the likelihood that respondents defined flirting as sexual harassment. In this case, women at the midsized newspapers (25,001-100,000 circulation) appeared to be least likely to consider flirting to be sexual harassment.

Finally, the six specific questions about definitions of sexual harassment were combined into a moderately reliable scale, and this scale was tested for correlations with the respondents' age, years of journalism experience, and the extent to which she had experienced both physical and non-physical sexual harassment throughout her career. Only age was significantly correlated with this scale, and the correlation, though significant, was quite low.

Sexual Harassment Policies

Each respondent also was asked whether her newspaper had a written policy regarding sexual harassment and if so, whether there were gender differences in awareness of the policy. About 71 per cent of the women said their newspapers do have a formal, written sexual harassment policy. About 13 per cent of the women said the newspaper did not have such a policy, and another 16 per cent were not sure whether or not a sexual harassment policy existed. Of the respondents whose newspapers did have a formal policy, the majority (70 per cent) said male and female employees were equally likely to be aware of the policy. About 19 per cent thought women were more likely to be aware of the policy, and 4 per cent thought men were more aware of it.

The respondents included in this survey were randomly selected, so these results should reflect fairly accurately the experiences and opinions of female journalists working at newspapers throughout the United States. However, one significant concern arises from the fact that the surveys have taken a relatively long time to complete. Interviewing began during the summer of 1993, and the last of the respondents whose data are included in this report were interviewed in February 1995. It's possible that events occurring during the intervening months may have increased the later respondents' awareness of sexual harassment issues. For instance, there was a fairly widely publicized fall 1993 case in which the Supreme Court ruled in favour of a woman who had sued her employer for sexual harassment under the "hostile environment" rule. Newswomen certainly would have been likely to have been exposed to at least wire service coverage of this case, which could have increased the likelihood that they would begin to redefine as harassment behaviour that does not include unwanted physical contact.

Another concern is the relatively large number of women who had left their jobs at the sample newspapers by the time we attempted to contact them. We have no way of knowing whether their experiences differed significantly from those of the women we interviewed. It is possible, for instance, that problems with sexual harassment contributed to their decisions to leave their newspapers, which would mean that our results underestimate the extent of sexual harassment newspaperwomen are encountering.

Despite these limitations, however, the results strongly suggest that sexual harassment is a significant problem for women working in America's daily newspapers. More than one-third of these women said sexual harassment has been at least somewhat a problem in their own careers as journalists, and three of every five respondents believe sexual harassment is a problem for women journalists in general. The difference in those two figures is interesting and may be explained, in part, by the fact that even women who have not themselves experienced blatant sexual harassment are aware when other women in their newsrooms have such experiences. During the openended questions at the end of our interviews, we found that many respondents who had not experienced harassment much themselves were deeply concerned about incidents involving other women with whom they worked.

While knowing about someone else's experience with harassment may not be as stressful as being harassed oneself, it almost certainly produces a less-thanideal working atmosphere.

Another important finding of this study was that, in comparison to the APME survey, we found a much higher percentage of women who said they experienced sexual harassment at least sometimes. Among our respondents, more than two-thirds experienced non-physical sexual harassment at least sometimes, when all possible perpetrators of harassment were considered, and about 17 per cent experienced physical sexual harassment at least sometimes. Only about 38 per cent of the APME survey's female respondents said they had ever been subjected to sexual harassment at their newspapers. Some of the difference may be explained by the wording of questions. We asked respondents about their experiences throughout their careers, while the wording of the APME survey question may have limited women's responses to those involving their present newspaper. Thus, the women in our survey may have been reflecting experiences over a broader span of time and more newspapers. It also is possible, however, that the APME's respondents were working for more enlightened employers; the papers involved in the APME study, after all, had volunteered to participate.

Another contrast with the APME study appears in the identity of persons doing the harassing. Among our respondents, problems with sexual harassment were most common in women's interactions with news sources, who were more likely than any category of coworkers to harass women journalists in either physical or non-physical ways. In the APME survey, on the other hand, 67 per cent of women who had been harassed said the harasser was a coworker, compared to 20 per cent who had been harassed by a source or client. This harassment by sources may be especially troubling to women journalists because many seem to feel powerless to do anything about it. In response to the open-ended questions, many women expressed the view that there was no effective way to prevent harassment by sources because the journalist must depend on these sources for information. One woman from a small Southeastern newspaper said, for instance, that most women reporters simply put up with harassment from sources rather than alienating them. This woman, who had had a police detective ask what colour panties she was wearing and throw a pair of underwear in her face during an interview, said she did not confront him about it. "I continued to work with him as a news source. To report it would have made it worse." Another woman said she wouldn't know what to do about a source's harassment because "in our case the person you would have to go to is the one person who makes women most uncomfortable in the newsroom."

Other women dealt with the harassment more aggressively. The business reporter who was sexually harassed by the bond trader reported the incident to her supervisor, who backed her in her decision to stop using the man as a source and to tell him specifically why she no longer would seek his opinions for stories. Another woman, who now works for a midsized paper in a North-Central state, reported that while working as a police beat reporter in Florida, she had been called out on a dark, rainy night to cover a wreck. The officer who had called her about the wreck suggested that she get into his car to write down the names of those involved, and when she did, he "attacked" her. She slapped him, got out of his car, and later reported the incident to her supervisors. "Luckily when I slapped him, he backed off. I think he was stunned -he was certainly way stronger than I was," she recalled. "It was part of what led him to be canned (fired)."

Harassment by sources may be most common, but the women we talked to also were, in many cases, deeply disturbed by harassment they experienced from coworkers and supervisors. In at least some cases, this harassment has had significant effects on women's careers, spurring them to leave the newspaper to get away from a harassing situation or even, in one case, to turn down a promotion that would have put the woman in more frequent contact with a harassing publisher. This woman, who works now at a newspaper in the Northwest, said the publisher had a habit of touching women employees on the buttocks and rubbing their shoulders. "It just never ended - and continual comments," the woman said. "The funny part is, I was offered the job of news editor, but I didn't take it because of his habits. So he was willing to offer a woman the job because he wanted to make money, and he wanted the experience I had. But he still had these other habits."

Again, women who dealt aggressively with their harassers seemed most likely to get positive results. A woman from a midsized New England newspaper reported that her male coworkers once put up a poster showing a woman surrounded by ten men, with the headline, "Put an end to rape. Say Yes." She said, "The poster was up for about five seconds, and I marched into the managing editor's office and asked him if he had seen it. He went back and took one look at it and immediately told them to take it down. In dealing with this stuff, the best thing to do is just go get a man with a brain in his head, as opposed to one of the ones with his brain between his legs."

Not surprisingly, the respondents in this survey were most likely to define as sexual harassment behaviours involving unwanted physical contact and a coworker pressuring a woman for a date. However, there also was substantial agreement that sexual remarks and comments with double meanings, displaying sex-oriented posters or calendars and telling sexual jokes to a woman who hadn't told the man similar jokes constituted sexual harassment. The only behaviour we asked about that wasn't defined as sexual harassment by at least 50 per cent of our respondents was flirting with a female coworker who hadn't previously flirted with the man.

We also found that about 71 per cent of the women worked at newspapers where there was a written policy regarding sexual harassment (16 per cent weren't sure whether the newspaper had a policy), and 70 per cent of those women said male and female employees were equally aware of the policy. The fact that harassment still is going on may suggest that male journalists, regardless of newspaper policy, simply aren't concerned about negative repercussions they might face if accused of sexual harassment. More likely, perhaps, is that male journalists do not understand that some of the more ambiguous behaviours, such as telling jokes or posting sexy photos, offend their female coworkers.

Some studies also have indicated that male managers in certain kinds of workplaces - including police stations, law firms, advertising agencies, and newspapers - view their workplaces as "unique environments, where sexual harassment can be excused." Women who want to work in these traditionally male environments are expected to play by the boys' rules or not play at all, and this may be particularly true in newsrooms still dominated by men. The finding that women working in newsrooms with higher percentages of male employees were more likely to experience sexual harassment is consistent with findings from other types of workplaces.

On the other hand, it's important to note that many of our more veteran respondents, in the open-ended section of the interview, stressed that their work environments had improved significantly over the course of their careers. One woman, for instance, said that she had been surprised to receive our initial letter because her work environment seemed fine; she said the fact that we were doing the study made her guess that harassment still was a problem in other newsrooms.

Having established that harassment indeed is a problem for women newspaper journalists, we now need to turn our attention to understanding why this harassment occurs and, perhaps more important, how it can be stopped. Further analysis of the open-ended responses from this study is helping us to understand how harassment victims typically respond to their harassers and which kinds of responses seem to be most effective. In addition, further research will be needed to determine how male journalists perceive the kinds of behaviours female journalists categorize as sexually harassing, the circumstances under which they may engage in such behaviours, and how action by newspaper management affects harassment of journalists both in the newsroom and by sources outside.

Regardless of the reason, it seems clear that newspapers must begin to do a better job of addressing the issue of sexual harassment if they want to keep their best and brightest female employees. Research in other fields has demonstrated that the negative work-related outcomes of sexual harassment include high employee turnover, lowered self-esteem and decreased selfconfidence among harassment victims, deteriorating coworker relationships, and decreased job satisfaction and commitment to the organization. From their recent meta-analysis of studies of job stress among journalists, Cook and Banks concluded that there is a strong relationship between job stress and burnout and between job burnout and intention to leave the profession. Sexual harassment may be only one source of job stress for women journalists, but it's an additional stress. Female journalists already face the same stresses male journalists face, and that one additional burden may be enough, in some cases, to send highly competent, top-performing women looking for somewhere else to work. As noted earlier, even when they stay in newspapers, sexual harassment may distract women from the work on which they really want to be concentrating. In that sense, sexual harassment of women journalists does a disservice not only to them but to newspapers' readers as well.

For these reasons, as well as concern for common human decency and fairness, newspaper owners, publishers, and managers would do well to heed the comments of one of our survey respondents, a reporter from a medium-sized Mid-Atlantic newspaper. She said of her supervisors: "Sometimes, these people don't seem to think all the publicity about sexual harassment and sex discrimination applies to them and their behaviour."

EXPERIENCE WITH SEXUAL HARASSMENT

Respondents also were asked to indicate how often they personally had been subjected to two types of sexual harassment - harassment that did not involve physical contact (sexual comments, jokes, etc.) and harassment that did involve physical contact (unwanted touching, etc.) - from a variety of professional contacts. The results indicate that news sources were the most likely to harass women journalists both physically and without making physical contact. More than 44 per cent of the women reported that sources at least sometimes subjected them to non-physical sexual harassment, and about 6 per cent reported physical sexual harassment by sources at least sometimes. More than one-fourth of the women had at some time experienced physical sexual harassment by a news source, and more than 70 per cent of the women had experienced non-physical sexual harassment by a source.

Overall, at least one-fourth of the women said they experienced non-physical sexual harassment at least sometimes from their supervisors or others in positions of authority over them (25.1 per cent) and from coworkers at their same level (29.1 per cent), and nearly one-fourth experienced such harassment from subordinates (23.6 per cent) or in other professional settings (22.5 per cent). Almost 5 per cent had been physically harassed at least sometimes by their supervisors and same-level peers. Because the results shown do not indicate whether the same women were experiencing harassment from a variety of professional contacts, we created two new variables that indicated whether the respondents had been subjected to non-physical or physical sexual harassment at least sometimes from any source.

In other words, had the women experienced physical sexual harassment at least sometimes, regardless of the person engaging in the harassment. More than two-thirds of the women (67.4 per cent) had experienced non-physical harassment at least sometimes by someone in their work environments, and 16.7 per cent of the women had been physically sexually harassed at least sometimes, regardless of the identity of the harasser.

In addition, nearly one in four women had experienced non-physical harassment by three or more professional contacts, and about 6 per cent had been physically harassed by two or more professional contacts. These results suggest that sexual harassment is occurring among women journalists in a relatively widespread manner; it isn't just a few women who are being affected by harassment from multiple professional contacts.

Cross tabulations were conducted to determine whether a woman's chances of being subjected to either non-physical or physical sexual harassment were related to her job title, age, immediate supervisor's gender, the size of the newspaper for which she worked, her years of experience as a journalist, or the percentage of women in the newsroom.

Analyses revealed no significant effects for any of these variables for the measures of combined experience with non-physical or physical sexual harassment. However, some significant differences did exist in measures of non-physical harassment by specific types of work contacts.

The percentage of women in the newsroom was significantly related to a respondent's likelihood of being sexually harassed by coworkers at her same level; women whose newsrooms were one-third female or less were more likely to experience non-physical harassment at least sometimes. This may simply reflect the fact that women are less likely to be harassed by their same-gender peers, so more women in the newsroom means fewer coworkers who're likely to harass them. It also may be, however, that predominantly male newsrooms create a more sympathetic environment for employees inclined to subject their peers to verbal or visual sexual harassment.

Reporters and photographers-women who spend more time outside the newsroom itself-were less likely to report having been harassed by subordinates than were copy editors, graphic artists, and others who spend all or nearly all of their work hours in the newsroom. Again, this may reflect a simple difference in opportunities; reporters and photographers may spend less time around subordinates and therefore have fewer chances to be sexually harassed. A more likely explanation may be that reporters and photographers are less likely to feel that they have any lower-level coworkers. On this question, women did not have the option of saying the question did not apply to them.

On the other hand, reporters and photographers' time outside the newsroom makes them more vulnerable to being sexually harassed by news sources. Nearly 60 per cent of reporters and photographers said sources had sexually harassed them at least sometimes, compared to more than one-third of copy editors, graphic artists, and others working primarily inside the newsroom.

Responses to the open-ended questions at the end of each interview indicated that the types of sexual harassment the women journalists experienced ranged from the merely irritating-being called "honey" and "sweetie" or "that little girl" - to the downright dangerous. One political reporter from a small Midwest newspaper said she deals with condescending name-calling by simply returning the favour: "After I treat them the way they treat me, by calling them 'sweetie' or something like that, it doesn't happen after that."

Other women, however, reported having to deal with much more disturbing instances of sexual harassment by sources. For instance, one police beat reporter from a small newspaper in a Mid-Atlantic state recounted two instances in which she went to a district attorney's office to conduct interviews and found him playing confiscated X-rated videotapes. He continued to watch them during the interviews, telling her, "We just got these tapes in, and I have to look at them." Not surprisingly, the woman found the experience unnerving: "It just didn't make sense that he would put them in the tape player. They're (videotape characters) having sex, totally nude, on TV. It was disturbing and uncomfortable, and I was trying to ask him questions. I just ignored it. I probably should have asked him to turn it off, but I didn't. He's a pretty intimidating man anyway."

Another woman, who works for a large Midwestern newspaper, was equally unnerved by the behaviour of a bond trader she interviewed at his office. She noticed that, while showing her a computer programme he used, he kept brushing his knee against her; she also noted that, as staff members left the office about 5 p.m., each seemed to make a point of letting her know they were leaving. Uncomfortable being left alone with the man, the woman got up to leave; as she did, the source brushed her long hair back behind her shoulder. "From your father, it might be endearing," the woman recalled, "but coming from someone like that, I found it very offensive."

Many of the respondents who work or have worked as reporters reported that sources often suggested going to a bar or to a motel to conduct interviews or that sources would joke with each other about whether the reporter was having sex with one of them or might be willing to do so. Other respondents described instances of blatant physical sexual harassment by sources. One reporter had a source who was a doctor approach her from behind and give her a "full body press." Startled, she responded by saying, "Rape," softly but loud enough for him to hear. The doctor left the room and had no contact with the reporter for the next few months.

One woman from a small Northeastern newspaper recalled being propositioned by a source whose house she had gone to. "He propositioned me, tried to force himself on me. I got out of it by talking fast. I had gone to his house to do the interview, so he considered it OK, I guess."

Unfortunately, sources were not the only perpetrators of sexual harassment. One woman recounted an incident during a news meeting in which the managing editor asked another female staffer, who was wearing a mini-skirt, to turn around so the group could appreciate her outfit and suggested that she ought to wear mini-skirts more often.

A photographer/photo editor who works for a midsized Southwestern paper reported that both sources and coworkers frequently make comments about her breasts. Once, during an assignment in Central America, she contracted a water-borne illness that resulted in significant weight loss. When she returned to the newsroom, a manager noted how much weight she had lost and said, "It's too bad it all came out of your boobs."

A night editor from a small paper reported that the newspaper's sports editor regularly comes by her desk and rubs her shoulders and touches her hair. When she finishes her work, she said, she sometimes asks if there's anything she can help him with because he has to deal with more latebreaking news. Her offer to help is greeted with more harassment: "He always- every single day- says, 'Yes, there is something you can do,' and then laughs."

A journalist from a Southeastern newspaper reported that her manager once had called her at home and asked her to meet him at a lounge to discuss something work-related. "When I got there, he was really drunk, and he said, `You want it, and you know you do.' I went out the fire escape to get out of there. When I left, I was fearful I had lost my job. But I think he was so drunk he didn't even remember doing it." A reporter from a midsized newspaper in the Northeast had a similar experience with her newspaper's former chief editor. The editor had invited her and a male friend to a party at his apartment and then offered to let the reporter drive his expensive sports car to the apartment, while her friend followed in his own car. "This man had always been very kind to me," she recalled. "I had no reason to expect anything." But after she got into the driver's seat, the editor began telling her that "the things he would like to do with me and to me would make him lose his job. He kept saying he was disturbed about the thoughts he was having about me." She got out of the car and left with her friend. Another of this woman's coworkers circulated throughout the newsroom a list of all the women in the newsroom, ranked according to how much he wanted to have sex with each one.

VARIATIONS OF JOURNALISM

FEATURE JOURNALISM

Newspapers and periodicals often contain features written by journalists, many of whom specialize in this form of in-depth journalism. Feature articles usually are longer than straight news articles, and are combined with photographs, drawings or other "art." They may also be highlighted by typographic effects or colours.

Writing features can be more demanding than writing straight news stories, because while a journalist must apply the same amount of effort to accurately gather and report the facts of the story, the reporter must also find a creative and interesting way to write the article, especially the lead, or the first one or two paragraphs of the story. The lead must grab the reader's attention yet accurately embody the ideas of the article. Often the lead of a feature article is dictated by its subject matter. Journalists must work even harder to avoid clichéd images and words when writing the lead and the rest of the article.

In the last half of the 20th Century the line between straight news reporting and feature writing blurred as more and more journalists and publications experimented with different approaches to writing an article. Tom Wolf, Gay Talese, Hunter S. Thompson and other journalists used many different approaches to writing news articles. Urban and alternative weekly newspapers went even further blurring the distinction, and many magazines fan more features than straight news.

Some television news shows experimented with alternative formats, and many TV shows that claimed to be news shows were not considered as such by many critics, because their content and methods did not adhere to accepted journalistic standards. National Public Radio, on the other hand, is considered a good example of a good mixture of straight news reporting, features, and combinations of the two, usually meeting standards of high quality. Other U.S. public radio news organizations have achieved similar results. However, a majority of newspapers still maintain a clear distinction between news and features, as do most television and radio news organizations.

Sports Journalism

Sports journalism covers many aspects of human athletic competition, and is an integral part of most journalism products, including newspapers, magazines, and radio and television news broadcasts. While some critics don't consider sports journalism to be true journalism, the prominence of sports in Western culture has justified the attention of journalists to not just the competitive events of sports, but also to athletes and the business of sports. Sports journalism in the United States has traditionally been written in a looser, more creative and more opinionated tone than traditional journalistic writing; however, the emphases on accuracy and underlying fairness is still a part of sports journalism. An emphasis on the accurate description of statistical performances of athletes is also an important part of sports journalism.

Science Journalism

Science journalism is a relatively new branch of journalism, in which journalists' reporting conveys information on science topics to the public. Science journalists must understand and interpret very detailed, technical and sometimes jargon-laden information and render it into interesting reports that are comprehensible to consumers of news media.

Scientific journalists also must choose which developments in science merit news coverage, as well as cover disputes within the scientific community with a balance of fairness to both sides but also with a devotion to the facts.

Many, but not all, journalists covering science have training in the sciences they cover, including several medical doctors who cover medicine.

Investigative Journalism

Investigative journalism, in which journalists investigate and expose unethical, immoral and illegal behaviour by individuals, businesses and government agencies, can be complicated, time-consuming and expensive — requiring teams of journalists, months of research, interviews (sometimes repeated interviews) with numerous people, long-distance travel, computers to analyze public-record databases, or use of the company's legal staff to secure documents under freedom of information laws.

Because of its inherently confrontational nature, this kind of reporting is often the first to suffer from budget cutbacks or interference from outside the news department. Investigative reporting done poorly can also expose journalists and media organizations to negative reaction from subjects of investigations and the public, and accusations of gotcha journalism. However, done well, it can bring the attention of the public and government problems and conditions that the public deem need to be addressed, and can win awards and recognition to the journalists involved and the media outlet that did the reporting.

Investigative journalism is a kind of journalism in which reporters deeply investigate a topic of interest, often involving crime, political corruption, or some other scandal.

An investigative journalist may spend a considerable period researching and preparing a report, sometimes months or years, whereas a typical daily or weekly news reporter writes items concerning immediately available news. Most investigative journalism is done by newspapers, wire services and freelance journalists. An investigative journalist's final report may take the form of an expose.

The investigation will often require an extensive number of interviews and travel; other instances might call for the reporter to make use of activities such as surveillance techniques, tedious analysis of documents, investigations of the performance of any kind of equipment involved in an accident, patent medicine, scientific analysis, social and legal issues, and the like. In short, investigative journalism requires a lot of scrutiny of details, fact-finding, and physical effort. An investigative journalist must have an analytical and incisive mind with strong self-motivation to carry on when all doors are closed, when facts are being covered up or falsified and so on.

People Journalism

Another, less reputable, area of journalism that grew in stature in the 20th Century is 'celebrity' or 'people' journalism, which focuses on the personal lives of people, primarily celebrities, including movie and stage actors, musical artists, models and photographers, other notable people in the entertainment industry, as well as people who seek attention, such as politicians, and people thrust into the attention of the public, such as people who do something newsworthy.

Once the province of newspaper gossip columnists and gossip magazines, celebrity journalism has become the focus of national tabloid newspapers like the National Enquirer, magazines like People and Us Weekly, syndicated television shows like Entertainment Tonight, Inside Edition, The Insider, Access Hollywood, and Extra, cable networks like E!, A&E Network and The Biography Channel, and numerous other television productions and thouasands of web sites. Most other news media provide some coverage of celebrities and people.

Celebrity journalism differs from feature writing in that it focuses on people who are either already famous or are especially attractive, and in that it often covers celebrities obssessively, to the point of these journalists behaving unethically in order to provide coverage. Paparazzi, photographers who would follow celebrities incessantly to obtain potentially embarrassing photographs, have come to characterize celebrity journalism.

Professional and Ethical Standards

Journalists are expected to follow a stringent code of journalistic conduct that requires them to, among other things:

Use original sources of information, including interviews with people directly involved in a story, original documents and other direct sources of information, whenever possible, and cite the sources of this information in reports;

Fully attribute information gathered from other published sources, should original sources not be available (to not do so is considered plagiarism; some newspapers also note when an article uses information from previous reports);

Use multiple original sources of information, especially if the subject of the report is controversial;

- Check every fact reported;
- Find and report every side of a story possible;
- Report without bias, illustrating many aspects of a conflict rather than siding with one;
- Approach researching and reporting a story with a balance between objectivity and skepticism.
- Use careful judgement when organizing and reporting information.
- Be careful about granting confidentiality to sources (news organizations usually have specific rules that journalists must follow concerning grants of confidentiality);
- Decline gifts or favours from any subject of a report, and avoid even the appearance of being influenced;
- Abstain from reporting or otherwise participating in the research and writing about a subject in which the journalist has a personal stake or bias that cannot be set aside.

Ambush Journalism

Refers to aggressive tactics practiced by journalists to suddenly confront with questions people who otherwise do not wish to speak to a journalist. The practice has particularly been applied by television journalists, such as those on the CBS-TV news show 60 Minutes and by Geraldo Rivera, currently on the Fox News cable channel, and by hundreds of American local television reporters conducting investigations.

The practice has been sharply criticized by journalists and others as being highly unethical and sensational, while others defend it as the only way to attempt to provide those subject to it an opportunity to comment for a report. Ambush journalism has not been ruled illegal in the United States, although doing it on private property could open a journalist to being charged with trespassing.

Gotcha Journalism

Refers to the deliberate manipulation of the presentation of facts in a report in order to portray a person or organization in a particular way that varies from an accurate portrayal based on balanced review of the facts available. It particular is applied to broadcast journalism, where the story, images and interviews are tailored to create a particular impression of the subject matter.

It is considered highly unethical to engage in gotcha journalism. Many subjects of reporting have claimed to have been subjected to it, and some media outlets are guilty of deliberately biased reporting.

Rights of Journalists Versus those of Private Citizens and Organizations

Journalists enjoy similar powers and privileges as private citizens and organizations. The power of journalists over private citizens is limited by the citizen's rights to privacy. However, many who seek favorable representation in the press (celebrities, for example) grant journalists greater access than others enjoy. The right to privacy of a private citizen may be reduced or lost if the citizen is thrust into the public eye, either by their own actions or because they are involved in a public event or incident.

Citizens and private organizations can refuse to deal with some or all journalists; however, the powers the press enjoy in many nations often make this tactic ineffective or counter-productive.

Citizens in most nations also enjoy the right against being libeled or defamed by journalists, and citizens can bring suit against journalists who they claim have published damaging untruths about them with malicious disregard for the truth. Libel or defamation lawsuits can also become conflicts between the journalists' rights to publish versus the private citizen's right to privacy. Some journalists have claimed lawsuits brought against them and news organizations — or even the threat of such a lawsuit — were intended to stifle their voices with the threat of expensive legal procedings, even if plaintiffs cannot prove their cases. This is referred to as the Chilling effect.

In many nations, journalists and news organizations must function under similar threat of retaliation from private individuals or organizations as from governments. Criminals and criminal organizations, political parties, some zealous religious organizations, and even mobs of people have been known to punish journalists who speak or write about them in ways they do not like. Punishments can include threats, physical damage to property, assault, torture and murder.

Right to Protect Confidentiality of Sources

Journalists' interaction with sources sometimes involves confidentiality, an extension of freedom of the press giving journalists a legal protection to keep the identity of a source private even when demanded by police or prosecutors; withholding sources can land journalists in contempt of court, or jailtime.

The scope of rights granted journalists varies from nation to nation; in the United Kingdom, for example, the government has had more legal rights to protect what it considers sensitive information, and to force journalists to reveal the sources of leaked information, than the United States. Other nations, particularly Zimbabwe and the People's Republic of China, have a reputation of persecuting journalists, both domestic and foreign.

In the present decade in the U.S., despite a long tradition of a journalist's ability to protect sources from government enquiry, the Supreme Court has upheld lower federal court rulings that restrict to varying degrees the rights of journalists to withhold information, and prosecutors on the state and federal levels have sought to jail journalists who refuse demands for information and sources they seek to protect.

Right of Access to Government Information

Like sources, journalists depend on the rights granted by government to the public and, by extension, to the press, for access to information held by the government. These rights also vary from nation to nation and, in the United States, from state to state. Some states have more open policies for making information available, and some states have acted in the last decade to broaden those rights. New Jersey, for example, has updated and broadened its Sunshine Law to better define what kinds of government documents can be withheld from public enquiry.

In the United States, the Freedom of Information Act (FOIA) guarantees journalists the right to obtain copies of government documents, although the government has the right to redact, or black out, information from documents in those copies that FOIA allows them to withhold. Other federal legislation also controls access to information. The Bush Administration, however, has been much more aggressive in asserting its right to restrict information from the press, which has led to claims that the government is attempting to circumvent FOIA, and to more ligitation between press organizations and the federal government. The federal courts have acted in different ways in different cases, but often have sided with the government against press access.

Bloggers enjoy Rights of Journalists

The growth of Internet do-it-yourself publishing in the late 1990s, especially the weblog or blog style of personal publication, gave rise to debates of "are bloggers journalists?" At issues are not only role-definitions, egos and relative status, but practical questions of access, as well as legal questions in jurisdictions where journalists have special privileges — such as protection against being forced to disclose confidential sources or information.

Bloggers are on the watch for cases that might set legal precedent concerning their rights as journalists. For example, in a 2005-2006 California case brought by Apple Computer, an Appeals Court judge said online writers who published information from anonymous sources were entitled to the same protection as other journalists. There was "no workable test or principle that would distinguish 'legitimate' from 'illegitimate' news," the court said.

Freedom of the Press

Freedom of the press is the guarantee by a government of free public press for its citizens and their associations, extended to members of news gathering organizations, and their published reporting. It also extends to news gathering, and processes involved in obtaining information for public distribution. In the U.S. this right is guaranteed by the First Amendment to the United States Constitution. Not all countries are protected by a bill of rights or the constitution pertaining to Freedom of the Press. For example, Australians have nothing in their constitution nor a bill or rights that suggests anything to do with Freedom of the Press.

With respect to governmental information, a government distinguishes which materials are public or protected from disclosure to the public based on classification of information as sensitive, classified or secret and being otherwise protected from disclosure due to relevance of the information to protecting the national interest. Many governments are also subject to sunshine laws or freedom of information legislation that are used to define the ambit of national interest.

In developed countries, freedom of the press implies that all people should have the right to express themselves in writing or in any other way of expression of personal opinion or creativity. The Universal Declaration of Human Rights indicates: *"Everyone has the right to freedom of opinion and expression; this right includes freedom to hold opinions without interference and to seek, receive, and impart information and ideas through any media regardless of frontiers"*

This philosophy is usually accompanied by legislation ensuring various degrees of freedom of scientific research (known as scientific freedom), publishing, press and printing the depth to which these laws are entrenched in a country's legal system can go as far down as its constitution. The concept of freedom of speech is often covered by the same laws as freedom of the press, thereby giving equal treatment to media and individuals. Besides said legal environment, some non-governmental organizations use more criteria to judge the level of press freedom around the world. Reporters Without Borders considers the number of journalists murdered, expelled or harassed, and the existence of a state monopoly on TV and radio, as well as the existence of censorship and self-censorship in the media, and the overall independence of media as well as the difficulties that foreign reporters may face. Freedom House likewise studies the more general political and economic environments of each nation in order to determine whether there exist relationships of dependence that limit in practice the level of press freedom that might exist in theory. So the concept of independence of the press is one closely linked with the concept of press freedom.

The Media as the Branch of Government

The notion of the press as the fourth branch of government is sometimes used to compare the press (or media) with Montesquieu's three branches of government, namely an addition to the legislative, the executive and the judiciary branches. Edmund Burke is quoted to have said: "Three Estates in Parliament; but in the Reportpooopers' Gallery yonder, there sat a Fourth estate more important far than they all".

The development of the Western media tradition is rather parallel to the development of democracy in Europe and the United States. On the ideological level, the first advocates of freedom of the press were the liberal thinkers of the 18th and 19th centuries.They developed their ideas in opposition to the monarchist tradition in general and the divine right of kings in particular. These liberal theorists argued that freedom of expression was a right claimed by the individual and grounded in natural law. Thus, freedom of the press was an integral part of the individual rights promoted by liberal ideology.

Freedom of the press was (and still is) assumed by many to be a necessity to any democratic society. Other lines of thought later argued in favor of freedom of the press without relying on the controversial issue of natural law; for instance, freedom of expression began to be regarded as an essential component of the social contract (the agreement between a state and its people regarding the rights and duties that each should have to the other).

THE INDIAN MOVEMENT AND POLITICAL DEMOCRACY

This work investigates the implications of the Ecuadorian Indian movement for democratic politics. While its empirical questions focus on Ecuador's political processes, a key purpose is to offer a Latin American perspective on the broader debate on the "civil society argument"; namely, the proposition that civil association has intrinsically positive effects on democracy.

The assumption herein is that particularization is essential for appraising this wide-ranging claim. Civil society and democracy are knotty concepts because they refer to complex realities that can be approached from different points of view. To cut through the complexity, this study follows a strategy of double specification, concentrating on social movements as a distinct type of civil association and demarcating discrete functional terrains to observe their bearing on democracy. Applied to the case at hand, this strategy provides a basis for a contextualized assessment of the putative democratic benefits of civil association and offers insights on the conditions of political engagement that social movements share with other kinds of civil society groups.

The pivotal claim of this study is that civil society actors may or may not contribute to democracy and that, in the particular case of social movements, the underlying tension between the participatory and insti- tutional dimensions of democracy may be expressed through a mixed bag of favorable and unfavorable effects on the different components of political democracy. The analysis of the Ecuadorian Indian movement demonstrates that to understand the varying impact of civil activism on democracy, scholars must adopt a nuanced, context-specific approach that does not lose sight of the particularistic orientations of civil associations and that pays close attention to their definition of means and ends, the institutional responses evoked by their initiatives, and the unintended consequences of their actions.

The relevance of the case cannot be overstated. The Ecuadorian Indian movement is often cited as the best-organized and most influential indigenous movement in Latin America. Its origins date back to the rise of local and regional organizations that, in the 1980s, came together in CONAIE, the Confederation of Indigenous Nationalities of Ecuador.

The spectacular battles of the 1990s transformed the movement into a powerful force that, in addition to pressing indigenous demands, took up a leadership role in the wider resistance to the imposition of neo-liberal reforms.

By 1997 CONAIE had launched the party Pachakutik to take part in elections, and its political clout had been boosted by its role in the developments that led to the fall of president Abdalá Bucaram and the convening of a constitutional assembly. In January 2000, amid an economic and political crisis of unprecedented proportions, CONAIE joined a group of military officers led by Colonel Lucio Gutiérrez in a non-violent coup that toppled President Jamil Mahuad but failed to hold on to power.

Three years later, the same actors made another bid for power as an electoral coalition, which succeeded in winning the presidential elections. The presence of Indian leaders in the government was a high point for the movement, but it did not last long. After six months of conflicts over President Gutierrez's neo-liberal turn, CONAIE withdrew its support and Pachakutik's ministers abandoned the cabinet.

Clearly, this is a movement that has reached well beyond the bounds of a bid for indigenous rights. Much more has been at stake, including matters of national economic and social policy and issues that are directly related to the struggle for political power and the fate of Ecuadorian democracy. In the context of contemporary Latin America, then, this case is highly relevant to the discussion of the various types of impact that social movements can have on democracy.

This chapter lays the groundwork for the analysis with a conceptual discussion elucidating the notion of civil society, the specificity of social movements as a variant of civil association, and the paradoxical relationship between social movements and democracy. The factors behind the rise of Ecuador's Indian movement, the broadening of its struggles, and the saliency of its political protagonism are then reviewed. The enquiry is framed as a scrutiny of the movement's consequences for the participatory and institutional dimensions of democracy. After exploring the bases of CONAIE's support, the study examines the movement's two main modalities of political engagement: its efforts to influence government policies and its struggles to conquer positions of power.

The appraisal of the effects on the democratic regime covers four areas: interest representation, control of state power, legitimacy, and political socialization. The conclusions assess the significance of the Indian movement for democracy, briefly rejoining the debate on the "civil society argument" and commenting on the present challenges for Ecuadorian indigenous activists.

CIVIL SOCIETY, SOCIAL MOVEMENTS, AND DEMOCRACY

This work adopts a modified version of Michael Walzer's definition of civil society, taking it to refer to the ensemble of social practices that generate a space of voluntary association and the sets of relational networks, or social actors, that occupy that space. Within this scope, the cast of civil society actors includes all voluntary groups formed for the sake of the common aspirations and concerns of its members. This formula is useful because it grasps civil society on its own terms, avoiding the pitfalls of definitions that imply assumptions about its relationships with the political institutions, such as the idea that civil society is necessarily autonomous from the state, necessarily opposed to the state, or necessarily good for democracy.

A good antidote to the mystifying sway of prescriptive definitions of civil society is to keep in mind that the realm of voluntary association is thoroughly marked by pluralism, particularism, and inequality.

Civil society is pluralistic because its practices are based on multiple forms of participation, express many social identities, and pursue a wide variety of goals.

Civil society is particularistic because its groups have their own norms and because, with rare exceptions, they restrict benefits to members and pursue goals that reflect their own priorities-even when, as often is the case, they claim to represent the public interest.

Moreover, civil society is tied up with inequality not only because different groups have different levels of opportunity to associate and further their ends, but also because a great deal of what associations do has consequences in terms of widening, maintaining, or narrowing existing social gaps.

Social movements are a particular form of civil association. They can be defined as organized drives to promote or resist change through collective practices that are embedded in a structure of conflict, involve episodes of mass participation, and challenge existing institutions.

The reference to conflict implies that social movements confront opponents in struggles over values and claims to resources, status, or power, a feature that sets them apart from civil associations that are not involved in such confrontations (*e.g.*, social clubs, churches, and charitable foundations). On the other hand, the emphasis on events in which large numbers of people engage in non-institutional forms of action foregrounds popular participation and defiance of prescribed rules, two elements that are absent in the case of associations whose activities are carried out by small circles of activists or professionals who follow" the proper institutional channels" (*e.g.*, interest groups and advocacy organizations). To understand movements, one must ascertain what is at stake in the conflicts in which they are involved. In empirical studies, the stakes can be inferred from their goals, their actions, and the context of their struggles.

The conceptual distinction between civil and political engagement is a useful tool for initiating that enquiry. In civil engagement, the conflict is located in civil society itself. There are two variants of this kind of engagement: construction of collective identity, in which movements seek to alter the self-consciousness of actual or potential followers; and cultural crusades, in which movements act on the general public to change dominant values or attitudes.

In political engagement, the conflict is played out through interactions with state actors or other agents from political society; that is, the arena of competition for control over the state apparatus and public policy. Here, the actions of movements are usually aimed at inducing policy changes. Sometimes, however, their struggles may turn into attempts to control the positions of power themselves.

Social movements are a modern form of participation that emerged with the changes related to the consolidation of capitalism, the national state, and liberal democracy. As a rule, movements have served as a medium for the participation of excluded groups and for the politicization of issues that the institutions are unwilling or unable to address.

By engaging in confrontational practices like marches, boycotts, and demonstrations, movements have shown that ordinary people can capitalize on numbers, unity, and determination to achieve goals against the will of the most adamant opponents or rulers. Movement practices, then, must be seen as practices of non-institutional power. Lacking other resources, excluded and powerless people use disruption. They generate might by withdrawing the tacit support that power holders derive from" business as usual," thus creating a political market in which they can trade the lifting of their sanctions for the changes they seek.

Some authors have argued that movements and revolutions are variants of contentious politics; namely, a particular kind of political activity in which challengers use non-institutional means in their interactions with elites and the state. By itself, though, the opposition of institutional and non-institutional means cannot capture the diversity that exists in civil society's political practices. In the view of this study, it should be combined with another distinction that, considering the actors' ends, marks the contrast between the politics of influence, which focus on swaying public policy decisions; and the politics of power, which are played as attempts to seize the positions from which the decisions are made. On the basis of the combinations of means and ends, identifies four alternative forms of civil society's political engagement.

As a static categorization, this matrix marks out the specificity of movements in regard to other forms of civil political involvement. But the framework can also serve as a dynamic referent for variants and transformations. Variants are relevant because movements often combine the use of non-institutional means with conventional modalities of action.

Transformations are also relevant because movements develop over time in a sequence of events that at some point is completed. At the peak of its cycle, a movement that initially focused on reforms may blend into a revolution, a sweeping challenge to the structure of power, which is usually violent and, if successful, involves dramatic changes in the organization and policies of the state.

Far more frequent, however, is institutionalization, which takes partial forms when movements spawn lobbying agencies or political arms and final forms when they abandon the unconventional forms of action and reorganize themselves as interest groups or political parties.

What is the relationship between movements and democracy? To elucidate this, we must first dispel the myth that civil society activities are always beneficial to democracy. It is true that civil associations can assist democracy by disseminating its values, representing social interests, resisting state arbitrariness, and educating people for democratic participation. But although associations can fulfill these positive functions, they may not always do so.

Indeed, they may also harm democracy in various ways, such as upholding antidemocratic ideologies, using corruption to get privileges, and seeking co-optation as state clienteles. The key point is that civil society actors may or may not contribute to democracy; and in both cases, what they actually do may vary greatly.

The groups that are not helpful run the gamut from associations whose activities are devoid of political consequence to organizations that may be conspiring to subvert a democratic regime. When associations contribute to democracy, by contrast, they rarely do it by design, but as a byproduct or contingent result of their efforts to attain their own particularistic goals.

All the foregoing holds true for social movements, but with a special twist: their status in democratic polities is haunted by an intrinsic ambivalence.

Definitions of democracy can be broadly divided into procedural definitions, which view democracy as a regime based on electoral representation and guaranteed civil and political rights; and substantive definitions, which see it as a principle of participation that guides all political practices.

This counterpoint highlights a fundamental tension between two ingredients of democracy: the principle that" the people rule" and the institutional procedures that, at any given time, embody that principle. Generally speaking, institutions produce social order by imparting stability and meaning to behaviour.· In their domain, democratic institutions contribute to that order by protecting citizens' rights and providing means for their participation in politics.

But institutions have a downside, aptly captured in Jean-Paul Sartre's assertion that they amount to" the systematic self-domestication of man by man". In dictating the acceptable ways of doing things, institutions foreclose alternatives, generating an effect of suppression that is magnified by their tendency to get entrenched in their own inertia.

The case of representative democracy is especially poignant because, for most citizens, the same institutions that enable them to choose their rulers also imply their exclusion from further participation. This tension underlies the paradox of social movements in democracies. As a form of political engagement that involves large numbers of normally excluded people, movements fulfill the principle of citizen participation. But their reliance on non-institutional means implies that they are often in breach of the rules that define how the polity works. What turns the inconsistency into a paradox is that it has not prevented the emergence of movements as a regular feature of political life.

To the contrary, viewed from the side of democracy, the key element in the relationship is that political democracy is an open invitation to social movements. Democracy offers fertile ground because it guarantees the rights of expression and assembly and, perhaps more important, because its own claim to legitimacy, grounded as it is in a discourse of popular sovereignty, citizenship rights, and inclusion, lends legitimacy to the claims of those who do not feel represented and want changes in public policies, in the definition of rights, or in the democratic institutions themselves. Viewed from the side of movements, however, the relationship cuts both ways. In positive outcomes, the paradox is resolved in the deepening of democracy; that is, in situations in which a movement helps make a polity more democratic by winning reforms that broaden citizenship rights and provide for greater citizen participation in politics. Europe and the United States offer many examples of movements that advanced democracy through struggles against slavery, for labor's freedom of association, for the enfranchisement of women and the poor, and for the civil rights of racial, ethnic, and religious minorities.

But there have been negative outcomes, too, including the Nazi and Fascist movements, which ushered in a catastrophic period when democratic institutions were wiped out, the political and civil rights of entire populations were revoked, slavery was reinstated, and genocide became state policy. Finally, there may also be cases in which a movement's impact is a mixed bag of favorable and unfavorable effects on different components of political democracy.

The paradox of social movements should give us pause. We cannot assume that movements always contribute to political democracy just because they involve popular participation.

But it is also a mistake to think that movements automatically detract from democracy because they infringe on institutional rules. Mindful of the complexities, political philosophers have long been engaged in discussing the circumstances in which civil disobedience may be justified in democratic polities. For social analysts, the challenge is different. We must use the complications as pointers for trying to provide more nuanced answers to empirical questions about the origins of social movements, the sources of their power, and their consequences for democracy. These are the questions addressed in this work on the Ecuadorian Indian movement.

The Contentious Cycle of the 1990s

In 1979, Ecuador turned from military to civilian rule. By way of background, it is worth calling attention to three aspects of that transition. First, the Ecuadorian generals did not display the repressive and probusiness zeal that typified military rule elsewhere in Latin America. Instead, they pursued a nationalistic agenda focused on the development of oil exports, agrarian reform, and "inward-oriented" industrialization.

During the 1970s, the economy expanded, and there were ostensible improvements in the living standards of the popular sectors. This, and the absence of severe repression, fostered attitudes of support for the military regime.

Second, the democratic transition was initiated and tightly controlled by the armed forces. The "handed down" democracy did not inspire the sense of commitment that could have existed if the political parties and civil society had played a greater role in wresting it from the military. Because they had not been crafted through political compromises, moreover, the new institutions proved ill-suited for the resolution of conflict, which set the stage for relentless strife between the executive and congress, constitutional tampering in all branches of government, and a chronic exacerbation of party fragmentation, regionalism, and personalistic politics.

Third, the transition to democracy offered opportunities for the political involvement of the indigenous population. The 1979 Constitution eliminated the literacy requirement, which had excluded most Indians from the vote.

The process was boosted by the first civilian president, populist politician Jaime Roldós, who promoted the participation of Indian organizations in rural development and literacy programmes.

The downsizing of these initiatives under president Osvaldo Hurtado (from the centrist Christian Democratic party, 1981-84) and their elimination altogether by León Febres Cordero (from the conservative Social Christian party, 1984-88) provided an early rallying point for criticism and contentiousness among the Indian activists.

These elements must be kept in mind to understand the developments of the 1990s. On the one hand, they draw a connection between the tumultuous nature of Ecuadorian politics and the reality that after a decade of civilian rule, Ecuador was still plagued by the flaws of its democratic institutions, the dubiousness of its politicians' allegiance to the rules of democracy, and the shallowness of its citizens' democratic political culture.

On the other hand they indicate that, by the late 1980s, favorable conditions for an Indian movement had appeared. The extension of political rights and the openings in government policy had stimulated indigenous organization. The subsequent withdrawal of state support, the policies of adjustment, and the downturn of the economy would provide strong motives for the Indian insurgency of the 1990s.

RISE OF THE INDIAN MOVEMENT

In the 2001 census, only 6.6 per cent of all Ecuadorians identified themselves as Indians. Including those who declared that they or their parents spoke indigenous languages, the proportion rises to 14.3 per cent, which is the best available approximation of the size of the indigenous population. The Quichuas of the Sierra account for about three-quarters of that population, with most of the rest distributed among smaller groups in the Amazon. Throughout Ecuador, the basic unit of Indian settlement is the community, which, despite variations, presents generic characteristics that will be discussed later.

The process of Indian organization was a classic example of bottomup networking based on local and regional associations of communities. In the Amazon, it came in response to the arrival of peasant colonists, oil companies, and state agencies. In the Sierra, the stimulus was the fight for the land, which peaked with the military's agrarian reform of the 1970s. With the return to democracy, the indigenous organizations continued to work for development and the defence of their culture and lands, coming together under umbrella federations in the Sierra and the Amazon and eventually under CONAIE, the Confederation of Indian Nationalities, in 1986.

Since its inception, CONAIE has combined livelihood goals and citizenship aspirations. The former have focused on economic improvements, education, health, and the protection of Indian lands; the latter on the redefinition of Ecuador as a plurinational state, the end of discrimination, territorial autonomy, representation in state institutions, control over education and development programmes, and official recognition and funding for the indigenous organizations.

CONAIE's first achievement came in 1988, when it negotiated with President Rodrigo Borja (the creation of a national programme of bilingual education, funded by the state and run by indigenous personnel connected with the Indian organizations. But the presentation of CONAIE's contentious credentials was the 1990 levantamiento (uprising), a huge mobilization that vented the frustrations of a rural population that had been severely punished by the adjustment policies and the long recession of the 1980s.

The uprising was a peaceful civic strike in which tens of thousands of highland Indians blocked highways and marched into cities to seize public offices. The protest continued for several days, until the government agreed to discuss the demands. There were measures to alleviate the situation in the rural areas and settle some pending land conflicts, but an issue that remained unsolved was the status of the ancestral lands in the lowlands. Two years later, CONAIE sponsored a large march from the Amazon. Once again, President Borja was forced to negotiate with the Indians, who stayed put in the capital until he agreed to demarcate and title their lands.

The Sierra uprising and the Amazon march revealed the depth of the Indians' discontent and opened the eyes of all Ecuadorians to their return as actors who could exert influence in national politics. The uprising, in particular, was a real shake-up. As a rural protest on a national scale, it had no precedent in the country's history. In most respects, it was a feat of collective creativity, the spontaneous invention of a new form of contention that turned into a blueprint for the string of mobilizations that would follow in the 1990s.

The Indian-Peasant Front

The 1992 election gave the presidency to Sixto Duran, a conservative independent candidate. His economic plan focused on deregulating trade and capital flows, reducing social spending, eliminating subsidies, and privatizing state enterprises and social security. But Durán lacked reliable support in the legislature, and his privatization initiative was also opposed by the military, which saw the state enterprises as an important legacy of the military regime.

In addition, Durán encountered resistance in civil society. The main challenges came from the Indian movement, which, buoyed by its initial successes, was displacing the labour federations as the beacon of popular opposition.

The first confrontation took place in 1993, over the plan to cut the social security budget and liquidate the health service for rural areas. CONAIE and other peasant organizations supported the strike of the social security employees and a massive protest of the beneficiaries of the rural health service. After two days of blockades and demonstrations, Durán was compelled to restore the budget and reaffirm the continuity of the health service.

The success of this struggle proved that well-organized protests could thwart an antipopular policy. In addition, it was an important precedent of collaboration between the Indian movement, other peasant organizations, and the unions from the public sector.

Next came the battle over the government's Law of Agrarian Modernization. The bill sought to abolish the legal basis for land expropriation, concentrate state support on capitalist agriculture, eliminate communal property, and privatize irrigation water. CONAIE sponsored the formation of the Coordinadora Agraria Nacional (CAN), a coalition that included smaller Indian and peasant organizations, such as FEINE (Indigenous Evangelical Federation) and FENOCIN (Federation of Peasant and Indigenous Organizations, influenced by the Socialist Party). CAN proposed its own bill and staged public debates on the issue.

In June 1994, the Coordinadora Agraria called an uprising that, once again, paralyzed the country for several days. Eventually, President Durán was forced to negotiate the bill. In its final version, the law defined peasant agriculture as deserving full state support, reaffirmed that water was a public resource, and recognized the legality of communal and cooperative forms of ownership.

The Popular Front

By 1995, CONAIE and its allies had participated in the formation of the Coordinadora de Movimientos Sociales, a broad coalition that included Indian and peasant organizations, unions from the public sector, and a large number of neighbourhood associations, feminist groups, and human rights activists.

Meanwhile, President Duran had called for a referendum that proposed constitutional reforms to strengthen the executive, weaken the unions, and allow the privatization of the state enterprises and social security.

While the business sector generously financed the "yes" advertising campaign, the Coordinadora de Movimientos Sociales and the labour federations mounted an intense grassroots effort to bring out the "no" vote. On the day of the referendum, the voters rejected all the reforms. The defeat closed the books on Durán's initiatives, leaving in place an empowered popular coalition. The success of the "no" campaign reinforced the position of the activists who had been calling for electoral participation. In its December 1995 assembly, CONAIE launched a political party that was intended to be based on the Indian movement and its allies. The Pachakutik Movement of Plurinational Unity (Pachakutik means "time of resurgence" in Quichua) entered the scene in the elections of 1996, in alliance with an independent group led by television commentator Freddy Ehlers. Ehlers did not qualify for the second presidential round, but Pachakutik won 10 per cent of the congressional seats and significant representation in provincial legislatures, local councils, and mayoralties.

The victory of Abdalá Bucaram in the 1996 election opened a period of enhanced turbulence in Ecuador. This clownish politician led the Roldocista Party, a populist force with its main base of support in the suburbs of Guayaquil. As mayor of that city, Bucaram had earned a reputation for corruption, but he had also extended his clientelist networks. During the campaign he attacked "the oligarchy" and Durán's aborted reforms.

As president, however, he focused on dividing the Indian movement, creating a Ministry of Indigenous Affairs and trying to buy the support of some Indian leaders. At the same time, Bucaram stuffed the government with relatives and friends, and it soon became evident that the country was sinking to new depths of corruption.

Bucaram's discourse had also changed. Now he spoke about promarket reforms, trying to ingratiate himself with the International Monetary Fund and inviting Domingo Cavallo, the architect of Argentina's neo-liberal programme, to be the consultant for his economic plan.

Bucaram announced that plan at the beginning of 1997, when the labour unions and CONAIE were preparing a rally opposing neo-liberal policies, corruption, and the Ministry of Indigenous Affairs. The measures included stiff budget cuts, higher electricity and gas rates, labour reforms, and a timetable to tie the currency to the dollar. The rally turned into a mobilization for the president's removal, and was supported by the main political parties.

As Quito swarmed with Indian demonstrators, Congress removed Bucaram on grounds of mental incompetence and named its speaker, Fabian Alarcón, as acting president. In the process, CONAIE and the other organizations extracted the promise that an assembly would be convened to reform the constitution. The 1997 elections for that assembly gave Pachakutik 10 per cent of the seats. Its delegates pushed through several reforms, including sections that defined Ecuador as a multicultural state and recognized social, cultural, and political rights for the indigenous peoples.

The next presidential election was won by Jamil Mahuad, from the Christian Democratic Party. The new president faced strong pressure from the IMF, which was vexed by the stagnation of Ecuador's reforms. At the same time, he confronted a popular coalition that rejected those reforms and had proven its oppositional power. To top it off, the economy sank into its worst recession since the 1930s. The economic collapse of 1998-99 was triggered by the fall of oil prices and the devastation of the coast by the climatic phenomenon of El Niño. When the banana and shrimp exporters stopped repaying their loans, the banks plunged into crisis and, despite Mahuad's billion-dollar bailout programme, the financial system collapsed. A massive flight of capital ensued, the gross domestic product shrank by 7.1 per cent, and it became obvious that the country would not be able to pay its external debt.

Mahuad devalued the currency, froze bank accounts, and focused on securing the support of the Social Christian Party, traditional advocate of the coastal exporters and banks. But the IMF's conditions for a stabilization loan were tough: eliminate all subsidies, privatize public enterprises, raise taxes on income and rent, and refrain from saving the banks. Mahuad's situation became untenable. On the one hand, the popular opposition fought back against the cuts and privatization. In 1998 and 1999, Mahuad had to deal with three large mobilizations in which the popular front led by CONAIE broadened to include middle-class sectors, such as truckers, bus operators, and small and medium-sized entrepreneurs. On the other hand, the IMF's insistence on tax reform and forsaking the banks alienated the business sectors. When the Social Christian Party pulled out of the negotiations, it became clear that Mahuad's presidency would not last long.

In the last days of 1999, Mahuad announced a plan to dollarize the economy and implement the IMF measures. Assisted by soldiers, Indian crowds flocked to Quito demanding his dismissal and occupying Congress and the Supreme Court. On January 21, 2000, indigenous activists and young military officers cheered in Congress as Colonel Lucio Gutiérrez and CONAIE's president, Antonio Vargas, proclaimed a "government of national salvation." After frantic consultations among generals, politicians, and U.S. diplomats, however, the armed forces announced that they were restoring constitutional order by installing Vice President Gustavo Noboa as the new president.

Gutiérrez and the other officers involved in the coup were arrested, and the Indian leaders were forced to order the protestors to retreat.3 In the ensuing months, the detainees were granted amnesty and discharged from the army. While dollarization was maintained, the IMF negotiations were eventually abandoned without an agreement.

Much speculation has been offered about who manipulated whom in the military-Indian coup. In some versions, the conspirators appear as victims of a plot to get rid of a weakened president and proceed with dollarization. But the truth is that the colonels had been pressing their superiors for decisive action against Mahuad and that their contacts with the Indian leaders intensified after the Parlamento Popular, an assembly in which more that three hundred delegates of CONAIE and other groups called for Mahuad's removal and the formation of a popular government.

Thus it is unquestionable that the coup's organizers were acting on their own initiative. Their inability to hold on to power, however, proved that the whole enterprise had been utterly misguided.

Disillusionment and Demobilization

In preparation for the 2002 elections, Colonel Gutiérrez founded the Patriotic Society Party, PSP, which put forward his candidacy for president. After failed attempts to forge a centre-left coalition, CONAIE and Pachakutik decided to form an alliance with the PSP. Benefiting from the Indian vote and a fragmented field of 11 candidates, Gutiérrez won the first round with 20.4 per cent of the total. In the second round he defeated banana tycoon Alvaro Noboa, an independent conservative, by 9.6 per cent. Like previous presidents, Gutiérrez lacked majority support in Congress, where the PSP-Pachakutik alliance had won only 17 of the 100 seats.

After the coup, Gutiérrez had cultivated the image of a progressive populist. As the elections approached, however, he toned down his discourse and included business leaders among his advisers.

He visited Washington to meet with IMF and U.S. officials and, immediately after his election, started to talk about austerity measures.

The new attitude was reflected by the make-up of his cabinet. Although Gutiérrez appointed some Pachakutik ministers, the posts responsible for economic policy were assigned to the advisers who had been functioning as links with the business sectors and the IMF.

Gutierrez's priority task was a deal with the IMF, which wanted the fiscal deficit elminated. Knowing that an agreement would open the door to loans for social investment and development, Pachakutik's cabinet ministers went along with the austerity measures, doing their best to moderate them. The result was a salary freeze in the public sector and higher prices for fuel, transportation, and electricity. Many activists saw this as a betrayal. The Indian federation of the Sierra, Ecuarunari, demanded the resignation of the responsible ministers. CONAIE echoed Ecuarunari's reproofs, calling for a rectification of the government's economic policies.

By mid-2003, disagreements over several issues, including the government's handling of strikes by teachers and oil workers, had aggravated the tensions in the coalition. Gutierrez's intense proselytizing in rural areas irritated the indigenous activists, who decried it as a scheme to bypass CONAIE and form clientelist networks. While the cabinet was torn by mutual accusations, the "allies" maneuvered in opposite directions in Congress, where Pachakutik tried to form a centre-left block and the PSP courted the Social Christian Party. The alliance collapsed in August 2003, when Pachakutik refused to support a bill that modified labour contracts in the public sector and Gutiérrez dismissed its ministers.

With the end of the alliance, CONAIE's internal divisions rose to the surface. Amazon groups criticized the leaders for leaving the government, and radical sectors of the Sierra reproached their delay in breaking with Gutiérrez. Meanwhile, Gutiérrez went on the offensive to weaken CONAIE further, issuing a decree that allowed him unilaterally to appoint the personnel of the state agencies that dealt with indigenous issues. This ended the practice by which the officials were nominated by CONAIE and ratified by the president. The next step was the replacement of the agencies' staff with activists who had signed up with the PSP and leaders from FEINE and FENOCIN.

By the end of his first year in office, Gutiérrez was facing accusations of nepotism and corruption. He had not succeeded in winning support from the Social Christian Party (Notisur 2003d). CONAIE proposed a rally to demand his dismissal, but the Amazon groups opposed it, and the other organizations ignored the call. FEINE had chosen to back Gutiérrez in exchange for programmes for the Protestant indigenous communities, and some of CONAIE's own groups, particularly in the Amazon, were involved in similar dealings. Despite the warning signs, CONAIE staged a protest in February 2004. The Indian federation of the Amazon and the other organizations refused to participate; the grassroots response was decidedly weak; and by the end of the first day, the mobilization was called off. Four months later, CONAIE organized another protest. The outcome was the same, aggravated by the Amazon groups' public support of Gutiérrez, who had just appointed his former fellow coup leader, Antonio Vargas, minister of social welfare. Vargas, himself a Quichua from the Amazon, had left CONAIE in 2002, eventually joining FEINE and becoming a staunch supporter of Gutiérrez.

The failure of the 2004 protests exposed CONAIE's crisis. But Gutierrez's success in neutralizing the movement did not solve his problems in Congress. In November he barely survived an impeachment vote amid charges that he had bribed legislators and had secured the Roldocistas' support by promising the return of their exiled leader, Bucaram. Then Gutiérrez dismissed 27 of the 31 Supreme Court justices, installing docile judges who overturned Bucaram's corruption convictions. On April 15, 2005, after three months of constitutional upheaval, Gutiérrez declared a state of emergency and ordered the police to repress protesters in Quito. The move backfired when the radio stations opened their microphones to an outpouring of indignation against his attempts to assume dictatorial powers. Following a week of demonstrations, the military withdrew its support, Gutiérrez abandoned the presidential palace, and Congress replaced him with Vice President Alfredo Palacio.

Once again, an Ecuadorian president had been ousted on the crest of street protests. This time, however, the main protagonists had been the urban crowds of Quito. CONAIE's leaders were slow in deciding to join in the protests, and when they finally did, their calls brought few Indians to the capital. Ironically, the fall of Gutiérrez offered further evidence of the prostration of the indigenous movement.

The Indian Movement and Democracy

This section elucidates the implications of the Indian struggles from the point of view df democracy. First, it looks at participation as a source of power for the Indian movement. Next, it assesses the consequences, through separate enquiries into the politics of influence and the politics of power. The last part examines the various impacts on Ecuador's democratic institutions.

The Secret of the Indians' Power

The Indian movement became a significant force because it was able to compel governments to pay heed to its demands. It was a classicexpression of the power that grows out of the effective use of disruption. To determine the sources of that power would entail exploring many factors, including the geopolitical assets of the Indian groups (strategic location in places where they could block the main national highways), the functional capabilities of their activists and organizations, and the financial and logistical assistance of external allies, such as progressive sectors of the Catholic Church and a variety of domestic and foreign NGOs. Some of these elements were addressed in a previous study; therefore the focus here is on what can be considered the main source of the effectiveness of the mobilizations: at the grassroots level, people were willing and ready to participate in them.

Throughout Ecuador, the decisions to respond to CONAIE's mobilization calls were taken by the Indian communities. Legally recognized as rural neighbourhood associations, these communities have roots that go back to the colonial system of resguardos, or reservations. Their revitalization was boosted by the land struggles of the 1960s and 1970s, which, insofar as they involved appeals to primordial loyalties of extended kinship and reciprocity, reinforced the old community as the natural framework for these relationships. At the same time, the agrarian reforms diluted the landowners' power, creating spaces in which the communities, by taking up the representation of the Indian peasants, gained prominence as relevant actors in local and regional politics.

Today, Ecuador has about 2,100 Indian communities, functioning as self-regulated entities based on the authority of their asambleas (in which everybody participates) and cabildos (executive committees of five members). All important issues are discussed in the asambleas, where agreement is usually reached by consensus rather than by voting. The decisions are binding for all members, with formal and informal mechanisms to ensure compliance. Thus, joining in a mobilization is always the result of a decision of the community, which exerts its influence to make sure that the members join in the roadblocks and rallies. The secret of CONAIE's power, then, lies in its ability to harness the resources for collective action that exist in the Indian communities. Pierre Bourdieu's concept of social capital helps elucidate this process. Bourdieu sees social capital as the aggregate of resources linked to the possession of a network of relationships of mutual acquaintance or recognition. Members of a group that, like the Indian community, is based on reciprocity and solidarity can claim access to the resources of their peers by virtue of belonging to the group. But the group as such can also use the resources embedded in the network. Indeed, the accumulation and use of social capital are always guided by contextual norms and institutions. This is particularly visible in communal groups, whose formal and informal rules define the available resources, the ways they can be claimed, and the sanctions that enforce delivery. The rules circumscribe and aggregate social capital, ensuring that its use is restricted to members and taking advantage of the effect of concentration to maximize benefits. In such circumstances, social capital is an asset that belongs to the group, which can institute itself as collective beneficiary in activities that benefit the group as a whole.

In practical terms, this means that a community that joins a mobilization is making a claim on its social capital, and that the members' readiness to participate is a resource that they owe to the community. As Alejandro Portes has shown, different motives may be at play when members contribute resources, including feelings of obligation (internalized norms), expectations of future repayment (norm of reciprocity), identification with the group (bounded solidarity), and fear of sanctions (enforceable trust). The same motives can explain the behaviour of each individual community within the networks of communities that make up the Indian movement. The general point is that the Ecuadorian Indian movement operates as a network of networks, whose activities can be analysed as a process of accumulation, concentration, and deployment of the social capital embedded in its grassroots community structures. By bringing that social capital to bear on the political system, CONAIE has been effecting its conversion into political capital; that is, into leverage that can be used to wrest concessions from governments or to compete for direct access to power.

The Politics of Influence

In the politics of influence, social movements seek changes in public policy decisions. We are interested, then, in these questions: On which issues did the Indian movement try to influence government policy? What was at stake in those issues? and How effective were the mobilizations in achieving their goals? Here, we should keep in mind that the issues changed with the evolution of the struggles. Initially, when the Indians were fighting alone, they focused on their own demands. Later on, CONAIE's coalition-building initiatives broadened the confrontation, incorporating issues that were relevant to the other rural groups and, eventually, to the popular sectors at large. Through the issues we can discern the stakes. The Indians' demands focused on achieving the status of recognized ethnic groups with terri- torial rights and some degree of autonomy. This challenged the existing notions of nationhood and citizenship; the former by defying the assumption that white-mestizo identity was the foundation of Ecuadorian identity, and the latter by questioning the liberal axiom that citizen rights could only be individual, not collective rights. The Indian claims, then, sought changes in the existing conditions. By contrast, the struggles over agrarian and national economic policy matters were attempts to resist changes. The fights over the Seguro Campesino and the Agrarian Modernization Law focused on thwarting initiatives that would have worsened the situation of the rural population. Similarly, the national protests against neo-liberalism were defensive responses to attempts to unload the burdens of reform onto the shoulders of the popular sectors. The stakes, then, had to do with the distribution of the costs of adjusting the economy to the new conditions of global capitalist development.

Did the struggles achieve their goals? We may start with the opposition to the neo-liberal agenda, the results of which are trickier to appraise. Studies have shown that Ecuador ranks among the least effective reformers in Latin America. Clearly, the popular struggles played a role in this outcome, but their influence cannot be disentangled from the effects of the lack of political support and the hostility of the business sector to some reforms. Besides, we should not forget that neo-liberalism was never really defeated in Ecuador, as its setbacks were always followed by renewed attempts to enact its reforms. We can conclude, then, that in this area the struggles had limited success. Interacting with other factors, they delayed the reforms and, in some cases, mitigated their impact on the popular sectors; but they were unable decisively to vanquish the neo-liberal agenda.

On the rural-agrarian front, CONAIE and its peasant allies were much more effective. After soundly defeating the attempt to scrap the rural health service, they succeeded in influencing the new agrarian legislation to keep water in the public domain, secure the status of communal property, and restore the state's support to the peasant economy. Eventually, the 1998 constitutional reform enshrined all these attainments in the Ecuadorian charter.

Concerning Indian ethnic demands, the initial fights established CONAIE's contentious credentials and led to significant gains on the land rights front, particularly in the Amazon. Later, the confrontations over broader national policy issues became an effective means for attaining the particularistic goals of the Indian movement. In the give and take after the fall of Bucaram, for example, CONAIE won one of its most important achievements: the creation of CODENPE (Ecuadorian Council of Indian Nations and Peoples), the agency that now coordinates all support programmes for indigenous groups with participation of their own organizations. Further concessions were wrested from Mahuad in the battles of the late 1990s, including an investment fund for Indian areas, the legalization of traditional medicine, and budget increases for the state's indigenous agencies.

On the whole, the movement was able to accumulate an uneven but substantial record of success in influencing government policies. One upshot was that CONAIE could reinvest political capital earned through the mobilizations in other forms o f action and more ambitious goals. On the one hand, its lobbying drives yielded significant gains without having to resort to protests, including the creation of PRODEPINE (Development Programme for Indian and Black Populations, initiated in 1997 with World Bank funding), the establishment of a health programme for Indian communities, and the launching of CODENPE projects of infrastructural works, water and irrigation, soil improvement, rural housing, and organizational capacity building. On the other hand, the Indian movement took steps to establish itself as a contender in the struggle for political power.

The Politics of Power

In the politics of power, agents participate in contests to occupy the positions that control and direct public policymaking. The three main manifestations of the Indian movement's struggles for power were the fight for control over the state's agencies of indigenous affairs, Pachakutik' engagement in electoral politics, and CONAIE's involvement in the coup against Jamil Mahuad.

For the Indian movement, the agencies in charge of bilingual education and indigenous health; the council of indigenous peoples, CODENPE; the development programme PRODEPINE; and the indigenous investment fund constituted a first major arena of power contestation. Steered by the movement, the agencies of indigenous affairs could serve as a means to attain objectives while fulfilling the programmatic ambition of exercising autonomy. Controlled by governments, they could be turned into tools of clientelistic domination. In the heat of the struggles, CONAIE wrested from the government an informal deal whereby the officials were appointed on the basis of its nominations. Later, however, President Gutierrez's actions showed that, in a less favorable climate, CONAIE's grip could be easily broken. The situation was complicated by the rivalry among indigenous-peasant organizations. Under the initial arrangement, CONAIE monopolized the representation of the Indians; this had always been resented by smaller groups like FEINE and FENOCIN. Thus, Gutierrez's repeal of CONAIE's privileges was more than a step to exclude it from the agencies' resources. It was also a gambit aimed at luring the other organizations into a network of patronage and using their example to entice CONAIE's local and regional chapters onto the clientelistic bandwagon.

The second front in the struggle for power was electoral competition. Pachakutik was launched in 1996 as a party based on CONAIE and its closest allies. In practice, however, it has been the political arm of the Indian movement, which provides most of its candidates for office. The best indicator of Pachakutik's overall strength are the congressional elections, in which its candidates have won, on average, 7.5 per cent of the seats. While this falls short of the estimated size of the indigenous population, it can still be seen as a fair result for a new party. Moreover, the 2002 presidential election proved that Pachakutik's vote can be decisive, since Gutiérrez qualified for the second round by a margin of less than 5 per cent. But it is at local and regional levels where Pachakutik's results have been especially significant. In the 2000 elections it won 4 governorships, 17 mayorships, and substantial representation in the provincial, municipal, and parish councils of the Highlands and the Amazon. The party's performance was similar in 2004, with 3 governors and 20 majors elected. Thus, while Pachakutik has not yet fulfilled its potential, it is clear that it is serving as a vehicle for self-government in the main indigenous areas.

We do not have enough studies to draw a panoptic picture of Pachakutik's performance at the different levels of government. One area in which the outcome can be readily recognized is the country's charter. In the 1997 constitutional assembly, Pachakutik negotiated important provisions, including the definition of Ecuador as a multicultural state, the designation of the indigenous groups as peoples, and the recognition of their rights to preserve their culture and their forms of political organization and administration of justice. Together with other clauses about the creation of indigenous territorial entities, these rights offer a framework for some degree of autonomy. But implementation depends on further legislation by Congress, where Pachakutik's moves have been conditioned by its minority status and its role as an opposition party focused on undercutting initiatives coming from the executive.

In contrast to its adversarial role in Congress, Pachakutik's gains in local elections created real opportunities for exercising power. The initial research on these experiences has focused on counties with dense Indian populations or visibility as touristic or artisanal centers, including Guamote, Otavalo, Cotacachi, Saquisili, and Bolívar.

The studies cast light on innovative efforts to encourage grassroots participation, establish practices that are free of corruption and clientelism, foster fairness in the distribution of resources, and promote multiculturalism by adapting traditional indigenous institutions. But they also show that the progress has been uneven and that, in some cases, Pachakutik's local authorities have been disappointing.

The third and by far the most dramatic incursion of the Indian movement into the politics of power was the January 2000 coup against Mahuad. In that episode, CONAIE conspired with military officers to overthrow the government and assume the powers of the state.

One way of coming to terms with the outcome is to look into the reasons for the coup's failure. In retrospective accounts, the Indian leaders have mentioned the generals' betrayal, the machinations of the elites and the U.S. embassy, the hostility of the press, the lack of popular response in the cities, and their own unpreparedness to take power. From this, one can conclude that the coup failed because it was marked by improvisation and, ultimately, because it reflected a gross misreading of the political scene.

Another way of assessing the coup's significance is to consider its repercussions for the Indian movement itself. The evidence indicates that there was public support for the removal of Mahuad but not for a military-Indian takeover. In the polls taken on the day of the coup, only 6 per cent believed that Mahuad could continue, 71 per cent approved the protests, and 79 per cent thought that Mahuad had to be replaced without breaking the constitutional order.

Two days later, the polls showed that 80 per cent were pleased that democracy had been maintained, 77 per cent supported the investiture of Vice President Noboa, and only 13 per cent would have preferred to keep the military-Indian junta. The overall pattern is clear.

While CONAIE fulfilled a well-regarded role in expressing public discontent, its attempt to take power by force was rejected. The payoff for the Indian movement was also ambivalent. At the time, its image as a powerful player may have been boosted and its undemocratic behaviour may have been glossed over amid the general complacency with Mahuad's removal. But in the long run, CONAIE's collusion with the colonels put it on track for further blunders whose consequences would be far more damaging.

Recapitulating, what can we make of the Indian movement's involvement in these diverse forms of the politics of power? As we saw in the conceptual section, it is not rare for a movement to launch a party and combine protest with electoral participation. The juxtaposition of CONAIE's struggles over the indigenous agencies and Pachakutik's electoral ventures, then, are an example of what a movement undergoing institutionalization typically does.

The coup, though, was a very different matter. If we were dealing with a revolutionary group, we might think about the use of force as part of the strategy of" combining all forms of struggle." But CONAIE and Pachakutik have never claimed to be revolutionary organizations.

We are left, then, with the sense that the coup was an anomalous deviation from the path that the movement had been following.

To account for it, one could make allowances for the magnitude of the crisis, the intensity of the public's outrage, and the leaders' rashness and lack of vision. What is difficult to fathom is why, to this day, the activists have not conducted a real evaluation of those events and their fallout. In the absence of soul searching, the naive opportunism that transpired in the coup kept haunting the Indian movement. Indeed, the leaders' decision to support Gutiérrez in the 2002 elections can only be seen as an attempt to cash in on whatever political capital they believed they had gained from the January 2000 adventure. Gutiérrez won the election, but the quick unraveling of the alliance showed that the move had been another serious mistake. The Indian movement could not stop Gutiérrez's neo-liberal turn, Pachakutik was forced to leave the government, and CONAIE was weakened by divisions. But the worst damage came from the disappointment at the grassroots, where Pachakutik's presence in the government had been hailed as an opportunity to access the resources that had been always denied to the Indians. Combined with the effects of Gutierrez's clientelist strategy, the loss of trust at base level became a major factor in the failure of CONAIE's latest mobilizations.

Impact on Democracy as a Political Regime

This assessment of the Indian movement's impact on the regime is grounded on elaborations of four ways that civil associations may impinge on democratic institutions. The first of these is interest representation. In democratic regimes, political parties are the prescribed medium for representing citizen interests. Very often, however, party systems cannot express the diversity that exists in society. Civil associations can compensate for this deficit by conveying the interests of specific sectors to the political system. The Ecuadorian Indian movement exemplifies this function.

It gave voice to excluded groups, projected their concerns into the public agenda, and opened new areas for policymaking. Furthermore, its strategy of alliances was instrumental in aggregating and expressing the demands of all the rural groups and, eventually, the popular sectors at large.

To this we can add the creation of a party that incor-porated marginalized interests into the system and spurred indigenous participation in elections.

Interest representation by civil associations can help fulfill three principles of democratic governance: responsiveness (serving all sectors), consensus orientation (mediating among different interests), and equity (treating everyone equally). Realizing this potential, however, does not depend on the civil groups alone.

It also depends on the institutional actors' willingness to consider their views and adhere to democratic principles. In Ecuador, incumbent governments had many opportunities to hear what the indigenous and popular sectors wanted and to fulfill their side of the democratic governance bargain.

But those governments chose to ignore the input that came from below. Insisting on the imposition of unpopular reforms, they wasted the opportunities for building the kind of consensus that would have strengthened democratic governance. This calls attention to a second function of civil associations: the control of state power. Liberal formulations emphasize the notion that citizens should protect themselves from state intrusion in private affairs and from violations of civil and political rights. Broader interpretations, however, include additional issues related to transparency and accountability. Once again, we find a connection with the principles of democratic governance, since the contribution of civil associations consists in holding governments responsible for fulfilling those principles.

In Ecuador, the popular opposition to neo-liberal governments repudiated the governments' insensitivity to the concerns of the majority, unwillingness to compromise, and unilateral commitment to the priorities of the business elites and the IMF. Thus, in the process of defending the interests of the popular sectors, the Indian movement and its allies were also fulfilling the watchdog role of trying to counterbalance what was widely seen as an unfair use of authority.

The foregoing interpretation leads to a third function: legitimation. In democratic polities, governments are acutely dependent on legitimacy because it is the people's support that justifies the right to exercise authority. Citizen groups can reaffirm legitimacy in two ways: explicitly, through actions that convey support; or tacitly, by doing nothing that might be construed as opposition.

The denial of support, however, must take the form of explicit oppositional action if it is to be understood as such. It is also worth noting that, in democracies, legitimation is rarely an all-or-nothing matter. The reason is that civil associations can legitimate or delegitimate authority at different levels.

Opposition to a policy does not necessarily imply disaffection with a government, and disaffection with a government does not necessarily entail rejection of the regime. Indeed, a common result of challenges at lower levels is the reinforcement of legitimacy at higher levels, as illustrated by cases in which a negotiated solution of a policy conflict boosts the image of a government, and situations in which the constitutional replacement of an unpopular government reaffirms the credibility of a democratic regime.

The legitimacy issue is particularly sensitive in the case of social movements because their motives are oppositional and their activities assume non-institutional forms. Still, taking into account the nuances of legitimation, there is much room for their fulfillment of this function.

The Ecuadorian Indian movement was certainly shoring up the political institutions when it created a party and urged its base to go to the polls. Beyond that, the routine challenges of the movement focused on policy matters that did not question the legitimacy of the governments or the regime as such. Through a different route we return to the point that, if the Ecuadorian governments had been more open to negotiation, the results could have enhanced their standing. Instead, their inflexibility became a factor in the escalation of conflict that led to their delegitimation. It was against this background that the Indian movement played an active role in the demise of two presidents. In the fall of Bucaram, the legitimacy of the regime was not at stake. The ousting of Mahuad was different because it involved a conspiracy to usurp power, which, had it succeeded, would have implied the breakdown of democracy. But the coup failed, and as a result, its actual impact on regime legitimacy is difficult to assess.

Intuitively, one would think that, by exposing the frailty of the institutions, the affair may have eroded their credibility. This inference, though, is not supported by the evidence. Over the last decade, the Latinobarómetro polls have shown a general softening of support for democracy, but the trend has been much less pronounced in Ecuador than in the rest of the Latin America.

Comparing the periods 1996-99 and 2000-2004 (before and after Ecuador's January 2000 coup), support for democracy declined by 12 per cent in the region as a whole but only by 6 per cent in Ecuador. One can speculate that, to some extent, Ecuadorians felt reassured that their democracy had survived the crisis.

Speculations aside, the movement's attempt to subvert the regime raises questions about a fourth function attributed to civil society: political socialization. In one of the most prominent formulations of the "civil society argument," associations are presented as frameworks in which citizens acquire the values and dispositions that are needed for a workable democratic polity. This claim relies on two basic assumptions about political socialization: that it is a matter of the formation of individuals, and that its results can somehow "free-float" into the public sphere as a resource that can be readily harnessed for the benefit of democracy.

What these assumptions miss is the significance of the mediation of the group, which becomes a collective subject of its own socialization process, inculcates its particularistic norms along with the more general dispositions, and regulates the use of the resources that make up the network's social capital. In so doing, civil society groups invariably condition the impact their socialization may have on the political system.

Taking this into account, we can tackle what appears to be one of the most puzzling questions about the Ecuadorian Indian movement. This study has demonstrated that the movement's struggles have induced vast changes in the behaviour of the indigenous groups. Because those changes would not have been possible without processes of socialization, it is clear that the movement has been doing a massive job teaching people to work together, cultivating interest in policy issues, and providing knowledge and skills for participating in public activities, such as mobilizations and elections.

The seemingly puzzling question is how these contributions to political socialization, which, according to the celebrated claim, should be functional to democracy, square with the attempt to take power by force. The matter is less baffling if we keep in mind that movements do not socialize people to help the workings of democratic regimes; they do it to attain their goals. The real question, then, concerns the movement's lack of commitment to Ecuadorian democracy.

This lack of commitment can be traced to three sources. One is the conviction that Ecuador's democracy is a fraud. Time and again the Indian militants have decried what they view as a corrupt democracy, with institutions that are discriminatory and governments that benefit the elites at the expense of the common people. Another source is the disrespect of all the political players for the rules of democracy. Willy-nilly, the indigenous activists have "learned the ropes" of practical politics within a system of interactions in which the prevailing attitudes are not distinguished by reverence for constitutional conventions.

The third source is the tension between the principles that inspire the indigenous internal practices and the liberal notions of democracy. At one level, it is a matter of the contrast between direct and indirect democracy; the former embodied in the participation of all in communal decisionmaking, and the latter in the elected officials who decide for all citizens in the broader Ecuadorian polity. At another level, it is a contrast between two canons of representation.

When the communities elect representatives to the associations, and when the associations elect representatives to the next-level federations, the elected persons function as delegates, whose powers are limited to specific mandates and whose authority can be revoked at will by those who elected them. In a liberal democracy, by contrast, elected officials operate as fiduciaries who use their discretion to interpret the interests of the represented and act on their behalf.

This raises the question of what the Indian movement's democratic ideals are, and whether these ideals and the standards of Ecuador's democracy are so incompatible as to justify the repudiation of the latter by the activists. In a political declaration approved in 1993, CONAIE called for a "plurinational communitarian democracy" based on equality, liberty, fraternity, and social peace. This goal would be achieved through a political reorganization aimed at guaranteeing the full participation of the Indian peoples and the other social sectors.

The platform adopted by the first congress of Pachakutik in 1999 was more specific, proposing a "radical democracy" based on a semiparliamentary system, decentralization, civil society representation in some state agencies, and direct participation through citizen initiatives, referenda, and recall of elected officials.

These proposals could be easily integrated into an agenda to "deepen" the democratic character of existing institutions. The activists' lack of commitment, then, is not rooted in an unbridgeable programmatic rift.

Rather, it seems to result from a double ideological distortion: a view of Ecuadorian democracy that chooses to dwell on its deficiencies (ignoring that the conquest of indigenous rights and the Indian movement itself would hardly have been possible without it), and an exaggerated sense of the contradiction between the indigenous principles and those of the existing institutions.

This work has investigated the consequences of the Ecuadorian Indian movement for democracy. Its enquiry was based on conceptualizations that defined the specificity of movements as a form of civil society's political engagement and offered guidelines for studying their effects on the participatory and institutional dimensions of democracy. The analysis showed that the Indian movement had roots in communal mechanisms of direct democracy, that its multilayered structure had been built through bottom-up networking based on delegative representation, and that its protagonism in the contentious cycle of the 1990s marked a historic milestone for the involvement of the indigenous groups in Ecuador's public life.

The participatory breakthrough came on two fronts. Practicing the politics of influence, the movement forced new issues onto the public agenda, wrested concessions from governments, and led alliances that repeatedly hindered the imposition of neo-liberal reforms.

Engaging in the politics of power, it contested the control of the state's indigenous agencies and spawned a party that made strides in the electoral representation of the Indian groups, the procurement of their collective rights, and their progress towards self-government. These initiatives fulfilled important functions for Ecuador's democratic institutions. In the areas of interest representation and control of state power, the demands and protests provided ideas and contributions for improving the quality of democratic governance and imposed restraints on policies that were widely rejected by civil society. The launching of a new party was also significant as a development that upheld the legitimacy of the democratic regime.

It is unquestionable, then, that the Indian movement has made remarkable contributions to Ecuadorian democracy. Yet we have also seen that the swell of activism was not an unmitigated blessing for democratic politics. The critical drawback was the January 2000 attempt to subvert the constitutional order. At that point, CONAIE transgressed the threshold beyond which, in a democracy, an opposition becomes disloyal.

The analysis here showed that the coup was inconsistent with the behavioural pattern of the Indian movement and that its negative impact was mitigated by its own failure and by the special conditions under which it happened. But the extenuating circumstances cannot absolve the movement of responsibility for threatening the democratic regime. Further scrutiny emphasized the reality that political socialization within the Indian movement had not fostered a sense of commitment to Ecuadorian democracy.

This evidence of contradictory consequences is consistent with the critique that the "civil society argument" plays up beneficial effects and ignores the possible downside. It also underscores that in Latin America, the study of the impact of civil associations on democracy cannot overlook three crucial points. The first is that the realization of the democratic potential of any civil society initiative depends on how the political institutions process it. Democratic governance is enhanced when decisionmakers take the concerns of civil associations into account. Conversely, democracy suffers when governments ignore citizen feedback, treat it perfunctorily, or demonstrate biases in their reactions to the bidding of different sectors.

The second point is that when civil associations mobilize broad support, the institutional responses to their functions of interest representation and control of state power can be highly consequential for regime legitimation. The legitimacy of democratic politics is strengthened when governments take notice of popular sentiment; but democratic regimes may fall into a tailspin of delegitimation when the inputs from below are repeatedly rebuffed.

The third point is that it is a mistake to view civil society groups as neutral purveyors of citizens trained for democracy. Like other social capital resources, the results of political socialization remain embedded in the networks of interaction that produce them. As collective structures that constitute the primordial source of social capital, regulate its uses, and mediate between individuals and society, civil associations impart their particularistic slant to socialization and influence its fallout in the political system.

For Ecuador's indigenous activists, the stark contrast between the successes of the 1990s and the more recent frustrations underscores the urgency of rethinking their bearings.

To a large extent, their present predicament is a result of their own inability to respond to the complexities of the movement's institutionalization process. Two tasks in particular were sorely neglected. One was in the area of strategic development. To maintain coherence in situations of partial institutionalization, social movements must define a roadmap for combining protest with the use of prescribed means, and they must do it in such a manner that the two forms of action reinforce rather than interfere with each other.

The other neglected task was ideological elaboration. In the politics of influence, social movements can afford to condemn unstintingly the poverty of democracy. But in a democratic system, whatever its shortcomings, a movement that acts in the name of democracy cannot make the transition to the politics of power without taking a more constructive stance towards the existing institutions.

Essentially, it is a matter of reframing the movement's ideology by shifting the emphasis from antisystem representations to imageries of democratic renovation from within. In Ecuador, the lack of strategic guidelines and the shortsighted attitude towards the democratic institutions jumbled the responsibilities of CONAIE and Pachakutik, muddled their priorities, and paved the way for the missteps that weakened the Indian movement. It may be a commonplace to say that a crisis can be turned into an opportunity, but that is precisely the challenge that the Ecuadorian indigenous activists face today. Whether or not they succeed will depend on their willingness to recognize that the time for reckoning and self-criticism is long overdue.

7

Role of the Media in Development Communication

INTRODUCTION

The role of media also changes in development communication. It plays the following four responsible roles:

- Circulate knowledge that will inform people of significant events, opportunities, dangers and changes in their community, country and the world.
- Provide a forum where issues affecting the national or community life may be aired.
- Teach those ideas, skills and attitudes that people need to achieve for a better life.
- Create and maintain a base of consensus that is needed for the stability of the state.

You must be knowing the meaning of 'empathy'. Daniel Lerner used this term with a particular emphasis on the aspirations for a new identity. Suppose, you have a goal of building a decent house so that you can live with the minimum hassles'. You dream about it, you aspire for it. We can say that you empathize with it. Here, Lerner said that people of any given society must think and aspire for a better life.

If they do so, then they are empathetic about a better life. To perform these roles, the media keep the development orientation in its perspective. Three approaches have been identified in relating communication to development. These are empathy, diffusion, and multiplying of information. We shall discuss each separately, individually.

Empathy: Daniel Lerner in his book, Passing of Traditional Society, saw the problem of 'modernizing' traditional societies. He saw the spread of literacy resulting from urbanization as a necessary precondition to more complete modernization that would include participatory political institutions. Development was largely a matter of increasing productivity. And to increase this productivity one must aspire, and it must begin in the psyche of the people. Hence, it is basically "psychological".

Urbanization → literacy → economic and political participation → the mass media exposure

According to D. Lerner, development failed to because peasants were unable to 'empathize' or imaginatively identify with the new role, and a changed and better way of life and so remained fatalistic –unambitious and resistant to change. Every change in society must originate and begin in the hearts of the people. If the people would like to change, only then the development would begin. What is required is that some means of providing such people with clues as to what better things in life might be. Lerner saw the media as filling this need of promoting interest among the people for a better life. Not only that, he saw the media as machines, inspiring people for better things in life. He said 'empathy' endows a person with the capacity to imagine himself as proprietor of a big grocery store in a city, to wear nice clothes and live in a nice house, to be interested in "what is going on in the world" and to "get out of his hole". He pointed out to the correlation between economic productivity and the media provisions in different countries in support of his theory. The richest country had the most newspapers, the radios and so on, and the poorest, the least.

Diffusion: Everett M. Rogers approached this with a perspective that had much in common with Lerner, but differed with him somewhat in emphasis. He saw the diffusion of the new ideas and their practice as a crucial component of the modernization process. According to him, "the mass communication influence appears to operate with a 'two step flow' process through awareness of the mass media, development of favourable attitudes and adaptation by interpersonal channels, particularly, "opinion leaders". We shall discuss this a little more.

It has been found that when a message is propagated, a segment of the population adopts it, and develops a positive attitude towards it. This can happen in the case of a product, fertilizer, seeds, ideas, journals, etc. Then, the people who adopt first, directly or indirectly shape the positive attitude of others who remain indifferent to the message. This is true in places where information and literacy levels are low. Simple people would like to get confirmation from the people living in their proximity. You can think about this process in your daily, life. How many times you need information about a product, a book, or about an incident from your friends, classmates, office-mates, neighbours and others. Women, especially, need a lot of confirmation from others before they adopt something. We can go on citing examples.

Magic Multiplier: Wilbur Schramm's Mass Media and National Development, which was produced for the UNESCO, became almost a blueprint for development communication. While Lerner and others saw all of the media cut put as having potentially modernizing effects, for Schrarmm it was their content that was the key to their use in development. "Social change of great magnitude is required. To achieve it, people must be informed, persuaded, educated. Information must flow, not only to them but also from them, so that their needs can be known, and they might participate in the acts and decisions of the nation-building; and information must also flow vertically so that decisions may be made.

Works should be organized, and skills should be learned at all levels of society for better utilization of the resources of society. Here is where the mass communication enters the calculus—the required amount of information and learning is so vast that only by making effective use of the great information multipliers, the mass media, can the developing countries hope to provide information on the rates their timetables for development demand". Let us elaborate a little. Schramm very clearly mentioned that a lot of feedback is required when one uses communication for development. It should never be one-way traffic. The users should be able to give feedback to the implements.

This would help the implementers to find out whether or not the communication is meeting their purpose or aim. Schramm has also said that each person could have the information required by the work that he would undertake. And there might be thousands and lakhs of workers requiring various information. The conventional channels of communication would never be able to meet this demand. Therefore, modem communication technologies would be of great use to meet this demand by multiplying the messages and reaching each and every worker.

COMMUNICATION NEEDS AND RESOURCES

So far, we have discussed the positive role of communication, and have seen how the communication inputs work to make a developmental programme. But how does one go about formulating the communication strategy or the inputs a programme? In planning communication strategy for development, the most important element is identification of communication needs and resources. Unless one is careful about this, or if one overlooks these elements, communication strategy and plan will not be effective, and all efforts will go in-vain. It is necessary to assess carefully the communication needs of the community and the country. To identify communication needs and resources of a country, the following process has been suggested by the UNESCO.

UNESCO Guidelines:

- The collection of basic data and systematic analysis of the country upon such bases as population densities, geographic limitations of communication, variety of social structures, ecology and agriculture transportation, physical communication, mobility, population, electrification, industrial capacity, manpower capacity, etc.
- The production of an inventory of the present communication

resources, including the modem and traditional media, and analysis of the variety of present communication structures. Such an inventory should also include the study of the audience, its communication consumption patterns, etc.

- Critical analysis of the present communication politics, including such considerations as ownership, structures, decision-making, etc.
- Critical analysis of the communication needs of each society, especially, in relation to the existing social and communication structures, and the uses to which communication is put.

Analysis of the communication components in all aspects of the national development plans and programmes in order to ascertain the communication requirements of the programmes, and the communication capacity which is essential to the execution of the plan. These needs must then be reconciled with the means and capacities that are available. A similar process may be followed to identify the communication needs and resources at the institutional or project level or wherever development activities are in progress.

THE ROLE OF THE MASS MEDIA

In order to perform their role effectively, the media personnel need to be fully conversant with the various aspects of human rights issues. They should arm themselves with the necessary information and then present the facts and analyses before the public. All this will have to be done at a sustained level. It is never possible to bring about favourable changes with just one stroke of the pen, or an infrequent programme or two. The poor would continue to live in conditions of insufficient food, clothing and shelter and the rich would maintain a luxurious lifestyle, even after this information were conveyed to them. Instead, what could be hoped for, is to make every citizen aware and conscious of their rights and to enable them to recognize a violation of human rights, when they come across such events in daily life. The news media can then bring about and maintain a healthy Human Rights Movement. Traditional folk media like Tamasha and Burakatha, which communicate with their audiences at a more personal level can inform and influence them. For this, the communicators themselves must be knowledgeable about human rights issues. They can narrate instances of violation of human rights and relate them to the daily lives of the masses.

THE ELECTRONIC MEDIA

The electronic media transcend the barriers of literacy and enjoy a widespread reach. However, these plus points are not taking advantage of, to the full extent possible. Government ownership and lopsided programming are their major drawbacks. Firstly, informative programmes needs to be based on healthy debates and discussions and not on propaganda and image-building exercises of leaders, as is usually the case. Secondly, only sensitive personnel can put across a point clearly and in a wholesome perspective. Such sensitivity cannot be found in people who equate a career in communication to a mere 'job'. It needs more than a mechanical approach to sensitize the public to the egalitarian goals of equality, freedom and justice. It is not in the fitness of things to project an image that "all is well with the world", when there are serious violations of human rights in different walks of life. The electronic media have the potential to act as information disseminators.

To fulfil this role, they have to provide complete information to the audience. The piecemeal treatment of issues causes both confusion and harm. Neither is ail informed public opinion generated by taking this approach. In general, there is inadequate coverage of human rights issues and problems. These could be anything from deprivation to gender inequality; from the health hazards caused by environmental pollution to malfunctioning of the electoral process. An occasional programme by a producer may expose the abuses of the electoral system or any other area. But such stories receive rare mention ill the daily news bulletins, One cannot wish away problems of such magnitude as those pertaining to the neglect of human rights, by simply ignoring their presence.

THE PRINT MEDIA

Quite naturally, the print media have literate audiences. A big industrial houses have a monopoly over ownership of the press. This fact determines the nature of relations between the press and the government. Newspapers openly take sides for or against the policies of the government. For instance, the 'Indian Express' has a penchant for writing against the government in power. The nexus between the print media and the government is strengthened by a sort of 'give and take' policy.

The press receives government patronage in terms of supply of newsprint and advertisements in return for favourable write-ups about the government. In such a situation, violations of human rights by the state are unlikely to surface. The same is the case if the rights of workers in the press Industry itself were to be violated. Personal rapport with the government is limited to senior journalists. It does not extend to junior journalists at the grassroots level. One such case, Gulam Rasool, a field reporter, was gunned down in a false encounter with the Andhra Pradesh police while investigating the issue of corrupt land-dealings.

He was apparently posing uncomfortable questions to those involved. This was reason enough for the authorities to "liquidate" him. The regional language press obtains scarce attention in competition with major national dailies. Few individuals attempt to start a newspaper or magazine at a local level, because of the large amounts of investment and the technology involved. Consequently, the first casualties are the freedom of the press and the standard of journalism. To its credit, investigative journalism has probed human rights issues like the working conditions provided to child labourers, the torture behind prison bars and illegal "encounter" deaths.

THE FILM MEDIUM

Socially relevant and purposeful issues enrich the cinematic value of any film. Themes like the caste system, subjugation of women, rural poverty and the feudal system, all of which are concerned with the area of human rights, have been dealt with time and again. Let us trace some landmarks in Indian cinema which have sought to solve the problems prevailing in society. "Chandidas" (1932) by Debaki Bose under the banner of the New Theaters and "Acchyut Kanya" (1936) by the Bombay Talkies carried a crusade against untouchability.

The film "Sawakari Pash" (The Indian Shylock or the trappings of a money-lender) made in 1925 by Baburao Painter of the Maharashtra Film Company was a shocking expose of the exploitation of the poor peasants by unscrupulous money lenders 'Jiban Maran' (1939) also from the New Theatres, dwelt on the social rehabilitation of the patients of tuberculosis, considered an infectious and deadly disease in the thirties. The Prabhat Film Company made a number of socially purposeful films like "Duniya Na Mane" (1937) which voiced a strong protest against the marriage of young girls to old men. The film "Padosi" (1938) by V. Shantaram idealized Hindu Muslim brotherhood even in the days of mounting communal tension. "Dharti Ke Lal" (K.A. Abbas) and "Neecha Nagar" (Chetan Anand) in the late Forties struck a note of idealistic social consciousness.

In fact "Neecha Nagar" earned international acclaim and is probably the first film to bring to focus the problems of environmental pollution. The Fifties marked the origin of socially relevant films in a rural setting like "Do Bigha Zameen" (Bimal Roy) and "Mother India" (Mehboob Khan). The Fifties also saw the emergence of Satyajit Ray, Ritwik Ghatak and Mrinal Sen. With the making of "Pather Panchali (1955), the Indian film scene underwent a qualitative change.

But it was only after "Bhuban Shome" (1969) by Mrinal Sen that a New Wave or Parallel Cinema Movement, gathered momentum. Such realistic films as Basu Chatterjee's "Sara Akaash" (1979), Moni Kaul's "Uski Roti" (1969), Kumar Sahani's "Maya Darpan" (1972), Avtar Kaul's "27 Down" (1973), Girish Karnad's "Kadu" (the forest, 1973) and M.S Sathyu's garam Hawa" (1973), were made on shoe-string budgets. A more traditional path was followed by Shyam Benegal whose films (Ankur, 1974, Nishant, 1975, Manthan, 1976) have been relatively realistic in form and deeply committed to socio-political themes. By the Eighties, a new generation of filmmakers was setting a new trend. They began to use the medium to focus attention on grave socioeconomic issues and raised questions against social injustice and atrocities, with passion and compassion. They have been described as “film activities”, who treat cinema as a pulpit. The trend started with Anand Palwardhan, Tapan Bose and Suhashini Mulay (of Bhuban Shome fame). Patwardhan’s “Hamara Sahar” a telling social commentary on the life in the slums of Bombay, offered a refreshing contrast to many commercial films dealing with the same theme. At great risk to his life and equipment, Tapan Bose made a shocking exposure about the Bhagalpur-scandal the blinding of prisoners by the police authorities. Bose also produced an outstanding film, “Beyond genocide”, on the Bhopal gas tragedy and its aftermath. The “Voice of Baliapal” by Vasudha Joshi and Ranjan Palit articulated the mute expression and protests of evicted villagers in an Orissa village. The film medium has the potential to portray the ills which all society, frequently in the narrative format. This is how films serve the cause of human rights and ensure their just implementation in society.

THE" DEVELOPMENT MEDIA" IN ASIA

Neglected by the authors of the four press theories were media in the poorer countries of the world-development media. The press in South Asia may best be described by the concept of development journalism, a concept developed later to supplement the four theories, as the development of communities and giving voice to the underprivileged are major goals of many of the local media in the region.

The development press is popular in the region perhaps because South Asia is the least economically developed region on the continent. More than half of the world's underweight children lived in India, Bangladesh, and Pakistan, said a recent UNICEF report on the global progress on children's issues.

In India, approximately 47 per cent of the under-five population was underweight. The report found that South Asia was the only region that showed a gender bias with regard to child nourishment, with girls more likely to be underweight than boys. The issue of undernourishment points to the problems of poverty, lack of education, and inequality in the region.

In India, communication not only means the transfer of information, but also includes the participation in the society and in the community. The Indian brand of development journalism" focuses on the needs of the poor, the deprived, and the marginalized and emphasizes their effective participation in developmental planning". It motivates the participation of the people and advocates for their interests instead of the views of the policy makers and the planners. And it promotes social justice for all.

Journalists in the country believe that the media should not only carry stories about health campaigns like the one against AIDS but also discuss issues that are important for a civil society because only the mass media can reach the vast rural population and give them a voice in debates affecting their lives.

The mass media can also play a crucial role in social progress, as any transitional society will encounter new attitudes, a new mindset, and a new value system. Development journalism enthusiasts in India conducted workshops for social activists to train them to write stories about development issues and workshops for local editors and journalists to familiarize them with realities and issues in local communities. Commercial newspapers also play a role in development journalism.

The Jharkhand-based Prabhat Khabar had been doing development journalism by giving people information on science, information technology, economics, and the comparative financial progress of different states. The paper also conducted" readers'courts," where readers could interact with journalists and discuss ways of improving the quality of the paper, much like the role of the focus groups in civic or public journalism in the United States.

Radio plays a special role in development journalism in South Asia because of its easy and wide reach in the vast rural areas, where literacy rate is still relatively low. The Indian communications NGO (non-government organization) had been highlighting the importance of community radio in India for over half a decade and called for the extension of community broadcasting.

In India, awards are given to mentors of development journalism for encouraging and nurturing journalists to investigate and write on development issues and for supporting journalism initiatives towards" a common social good". Journalists and media researchers in India and Pakistan criticized some of the mainstream media for their elitist approach, focusing on the prominent while ignoring the plight of the underprivileged in rural communities by following Western news values.

The degree of press freedom in South Asia, however, varies considerably from country to country. Once the largest colony in the world, India is the largest democracy in the world today. Only under Prime Minister Indira Gandhi was an attempt made to curtail press freedom by declaring a political emergency to suspend civil rights. The government of Narasimha Rao tried to prevent exposés of government corruption under the pretext of protection of privacy. Despite such government attempts at control, the press in India has largely remained private, free, and vibrant. Cushrow R. Irani, editor-in-chief and managing director of The Statesman, said that India's press today is as free as it chooses to be. N. P. Chekkutty, editor of Media Focus, wrote," The Indian media works in an atmosphere of freedom. We are the purveyors of free thoughts and opinions. We do reflect the freedom of expression the Constitution guarantees to our citizens, and we, therefore, are the epitome of a free, liberal society".

With the freedom it enjoys, the press in India often plays its watchdog role seriously." Newspapers in India are completely free, as free as the newspapers in the United States, as they are privately owned and free of censorship". It is the newspapers that have exposed corruption in India, though some journalists are attacked for their investigative reporting. The Indian press has always been vigilant about protecting its freedom and aggressive in reporting. Free as it may be as the press in the United States, the Indian press clearly differs from the Western libertarian press system in the perception of its mission. For its social role, the Indian press may be closer to the civic or public journalism in America, which also prescribes an advocacy role for the press. However, in India development journalism represents the aspirations of many journalists, while in America the ethical implications of civic and public journalism are still being debated.

In India, press freedom is guaranteed by the Constitution and the independent court system, which is very similar to the situation in neighbouring Pakistan, formerly a part of India before its independence. Behind India, which has a relatively low literacy rate of 65 per cent, Pakistan's literacy rate is even lower at 38 per cent, which limits the growth of its press industry.

There are about 1,330 newspapers in print in Pakistan, but only 1 per cent of the population buys a newspaper. The press in Pakistan is independent of the government and mostly privately owned.

Major public issues are debated in the press, which has become an instrument for change. In Pakistan no law governs the registration of publications. In recent years, Pakistan has been moving towards greater press freedom, and its press is among the most outspoken in South Asia. In both India and Pakistan when the government tries to crack down on critical press coverage of the government, the courts often strike down government charges in support of press freedom.

There are exceptions to the constitutional guarantees of the freedom of speech and of the press in Pakistan, the most important of which is the" reasonable restrictions imposed by law in the interest of the glory of Islam". The Constitution prohibits the ridicule of Islam, of the armed forces, or of the judiciary. Development journalism is perhaps less developed in Pakistan than in India. Circulation of newspapers in the rural areas of the country is one of the lowest in the world because of the urban orientation of the papers and the cost of subscription in addition to a low literacy rate. The rural market is largely untapped.

The dramatic increase in the number of publications in recent years is not supported with trained staff. Many journalists, especially rural ones, lack the basic skills to cover the complex issues important to their communities. However, electoral politics has increased the importance of rural centres in the emerging democracy of Pakistan.

Supporting development journalism, the Pakistan Press Foundation (PPF) was established to help raise the standards of journalism, particularly of the vernacular and regional press, and to promote greater awareness of social and development issues through the media. In 1999, PPF restarted the rural journalists'skills development project. By 2002 hundreds of Pakistani rural journalists have attended the workshops. The emphasis of the workshops is on improving basic skills of newsgathering and news writing, as participants are given exercises using actual issues, such as violence against women, environmental issues, child labour, bonded labour, and crime rates. The end of monopoly of the electronic media in Pakistan provides new hopes of reaching a rural audience as radio is acknowledged to be a more suitable and affordable means of providing local communities with a voice of their own. It is more interactive and more suitable for community development. In less than six years, between 2000 and 2006, the broadcast sector completely changed the monolithic landscape that existed for about fifty-three years.

But the proliferation of radio stations has created the co-existence of robust liberty and open lawlessness, and commercial interests dominate the airwaves while development journalism still needs time to take hold. Research on the topic, however, is several steps ahead of the media industry.

Development journalism is regarded as an Asian model of journalism, stemming from the dissatisfaction with the Western news values that do not serve the cause of national development. Western news values of timeliness, prominence, proximity, conflict, and the bizarre exclude the ordinary people in the news unless they are involved in accidents, violence, or catastrophes.

Development journalism, on the other hand, should focus on the educational function of the news, stories about social needs, self-help projects, and obstacles to development. In the exploration of the development journalism model by Asian media researchers, the watchdog role of the media was emphasized, and the media were urged to remain vigilant against government involvement.

In Sri Lanka, three newspaper groups dominate the island's newspaper scene - the ANCL, the Upali Newspapers Ltd. and the Wijeya Newspapers Ltd. The ANCL has been under government control since 1973, while the other two are privately owned but have close family connections to political parties. In the broadcasting sector, Sri Lanka was perhaps the first British colony to introduce radio broadcasting a few years after its inauguration in Europe in 1920s. The country liberalized its radio and TV sectors ahead of the rest of Asia. It permitted the establishment of more commercial radio stations than any other country in the region and put the state-controlled Sri Lanka Broadcasting Corporation under considerable competitive pressure. It also allowed private radio stations to broadcast news and current affairs, unlike some of its neighbouring countries.

Efforts at setting up community radio have never stopped in Sri Lanka. Universities in Sri Lanka and UNESCO played host to regional workshops on community radio for participants from South Asian countries. The goal of such workshops was to make community radio a reality in South Asia and encourage-cooperation among community radio advocates in the region. Radio still is a popular medium in South Asia, particularly in rural areas. In Sri Lanka telephone boxes, where a radio station button is installed, allow listeners to contact a station without paying a fee. The system makes it easier for listeners to participate in the programmes and solve problems in the communities.

The mass media in Sri Lanka also play a role in environmental education. Most people in both urban and rural areas use different media outlets as their primary source of environmental education, especially the print media. Television is the next major source of information for the urban population, while radio for the rural population. The media cover environmental issues in the form of news, editorials, investigative stories, entertainment, and educational programmes.

Development journalism in the country can have a bigger potential if the government allows even greater participation by the public in media discussions, which is often limited when there is an increase in guerrilla warfare in the country. It is evident from the above discussions that the degree of press freedom under the development concept varies from country to country, and that is where the controversy with the concept lies. While one scholar describes it as" the pursuit of cultural and informational autonomy" and" support for democracy" among other goals, another scholar criticizes it as" a rationale for autocratic press control" and" guided press".

Where do all the discussions about the press systems in Asia leave us theoretically? When theories encounter major difficulties in serving as a guide to the understanding of the realities they are supposed to describe, new paradigms are needed. So are the criteria of the Freedom House for assessing global press freedom and civil liberties when their rankings fail to reflect changing realities. Obviously, more factors should be taken into consideration than the current criteria. The Last Rights concluded that the four theories were a" durable" but now" questionable" map and that a" more adequate" map is needed. The book presented inspiring criticism of the four press theories but stopped short of proposing a new paradigm.

STRATEGIES IN DEVELOPMENT COMMUNICATION

A strategy is the careful formulation of plans towards achieving a goal. Since development communication is goal oriented, one has to be careful in planning communication strategies. There may be a number of communication strategies for the achievement of a particular communication goal. There is a need to analyse these very carefully.

Since these strategies are formulated in the context of the developing countries, one should give keen consideration to cost-benefit factors before selecting the right strategy. In the modern world, there are a number of new technologies, media and techniques, which are available to a communication strategy planner. One has to evaluate these alternatives available to him, using cost-benefit analysis and administrative feasibility. Always, one has to keep in mind the target audience.

DEBATES AND DEVELOPMENTS

We have already familiarized you with the essentials of the international communication the monopolization of news and information flow by a handful of transnational media giants, such as AP, AFP, Reuters, UPI, ITAS-TASS, VISNEWS. International organizations and regulatory bodies like ITU; and the imbalances in news and information flow arising out of the monopoly by transnational media conglomerates and the guiding principles of 'free flow' of information. A major consequence of the monopoly of news and information flow was the 'one-way flow' of news and information, generally from the developed to the developing world.

The nature of flow, as the eminent journalist, D.R. Mankekar, describes, was "imbalanced, iniquitous, sometimes even biased and West-oriented, impervious" to the needs of the developing world. As this was detrimental to their interests in more than one way, the developing nations attacked the free-flow concept and its concomitant—the transnational media empires. For they believed that the monopolistic media empires of the west created and sustained distorted pictures of the world that were far away from the reality.

These developing nations campaigned for a 'new order' in the field of international information and communication, which would facilitate a 'free and balanced flow' of information capable of breaking through the stereotypes created and nurtured for over 50 years by the Western media empires. The new order, they maintained, would create a new international information climate that would foster a closer and better understanding among nations and individuals. The ensuing debates in the international forum lasted for nearly a decade, beginning from the early 1970s.

This period is reckoned as a watershed in the history of international communication. Indeed, it was a period of many significant developments. First, the developing nations, under the non-aligned umbrella resolved to address themselves to the international communication issues.

Second, to offset the ill effects of One-way flow, alternative means of exchange for meaningful and relevant news and information among the non-aligned nations took roots. The most important step in this direction was the hunching of the Non-aligned News Agencies Pool, in 1975, followed by the establishment of many other news distribution systems at national, regional and international levels. Third, notable revisions also occurred in the concepts and thoughts governing international communication. The 'free-flow' concept was amended to 'free-and balanced flow', when a declaration on the role of the media in the promotion of international understanding and peace was approved by the UNESCO, in 1978. Commensurately, the corollary doctrine, the 'the right to know' was transformed into 'the right to communicate'. Fourth the new order debates led to the setting up of an International Commission for the study of communication problems better known as the "MacBride Commission", whose report was accepted by UNESCO, in 1980. Fifth, resolution 4.19 of the 21 UNESCO General Assembly, held in 1981, outlined the basic character and content of the 'new order'. Sixth, in the same year, the International Programme for the Development of Communication (IPDC) was set up to provide assistance for the development of the communication infrastructure in the developing countries.

Nomenclature: Before we proceed further, please note that there has been no uniformity with regard to the nomenclature of the 'new order' concept. The non-aligned nations coined the phrase, New International Information Order (NIIO), The MacBride Commission broadened the schism by substituting the term 'word' for 'international' and incorporating 'communication' along with 'information'. Since then the phrase the 'New World Information and Communication Order (NWICO), or its shortened form the NWICO, has been widely used. In this unit the nomenclature NWICO is used. Also note that the terminologies of the Third World and Developing World, and the First World and Developed World are used interchangeably.

News Flow Controversies: Most of the scholars trace the origin of the demand for new international information and communication order to the cold war era, and the emergence of the Third World consciousness in the 1950s. Some of the contentions and problems aired now by the mind World that a handful of media-rich countries determined the nature and kind of news and information flow between nations, that the international news and information business operations benefited only the media-rich nations, and that such operations are detrimental to the interest of media-poor countries, were as fundamental to the media controversies of the early decades of the 20th century as to the 1970s new order debates. Ever since the birth of the international news agencies, the monopolistic practices in the international news business have been in evidence.

First, their home regions came under their monopoly. Subsequently, through the cartel agreements of the 1870s the European agencies extended their monopoly in regions under the influence of their home countries. But, in several aspects, the relationship among the cartel members was unequal. In terms of territory, Britain's Reuters had an area as vast as the British empire, spread across Africa, Asia, America, Australia and Europe, covering almost one-fifth of the globe. In terms of influence too, it was the Reuters that mattered. Its extensive network supported by Britain's control of the world's transoceanic cables, helped it to become the most powerful agency in the world. The monopoly of the international news business by the European triumvirate was not to continue unchallenged in the fast changing political climate of the 20th century. Much of the resistance to the European agencies came from the US, which, by the end of World War I, was switching its role from an international debtor to that of a major creditor. Its increasing control over transoceanic cables and an expanding medium at home provided the much needed muscle power to its agencies to challenge the European cartel. Many in the US had come to realize the advantage that would accrue out of the international news business. At this juncture, the AP synthesized its commercial interest with diplomatic interest of the US by stressing how the Reuters, through European news cartels, controlled all foreign news sent into the US, and all American news to the rest of the world, and how such practices promoted Britain's interests while affecting the interests of both the US and the AP. Finally, the AP ceded from the cartel, in 1934, and independently went into the business of news collection and distribution around the world, heralding the impending domination of the US in the coming years.

Free Flow Ideas: A major factor that helped the growth of US agencies was the wireless transmission technology, perfected at home, which reversed the world communication imbalance to the overall advantage of the American interest.

Yet another forum responsible for the growth of the US communication network abroad was a general realization in the US of the advantages that world communication controls bestowed on foreign trade and commerce. Following such realizations, ideas on the unrestricted flow of communication between nations began to crystallize in the US. Fit, the American Society of Newspaper Editors adopted a resolution urging the political parties to support freedom of information and unrestricted flow of communication throughout the world. Subsequently, with the Democrats and Republicans adopt these aims, the free flow doctrine became an integral part of the US political ideology and foreign policy. The UN too came under its influence. Its declaration on Freedom of Information, issued m 1946, made the first reference to the free flow of information:

- "All states should proclaim policies under which the free flow of information, within countries and across frontiers, will be protected. The right to sell and transmit information should be insured in order to enable the public to ascertain facts and appraise events."

The US was also successful in incorporating some of its viewpoints in the Universal Declaration of Human Rights, which was passed by the UN General Assembly in 1948. Article of the declaration reflects the American concept of free flow. It reads:

- "Everyone has the right to freedom of opinion and expression; this right includes freedom to hold opinions and to seek, receive and impart information and ideas through any media regardless of frontiers."

With its lead in communication technology, the US had everything to gain from the free flow doctrine. In about two decades, its grip on international communication was complete.

DEVELOPMENT REPORTING FOR MASS MEDIA

In this section we shall discuss how a development reporter should adopt the media and adapt his/her skills to suit the characteristics of various media.

DEVELOPMENT REPORTING FOR PRESS

In this chapter, you will learn how a particular mass medium can effectively serve the cause of development. As a development reporter, you will be required to process and present facts in an intelligible form to the reader/ viewer/ listener. Although electronic media, radio and television, have made a veritable impact on the masses, print media will remain most decisive and educative for a long time to come.

In India, print medium occupies an important place. There are more than 1500 daily newspapers published in all the 18 national and other languages. Several newspapers devote full pages to development news. For example The Indian Express, The Pioneer, and The Hindu in English set aside one full page for "Development News" once a week. Development storks are best done in the form of a feature article.

In another unit, you would have learned as to how a feature is written. Besides, newly started development work or those proceeding at a snail's pace, thereby leading to tremendous loss in funds or causing terrible inconvenience to the public can be presented in the form of news items or featured news stories. In fact, photo features on development projects can also be presented effectively. Interviews with the recipients of the benefits of the projects already completed can also help evaluate their impact on the masses. Such writings can also induce the authorities to expedite other projects under implementation. Development stories pertaining to the topics mentioned earlier, appear on the development pages of the newspapers from time to time.

The Hindu published a separate page on agriculture issues and farming research, and how these can be taken to the land from the lab. In addition, other subjects relate to particular crops, seeds, marketing, fertilizers, pesticides, rural life and allied areas. The reporters visit the countryside regularly, to collect material for the page.

Similarly, a number of newspapers in almost all national languages carry news, features, interviews, interpretative and investigative stories on development subjects. In fact, the two national news agencies, PTI and UNI, maintain separate desks to focus on developing stories. An imaginative development writer can do freelancing for the press, radio, and television. Besides employment, opportunities exist in different newspaper establishments to cover development news. A development reporter however has a challenging job and requires hard work, commitment and dedication. But the compensation in terms of contribution to the national development are tremendously satisfying.

DEVELOPMENT REPORTING FOR RADIO

In India, radio has proven its utility as a potent audio medium for creating awareness among people in several areas of human endeavour, including development. It helps in promoting an instinctive urge for development consciously, by broadcasting programmes designed to help people diagnose their problems and clarify their objectives so that they may be able to make their decisions wiser.

India has of late witnessed tremendous expansion in the two electronic media, radio and television. From six radio stations in 1947, All India Radio (AIR) has grown to nearly 200 radio stations, catering to the local and regional audiences. Rural Radio Forums were started with 149 stations. Seven radio stations were used for broadcasting 20 programmes to 150 village groups clustered in five unilingual districts of one state in the first pilot project. Each forum consisted of 10 to 20 villages. They gathered to hear and discuss programmes. An elected secretary kept minutes of the meetings, while a chairperson (who was elected for short term) led discussions.

The forums often raised questions about new problems and appealed to AIR for additional information or for advice on how to adapt information to the local conditions. A typical programme devoted 20 minutes to a substantive agricultural issue and ended with a 10 minute dialogue in response to questions raised by previous programmes. Brief comments on market reports and weather were also aired. Listeners and participants in forum groups could hear as many as 50 hours of radio programming.

They could also experience as many as 100 opportunities to participate in, or hear subsequent local discussions. Evidence from carefully conducted field experiments confirmed that the Indian government's "grow more food" campaign had been stimulated by this combination of mass media, interpersonal communication and subsequent feedback. Field experiments which compared villages with "rural radio forums to villages without them were filled with praise.", a success beyond expectations.

Increase in knowledge in the forum villages was spectacular, whereas in the non-forum villages it was negligible. Growth of the relatively cheap transistor radio, reduced the villagers' desire to attend forum meetings. They preferred to stay home and listen to other types of programmes. This led to their demise, although some listeners' clubs are still operating.

Regular radio farm and home units have been established in all the radio stations headed by farm radio officers to run agricultural and rural development programmes. About 20 radio stations have science cells headed by "science officers." Various campaigns against smoking and drugs were carried through radio with the help of experts. Thus, as a development reporter for radio, there is plenty of scope to write scripts, to devise special programmes and also the work in the capacity as a freelancer to do development field stories. While reporting development for radio, you must remember that you are talking to the people.

Of course, you can always read your scripts if the broadcast is in your own voice. However, you should not appear as if you are reading. To achieve this, you must write your scripts in simple language. In the spoken word, your approach has to be personal, with a person to person or a special I-and-you quality. When you want to reach people who cannot read or write, or the people who live in remote villages, and when you want to reach people speedily, the radio is the answer.

The "development" is actually meant for these people, who have been left out of the development due to various reasons but the foremost barrier has been their own ignorance. Your radio talk, radio-feature, radio-drama, radio-discussion must be able to break that barrier. You use radio to inform, alert, suggest, direct, interest, stimulate and motivate people. A good development programme to be put on the radio must be recorded in the field. It will give an impression of informality and intimacy to the listener. These factors make radio programmes impressive, effective, and purposeful.

Development Reporting for Television: Television was first started in India in a small way in 1959. As a development reporter, you can use television to spread know-how; to as many people as within the reach of a television centre or even to the whole country through national hookup. However, to be effective, your development programme must be field-based. You must remember that television is a visual medium.

And if the visuals are missing or the cameraman fails to focus on the relevant visuals, then the television's impact will be completely lost. For making a good television programme with a view to motivate people for development, requires a lot of effort, research, and commitment. In 1975, some researchers undertook the task of developing audience profiles of the people who were likely to receive television programmes through SITE—Satellite Instructional Television Experiment transmission. Each profile contained information on a cluster of three to four districts in a state, covering aspects such as language, customs, values, beliefs, social structure, economy, agriculture, health, hygiene, nutrition, mother-child care and family planning.

Television programmes could be telecast to support development programmes in all these spheres. For writing a good television script, fewer words and more visuals are needed. Much more is communicated through visuals. You may first shoot the film according to a rough script or you may first write the complete script and then take up shooting according to it. It works both ways. It is best to involve yourself at every level of the production of such a programme. If you just write the script and give it to a producer and do not accompany the camera team for shooting at the site, the programme may miss some of the vital points. Besides, you must also sit with the video editor to prepare the final version of the programme. Never make only studio based development programme for television. Go to the spots. Visit the remote areas. The development will never remain an exercise on paper, if television is used properly and fearlessly. A well made television programme can help you expose the loopholes in our planning and implementation of the development plans.

Reporting on Sustainable Development: The ten "sustainable development" was popularized by the report of the World Commission Environment and Development (WCED), also called the Bruntland Report with the title "Our Common Future" published in 1987. A strategy for sustainable living titled "Caring for the Earth" prepared by the International Union for Conservation (IUCN), the UNEP (United Nations Environment Programme) and the World Wide life fund (WWF) defines sustainable development as "improving the quality of human life while living within the carrying capacity of supporting ecosystems." According to Dr. M.S. Swaminathan "A dynamic concept of carrying capacity would imply in operational tens the conservation of natural ecosystems as well as their continuous improvement through research, training, technology, community cooperation and public policies.

To some, sustainable development is a long awaited call for political recognition of global environmental decay, economic injustice and limits to material growth. Economics driven growth has led to a 20-trillion global economy. The decline in environmental quality has however underlined the need for harmonizing the logic of economics with that of ecology. A destructive consequence of human action is the gradual conversion of the surface of the earth into wastelands and degraded lands. Globally, 15 per cent of the total earth surface has undergone human induced soil degradation. About 24 per cent of the human-occupied territory of the earth is degraded only by human activities.

At least 66 million hectares of irrigated land are affected by Stalinization. About 1 million hectares of its prime farmland in rain-fed areas are being lost each year to urbanization. There are also similar frightening figures with reference to water pollution and ground water exhaustion. Compounding these problems is the gradual diversion of forest lands for a variety of other uses, thereby resulting in the loss of habitats rich in biological diversity. The new paradigm of development places as much stress on ecological sustainability as an economic and social sustainability. The sustainable development, therefore, represents an opportunity for humanity to correct a historical error and develop a gentler, more balanced, and stable relationship with the natural world. This view of sustainable development also raises moral considerations such as the need in a limited world for a more equitable sharing of the world's resources. The industrialized countries have intensified their efforts to arrest soil erosion, conserve water and biological diversity and reduce the consumption of mineral fertilizers and chemical pesticides and at the same time stabilize the per hectare productivity at the current high levels. According to Dr. M.S. Swaminathan, the problem facing us today is not so much about discovering what must be done to ensure sustainability, as learning how to do it. The technologies which can promote sustainability rely heavily on knowledge as a substitute for capital, farm grown inputs as substitutes for market purchased ones and community co-operation as a supplement to individual action.

With this background, a total reorientation is required in development reporting in India. When writing about any development project, you must ask questions like how it will improve the quality of life of the people without damaging the quality of air, water, and soil and also without eroding the moral and social values.

CONTEMPORARY TRENDS IN MEDIA AND INTERNATIONAL RELATIONS

With the end of the cold war between the Soviet Union and the United States of America, there seems to be a new, more relaxed and more cooperative environment prevailing in the world politics. But this situation is very deceptive. Developments in the US, on the domestic front, and their balance of payment position, and, in Russia, on the political and economic front, have dampened the dominant outlook presented at the beginning of the current decade. The fight to influence the developing countries has ended. Most of the communist countries are now desperately trying to get aid and cooperation possible fare restructuring their own countries.

In India, the new economic policy has been formulated, and is being implemented now. The economy is opening up for the participation of the foreign companies. But this is not shaping up as planned, and already there are misgivings, internally, and fears expressed about the stability of the country by the foreign investors. Ironically, in such a fluid situation, the experts from both the West and Third World countries, like India, are discussing such issues-like environment protection, AIDS, NPT, etc., to salvage mankind from being wiped off from the face of the earth.

This contradiction needs to be resolved before any meaningful effort could be made to reverse the trend in the Third World. All these issues are reflected in the television and radio programmes, Satellite communication has wired the whole earth. People sitting in any town in any country can hook their TV sets to the satellite and watch programmes of their choice. Due to the speed with which things are happening, decades or even centuries could be compressed in a few years time. In the Third World, there is a sharp decline in autocratic and dictatorial rules. The military-led regimes in South American, African and Asian countries have gone back to the barracks. The popular governments are taking over be reins of running their countries. There is a marked visibility of people at the grassroots level participating in government. What we are witnessing is a phase of maturity in the former colonies of the imperialist powers. The media of the Third World does realize this change in the national and international political and economical spheres.

The exchanges of the TV programmes, especially educational programmes, are quite frequent, though the flow is still imbalanced, because more western programmes are seen on the TV screens of the Third World countries. At the recently concluded International Film Festival in New Delhi, the quality of the movies from the West left much to be desired. This revealed the status the West still gives to such an important country like India. Thus, despite the large-scale changes brought about by technology, imbalance persists in the media and coverage of the developed West vis-a-vis the developing countries of the Third World.

INFORMATION IMBALANCES BETWEEN DEVELOPEDAND DEVELOPING COUNTRIES

Before going into the issue of information imbalance, one has become familiar with concepts that are central to international communication. International communication, at a simple level, could be conceptualized as a communication process between two or more national and cultural systems. Theoretically, nations are free to assume any role in this process. But the ground realities are different.

The status of a given nation and its media institutions in the international news flow system is determined by the role a national media system is destined to play: the role of a producer-distributor or that of a consumer-buyer. Economics determines the ability of a nation to establish its own infrastructures for newsgathering and transmission. The importance of the Technology factor hardly needs any emphasis.

Those having access to modern communication technology as the ‘producer-distributor’ of media products. The UNESCO was made a willing tool in promoting the interests of the ‘producer-distributors’ of the media products and technology.

In 1961, the UNESCO proposed that for each 100 inhabitants of a country, the minimum standard be, at least, 10 copies of daily newspapers, 5 radio receivers, and 2 television sets. Lacking the financial resources, manpower and technology, the new nations had no other option but to be “consumer-buyers” of what the Western media produced and distributed worldwide in terms of hardware and technology, and software programmes.

The major implications of such a domination are that:

- These agencies determine the very nature of the news flow in the world,
- The news consumers everywhere view the world as these agencies report it,
- The news flow, by-and-large, is one-way from the developed nations to the developing nations,
- In the one way flow, the developing nations are under-reported and, when reported; they are presented in a bad light.

These are the consequences of the spread of the Western media, in general, and the US media, in particular, it was not surprising that in the early 1970s a large number of new nations began to complain about the ill effects of the monopoly of international communication. In the pre-eminent position of the US and a few of her allies, a threat to 'national sovereignty' was seen in the US export of cultural products such as books, films, the TV programmes and magazines, a growth of a new kind of imperialism, 'cultural imperialism', was perceived, and the free-flow doctrine was accused of having promoted one-way flow, from the US to the rest of the world.

Bibliography

Akshay Kumar Nayak and Samir Kumar Singh: *Mass Communication Today*, Jnanada Prakashan, Delhi, 2009.

Archana Rakesh Singh: *Mass Communication in Prevention and Control of AIDS : Strategies for Adolescents*, Concept Publication, Delhi, 2006.

Arun Bhatia: *Theory and Research in Interpersonal and Mass Communication*, Akansha Publication, Delhi, 2005.

B. K. Chaturvedi and S.K. Mittal: *Mass Communication Principles and Practices(3 Vols Set)*, Global Vision Publication, Delhi, 2010.

Bhanu Pratap Singh: *Mass Communications Theory*, Anmol Publication, Delhi, 2011.

Deepak Nayyar: *Modern Mass Communication*, Oxford Book Company, Delhi, 2007.

Denis Mcquail: *Mcquail's Mass Communication Theory*, Sage Publication, Delhi, 2010.

Dharmendra Singh: *Mass Communication and Social Development*, Adhyayan Publication, Delhi, 2004.

Dileep Kumar, K.S. Kadian and O.P. Garhwal: *Mass Communication in Agricultural Extension*, Satish Serial Publication, Delhi, 2012.

Girish Saxena: *Mass Communication in Digital Age*, Vista International Publishing House, Delhi, 2009.

Hema Agrawal: *Society, Culture and Mass Communication : Sociology of Journalism*, Rawat Publication, Delhi, 1995.

J K Singh: *Textbook of Mass Communication*, APH Publication, Delhi, 2012.

J.P. Ahluwalia: *Modern Mass Communication : Critical Approach*, Altar Publication, Delhi, 2012.

J.V. Vilanilam: *Mass Communication in India : A Sociological Perspective*, Sage Publication, Delhi, 2005.

Jagadish Chakravarthy: *Net, Media and Mass Communication*, Authorspress, Delhi, 2004.

John Vivian: *The Media Of Mass Communication*, PHI Learning, Delhi, 2011.

Kamal Shankar Srivastava: *Principles of Indian Journalism and Mass Communication : Historical Approach, Trend and Development*, APH Publication, Delhi, 2007.

Kameshwar Dayal: *Mass Communication in Information Age : Concepts and Applications*, Cyber Tech Publication, Delhi, 2011.

Keval J. Kumar: *Mass Communication in India*, Jaico Publication, Delhi, 2002.

Manohar Puri: *Outlines of Mass Communication*, Pragun Publication, Delhi, 2006.

Monita Singh: *The Law of Journalism and Mass Communication*, Centrum Press, Delhi, 2010.

Praveen Kumar: *Mass Communication and Writing Skills*, Centrum Press, Delhi, 2010.

Rajat K Chaudhary: *Research Method in Mass Communication*, Pearl Books, Delhi, 2007.

Rajiv Saxena: *Mass Communication: Research and Analysis*, Centrum Press, Delhi, 2010.

S.C. Sharma and Sweta Bakshi: *Modern Journalism and Mass Communication*, A.K. Publication, Delhi, 2009.

S.K. Bhatnagar: *Media and Mass Communication*, Shri Sai Printographers, Delhi, 2010.

Sachin Bharti: *Mass Communication and Society*, Aavishkar Publication, Delhi, 2008.

Subrato Ghosh: *Modern Trends in Journalism and Mass Communication*, Adhyayan Publication, Delhi, 2008.

Uma Narula: *Mass Communication: Technology: New Perspectives*, Har-anand Publications, Delhi, 2010.

Urmila Devi: *Mass Communication Today*, Ace Books, Delhi, 2010.

Ved Prakash Gandhi: *Principles and Practices of Mass Communication : A Theoretical Perspective*, Kanishka Publication, Delhi, 2007.

Index